Why We Think What We Think

Dan LeRoy

WHY WE THINK WHAT WE THINK

The Rise and Fall of Western Thought

SOPHIA INSTITUTE PRESS
Manchester, New Hampshire

Cover by LUCAS Art & Design / Jenison, MI

Cover image: *The Thinker* by Auguste Rodin (Shutterstock 6440767)

Sophia Institute Press
Box 5284, Manchester, NH 03108
1-800-888-9344
www.SophiaInstitute.com

Sophia Institute Press is a registered trademark of Sophia Institute.

paperback ISBN 978-1-64413-728-4

ebook ISBN 978-1-64413-729-1

Library of Congress Control Number: 2023951707

first printing

Acknowledgments

As I TELL MY students all the time, writing a book is the loneliest process you can be part of that involves so many people. The truly lonely part of it is knowing that the errors, as always, are yours and yours alone. That acknowledgment — as close as I'll probably ever come to existentialism — seems like the right place to begin.

Happily, the people who have inspired you, and whom you meet along the way, more than make up for any downside to writing a book. For this project, that cast includes:

✠ The Catholic philosophers and authors whose considerable work paved and pointed the way, Peter Kreeft and Edward Feser in particular.

✠ The other writers whose work I drew on again and again for inspiration, especially Richard Rubenstein and Arthur Herman.

✠ The entire team at Sophia Institute Press. I'm so happy to be working with such a great publisher once again!

✠ My editors, John Vella and Kevin Schmiesing, whose careful and thoughtful reading of this text enhanced it substantially — and saved me from many errors in the process.

✠ My writer friends — in particular, Michael Lipton, Larry Groce, D.X. Ferris, Peter Relic, Jim Daniels, Greg Renoff, and Neil McCormick.

- ✠ Fr. Kim Schreck, Fr. John Naugle, Fr. Ladis Cizik, Fr. Bill Schwartz, and Deacon Harry DeNome, who shepherd the best and most faithful Catholic parish in America: St. Augustine, in the Diocese of Pittsburgh.

- ✠ The administration, faculty, staff, and students at Lincoln Park Performing Arts Charter School and Lincoln Park Performing Arts Center. In particular, I recognize the other past and present members of the Writing and Publishing Department: Deanna Baringer, Cindy West, Wende Dikec, and Fred Durbin, as well as all my wonderful students.

- ✠ My best friend, Stephen Catanzarite, who played a major role in bringing me back to the Catholic Faith, as well as his always-gracious wife, Rachel, his sons, Thomas and Henry, and the rest of their relations.

- ✠ My incredibly supportive family, including my brother, Drew LeRoy, and my nephews, Alex, Matt (and his wife, Victoria), and Connor; my brother-in-law, Devin Nutter, his wife, Melissa, and my niece, Charlotte; Carolyn Tallman, Jamie Tallman, Heather, Chad, and Lily Sigmon; and Nancy, Steve, Adam, and Rachel Kovac.

- ✠ The best parents in the world, Louie D. and Polly G. LeRoy, who set me forth on a blessed life filled with God and writing.

- ✠ The best children in the world, Carys, Greer, and Grant. Reading and writing about so many childless philosophers makes me extra-grateful for the uncountable blessings my daughters and son have brought to my life.

- ✠ Finally, the best of wives, and best of women, Kiena Nutter, who has been patient, indulgent, and truly loving in the way that only a writer's spouse is called to be. I love you for that — and for everything else as well.

— Dan LeRoy
Pittsburgh, September 2023

There is nothing so absurd that it has not been said by some philosopher.

— *Marcus Tullius Cicero,* On Divination

In so far as religion is gone, reason is going. For they are both of the same primary and authoritative kind. They are both methods of proof which cannot themselves be proved.... The whole modern world is at war with reason, and the tower already reels.

— *G.K. Chesterton,* Orthodoxy

I stopped outside a church house
Where the citizens like to sit
They say they want the kingdom
But they don't want God in it

— *"The Wanderer" by U2 with Johnny Cash*

Contents

SECTION THREE

THIS IS THE MODERN WORLD: BREAKING FREE AND FREE FALLING

SECTION FOUR

THE DARKENING WOOD

Prologue

Sometimes, a joke is the fastest way to reach a difficult truth.

> *How can you make a philosophy student get off your porch?*
>
> *Just pay him for the pizza.*

How did we get from a world in which some of the smartest people in recorded history were philosophers — a world in which philosophy gave birth to science and made sense of religion — to a world in which philosophy has become, at best, the setup for a punchline?

Not many people ask that question these days. The idea that philosophy is irrelevant seems self-evident.

There's another set of questions that people ask every single day, however.

How did we get to a world where we can't agree on *anything* — even the most elementary, objective, and obvious truths? How did we get to a world where it seems like everyone is, in the final analysis, utterly *alone*, where every tie that might connect us has been cut? And how did we get to a world where, despite all the promises of research and technology, the future seems more fragile, and the truth more unknowable, than ever before?

How *did* we get to that world?

And is there any way out of it?

Those are good questions. But it's impossible to answer them without first figuring out what happened to philosophy.

Many histories of philosophy don't even attempt this. They politely ignore its embarrassing decline. It's a tragic story in many ways. Yet only by understanding it can we truly know how we got here.

The purpose of this book is simple, then. It tries to answer why philosophy no longer seems to matter, so that we can figure out why nothing *else* seems to matter, either — and what, if anything, we can do about both problems.

Philosophical Suicide

The simple answer to the first question is this: philosophy became irrelevant by choice. It *made* itself irrelevant. In short, it committed suicide.

This process took the better part of a thousand years, so it happened gradually. There were dramatic moments along the way, but it wasn't an epic blowup. It was, instead, an unsexy decline. More like suicide by erosion.

Here we should stop for a moment to define terms. What do we mean when we say *philosophy*? Or *science*? Or *theology*?

The late, great British philosopher Sir Roger Scruton proposed thinking about the three terms this way. He defined science as "the realm of empirical investigation."[1] We test observable events and try to use those tests to predict what might happen next. Those tests may show that there are natural laws that are always in effect.

But science, Scruton pointed out, often asks questions it can't answer — questions that lie outside the observable. These are *metaphysical* questions — questions that go beyond the physical.

Theology is a way to try to answer these questions. We attempt to fit them into a framework, a system of religion.

Philosophy, however, can contain elements of *both* science and theology — and it always has. It examines empirical data, like science. But, like theology, it also speculates about what lies *beyond* that data.

The first philosophers, as we'll see, were also scientists. And many of the greatest theologians in history were also philosophers.

For some time, the three fields were more or less interchangeable. This reached a peak during the medieval era, when Catholicism produced great

[1] Roger Scruton, A Short History of Modern Philosophy: From Descartes to Wittgenstein (London: Routledge, 1995), 4.

scientists, great theologians, and great philosophers. Sometimes, these were just three facets of the same person.

Then, roughly eight hundred years ago, this trio of disciplines began to go their separate ways. Why?

The popular view is that science could no longer be held back by theology or philosophy. It became the dominant field because it had all the answers. Facts, as opposed to speculations. Certainty, in short.

Even most skeptics realize this caricature isn't true. For all its miraculous discoveries, the list of things that science has no answers for is long. And science itself is *based* on a series of philosophical assumptions — including the existence of a world outside our minds, and our ability to examine it accurately.

But there's no doubt science had a huge effect on philosophy. Primarily, it began to dictate the questions that philosophy — once the most wide-open of disciplines — should tackle.

There are four major branches of philosophy, and each one exists to answer a specific query. There's *metaphysics* (What is the nature of reality?), *ontology* (What is the nature of being?), and *ethics* (How should we act?).

But it's the fourth branch that has become dominant. This field concerns what we can know and how we can know it. It's called *epistemology*.

For the past several centuries, philosophers have made epistemology their main concern, trying to determine what, exactly, we can know for certain. Over and over again, the results have been disappointing, horrifying, or just plain ridiculous. This is because philosophy asked science questions that science could not possibly provide. And because philosophy rejected the answers that theology *could* supply — since those answers were inconvenient.

In fact, every time philosophers tried to answer the epistemological question, the number of things we could know for certain seemed to shrink. As we'll see in this book, by the end of the Enlightenment, philosophy was left admitting that there was almost nothing we could know for sure. Skepticism ruled.

By that point, philosophy had become good for a single purpose: casting doubt on pretty much everything — including science.

That was convenient, though. Science was useful as long as it was inventing things to benefit the individual and make him more and more free. If science proposed that there might be limits on that freedom, however ... then it had to go as well.

With Friends Like These ...

Some of the greatest absurdities uttered by philosophers over the centuries have been motivated by the same desire: liberating the individual.

This was a process that started early on, in the days of classical Greece and Rome, through the work of groups like the Sophists and the Skeptics. But since the late medieval era, the main project of philosophy has been to help free man from all his obligations. The obligation to God would take a long time to overcome. Yet Western philosophy has certainly made a good go of it.

Sometimes this process of liberation was deliberate. At other times, it's been accidental. A supreme irony — philosophy is full of them — is that some of the greatest philosophers in history, who participated in this project to liberate the individual, were believing Christians. As this book argues, their efforts did more to destabilize, delegitimize, and demonize Christianity than the work of any atheists or enemies of the Church.

The issue, once again, has usually been certainty. Certainty about what we can and can't know — about God's workings, and about the world around us.

During the medieval period, St. Thomas Aquinas worked out a philosophy that seemed to answer many crucial questions — about what humans could know about their own existence, as well as the world around them, and how these things connected us to God. He harmonized this system with the work of the great classical philosopher Aristotle, giving it a solid grounding in empirical thought.

But Aquinas's system was challenged by other leaders of the Church, who said St. Thomas was presuming to know far too much about the mind of God. They felt he was proposing *too much certainty*. So they chose skepticism instead.

Though no one realized it at the time, this was the beginning of the end for philosophy.

Free at Last, Free at Last, Thank ... William of Ockham?

No one person could be completely responsible for such a momentous shift, of course. And since Aquinas's views were later upheld by the Church, some look for culprits much later in history.

In a 2002 article titled "The End of Philosophy," the Catholic professor Ralph McInerny suggested that the seventeenth-century French philosopher René Descartes was the thinker who made the definitive break with the past.

"The mark of the modern," McInerny wrote, was "to announce that all previous philosophy was meaningless or based on some mistake which could now at last be corrected."[2]

Descartes definitely did make such a claim. He definitely did break with Aquinas's and Aristotle's views. And he definitely is one of the pioneers of modern science, as we'll see in chapter 12. So McInerny was only one of many distinguished scholars to pin the blame for philosophy's decline on Descartes.

But in this book, I join some others — both Catholics like Edward Feser and non-Catholics like Richard Weaver and Richard Rubenstein — in arguing that the decline started much, much earlier.

Not long after Thomas Aquinas's death in 1274, Catholics friars like John Duns Scotus and William of Ockham rejected the conclusions he drew. They claimed these conclusions were based on knowledge humans could never hope to possess. The only way to know anything about God, they contended, was through *individual faith* alone.

This was a radical and influential doctrine. It undermined Aquinas's revolutionary, yet common-sense, system of thought. It also undermined the Aristotelian principles that system was based upon. As we'll see, it helped pave the way for the Church's breakup during the Protestant Reformation and opened the door for a new, results-oriented science, free of Christianity's constraints.

In this new science, the idea that things — especially man —were created for some *purpose,* that they have what Aristotle called a "final cause," had to be abandoned. After all, final causes couldn't be proven empirically. More important, they suggested that there were natural *limits* to what man could, and should, do. In other words, these limits were getting in the way of the experiments.

These final causes and natural limits were never *disproven* —not by scientists, nor by anyone else. Aristotle's and Aquinas's systems were not disproven, either. They never *have* been disproven, in fact, despite what many people believe. But these limits, these systems, and Aristotle and Aquinas — they were all cramping Liberated Man's style. So they had to go.

Meanwhile, Duns Scotus and Ockham also argued against using the world's physical reality as a way of understanding God, as Aquinas had shown was possible. This would eventually leave the religious with only faith to defend their beliefs.

2 Ralph McInerny, "The End of Philosophy," *Anuario Filosófico* (January 2002): 677.

Over time, both Aquinas and Aristotle would be abandoned by Western thinkers.

It didn't happen all at once, but in chapter 10 I'll argue that this rupture was the turning point in human history.

"Views like Ockham's," writes Edward Feser, "prefigured themes that would come to define modern philosophy and modern civilization more generally."[3]

Duns Scotus and Ockham, of course, were believing Christians. But many of the Western thinkers who followed them were far less orthodox. Some weren't Christians at all. And for those who wanted to liberate humans — theologically, economically, and morally — Ockham's skepticism gave them the perfect tool. It cast doubt on nearly everything — including, paradoxically, science.

Nevertheless, the modern philosophers who took their cues from Duns Scotus and Ockham were confident they could discover the certainty that Christianity seemed unable to provide. It turned out to be a lot harder than they thought.

René Descartes usually gets credit for his famous thought experiment, where he stripped away everything uncertain in his quest for ultimate truth. Most people remember the experiment, but not the result: minus God, Descartes showed us a dystopia right out of *The Matrix*. We are nothing but unconnected minds, cut off from everything but our own thoughts. It's a horrific idea. But it's the best Descartes could do ... without God to bail him out.

As Descartes's example proves, the demand for certainty has consistently led philosophy into dark, tight corners from which it can't extricate itself. Often, the only way to escape seems to be to go deeper and deeper into the cave.

But even though philosophers stumbled around in the dark in their quest for certainty, their search had a momentous side effect. Some (like me) would say that this side effect was really the point of the whole exercise.

If there's no certainty — about how we should act; about cause-and-effect relationships; about the objective reality of things (the color red, dogs and cats, men and women); about the existence of the material world itself — then the individual wins, because there are no certain truths. We can all do whatever we want, because who can show us otherwise?

If we're lucky, a world without certainty is a world of tolerance, where we all live and let live, since nothing can be proven. That's more or less been the story of the West — that is, with a few inconvenient and incredibly bloody

3 Edward Feser, *The Last Superstition* (South Bend, IN: St. Augustine's Press, 2008), 170.

interruptions — since the Enlightenment. But ultimately, the contradictions of that tolerant, uncertain world mean that it can never last. This has become more and more clear in the intolerant, uncertain, early twenty-first century.

So if you wonder how we got to the world of today, where people are compelled to accept outrageous lies or suffer the consequences, and where no relationship carries any obligation whatsoever, then philosophy is your answer, as the pages that follow will prove. It's just that nobody blames philosophy anymore, because it's all but disappeared from the scene. This book will finally hold it to account.

It will also argue that philosophy can, and *must*, be rehabilitated—that it is far too important and valuable to languish as the joke it's allowed itself to become. And to do that, we have to look back, to know what we've lost, and how to recover it.

Until then, the West trudges further and further from the light generated by the ancient philosophers, and by saints like Augustine and Aquinas. Deep down, we know what this light reveals: that we are not sovereign. We are not free.

Ignoring that light of tradition, the modern philosophers tried again and again to find *another* light that they hoped would show us the opposite — the reality that rebellious man wants to believe. And even if we don't think about philosophy at all, most of us are blindly following in the circles in which these thinkers wandered.

In the darkness we've chosen, no one can read the words of Proverbs: "There is a way that seemeth right unto a man, but the end thereof are the ways of death" (14:12, KJV).

The Ultimate Question: Why Another Book about the Ultimate Questions?

This book is primarily for the beginner. As I have tried to do in the philosophy classes I've taught at the high school level over the years, I set out to create as clear and understandable an explanation of Western thought as I could manage.

My second goal, however, was to give that explanation in the context of a story — because there really *is* a story of Western philosophy. In many ways, it's an appalling one. But it's appallingly coherent, too — just like *Oedipus Rex* or *King Lear*.

Modern philosophy actually makes perfect sense if you view it as a means to an end. The end was human freedom. The means were whatever would allow man to escape the bonds and boundaries of God and nature. Some puzzling ideas may have resulted, but the goal is entirely understandable — even if the consequences have been disastrous, for both the world, and for philosophy itself.

My hope is that even experienced philosophers might find something of interest in this retold history. No doubt, some of that interest may take the form of disagreement. Debates are welcome. Many of the great philosophers in this book insisted that disagreements can be healthy and actually generate deeper understanding.

Why a *Catholic* history of philosophy? For one thing, most of the history of Western philosophy to date — about 1,500 years worth — is either explicitly Catholic, or occurred when Catholicism equaled Christianity. (However, I have tried to give appropriate weight to the Jewish and Muslim scholars who played such a critical role in this story.)

For another, while there are lots of indispensable Catholic surveys of philosophy — to cite just three authors, I would mention works by Fr. Frederick Copleston, Peter Kreeft, and Edward Feser — this book tries to stake out a spot that I thought remained vacant. There was no single-volume, accessible history of Western thought from a Catholic perspective that I could find. I hope this one can fill that gap.

In any survey like this, there's the tricky decision about who does and doesn't count as a philosopher. I think my choices here are pretty conventional. But I do make the argument that in the modern era, historians have unjustly neglected the philosophical contributions of several popes.

I think this book is an overdue introduction, not just to Western philosophy, but also to its *decline* — and to the ways that decline affects us daily. But obviously, it's only an introduction. The nice thing, however, is that if anything you read here gets you interested, then this could become the start of a lifetime project.

That's the way it happened for me when I read Bryan Magee's *The Story of Thought*. In my early twenties, I received a copy of Magee's survey of Western philosophy from the Quality Paperback Book Club. And I've been thinking about this subject ever since.

I still love the book — even the parts I disagree with wholeheartedly. And the parts that opened up an entire new universe for me remain every bit as fascinating today. I want to pass on that fascination — but I also want to pass on a sense of duty. Philosophy seems not just dead, but discarded. It's the job of smart people — faithful Catholics first and foremost — to reclaim and rehabilitate it.

The word *philosophy* combines two Greeks terms. *Philo* means "love," and *sophia* means "wisdom." So a philosopher is, by definition, a lover of wisdom.

That love, Aristotle believed, always begins with a sense of wonder about the world around us, and our place in it. In this, as in so many other things, the man they simply called "*The* Philosopher" was right. My wish, then, for every reader of this book, is that wonder — and, I hope, wisdom — will be the result.

Why We Think What We Think

Section One

IT'S (MOSTLY) ALL GREEK: HOW THE GREEKS (MOSTLY) GOT IT RIGHT

WHY DID WESTERN PHILOSOPHY begin in ancient Greece? It really wasn't an accident. There were certain conditions that made it possible.

First, while there were wars and insurrections, Greek society was largely stable and relatively prosperous in what we think of as the classical era, around the fifth and fourth centuries B.C. So the time and resources to devote to philosophy were available. Second, people have always had a natural curiosity about the world around them, and the Greeks were no exception. And third, that curiosity was, for the most part, uninhibited by a religious system that discouraged those inquiries.

Greece's religion was more about entertainment than enlightenment. Its stories of humanlike gods and goddesses made for great literature. Occasionally, these tales would offer an explanation for natural phenomena — such as Zeus, the king of the gods, tossing his thunderbolts like lightning.

What these stories didn't do, for the most part, was stop people from developing other — often more practical — explanations for why the world worked as it did. These people, who observed the world carefully, are the philosophers in this section.

The pre-Socratics in the first chapter were, as their name suggests, the philosophers who came before Socrates — which tells you something about what a big deal he was. Most of them were concerned with metaphysics, the nature of reality. What makes up the world, and why is nature the way it is?

The Big Three come next, starting with Socrates, his prize student, Plato, and then Plato's prize student, Aristotle. We call them the Big Three because they remain among the handful of the most important philosophers who ever lived. Some would say they *are* the most important philosophers who ever lived.

After the Big Three leave the scene, the de facto capital of the Western world shifts from Athens to Rome. The Battle of Corinth, in 146 B.C., marks the end of the Greek city-states. And the birth of Christ, of course, changes the course of history.

During this time, there are no more philosophers on the level of the Big Three, but several splinter groups offer their own competing theories. The surprising thing is that many of those ideas are very much with us today.

Yet the story of Western thought really starts, appropriately enough, where life begins: in the water.

CHAPTER ONE

A BIG SMALL WORLD

1.

Water. It's everywhere you look in the city of Miletus.

Muddy brown water between the banks of the Meander River, where the city is located. Deep green water in the city's bayside harbor. And dazzling, turquoise blue water where the river and bay empty into the Aegean Sea.

The man standing on a grassy hillside, shading his eyes and staring out into the widening expanse of the ocean, is thinking a lot about water. To him, it seems like the key to everything.

Humans, plants, and animals all need it to grow, he observes. It can alter its form — from liquid to solid to gas. It can move. It can change.

So water is going to become the key to this man's philosophy. But it's also going to become the key to philosophy, generally. Six hundred years before the birth of Christ, this man, gazing out at the Aegean from a hillside in ancient Greece, is going to become the father of Western thought.

And it's all because he saw water as the world's most significant substance — the one thing that all things had in common.

2.

The man on the hillside was Thales of Miletus. Today, most people think of him as the first true Western philosopher.

Thales's beliefs would be revised and rejected by future philosophers. "He thus set the tone for all future philosophy," quips author Paul Strathern, "by getting it wrong."[1]

But we should marvel instead at what Thales got right. His insistence on the importance of water was surprisingly prescient. After all, he was theorizing long before we could know that 90 percent of our body weight, and 60 percent of our body overall, really *is* made up of water.

Thales was one of the Seven Sages of Greece — a group of the wisest men of the seventh and sixth centuries B.C. He was brilliant at math, especially geometry. Some argue he was the first outstanding mathematician in the West.

He was a pioneering astronomer as well. The historian Herodotus claimed that Thales predicted the great solar eclipse of May 28, 585. Thales studied the constellations and calculated ways they might be used to improve navigation at sea. He may even have once fallen down a well while stargazing. This reportedly prompted a serving girl to voice what would become a common criticism of philosophers over the centuries. She ridiculed him "for being eager to know the things in the heavens but failing to notice what was just behind him and right by his feet."[2]

Thales also had an entrepreneurial side. According to one story told by Aristotle, Thales was able to successfully predict the weather. Knowing conditions were right for a large olive harvest, Thales cannily reserved olive presses in advance — then rented them out at a big profit.

Today, Miletus is part of Turkey. Once, it was one of Greece's wealthiest and most culturally significant cities. But only ruins now survive of that once-prosperous seaport — like the sun-bleached shell of the ancient theater, built facing southwest so that spectators could enjoy the ocean view.

1 Paul Strathern, *Socrates in 90 Minutes* (Chicago: Ivan R. Dee, 1997), 9.

2 Marc S. Cohen, Patricia Curd, and C. D. C. Reeve, eds., *Readings in Ancient Greek Philosophy: From Thales to Aristotle* (Indianapolis: Hackett, 2011), 11. The quoted material in this chapter can be found in a variety of ancient sources, but for ease of use and consistency, I've sourced much of it from this compilation, which is still the academic gold standard for information about the pre-Socratic philosophers.

The most important part of Miletus that remains is Thales. And the most important part of Thales that endures is his idea that the basic substance of the cosmos is water.

In his *Metaphysics*, Aristotle suggests that Thales came up with this idea by noticing that all living things need water to survive. Even seeds, Aristotle notes, have a "moist nature,"[3] and heat itself, he adds, is generated by moisture. And whatever this universal substance was, Thales proposed, it had to be capable of motion — and, therefore, change. Water fulfilled all these requirements.

Earth, Thales further believed, floated on a huge body of water like a piece of wood. He came up with this concept, perhaps, by standing on the banks of the Meander River, or on the docks in the harbor at Miletus. Thales saw that land masses seemed to end at water's edge, and used this observation to imagine earth as an island.

It's not entirely clear whether Thales was arguing that water is the *originator* of living things, or that everything actually *is* water. There are no records today of Thales's writing. And even by the time of Aristotle, a couple of centuries later, it seems those records might no longer have existed either — if they ever existed at all.

But whichever interpretation is true, it seems apparent that Thales was trying to do three things.

The first is that Thales was breaking with the tradition of resorting to myth for explanations of the natural world. A common story of the time, for example, stated that human beings had been created from mud by the Titan god Prometheus. But Thales searched instead for actual occurrences in nature to explain man's existence, and the world around him. It's for this reason that many people consider Thales the first Western scientist.

The second, equally significant, point is that Thales passed on to his followers — sometimes called the Milesian School — a way of thought we used to call "critical thinking." Today, that term has been co-opted by political groups who seem to encourage anything *but* thinking critically. But beginning with Thales, Western philosophers encouraged their students "to discuss, debate, criticize — and to produce a better argument or theory if [they] could."[4]

So one of Thales's own students, Anaximander, came up with a theory that contradicted his teacher's. He imagined the earth as a kind of double-sided

3 Cohen, Curd, and Reeve, *Readings*, 2.

4 Bryan Magee, *The Story of Philosophy* (New York: Dorling Kindersley, 1998), 181.

drum floating in space, "held up by nothing." This idea, the twentieth-century philosopher Karl Popper would say, "is one of the boldest, most revolutionary, and most portentous ideas in the whole history of human thought. It made possible the theories of Aristarchus and Copernicus."[5]

Then one of Anaximander's pupils, Anaximenes, contradicted *his* teacher by proposing instead that the earth was a stable, flat surface that covered the air beneath it "like a lid."[6] From these civilized disagreements came the spirit of scientific inquiry we now take for granted.

Third, and perhaps most important of all, Thales was trying to find a common denominator in nature: something that linked all beings, living and inanimate. In philosophy, this is known as *monism*. The root word is *mono* — Greek for "one," or "single." You could think of it as an idea that suggests unity: a connection that binds everything together, even things we think are distinct and separate.

Specifically, we could call Thales's idea *substance monism*: the concept that all things can be explained in terms of a single substance. In Thales's case, this substance would be water.

Many other philosophers would adopt this monistic approach. Several philosophers in this section did it — though they didn't agree on the single, uniting factor.

The next philosopher who did is a person whom you probably know already. What you may not realize is that he took a radically different approach to monism.

3.

Our next stop is fifty years after the birth of Thales, and thirty miles to the northwest of Miletus, just off the coast of present-day Turkey. The philosopher born on the island of Samos is someone you've probably encountered if you've ever taken a geometry class. Yet Pythagoras is also one of the most mysterious figures in philosophy.

The legends about Pythagoras are numerous. He was known as the "long-haired Samian,"[7] and was apparently good-looking enough to be described as

5 Karl R. Popper, "Back to the Pre-Socratics: The Presidential Address." *Proceedings of the Aristotelian Society* 59, no. 1 (June 1959): 4, https://doi.org/10.1093/aristotelian/59.1.1.

6 Cohen, Curd, and Reeve, *Readings*, 17.

7 *Iamblichus' Life of Pythagoras, or, Pythagoric Life. Accompanied by Fragments of the Ethical Writings of Certain Pythagoreans in the Doric Dialect . . .*, trans. Thomas Taylor (London: A. J. Valpy, 1818).

the "son of Apollo,"[8] the Greek god of the sun. He reportedly had a "golden thigh,"[9] which he once displayed at the Olympic games. Others said he possessed a magic arrow that allowed him to fly, and he could tame animals with his voice and his touch.

Like Thales, nothing survives of Pythagoras's writings, so all we know about him comes from a handful of ancient sources. They tell us he led a society that was partly scientific, partly religious, and utterly secretive. The Greek philosopher Porphyry later wrote that the members "kept no ordinary silence"[10] about their activities.

Pythagoras, who was a teenager when Thales died, may have been a student of the Milesian philosophers, and perhaps even of Thales himself. His father was a merchant and traveled widely, so Pythagoras may also have visited Egypt and studied geometry there — though this was often speculated about Greek philosophers with an interest in mathematics.

The story for Pythagoras really began when he was about forty years old. He moved to Croton, a town in the heel of Italy's boot, and set up a school there. Some might describe the school as more of a cult: the members of its inner circle, the *mathematikoi,* gave up their possessions and were vegetarians. (However, Pythagoras reportedly wouldn't let his followers eat beans, which caused gas.)

It's speculated that Pythagoras might have gotten some ideas for his school — including its dietary restrictions and code of secrecy — from priests he observed in Egypt. He also allowed female students at his school, an unusual move at the time.

This cross between mathematics and religion, however, isn't as hard to imagine as it might first seem. For the Pythagoreans, numbers were sacred. And for Pythagoras himself, the mathematical discoveries he made pointed to the divine.

The best example of this might be the Pythagorean theorem, which most of us learn by high school. Pythagoras found a ratio that is true in all right triangles: the square of the hypotenuse equals the sum of the squares of the other two sides.

8 *Iamblichus' Life of Pythagoras.*

9 *Iamblichus' Life of Pythagoras.* What, exactly, is a "golden thigh"? There are a number of references in ancient sources to this attribute of Pythagoras, who apparently displayed it to onlookers on several occasions. Some insist it was literally a golden thigh; others see it as a euphemism for genitalia. Those who support this theory note that "thigh" is sometimes synonymous with genitals in the Bible and in Greek mythology: for example, the story of Dionysus being born from the thigh of Zeus.

10 Cohen, Curd, and Reeve, *Readings,* 20.

The key thing here is that Pythagoras didn't *invent* this universal ratio: he *discovered* it. It was there all along, just waiting to be uncovered. But who or what created it in the first place?

This principle applied to other discoveries. One of them was Pythagoras's unlocking of harmonic intervals between musical notes. As legend has it, by listening to two blacksmiths — one of whom was striking an anvil half the size of the other — Pythagoras worked out the eight-note ratio of octaves that produces pleasing harmonies.

Pythagoras would speculate that similar ratios could be found throughout creation: in the spaces between stars, the planets, and the elements. This last speculation was proven true centuries after Pythagoras's death: the "Law of Octaves" was responsible for the formation of the Periodic Table of Elements.

It's no wonder that these discoveries hit Pythagoras and his followers like a divine revelation. It's also not surprising that these ratios led them to speculate about the nature of numbers themselves. Even numbers were good, odd numbers were evil, and ten was the "perfect number."[11] (This was because ten is a *tetractys* — a number made up of the sum of the first four numbers: 1, 2, 3, and 4.)

Creation itself, therefore, followed a pattern: "[O]n the Unlimited (the infinite that existed before the universe), God imposed a Limit, so that all that exists came to have an actual size. In this way God created a measurable unity from which everything else was formed."[12]

In short, Pythagoras came to believe that "number is the ruler of forms and ideas."[13] Like Thales, he practiced a form of monism — replacing *water* with *numbers* as the single common denominator in the cosmos.

As Aristotle put it in his *Metaphysics*: because "numbers seemed to be primary in all nature," Pythagoreans "supposed the elements of numbers to be the elements of all things that are."[14]

But the difference between Thales and Pythagoras — between water and numbers — is noteworthy for another reason. Very early in Western philosophy, we see the beginnings of a split that exists to this day.

Thales's monism is based primarily on evidence he gathered from his senses. We could call it empirical data. When Thales observed the moisture in

11 Cohen, Curd, and Reeve, *Readings*, 22.

12 Will Buckingham, *The Philosophy Book*, 1st ed. (London: Penguin, 2011), 28.

13 Buckingham, *The Philosophy Book*, 26.

14 Cohen, Curd, and Reeve, *Readings*, 22.

seeds, animals drinking water, and the river, bay, and ocean around Miletus, he was forming a theory based mostly on sensory input.

Pythagoras, meanwhile, worked out his numerical ideas using reason. Abstract thought, not observations, gave him his information. Thus, he felt that reason was superior to the evidence of the senses.

Taken to extremes, these two branches of philosophy—we'll call them *empiricism* and *rationalism*—have created what seems like an insurmountable divide over the centuries. One side prizes the physical, the other the mental.

At its edges, empiricism denies anything that can't be seen, heard, smelled, tasted, or touched. And on its outskirts, rationalism is skeptical that anything material—even human beings—exists at all.

Like just about everything else in his career, the way Pythagoras's life ended is unclear. He appears to have been chased out of Croton around 508 B.C., after his cult attracted unfavorable attention.

The woman most believe was his wife, Theano, was far younger than him. She may have been his student, and this may have aroused controversy. There's also a story that a rich man from Croton, named Cylon, wanted badly to join the Pythagoreans. But he was rejected because of certain "character defects."[15] Vowing revenge, he and his friends attacked the group.

Pythagoras reportedly escaped to Metapontium, a coastal city to the north. There, he may have died—or perhaps even committed suicide, in despair over the end of his society. The Pythagoreans survived his death, but were violently suppressed in 460 B.C. By the end of the fourth century, the group had all but disappeared.

Nevertheless, just like the numerical ratios Pythagoras discovered, his ideas would endure. Centuries before Christianity, the numbers he found in nature would pose a serious problem for those who wanted to deny the divine.

4.

Though many people don't realize it, they've been exposed to the philosophy of the next Greek thinker on our list by watching the 1995 Disney film *Pocahontas*.

[15] Errol Morris, "The Ashtray: Hippasus of Metapontum (Part 3)." Opinionator, *New York Times*, March 8, 2011. https://archive.nytimes.com/opinionator.blogs.nytimes.com/2011/03/08/the-ashtray-hippasus-of-metapontum-part-3/.

It comes at the beginning of the song "Just Around the Riverbed," when Pocahontas observes, "You can't step in the same river twice." This was the primary insight of Heraclitus, who used it to make a bigger case for the ever-changing nature of the world.

Heraclitus was born in 535 B.C. — a decade after the death of Thales — in the city of Ephesus. Ephesus was a coastal town in what is now Turkey, roughly equidistant from both Miletus and Samos. At the time, it was the major city in the Greek province of Ionia.

Heraclitus was born to an aristocratic family and was apparently the oldest son. But he had no interest in politics, and let his younger brother take on that role. Instead, he withdrew to practice philosophy. He acquired the nickname "The Riddler" — presumably because he liked to present his views in paradoxes.

Heraclitus apparently didn't have much patience when people failed to understand his brainteasers. Ancient historians record quite a few examples of his putdowns. Like this one: "What understanding or intelligence have they? They put their trust in popular bards and take the mob for their teacher, unaware that most people are bad, and few are good."[16]

About his listeners, he also offered this insult: "Uncomprehending when having heard, they are like the deaf. The saying describes them: being present they are absent."[17] About his fellow citizens, he wrote, "Every grown man of the Ephesians should hang himself and leave the city to the boys."[18] And he once suggested that the writer Homer ought to be flogged.[19]

Perhaps Heraclitus's frustrations were what led to his other nickname: "the weeping philosopher." Things probably would have been worse had he known that what was apparently his single book would only survive as a series of about a hundred fragments — although this volume was widely read in his day, led him to some fame, and attracted a following.

His touchy temperament aside, Heraclitus believed that the cosmos was ruled by a force he described as *logos*. Fittingly for someone who loved

[16] Cohen, Curd, and Reeve, *Readings*, 31.

[17] Cohen, Curd, and Reeve, *Readings*, 32.

[18] Cohen, Curd, and Reeve, *Readings*, 39.

[19] The quote about Homer being flogged (or whipped) comes from John Burnet, *Early Greek Philosophy* (First Rate Publishers, 2014), 141.

paradoxes, Heraclitus saw this logos as something that produced unity through the use of opposites

Everything, he believed, was in a constant state of flux — which we could also call motion. The reason you can't step in the same river twice is because the motion of the water changes the river from moment to moment.

We've all heard this idea expressed in various ways. For example, you're not the same person you were a year ago, or even a day or an hour ago. With each passing second, we change, however imperceptibly, and so does the world around us.

Scientific observation would prove that this is true. For example, humans shed cells constantly. The wind and water erode buildings and other structures. Organisms grow, even when we can't see their growth with the naked eye.

Heraclitus was therefore an empiricist, like Thales. He wrote that the senses are the best source of information, and added, "All that can be seen, heard, experienced — these are what I prefer."[20] Although he obviously didn't have access to scientific instruments that could prove his conjectures were valid, Heraclitus's insistence that change is constant has been one of the most influential ideas in philosophy.

However, he didn't see this constant change as a source of chaos. Instead, Heraclitus felt that the constant tension between opposites — between "day and night, winter and summer, war and peace, satiety and hunger"[21] — was what maintained balance in the universe.

In his *Nicomachean Ethics,* Aristotle quotes Heraclitus as saying, "What is opposed brings together; the finest harmony is composed of things at variance, and everything comes to be in accordance with strife."[22]

If we believe things are permanent, then, we're mistaken, according to Heraclitus. Plato gets credit for the quote "Everything is becoming; nothing is." But the idea is clearly Heraclitus's.[23]

It would be challenged, however, by our next philosopher. Heraclitus may have been a lover of paradoxes, but Parmenides came up with one of the trickiest yet.

20 Cohen, Curd, and Reeve, *Readings,* 36.

21 Cohen, Curd, and Reeve, *Readings,* 37. In the full quotation, Heraclitus says that *God* is all of these opposites.

22 Cohen, Curd, and Reeve, *Readings,* 35.

23 "Everything is becoming; nothing is" is one of the pull quotes in Bryan Magee's section on Plato in *The Story of Thought* (page 28), for example.

5.

Just as Heraclitus shares the *empirical* views of Thales, Parmenides has links to the *rational* philosophy of Pythagoras.

Parmenides was born around 515 B.C. to a wealthy family in Elea, a town near Naples in present-day Italy. Some believe he studied with the poet Xenophanes of Colophon.[24] This might be where he picked up the habit of writing in verse. Other ancient accounts suggest Parmenides also had a teacher who was a Pythagorean — a theory that would make a lot of sense.

As is the case with Heraclitus, only fragments of Parmenides's work survive. They all appear to be from an untitled poem that most call "On Nature." But in those fragments, written in the standard form of Homeric hexameters, Parmenides lays out a philosophy 180 degrees from that of Heraclitus.

"On Nature" tells the tale of a young man who meets a goddess. In the second section of the poem, called "Truth," the goddess instructs the young man on the nature of reality. "It is right both to say and to think that it is what-is: for it can be," the goddess says, "but nothing is not."[25]

This is both a tongue-twister of a passage and tricky to unravel. The translation is: the goddess is telling the young man that it's not possible for *something* to come from *nothing*. Something can only come from *something*, in other words.

From this observation, Parmenides — through the character of the goddess — uses reason to draw a series of other conclusions. If something can't come from nothing, then something must always have existed. And if something has always existed, and is therefore permanent, then true change must be impossible — or else that *something* wouldn't be permanent after all.

What we think is change, then, is just an illusion. In the next section of the poem, the "Doxa," the goddess challenges her young listener. Should he really trust the evidence of his senses, instead of her logic? His senses might tell him that the world around him is changing, but reason shows this is impossible.

If we look at the world around us, Heraclitus had said, we'll see things we think are solid, unchanging, and stable. But that was an illusion, he thought. If we look harder, we'll see that what appears permanent is actually in constant flux.

24 As Peter Kreeft points out in *Socrates' Children*, Xenophanes was "the first philosophical theologian." He was "a *monotheist*, teaching a single God *transcendent* to the world of things, rather than Parmenides' pantheistic 'one,' which was all things." Kreeft, *Socrates' Children*, vol. 1, *Ancient Philosophers* (Elk Grove Village, IL: Word on Fire, 2022, e-book), 59.

25 Cohen, Curd, and Reeve, *Readings*, 43.

In "On Nature," Parmenides simply took Heraclitus a step further. If you look beneath those more detailed observations, he thought — if you put the evidence you gathered aside and looked at things logically — you'll see that the changes you're observing aren't actually what they seem. They're another, deeper, illusion.

There is nowhere for change to come *from*, Parmenides believed. So the world is really one single thing, permanent and unchanging.

This is, for most people, a harder view to accept than Heraclitus's idea, which seems to have science backing it up. But the thing we shouldn't miss is that both Heraclitus and Parmenides essentially insisted on the same thing: the fundamental unity of the universe. They just expressed it in very different ways. Heraclitus believed that unity was expressed through eternal, unending *change*. Parmenides believed it was expressed through eternal, *unchanging* reality.

Parmenides had several students. One of the most famous was Zeno, also from Elea, who came up with a paradox that stumped many thinkers of his day. The parable of Achilles and the tortoise goes like this: Achilles can run as fast as he wants. But if the slow-footed tortoise has a head start, Achilles will never be able to catch up.

This seems impossible, and yet the explanation seems sound. As Zeno pointed out, "The pursuer must first reach the point from which the pursued departed, so that the slower must always be some distance in front."[26] To get from his starting point to reach the tortoise, Achilles first has to travel half the total distance. The math seems to show that by the time Achilles has done this, the tortoise will still be in the lead, no matter how many times you subdivide the distances.

Solving Zeno's problem actually requires physics — accounting for velocity — instead of just math.[27] But Zeno's conclusion was more than just a clever puzzle. Like his mentor Parmenides, he was really trying to show that motion was impossible. And if motion is impossible, then so is change — no matter what our senses tell us.

It's maybe a little too easy to line up Thales and Heraclitus on one side and Pythagoras and Parmenides on the other. But these four examples show us that,

[26] Cohen, Curd, and Reeve, *Readings*, 50.

[27] Astrophysicist Ethan Siegel gives a great explanation of the solution to Zeno's famous riddle in "This Is How Physics, Not Math, Finally Resolves Zeno's Famous Paradox," *Forbes*, May 5, 2020, https://www.forbes.com/sites/startswithabang/2020/05/05/this-is-how-physics-not-math-finally-resolves-zenos-famous-paradox/?sh=320bb46933f8.

over the first couple of centuries of Western philosophy, a split had formed between the evidence of the senses and the evidence of the mind.

Yet focusing on this divide ignores something that this quartet of philosophers had in common. Whatever their beliefs, all four men acknowledged the role of a god or gods at the head of the universe.

Thales was quoted as saying that all things are full of gods. (This is usually taken to mean full of *water*, but Thales also thought water had divine properties.) Pythagoras was the head of a religious cult which believed in reincarnation and worshipped the god Dionysus. Heraclitus believed in *logos* as a mystical, unifying force. And Parmenides seems to be saying that the universe is really a single, undifferentiated thing — which, logically, could only be God.

Other pre-Socratic philosophers had their own ideas of God. One example is Diogenes of Apollonia — a colony located near the Black Sea. During the mid-fifth century B.C., he came up with a monistic theory that *air* is the common element that unites the world.

"In my opinion, that which possesses intelligence is what people call air, and all humans are governed by it and it rules all things," he wrote. "For in my opinion this very thing is god, and it reaches everything and arranges all things and is in everything."[28]

All of those beliefs are a long way from the monotheistic religions that would follow. But they're even further away, in a sense, from the thoroughly modern philosophers we'll look at next.

6.

We don't know much about many of the pre-Socratic philosophers. But we might know the least about Leucippus. As proof of this lack of knowledge, one slightly later thinker, Epicurus — more about him later — even denied that Leucippus ever existed.

Where was Leucippus born? The Greek biographer Diogenes Laërtius suggested he might have been from Miletus, Abdera, or Elea — a wide range of possibilities that includes sites in present-day Turkey, Greece, and Italy.

There are reports that between 440 and 430 B.C., Leucippus started a school at Abdera. Some even claim that Leucippus founded the city of Metapontum, near the heel of Italy's boot.

[28] Cohen, Curd, and Reeve, *Readings*, 101.

The great philosopher Aristotle assumed that Leucippus was a real person, and what was good enough for Aristotle should probably be good enough for us. But the lack of information about Leucippus is probably why his name is usually just a footnote in philosophy textbooks.

Leucippus deserves more attention. He seems to have contributed several particularly important insights. The first is that he apparently developed a monistic theory about the world that anticipated the work of scientists centuries later.

Leucippus advanced the idea that the universe is infinite and is made up of tiny, invisible particles called atoms. These atoms existed in what Leucippus called a "void"—empty space that separated these atoms, but also allowed them the freedom to move.

These atoms, Leucippus speculated, could combine and recombine to create different forms. Even the atoms that make up our bodies don't simply disappear when we die. They can recombine with other atoms to make up entirely new substances. The Greek word for atoms is *atomos,* which means "uncuttable." We now know that atoms *can* be split, a fact the Greeks couldn't have realized without the help of modern science.

Given these limitations, however, the fact that Leucippus came up with this idea without access to today's scanning-tunneling microscopes—which finally allow us to "see" atoms—is truly remarkable. And it's more than a little ironic that a concept which depends heavily on the evidence of our *senses*—making these tiny particles visible—was at first a theory that depended more on *reason.* In other words, Leucippus thought, it *must* be the case that there were particles this small—even if we couldn't see them yet.

But there's a second way that Leucippus's theory is significant. This idea "offered the first complete mechanistic view of the universe, without any recourse to the notion of a god or gods."[29]

In other words, if the universe is simply a collection of atoms, which randomly knock into one another, then there is far less need for a *creator* of this universe.

No one seems to deny the existence of Leucippus's student, Democritus. He's believed to have been born in Abdera, a coastal city in northeast Greece, around 460 B.C. Some sources say he may have lived to the ripe old age of one

[29] Buckingham, *The Philosophy Book,* 45.

hundred. That would have meant he was around during the lifetimes of the Big Three philosophers we'll meet soon — Socrates, Plato, and Aristotle.

Democritus apparently wrote books — perhaps as many as seventy — on a wide variety of subjects, from math to grammar to farming to accounts of his own travels. But like many of the pre-Socratic philosophers, very little survives of his work.

We get most of our accounts of Leucippus and Democritus from later Greek writers, including Aristotle. These writers pay a lot of attention to the theory of nature being made up of atoms. Some are also skeptical about the idea of the "void." This vast, empty space seems to contradict Parmenides's concept that something can't come from nothing.

But Democritus suggsted that the void is actually a thing, and not a *nothing* — that the void "has some nature and existence of its own."[30] And the void is also *necessary* in the philosophy of Leucippus and Democritus, because atoms need space to move.

This motion of atoms, which the void permits, is necessary for change. And this idea of constant, unending change makes Leucippus and Democritus natural heirs of Heraclitus, who suggested that "everything is flux."[31]

Of course, how this change actually *begins* is trickier to pin down. Leucippus believed "that there are an infinite number of atoms moving for all time in an infinite void, and that these can form into cosmic systems or *kosmoi* by means of a whirling motion which randomly establishes itself in a large enough cluster of atoms."[32]

But as Aristotle noted of Leucippus and Democritus in his *Metaphysics*, "They say that there is always motion. But why it is and what motion it is, they do not state, nor do they give the cause of its being of one sort rather than another."[33]

Meanwhile, Plutarch, who lived in the first century A.D., thought that Democritus believed atoms had simply always existed: "All things are atoms, which

[30] Cohen, Curd, and Reeve, *Readings*, 86.

[31] Buckingham, *The Philosophy Book*, 40.

[32] Sylvia Berryman, "Ancient Atomism," *Stanford Encyclopedia of Philosophy* Archive. August 23, 2005; revised December 15, 2016, https://plato.stanford.edu/Archives/win2021/entries/atomism-ancient/.

[33] Cohen, Curd, and Reeve, *Readings*, 86. While Democritus and Leucipuus get credit for originating Greek atomism, scholars trace the roots of atomism several centuries earlier, to classical Indian philosophy. As *The Stanford Encyclopedia of Philosophy* notes, "Two distinct systems that regard Vedic texts as authoritative, Nyāya and Vaiśeṣika, favoured atomist accounts of the material world. Quite different atomist theories are found in Buddhist and Jaina systems" (Berryman, "Ancient Atomism").

he calls forms; there is nothing else. For there is no coming-to-be from what-is-not, and nothing could come to be from things that are, because on account of their hardness the atoms are not acted upon and do not change."[34]

What isn't often mentioned about Democritus is this irony: for someone who seems to be a natural empiricist, he was surprisingly skeptical about the evidence of the senses.

There are several passages from Greek writers that quote Democritus as having a dim view of empirical data. Like this one, from second-century philosopher Sextus Empiricus: "There are two kinds of judgment, one legitimate and the other bastard. All the following belong to the bastard: sight, hearing, smell, taste, touch. The other is legitimate and is separate from this."[35] Reason, Democritus seems to suggest, is this "legitimate" judgment.

In fact, Democritus seems to be the first example of a paradox we'll see again later in this book: an empiricist who was extremely picky about empirical data. He was *so* picky about the data he gathered, in fact, that it caused him to doubt we could ever get *any* truly reliable data from the senses.

Sextus Empiricus quotes him as saying, "In fact, it will be clear that to know in reality what each thing is like is a matter of perplexity."[36] This idea — that we can't ever know what a thing truly *is* — would be echoed much later by such seventeenth-century empiricists as John Locke and George Berkeley.

But unlike those philosophers, Democritus seems to have had no real interest in a god or gods who might help us make sense of an unknowable world. About atoms, he apparently said, "There is no other god aside from these."[37]

He also believed that free will is an illusion: everything happens "by necessity."[38] The universe is made up of pre-determined outcomes, which we have no control over. This belief would later be called *determinism*.

[34] Cohen, Curd, and Reeve, *Readings*, 88.

[35] Cohen, Curd, and Reeve, *Readings*, 91.

[36] Cohen, Curd, and Reeve, *Readings*, 92.

[37] Democritus did hold a weirdly godlike belief: that "certain images of atoms approach humans, and of them some cause good and others evil, and as a result he prayed 'to meet with propitious images.' These are large and immense, and difficult to destroy though not indestructible. They indicate the future in advance to people when they are seen and emit voices. As a result people of ancient times, upon perceiving the appearances of these things, supposed that they are a god, though there is no other god aside from these having an indestructible nature" (Cohen, Curd, and Reeve, *Readings*, 92).

[38] Cohen, Curd, and Reeve, *Readings*, 81.

This universe made up of atoms and void, where true knowledge is impossible, and free will doesn't exist, seems pretty bleak. So the main thing, Democritus thought, was to be cheerful — "through moderation of enjoyment and due proportion in life."[39] (How you can choose to "be cheerful" without having free will is another puzzle that materialists struggle with, even today.)

Moderation, though, does seem like good advice. Aristotle, among others, would later adopt it. But Democritus's fellow Abdera resident, Protagoras, would call those ideas into question. What does it really mean to be "cheerful"? What are "moderate" and "enjoyment," really? And how can we ever hope to know?

7.

It might not surprise you to learn that the most thoroughly modern of the ancient philosophers was a lawyer.

Many of our ideas about Greece as an incubator of culture come from the city-state of Athens during the fifth century B.C. During the rule of Pericles, the city experienced what most historians agree was a "Golden Era."

Pericles was a general, but in this period between the Greco-Persian Wars and the Peloponnesian War, he had time to focus on ruling Athens. And he turned it into a showplace.

He supported democracy, so much so that his enemies accused him of being a populist. He beautified Athens, overseeing the construction of several iconic buildings, including the Parthenon. And he patronized the arts and literature — in fact, he once proposed that the poor should be able to attend plays free of charge. (The cost would be paid by the state.)

During this peaceful time in Athens where democracy thrived, a jury system was developed to settle disputes. As a result, a group of legal advisors emerged. They were called Sophists. *Sophia* is the Greek word for wisdom, and these advisors offered to help people win disputes in the Athenian courts. The best-known of these Sophists was named Protagoras.

Once again, we lack solid information about a pre-Socratic philosopher. Protagoras was born in Abdera, perhaps around 490 B.C. He seems to have traveled, not just in Greece, but also through part of present-day Italy.

39 Cohen, Curd, and Reeve, *Readings*, 92.

He was also a student of Democritus, which seems appropriate. Protagoras would bring the skepticism that Democritus had about our knowledge of the natural world to a different field: ethics.

Protagoras was the first of the Greek philosophers to not focus on the question of *metaphysics*: "What is the nature of reality?" Instead, he tackled the question of *ethics*: "How should we act?" And his answer to that latter question was "We should act in whatever way serves our interests."

Like the other Sophists, Protagoras offered his services as a teacher and legal advisor. By all accounts, he was a truly gifted speaker — one who became rich and famous as a result. He had definite ties to Pericles, and appears to have been involved in Athenian government.

Plato, who gives us much of our information about Protagoras, shares with us the pitch Protagoras gave a prospective student: "My boy, if you associate with me, the result will be that the very day you begin you will return home a better person, and the same will happen the next day too. Each day you will make constant progress toward being better."[40]

It's true that Plato "was not an impartial witness"[41] when it came to the Sophists. He was critical of their ideas — especially the belief that seems to have been the cornerstone of Protagoras's philosophy: "Of all things the measure is man."

But if you accept this statement — and scholars are in agreement that it did come from Protagoras and is an accurate quote — then you also have to deal with the problems that come with it.

The significance of this statement — and of the other related beliefs of Protagoras — is summed up by professor Will Buckingham: "By placing human beings at its center, it continued a tradition of taking religion out of philosophical argument, and it also shifted the focus of philosophy away from an understanding of the nature of the universe to an examination of human behavior."

This was, in part, because Protagoras didn't think worrying about the gods was worth much effort. "Concerning the gods, I am unable to know either that they are or that they are not or what their appearance is like," he wrote. "For many are the things that hinder knowledge: the obscurity of the matter and the shortness of human life."[42]

40 Cohen, Curd, and Reeve, *Readings*, 105.

41 Cohen, Curd, and Reeve, *Readings*, 105.

42 Cohen, Curd, and Reeve, *Readings*, 106.

Therefore, he felt, we should focus instead on the here and now: on man, and how to make man's life better. To do this, however, we have to solve conflicts — which inevitably arise when people argue about the truth, both in and out of court. And everyone, Protagoras observed, believes different things about the truth, based on their experiences.

So if man — not a god, or gods — is the measure of all things, then we have to give priority to *individual experience,* instead of *universal truths.* There really *are* no universal truths: I have my truth, based on my personal experience. And you have your truth, based on your personal experience.

All truth, in other words, is *relative.* It can only be judged in *relation* to the truths of other people — and not measured against some universal, unchanging standard. Because, according to Protagoras, there isn't one.

As you might expect, Protagoras defended himself from the claim that he was trying to call universal truth into question. "As for wisdom (*sophia*) and the wise man (*sophos*), I am very far from saying that they do not exist," he said, "but I also call the man clever who, by transforming things, makes them appear to be good and be good for someone to whom they appeared to be bad and were bad."[43]

The key word here is "transforming." By the *quality* of his argument, a sophist like Protagoras can transform what amounts to a bad argument into a functionally good one — and convince others to follow along.

The Stanford Encyclopedia of Philosophy points out that this strategy is practical: it's a way of resolving disputes. But it resolves them not by resorting to a singular, objective truth. It does so instead by "clever" use of rhetoric — by making "the worse case the better,"[44] as Protagoras boasted he could do.

You may have noticed that a philosophy which can be boiled down to this statement — that there is no way of knowing whether something is objectively true — seems to contain a fatal contradiction. That is, the person who makes such a statement is saying that there are no universal truths — *except* for the statement "There are no universal truths."

Or you could make an objection this way. If everyone's beliefs are "true" to them, then there is no real defense against someone who says that the belief "There is no objective truth" is *false.* This objection was raised by several philosophers of the time, including Democritus, and later by Plato and Aristotle.

[43] Mauro Bonazzi, "Protagoras," Edited by Edward N. Zalta. *Stanford Encyclopedia of Philosophy* (Fall 2020; revised Fall 2023), https://plato.stanford.edu/entries/protagoras/.

[44] Buckingham, *The Philosophy Book,* 43.

True Sophist that he was, Protagoras apparently tried to refute this claim. But the response is not terribly convincing. It goes like this: If someone says that Protagoras's claim is false, then they're really just saying it's false *to them*. Other people will say his claim is true — and who can tell the difference? But that means we've created a bigger problem, which is known as *solipsism*.

In simple terms, solipsism means that a person can't know for sure that *anything* exists except himself — or, even more pointedly, except his own *mind*. This is why we sometimes use the term *solipsist* to describe people who are self-centered, or even narcissistic. This is a problem that modern philosophers, many of whom were sympathetic to Protagoras, would face.

It's unclear how things ended up for Protagoras. There are reports that he was tried and put to death for impiety — a lack of reverence — and that his books were burned. But Plato seems to suggest that Protagoras died instead in old age, as a respected elder statesman.

We can say this for certain: as the most modern of the ancient Greek philosophers, his ideas would become more and more fashionable over time. If Protagoras's philosophy sounds familiar, it should. His beliefs about a subjective, godless existence where the most clever argument wins predict the modern world with uncanny accuracy.

Another Sophist of the time, Gorgias, came up with an elegant three-part argument. It goes like this:

1. There is no being. (*Being*, in this case, means a stable and established order, form, or meaning.)
2. Even if there *were* being, we couldn't know it.
3. Even if we *could* know it, we couldn't communicate it.

These three statements sum up a radical skepticism about existence, about the possibility of human knowledge, and about communication. They aren't just skeptical, they're solipsistic — using the definition we just gave. And this skepticism and solipsism have "haunted the whole history of Western philosophy"[45] ever since.

As Peter Kreeft notes, Protagoras and the Sophists may have gone out of fashion, but they seem to have had the last laugh. Nearly 2,500 years after their heyday in Athens, "The Sophists have convinced the majority in the legal

[45] Kreeft, *Socrates' Children*, vol. 1, 95.

establishment of their main point."[46] Their relativism has taken the place of what law schools used to teach: a *natural law* that is universal and has always existed.

And former U.S. Supreme Court Justice Anthony Kennedy might as well have been channeling the Sophists when he wrote in 1992, "At the heart of liberty is the right to define one's own concept of existence, of meaning, of the universe, and of the mystery of human life."[47]

In other words, freedom means the freedom to choose your own truth. In this case, *Planned Parenthood of Southeastern Pa. v. Casey*, it was the freedom to choose when "the mystery of human life" begins — and when to end it.

This moral relativism "divides our society," Kreeft writes, "and is at the heart of our ongoing 'culture wars.' "[48] But it isn't always popular. Even in the days of Ancient Greece, Aristotle would observe that "people were rightly annoyed at Protagoras's promise"[49] to make "the weaker argument stronger" by using slick rhetoric.

Yet Protagoras's genius was seeing past the contradictions to a fundamental human truth: everybody wants to be right. And if being right means making "the weaker argument stronger" — or throwing out any standard of objective truth — then there will always be people willing to make that bargain.

[46] Kreeft, *Socrates' Children*, vol. 1, 88.

[47] *Planned Parenthood of Southeastern Pennsylvania v. Casey* (1992). Legal Information Institute, https://www.law.cornell.edu/supremecourt/text/505/833.

[48] Kreeft, *Socrates' Children*, vol. 1, 88.

[49] Cohen, Curd, and Reeve, *Readings*, 106.

Introduction

THE BIG THREE

Of the Big Three philosophers of the fifth and fourth centuries B.C., Plato is probably the best known. We have more of his writing than the others, for starters: Socrates wrote nothing during his lifetime, which isn't terribly surprising for someone who once said that "even the best of writings are but a reminiscence of what we know."[50] And most of Aristotle's writings were lost, leaving us, in most cases, with what amounts to lecture notes.

Plato's works are also packed with ideas about the biggest subjects — ideas about life and death; good and evil; the body and the soul; the proper society; the nature of love and relationships. People have been debating these things for the past two-and-a-half millennia. And Plato's books are beautifully written — something that's unfortunately unusual in the field of philosophy. The dialogues of Plato, Peter Kreeft contends, "are to philosophy what the Bible is to religion."[51]

But perhaps the best way to consider these three philosophers is as a trio. They are, after all, directly linked: Socrates was the teacher of Plato, who was the teacher of Aristotle. And while Plato is the most visible of the three, he would never have become what he became without the influence of Socrates.

He also would not have become what he became without the influence of Aristotle. While Aristotle was Plato's star pupil, he also frequently challenged his teacher. And those challenges have become fundamental to Western thought and how it developed.

Yet for all the differences between these three philosophers —especially the differences between Plato and Aristotle — their similarities may be even more significant.

For starters, all three believed in a single god. It was not the Christian God, of course, and it was not a god who involved himself with the day-to-day affairs

50 Plato, *Phaedrus*. Translated by Benjamin Jowett. Project Gutenberg. Last updated January 15, 2013. https://www.gutenberg.org/files/1636/1636-h/1636-h.htm.

51 Kreeft, *Socrates' Children*, vol. 1, 108.

of people. For Socrates and Plato, this god was the "One," the form of the Good. For Aristotle, it was an "Unmoved Mover." This god was eternal, unchanging, and the source of the ultimate truth.[52]

All three philosophers also believed in the existence of *universals* — including a universal standard of truth. There's much more to say about the subject of universals. But for the moment, it's important to note that this was a direct contrast with the Sophists, like Protagoras, who thought that truth — and therefore, morality — was relative.

There's another similarity in the three men that isn't often noted. As the Italian scholar Carlo Natali points out, none of the trio were paid for their lectures — unlike many other philosophers of the time, like the Sophists. This decision affected Socrates more than Plato and Aristotle, since he did not come from a wealthy family and chose philosophy "at the price of a life spent in miserable conditions."[53]

For Plato and Aristotle, however, philosophy was a response to a persistent question among many Greek men of the time: how to spend your time if you didn't have to work. This was a critical decision, since it defined "what sort of person we are."[54] And for Plato and Aristotle, philosophy was "a way of spending one's life, and of best actualizing one's human capacities; it was, in a word, the choice of a way of being happy."[55]

This happiness, as we'll see, was linked to their pursuit of knowledge — which, for all three men, equaled virtue. Man is good when he seeks the truth.

In short, three of the smartest people who ever lived all acknowledged the existence of a supreme being, the importance of virtue, and the existence of objective truth. And they shared these beliefs because they believed it was necessary, and not just for financial gain. So maybe it's worth paying attention to what they had in common — and why they believed it.

[52] Plato suggested that the world was created by a "demiurge," a manifestation of the Good who did its work.

[53] Carlo Natali, *Aristotle: His Life and School* (Princeton, NJ: Princeton University Press, 2013), 65.

[54] Natali, *Aristotle*, 66.

[55] Natali, *Aristotle*, 66–67.

CHAPTER TWO

THE GADFLY

1.

As the sun outside sinks into the ocean, a smoking charcoal brazier smudges shadows onto the walls of the cell. Several men are crowded around a bed. Some of them are laughing; some are weeping openly into their robes. All these sounds echo from the stones of the prison, until the old man on the bed urges his friends to hush.

He's seventy years old, and by any standard, he's extraordinarily unattractive. He's short, squat, and looks a lot like a frog. Partly this is because of his eyes, which are so wide-set that it seems he's gazing in two directions at once. He also has a snub nose; thick, fleshy lips; a pot belly; and a bald head. Some people compare him to a satyr, thanks to his hairy back and shoulders. He rarely bathes and owns only a single filthy cloak.

But none of this matters when he starts talking. As of today — February 15, 399 B.C. — he's probably the greatest speaker of his time. He'll be acknowledged as one of the greatest in history, in fact. Centuries later, more than one observer will say that only Jesus was a more significant figure.

Like Jesus, the scruffy little man on the bed has been sentenced to death. Like Jesus, the charges against the man have been exaggerated. Like Jesus, he's accused of not respecting the established religion.

And like Jesus, the man on the bed is taking his death sentence calmly. Some of his supporters are crying, knowing they're about to lose someone "whom I may truly call the wisest, and justest, and best of all the men whom I have ever known," as one of them will later say.

But the man on the bed tells his followers not to worry. He straightens his tattered robe and holds up his hands for quiet.

To die, he says, is the job of a philosopher. And the man on the bed will become, in the eyes of many, the greatest philosopher of all — even though he will leave behind no books, and even though his core belief is that wisdom means acknowledging you don't really know anything.

You can't get true wisdom, the man says, until you die. Committing suicide to acquire such wisdom would be wrong, he adds. But embracing death when it comes is the only real path for a philosopher. That's because the soul is immortal. And when it's separated from the body, it can finally gain the knowledge we all seek.

As the firelight flickers on the walls, as the charcoal smoke thickens, and as his followers sniffle, the man makes four arguments to explain what he means. After all, he has made his reputation through discussion.

"It is talk, sheer talk, and the joy of talking," he once said, "that is the prime attraction of Athens."[56] *And right to the end, he's going to keep it up.*

2.

The man on the bed, Socrates, was eventually put to death. The rulers of Athens had found him guilty of impiety and corrupting the young, though they were probably also tired of the way Socrates embarrassed them with his constant questions.

So who was this ugly, seemingly unremarkable man? And why did he threaten so many people?

Socrates was born in 469 B.C. in the village of Mount Lycabettus, a hillside town that was a twenty-minute walk from Athens. He was the son of a stonecutter and a midwife. He may have worked for a while in his father's trade, but he

[56] I. F. Stone, *The Trial of Socrates* (Boston: Little, Brown, 1989), 211.

also inherited part of his father's estate — so he might not have had to work at all. Not that Socrates ever cared about money — or earned much of it.

Instead, he studied with several early philosophers. One of them was Anaxagoras, who taught that the sun was a fiery star. His view would reportedly get him charged with impiety and run out of Athens. This eerily foreshadowed Socrates's eventual fate — although it doesn't seem to have given him any pause.[57]

Socrates was married twice and had three children. The mother of his children, Xanthippe, apparently had little patience for her husband the philosopher, who preferred hanging out and debating people in the Agora, the outdoor marketplace of Athens. Once, Xanthippe became so frustrated during an argument that she emptied a chamber pot on Socrates's head. (His witty response was, "After the thunder comes the rain.")[58]

Socrates also apparently served with some distinction as a private during the Peloponnesian War. In one combat story, he found one of his admirers, Alcibiades, lying wounded on the battlefield. Bravely, Socrates hoisted the young man onto his shoulders and carried him through enemy lines, to safety. But just as money was no concern to Socrates, neither family nor glory was his main motivation, either.

"He doesn't care if someone is beautiful, or rich, or has any of the distinctions the public thinks are so great," Alcibiades said approvingly. "He thinks of these things as nothing."[59]

Instead, Socrates spent his life following the advice inscribed over the doorway of the temple of the Delphic Oracle: "Know thyself." He would turn this quest into his own catchphrase: "The unexamined life is not worth living."[60]

57 In *The Trial of Socrates*, I. F. Stone contends that Socrates had no need to be cautious, because Anaxagoras was never actually charged with impiety for his views. If he had been, Stone says, then surely it would have been mentioned by Thucydides, Xenophon, or Plato. Stone also points out that stories about the Sophist Protagoras having his books burned are similarly suspect.

58 H. A. Guerber, *The Story of the Greeks* (New York: American Book Company, 1896), Project Gutenberg, https://www.gutenberg.org/files/23495/23495-h/23495-h.htm.

59 Kreeft, *Socrates' Children*, vol. 1, 104. Alcibiades apparently fell in love with Socrates and attempted to seduce him. "One can only assume that Alcibiades suffered from defective eyesight," jokes Paul Strathern. He tells the story of these foiled attempts in his *Socrates in 90 Minutes*, adding that resisting "the advances of a good-looking young man" would have shown "superhuman restraint" in Greece at the time (Strathern, *Socrates in 90 Minutes*, 35–37).

60 Plato, *Apology* (Section 31d), *Plato in Twelve Volumes*, vol. 1, ed. Harold North Fowler (Cambridge, MA: Harvard University Press, 1966), Perseus Digital Library, https://www.perseus.tufts.edu/hopper/text?doc=Perseus:text:1999.01.0170:text=Apol.:section=31d&highlight=voice.

It was in this pursuit of self-knowledge that Socrates discovered a paradoxical truth. The priestess of the temple at Delphi told him that no one was wiser than he was. Socrates struggled to understand how this could be so.

He approached a man who had the reputation of being wise, determined to show that the oracle was mistaken. But Socrates was startled to discover that the man was inflated with self-importance.

"I went away thinking to myself that I was wiser than this man," Socrates said. "The fact is that neither of us knows anything beautiful and good, but he thinks he does know when he doesn't, and I don't know and don't think I do. So am wiser than he is only by this trifle."[61]

But this "trifle" turned out to be the cornerstone of his philosophy. His famous quote, "I know nothing except the fact of my own ignorance,"[62] captures the humility of Socrates.

It also illustrates how he ran afoul of Athenian society. Determined to find out how many *other* people weren't as wise as they seemed, Socrates put a bunch of his fellow citizens to the test. They failed. And they weren't too happy about it.

"I went to one after another after that, and saw that I was disliked," Socrates said, "and I sorrowed and feared, but still it seemed necessary to hold the god's business of the highest importance, so I had to go on trying to find out what the oracle meant."[63] And so he did.

This took the form of Socrates asking an endless series of questions to do the god's business. These questions were an effort to find the essence of concepts like justice, piety, and goodness.

Socrates would ask, for example, "What is justice?" When people answered, he would expose the contradictions in their answers. This form of questioning, which we now call the *Socratic method*, is a way of getting at the truth by trying to precisely define a concept. The first goal is usually to show what a thing is *not*.

The Socratic method, which is still used today, was an early form of logic. It evolved into a style called the *dialectic*, which uses the collision of opposing ideas to generate new solutions.

The Socratic method is a negative style of interrogation. It's better at generating questions than answers. But it helps clarify issues where there may be a lot of preconceived ideas. And it forces participants to actively defend their positions.

61 Kreeft, *Socrates' Children*, vol. 1, 102.
62 Buckingham, *The Philosophy Book*, 49.
63 Kreeft, *Socrates' Children*, vol. 1, 102.

This last part of his method made Socrates unpopular with prominent Athenians, who didn't appreciate being shown up by this dirty, barefoot philosopher. They mockingly called him "The Gadfly." But he had another nickname, one that referenced his mother's profession. He was also known as "The Midwife" — in the sense that his questions helped give birth to knowledge.

3.

On a normal day, you might find Socrates holding court in a cramped shoe shop owned by a cobbler named Simon. This shop, located at the edge of the Agora in Athens, is where Socrates holds informal classes. You can hear him questioning his students over the din of Simon pounding hobnails into boots.

Today, however, is the feast day for the goddess Bendis.[64] *Socrates and his companion Glaucon*[65] *have celebrated at The Piraeus, the port of Athens. It's been a loud, hot summer day by the seaside, and they're both looking forward to getting back home. But they've just met a young nobleman named Polemarchus, who insists they first stop by the home of his elderly father, Cephalus.*

At Cephalus's estate, the discussion turns to a favorite topic: What is justice? Glaucon tells the story of a shepherd who was a descendent of King Gyges of Lydia. One day, there was an earthquake, and the shepherd discovered his ancestor's hidden tomb. Within this gravesite, the awestruck shepherd uncovered an incredible treasure: a ring that could make its wearer invisible.

What should the shepherd do with this unexpected gift? For Glaucon, the answer is simple. He argues that anyone who has a ring with the power of invisibility would be a fool not to use it for his own benefit.

"For all men believe in their hearts that injustice is far more profitable to the individual than justice, and he who argues as I have been supposing,

[64] The goddess Bendis was worshipped by the Thracians, who were allies of Athens during the Peloponnesian War. Some think that worshipping Bendis was a way for Athenians to acknowledge Thrace's wartime support.

[65] Glaucon was the older brother of Plato. He is a character in several of Plato's dialogues.

will say that they are right," Glaucon says, a smug grin spreading across his lips. "If you could imagine anyone obtaining this power of becoming invisible, and never doing any wrong or touching what was another's, he would be thought by the lookers-on to be a most wretched idiot."[66]

The only reason people would publicly praise this man, Glaucon adds, is that they would be afraid of suffering injustice themselves. Everyone really wants to be unjust; not everyone has the guts.

Injustice, Glaucon contends, should be treated like any other distinguished profession, "like the skilful pilot or physician, who knows intuitively his own powers and keeps within their limits.... So let the unjust make his unjust attempts in the right way, and lie hidden if he means to be great in his injustice."[67]

But through a series of questions, Socrates exposes the flaws in Glaucon's argument. He points out that Glaucon himself doesn't live the way he proposes, but is instead an honest man. Eventually, he reveals his first principle: that God can only be good. And if God can only be good, then it follows that he would not deceive humanity — as did Greek gods such as Zeus.

And if all that is true, Socrates suggests, then we should not deceive one another, either.

"Justice in her own nature has been shown to be best for the soul in her own nature. Let a man do what is just, whether he have the ring of Gyges or not."[68]

4.

The quest for knowledge and truth, Socrates thought, was the *telos* — the true purpose — of human beings. And seeking truth, he felt, was what truly makes us good — and therefore, happy.

66 Plato, *The Republic*, trans. Benjamin Jowett, Project Gutenberg, July 26, 2017. https://www.gutenberg.org/files/55201/55201-h/55201-h.htm.

67 Plato, *Republic*.

68 Plato, *Republic*.

"Seeing that all men desire happiness, and happiness, as has been shown, is gained by a use, and a right use, of the things of life, and the right use of them, and good fortune in the use of them, is given by knowledge," he said, "the inference is that everybody ought by all means to try and make himself as wise as he can."[69]

All error, Socrates believed, was the result of ignorance. Those who want bad things don't realize these things are bad — or else people would not want them. This is why Socrates stressed the importance of seeking knowledge. The more we know about ourselves, the more likely we'll be to seek — and find — true happiness, which is virtue.

But this belief, in the view of author I. F. Stone, was part of the reason Socrates was charged with impiety in early 399 B.C. Stone felt that these charges had less to do with Socrates not being *reverent* — and more to do with him not being *realistic*.

If no one does wrong willingly, Stone pointed out, then no one can truly be guilty, "and every criminal can go free."[70] In the developing legal system of Athens — a city which was, at the time, just emerging from a period of great turmoil — this was a frightening thought. Order and stability were real concerns.

"One has to remember that most Athenian families had suffered violence within the last three or four years, and were still lamenting a murdered father, brother, or son," Paul Johnson added. "The atmosphere was raw, bitter, and brutal."[71]

There was an even bigger problem, Stone thought. Socrates had made a habit of showing that no one truly knew anything. That included the rulers of Athens. "No one was fit to rule. Where did that leave the city? Up a creek. His dialectic was a dead end."[72]

The miracle may be that someone as provocative as Socrates wasn't charged earlier. But for the previous five years, he had somehow managed to survive several political firestorms in Athens.

After being humiliated by Sparta in the Peloponnesian War (431–404 B.C.), Athens had been ruled by the Thirty Tyrants. One of them was a former

[69] Plato, *Euthydemus,* trans. Benjamin Jowett, Internet Classics Archive, http://classics.mit.edu/Plato/euthydemus.html.

[70] Stone, *The Trial of Socrates*, 87.

[71] Paul Johnson, *Socrates: A Man for Our Times* (New York: Classic Penguin, 2011), 169.

[72] Stone, *The Trial of Socrates*, 87. As Stone pointed out, this sowing of doubt was one reason Socrates was sometimes accused of being a Sophist.

pupil of Socrates named Critias. Critias had forbidden the teaching of philosophy on the streets — a policy that directly targeted his old teacher. Yet Socrates managed to avoid prosecution.

After a violent uprising, the Tyrants were eventually replaced by democrats — which was even worse for Socrates. He had been a longtime skeptic of democracy, equating it to being ruled by sheep. And one of the democratic leaders was Anytus. He blamed Socrates for his son — a former pupil of Socrates — deciding to leave the family business and pursue a career as a philosopher.

Clearly, Socrates had made some powerful enemies. Yet at his trial before five hundred members of the Athenian ruling council, Socrates seemed to go out of his way to provoke the jurors.

For starters, he doubled down on his views about goodness and truth — views that seemed to call into question traditional Athenian beliefs about the role of the gods.

"Socrates' theory of the divine seemed to make the most important rituals and sacrifices in the city entirely useless, for if the gods are all good, they will benefit human beings regardless of whether or not human beings make offerings to them."[73]

That gave possible evidence of an irreverent nature. Then Socrates went further. He referenced a divine "sign" — sometimes called a "daimon" — which he said had been advising him his whole life.

"It is a sort of voice that comes to me, and when it comes it always holds me back from what I am thinking of doing, but never urges me forward," Socrates said.[74] (Then he couldn't resist getting in a dig at some of his accusers: this voice was what kept him from being a politician.)

If the jurors of Athens were looking for evidence that Socrates was a religious rabble-rouser, his claim to be in contact with a "daimon" probably clinched the deal. But not only did Socrates keep broaching controversial topics, he didn't seem to be taking the trial too seriously, either.

When he had a chance to suggest an alternate sentence, Socrates first advised that he be honored like a hero. He asked to dine for the rest of his life — at the public's expense — in the Prytaneum, the sacred hall in Athens.

[73] James M. Ambury, "Socrates," Internet Encyclopedia of Philosophy, https://iep.utm.edu/socrates/, 2002.

[74] Plato, *Apology* (Section 31d).

His friends begged him to be reasonable. So he proposed a fine — of one mina, enough to buy a scroll, or a bottle of wine.

The council was not amused. The final vote was 360 to 140 in favor of the death penalty.

Had Socrates asked to be sent into exile, the council would undoubtedly have agreed. And right up until the end, he could have escaped from jail: some of his disciples had arranged it. But Socrates believed that two wrongs could not make a right, and he refused.

In fact, Socrates concluded his defense by asking the jurors to "punish" his sons when they grew up, "if they seem to you to care for money or anything else more than for virtue, and if they think they amount to something when they do not." If the jurors agreed to do this, he said, "both I and my sons shall have received just treatment from you."[75]

5.

As the shadows in his cell lengthen, Socrates's time with his friends grows short. He has bathed, then sent his wife and children home. Now he needs to reassure his sorrowful friends that his death is not, in fact, the end.

The first argument he makes is called the Argument from Opposites. The world is made up of opposites, Socrates says. Therefore, there has to be an unchanging, indestructible opposite of our perishable bodies — a soul, in other words.

His second point is called the Theory of Recollection. We don't so much learn things as recollect things, he says. We were born knowing these things, but have forgotten them. And the fact that we were born with this knowledge suggests that we had to get it from some other place, where our souls reside.

Point number three is known as the Argument from Affinity. Some things are material, and perceivable by our senses, Socrates says. These things are mortal: they won't last forever. But there are other things that we can't perceive with our senses. Thoughts, for example, and other abstractions, like numbers. We know these things exist. The soul, therefore, must be like them.

[75] Plato, *Apology* (Section 31d).

The final point Socrates makes comes in something called the Theory of Forms. This will turn out to be the most important point of the four. Everything in the world is just an imperfect copy of a perfect idea, or form. And these perfect forms must be unchanging and eternal — including our souls.

"All men will agree that God, and the essential form of life, and the immortal in general, will never perish," Socrates reassures his friends.[76] *He turns to Cebes, an earnest disciple who has questioned him repeatedly.*

"Seeing then that the immortal is indestructible, must not the soul, if she is immortal, be also imperishable?" Socrates asks.

Cebes strokes his beard and considers. "Most certainly," he replies.

"Then when death attacks a man, the mortal portion of him may be supposed to die, but the immortal retires at the approach of death and is preserved safe and sound?" Socrates asks. Once again, Cebes nods.

Socrates smiles, and for a moment, his homely features become almost handsome. "Then, Cebes, beyond question," he says, smacking a fist into his palm, "the soul is immortal and imperishable, and our souls will truly exist in another world!"

6.

This belief in an immortal soul may be the most surprising teaching of Socrates. As author Peter Kreeft points out, it was a truly radical concept at the time.

The word *soul* (or *psyche*), prior to Socrates, meant "ghost." The idea we sometimes have of the soul being a ghostly version of our flesh-and-blood bodies is actually an old, old idea.

But "Socrates reversed the conventional relationship between body and soul: instead of the soul being a pale copy of the body, the body was a pale copy of the soul," writes Kreeft. The soul "is more real, solid, substantial, and alive than the body."[77]

[76] All quotes in this section come from Benjamin Jowett's translation of Plato's *Phaedo*.
[77] Kreeft, *Socrates' Children*, vol. 1, 106.

Therefore, Kreeft adds, "the fundamental task of life is the care of the soul."[78] This is because the soul—not the body—is the *true* self. "Others can harm my body, but only I can harm my soul, by ignoring its true goods, which are wisdom and virtue."[79]

If people wondered why Socrates was so cavalier about being sentenced to death, the answer is probably here. He didn't fear death because he believed that by humbly seeking wisdom and virtue, he had already done what was right.

That also included revealing the errors of others. "I help the god," Socrates said, "by proving that man is not wise."[80] But we need to make an important distinction: unlike the Skeptics and Sophists, Socrates believed that "the truth is out there"—and that it was man's job to try to find it.

7.

You might wonder, since Socrates didn't write down any of his thoughts, how we know so much about them.

The answer is that two former pupils of Socrates published their recollections of him. One was Xenophon, a former soldier who later turned to writing. His *Memorabilia* gives a basic portrait of Socrates that has often been criticized for missing the point: Socrates's philosophy. "If he were our sole authority for Socrates," Paul Johnson writes, "we would never have learned to venerate him as the founder of philosophy as an expert science."[81]

This is where Plato comes in. The most famous of all Socrates's students would later become, in the opinion of many people, the most important philosopher of all time. We'll read much more about him in the next chapter. For now, we'll only talk about him as the "biographer" of Socrates.

Plato used Socrates as the main character in a series of "dialogues." In these encounters, Socrates confronts a variety of adversaries, and almost always gets the better of them. His dialectic exposes contradictions and forces his opponents to concede Socrates's points.

These dialogues are some of the best-known philosophical works in history. The *Apology, Crito, Euthryphro,* and later, *Phaedo* (translated as *On the Soul*),

78 Kreeft, *Socrates' Children,* vol. 1, 108.
79 Kreeft, *Socrates' Children,* vol. 1, 106.
80 Kreeft, *Socrates' Children,* vol. 1, 103.
81 Johnson, *Socrates,* 9.

make up a quartet that describes the trial, imprisonment, and execution of Socrates. The *Republic,* meanwhile, doesn't just tackle the subject of justice: it lays out a plan for the ideal society.

Plato's dialogues have their reputation in part because he was, simply, a great writer. His Socrates — patient, witty, sly, and occasionally maddening — is one of the great literary figures in the Western canon, "a complex blend of the buffoon and the saint."[82]

The question that's often asked is: How much of this character is actually Socrates — and how much is actually Plato? Did Plato use poetic license to turn his Socrates character into a mouthpiece for his own ideas?

As one example, in *Phaedo,* Socrates mentions a theory of forms. This theory seems to be the same concept that Plato would use as the centerpiece of his own philosophy. So did this idea belong to Socrates or Plato? Did Socrates even agree with it?

There's a general consensus among scholars that the early dialogues of Plato reflect more of the "authentic" Socrates. In the later dialogues, these scholars believe, Plato begins to take over.

However, a major point is often overlooked: Plato's dialogues were written and circulated during the lifetime of people who knew Socrates. "So he could not have gotten away with great lies among the Athenians who had known him," Peter Kreeft contends, "any more than the disciples of Jesus could have gotten away with a fundamentally false account of Jesus if this account, oral or written, circulated within the lifetime of those who had known him."[83]

Kreeft further points out that "many other ancient sources corroborate, and none refute, the essential picture of Socrates that Plato gives us."[84] The simplest explanation, as we'll see later in this book, is sometimes the best.

8.

If our picture of Socrates is more or less accurate, then what effect can we say he had on philosophy — and on the world?

[82] Strathern, *Socrates in 90 Minutes,* 20.

[83] Kreeft, *Socrates' Children,* vol. 1, 103–104.

[84] One of the ancient writers who gave us a somewhat contrary picture of Plato is Aristophanes, whose play *Clouds* lampooned Socrates as a Sophist.

There is agreement about Socrates's importance. He was the first of the Big Three philosophers. And his dialectic — the Socratic method that tries to gain the most accurate information possible through a series of questions — is one of the most influential forms of inquiry in Western history. It was the ancestor of logic. And it's still used every day, all over the world — even if people don't recognize its origin.

The Socratic method also turned Western philosophy away from *metaphysics* — the nature of reality — toward *ethics* and *epistemology*: how we should act, and how we can know what we know.

In this way, Socrates is a lot like two of the greatest Eastern philosophers: Confucius and the Buddha. Confucius was a philosopher and politician who lived during the sixth century B.C. in China. Meanwhile, in Nepal, Siddhartha Gautama renounced his royal heritage for a life as a traveling religious teacher. He became the Buddha sometime between the sixth and fifth centuries B.C.

Both Confucius and the Buddha developed ethical systems of belief. Confucius taught a moral code that was similar in some ways to that of Socrates: it equated virtue with knowledge. It also included a variation of the Golden Rule that is sometimes called the Silver Rule: "Never impose on others what you would not choose for yourself."

The Buddha's system pinpointed suffering as the main roadblock to human happiness. Suffering, the Buddha taught, was caused by desire. So only by eliminating desire could humans be free from suffering.

There's a third great moral teacher, of course, to whom Socrates is often compared. His ethical philosophy — and its belief in an immortal soul — would have similarities to the later teachings of Jesus.

It's clear that Socrates took philosophy in a radically different direction than the pre-Socratics of ancient Greece: less worried about the world *outside* us than our place *within* it. Some later thinkers would argue that philosophy needed to return to metaphysics. Socrates more or less neglected it — which some philosophers saw as decadent. Why spend so much time on our own individual problems, they asked, instead of the shared problems of the world?

Yet far from being a prototype of the navel-gazing philosopher, Socrates was something much more important, much more practical — and much more fundamentally human. As Paul Johnson puts it:

For Socrates saw and practiced philosophy not as an academic but as a human activity. It was about real men and women facing actual ethical choices between right and wrong, good and evil. Hence a philosophical leader had to be more than a thinker, much more. He had to be a good man, from whom the quest for virtue was not an abstract Idea but a practical business of daily living. He had to be brave in facing up to choices and living with their consequences. Philosophy, in the last resort, was a form of heroism, and those who practiced it had to possess the courage to sacrifice everything, including life itself, in pursuing excellence of mind. That is what Socrates himself did. And that is why we honor him and salute him as philosophy personified.[85]

9.

In Socrates's prison cell, as the smoking brazier sputters and darkness arrives, the jailer brings in a cup. In it is a tea brewed with ground hemlock, or Conium maculatum, a flowering herb common to the Mediterranean region. This poisonous plant brings on paralysis and death by suffocation.

Even the jailer weeps before giving Socrates this fatal solution, yet the philosopher drinks the whole cup "quite readily and cheerfully."[86] All his friends can no longer control their tears, but Socrates hushes them once again.

In his final moments, he shares his hopes about what is to come next. Philosophy, he imagines, is the thing that will free his soul to pursue knowledge on a higher plane.

Those who have "purified themselves with philosophy" will be able to escape the prisons of their earthly bodies, he reassures his red-eyed friends. And they will live in mansions, he adds, that are too wonderful to be described.

Then Socrates must have his disciples help him lie down. He can no longer walk, as the hemlock tea has paralyzed his legs. His friends begin weeping once again, but Socrates can't hush them this time. His body now grows cold, and his soul is headed toward those beautiful mansions of his dreams.

✠ ✠ ✠

[85] Johnson, *Socrates*, 193–194.

[86] All quotes in this section come from Benjamin Jowett's translation of Plato's *Phaedo*.

CHAPTER THREE

THE SWAN

1.

The prisoner is finally, finally free.

Yet freedom may be worse than captivity. Everything hurts. Everything is strange. Everything is frightening.

For as long as he can remember, the prisoner has been chained by the legs and the neck deep within a cave. Now he can barely stand. His eyes squeeze shut at the barest hint of light.

But it's toward the light that his liberator is leading him. Shielding his face, and trying to hide his terror, the prisoner staggers along.

His liberator seems intent on making things worse. He keeps whispering to the prisoner. But he's not whispering words of encouragement. Instead, he's telling the prisoner that everything he's ever experienced has been a lie. "That is a statue," he says, pointing to a stone figure. "And this," adds the liberator, indicating a form flickering behind the statue, against the wall, "is the statue's shadow."

The prisoner doesn't understand. This thing, this shadow, is the only reality he's ever known, and he reaches feebly for it. But the liberator is impatient.

"It's only a copy of a man." The liberator grasps the prisoner's arm more tightly, pulling him toward the entrance. "A man. Like us."

None of this makes sense to the prisoner. And things are about to get worse. In a moment, he's pulled from the mouth of the cave. His head now feels like it's about to explode.

The prisoner falls to his knees for hours, curled into a ball, cowering and whimpering. He can't comprehend the sight that has blinded him, the sight that has laid bare an entire landscape of unfathomable wonders. He simply lies there, shuddering and dumbfounded by the rays of the sun.

2.

The scene you just read is based on the most famous image in the history of philosophy. And the man who came up with it very well may be the most famous philosopher. The "Myth of the Cave," as it is commonly known, is the creation of Plato.

More than 2,500 years after Plato told this fable in his book The *Republic*, it's as fresh, challenging, and mysterious as ever. It gives hope to some, and angers others. But like Plato himself, it simply can't be ignored.

One of the most-repeated quotes about Plato comes from Alfred North Whitehead, the British mathematician and philosopher. In 1929, he wrote, "The safest general characterization of the European philosophical tradition is that it consists of a series of footnotes to Plato."[87]

The second part of Whitehead's quote is important, but doesn't always get shared. He added, "I do not mean the systematic scheme of thought which scholars have doubtfully extracted from his writings. I allude to the wealth of general ideas scattered through them."

In other words, Plato is best known not for his overall philosophy — which can be hard to follow — but for the number of big ideas his writings contain.

There's no bigger idea than the one in the Myth of the Cave. That's because this myth is a metaphor for Plato's Theory of Forms.

All these years later, the Theory of Forms is still an incredibly controversial idea. It's confusing. Skeptics have poked multiple holes in it. Because of all this, some people deny it altogether.

[87] Alfred North Whitehead, *Process and Reality* (New York: Free Press, 1978), 39.

Yet as the philosopher Edward Feser points out, "something *like* Plato's theory is notoriously hard to avoid if we are to make sense of mathematics, language, science, and the very structure of the world of our existence."[88]

Why do people have such a problem with the Theory of Forms, then? Probably because of what it suggests — and because of who later adopted it.

3.

The man on the ground has been lying there all night.

It was a long, long evening, and not without its uneasy moments. Yet as the shadows fell, the man felt more at home. The darkness, after all, was a lot like the cave where he'd lived his whole life.

The man finally sits up and stares furtively into the void above his head. He squints at the large, bright object there, but gradually his clenched eye sockets relax. And he draws in a breath at the pinpricks of light that fleck the — well, it won't be until later that he will call it a "sky."

Suddenly thirsty, he crawls uncertainly until he reaches the edge of the ground. Looking down, he sees a face shimmering. He recognizes it as a man's face. But it takes quite some time before he understands that it is his own. And it takes even longer for him to realize that it is water — the same water he'd sipped in the cave — that's casting the reflection.

Now the sun is rising in the heavens. But while the man is cautious, he no longer feels so afraid. The glow reveals so much. And the man is not averting his gaze anymore. He's watching. Then crawling. Then walking. Then touching. And learning.

4.

As is true of many famous one-name celebrities, "Plato" was an adopted identity.

He was born Aristocles, after his grandfather. "Plato" — based on the Greek *platos*, which is the word for "broad" — was apparently a nickname that referred to either his forehead or his shoulders. (Plato was a wrestler of some repute, although he apparently just missed competing in the Olympics.)

88 Feser, *The Last Superstition*, 201.

Born in 427 B.C., he came from a wealthy family — both his father and mother came from high society in Athens. But Plato's father, Ariston, died when he was young. His mother, Perictione, remarried a man named Pyrilampes. It's hard not to wonder how much Plato's later ideas about the family — including his controversial suggestion that the state, not parents, should raise children — were shaped by his own childhood.

Like many young men, Plato drifted for a while. He apparently served as a cavalryman near the end of the Peloponnesian War. Then he considered pursuing a political career, although he quickly became disenchanted with the government of the Thirty Tyrants, who ruled Athens after the war. His potential career as a poet also went up in smoke — literally. Plato reportedly burned all his poems after hearing Socrates speak.

For his part, Socrates may have also recognized something special in Plato. There's a story told by some of Plato's ancient biographers about a dream Socrates had the night before the two first met. In the dream, a baby swan flew into Socrates's lap, where it instantly grew to adult size. This precocious swan, Socrates reportedly said, was Plato.

Whether that dream was true or just a literary invention, it's easy to understand how the fate of Socrates inspired Plato's philosophy. As we read in the last chapter, Socrates revolutionized philosophy in Athens. He turned it away from questions about the nature of the world around us, and focused instead on trying to define concepts like goodness and justice, and how humans could achieve them.

He also made lots of enemies. And as we saw, he was eventually sentenced to death. Plato, who studied with Socrates for nearly a decade, was devastated. He left Athens in disgust and would spend most of the next dozen years in exile, traveling to many countries. These included Cyrene, Megara, and possibly Egypt. But his most eventful stop was in Sicily.

It was in Sicily where Plato met some of the followers of Pythagoras, who believed that numbers were the key to understanding the world. This made a big impression on Plato. His own developing philosophy would also focus on things men could learn by reason (like numerical concepts), instead of the senses (like physical objects).

Before he left Athens, Plato had declared that "Until kings become philosophers, or philosophers, kings, things will never go well in this world."[89]

[89] Dave Robinson and Judy Groves, *Introducing Plato* (Duxford, U.K.: Icon Books, 2000), 9.

Later, Plato would turn this idea into a foundation of his political theory. He proposed that the ideal society would be ruled by philosopher kings. Naturally, they would be the wisest people in society, who cared only about knowledge — instead of glory or possessions.

While that high-minded proposal never came to pass, Plato got himself into trouble occasionally by trying to meddle in regular old worldly politics. In 388 B.C., on the island of Sicily, in the Greek-speaking city-state of Syracuse, Plato met a young man named Dion. Intelligent, attractive, and charismatic, Dion seemed to Plato to be the perfect candidate to become one of his "philosopher kings."

It didn't work out that way. Dion was also the brother-in-law of Syracuse's leader, Dionysius I, a legendarily paranoid tyrant. Dionysius was so impressed with Plato that he immediately imprisoned him, and made plans to sell him into slavery. "Don't worry," Dionysius I reportedly said, coining one of history's greatest lines. "He's so much of a philosopher that he won't even notice."[90]

An old friend, Anniceris the Cyrenaic, was surprised to see Plato in the slave market on the Greek island of Aegina. He paid twenty mina to win Plato's freedom. But despite this near-miss with disaster, Plato would return to Syracuse twice in later years to help Dion. (Neither trip went well, and Dion was later assassinated. The dream of the philosopher king was a hard one for Plato to abandon.)

However, in 387 B.C. Plato finally returned to Athens. He was now forty years old, and it was time to do something serious with his life. Anniceris had given him some money, and Plato used it to buy a piece of land about a mile northwest of the city, near the river Cephissus. "It was a region of parkland dotted with plane trees, in whose shade stood a number of statues and temples," writes author Paul Strathern. "Here, amidst the cool avenues and tinkling streams, Plato opened the Academy."[91]

The Academy is one of the most famous schools in history. It's usually considered the first university. Here, in this picturesque setting, Plato began assembling a group of followers. Some of them, unusually for the time, were women. One student, Aristotle, would later become as revered as Plato himself.

The Academy's course of study, as Peter Kreeft notes, "became the 'core curriculum' of Western education for the next two thousand years."[92] Students took classes in arithmetic, geometry, astronomy, and music. (That last subject was no

[90] Paul Strathern, *Plato in 90 Minutes* (Chicago: Ivan R. Dee, 1996), 31.

[91] Strathern, *Plato in 90 Minutes*, 33.

[92] Kreeft, *Socrates' Children*, vol. 1, 110.

accident, thanks to Plato's interest in Pythagoras's theories — which linked music and math.) And, of course, Plato's students also studied grammar, rhetoric, and logic.

In these classes, students sat in the shade of olive trees and listened while Plato strode around the gardens and lectured. But it wasn't just a one-way conversation. Students were free to disagree with each other, and with Plato himself.

Yet it was here, in the Grove of Academe, that Plato also began developing the philosophy for which he would become legendary. He would explain it in a series of dialogues that paid tribute to his own teacher, Socrates.

5.

If you'd seen the prisoner when he first emerged from the cave, you would hardly recognize him now.

The man who walks upright in the glow of the sun is no longer afraid of the world he sees revealed around him. The trees, the rocks, the rivers, the grass — all fill him with wonder. And he fills himself with wonder, too. No longer does he think of himself as a shadow on a cave wall. The sun has showed him who he really is: a man.

You might imagine that he'd be angry about the time he wasted in the cave. But the world he sees now is so amazing that he has no time for regret, nor does he want revenge.

Instead, he just feels pity for all his fellow prisoners, chained there in the cave and experiencing what he now realizes was a false reality. He shudders as he imagines going the rest of his life without seeing the truth. But what can he do?

The man stares into the majesty of the sun — now he can look upon it without flinching — and as he basks in its brightness and warmth, he reaches a decision. He will tell the prisoners about this world, this real reality.

He smiles, and begins to walk back in the direction of the cave.

6.

Plato's early writings — the *Apology*, the *Crito*, and the *Phaedo* — tell the story of Socrates, especially his trial and final days. They were Plato's attempt to set the record straight about his mentor, who apparently did not write anything during his own lifetime. And they used the dialogue form, featuring accounts of conversations between Socrates and other Athenians.

Often, these other characters disagree with Socrates, who reveals the flaws in their positions. Plato, of course, wanted to show his old teacher getting the better of the men who would one day put him to death — even though many of the dialogues end without definitive conclusions.

But Plato wanted to do more than just reproduce Socrates's arguments. He also wanted to recount the method that Socrates used to challenge his challengers. That's why he chose the dialogue form.

"His dialogues give us the *process* of thinking as well as the conclusions," Peter Kreeft writes, "and we have to steer our own mind along each step of the winding road before we get to the destination."

If that makes Plato's dialogues seem like a difficult read, you might be surprised. Much more of Plato's work survives than that of any other early Western philosopher. But Plato was also the first great philosopher who was a great *writer*, as well. The dialogue form may be a little strange to modern readers. The conversations, however, are clearly expressed, and full of memorable imagery.

The following questions are usually asked: How do we know Plato is accurately representing the ideas of Socrates? Isn't it possible that Plato was just using Socrates as a mouthpiece for his own beliefs?

While it's impossible to say for certain, scholars generally divide Plato's dialogues into three categories. As Peter Kreeft explains, they believe the early dialogues are fairly accurate representations of Socrates's conversations and thoughts. The middle dialogues — which include the most famous of Plato's writings, the *Republic* — are where Plato's own ideas start to merge with Socrates's. And by the later dialogues, Socrates becomes less important. In the final dialogue Plato wrote, *The Laws*, Socrates isn't even a character.

Plato covered an amazing amount of ground in these dialogues. He talked about the nature of beauty, evil, and love; the best form of education; and the importance of friendship and courage. He set out a comprehensive political philosophy, examined the origins of language, and even retold the legend of Atlantis.

But throughout these dialogues, there was one central idea that dominated. Plato was searching for something: he wanted to know the truth about reality. That truth, he believed, could only be found in the ultimate expression of goodness. And Plato finally concluded that there was only one way to discover this ultimate good: through a concept he called the Theory of Forms.

7.

It's said that just before he died, Plato had a dream. Like Socrates's dream before meeting his future student, it also involved Plato as a swan.

Plato imagined he was trying to escape fowlers by flying from tree to tree. Simmias the Socratic, who was also a character in one of Plato's dialogues, interpreted Plato's swan dream this way: many people would try to grasp Plato's thoughts, but no one would be able to do so.

Sometimes it seems that Simmias was right. Even if we try to focus on Plato's one big idea, so much has been written, debated, and suggested about the Theory of Forms over the past two thousand-odd years that it can seem impossible to understand.

It isn't. But it *has* attracted a lot of baggage that obscures our view of what Plato apparently had in mind.

The Theory of Forms begins with the split that had already emerged in philosophy: between knowledge people could gain from their *senses,* and knowledge they could gain from *reason.*

We saw this split in chapter 1. For example, the philosopher Heraclitus saw the world as constantly changing. That was because the evidence of his senses showed him these changes. Parmenides, on the other hand, used reason to conclude that true change was impossible. Everything in the world had to be a single, unchanging thing, he said, no matter what our senses told us.

Plato, however, looked for a third possibility—one that would combine these contradictory views.

To borrow from the philosopher Edward Feser, imagine a triangle. You can know a triangle by using your senses—if you pick up an object shaped like a triangle, or if you see a triangle that is drawn in ink, pencil, or chalk. You can also know a triangle by using your reason. If someone says "triangle," you immediately imagine a three-sided figure.[93]

[93] You can find the triangle example of Plato's Theory of Forms in Edward Feser's *The Last Superstition,* pages 32–36. The squirrel example that follows appears on pages 36–37.

But we have to acknowledge something else about triangles. Whether we *draw* them, or whether we *imagine* them, we didn't *invent* them. Instead, we *discovered* them.

A triangle is a three-sided figure whose angles always add up to 180 degrees. Human beings didn't invent this concept, and we can't change it, either.

The concept of triangles must be permanent, then. That means triangles can't exist solely in the physical world of the senses. But they also can't exist solely in our thoughts. Neither the world of the senses nor the world of the mind can be permanent.

So that means triangles must have originated in a place beyond the physical world, and beyond human minds as well.

Where is this third place? According to Plato, it is the Realm of Ideal Forms.

In this Realm of Ideal Forms, we can find triangles in their highest, most perfect (or "ideal") form. The *concept* of triangles, in other words, is perfect in a way no physical triangle could ever be. And even if we can *imagine* a perfect triangle, we didn't *create* it with our minds.

The same thing is true for other geometrical figures, and for numbers generally. You can represent the number three using a variety of physical objects — three pencils; three cars; three dollar bills. You can also represent it physically by writing the numeral 3.

You can also imagine "three" in infinite ways. But even if every brain in the universe ceased to exist, the perfect *concept* of three would still exist. *Where* would it exist? Again, Plato would have said that it could be found in a permanent "third place" — the Realm of Ideal Forms.

Things get trickier when we start applying this principle to physical objects and to abstract concepts. It's not impossible to grasp the idea of a perfect triangle, for example. It's harder to understand what we might mean by a "perfect squirrel," for example, or "perfect justice."

Once again, Edward Feser is valuable in making sense of this idea. To use his example, when we call something a "squirrel," we mean not only that it has the *form* of a squirrel, but that it lives up to a set of criteria that we agree squirrels ought to possess. A squirrel with four legs, a tail, and which gathers nuts for the winter, more or less lives up to this form of the ideal squirrel. It isn't a "perfect squirrel," but it checks a lot of the boxes.

However, a squirrel that "prefers to eat toothpaste spread on Ritz crackers, and to 'lay out' spread-eagled on the freeway," is a much less perfect example of squirrelhood. That doesn't mean it's no longer a squirrel. It just means that we have an idea of what a perfect squirrel is, and this squirrel is checking a lot fewer boxes.

What about abstract concepts like love, justice, and government? It seems harder to align these concepts with "perfection." After all, people have many different ideas about what makes a "perfect government" or a "perfect love."

To make sense of this problem, Plato identified the highest of all these forms: the form of the Good. This is the source of all the other forms, and the best way of understanding them.

Someone may argue, for example, that a dictatorship is a perfect form of government, or that an abusive relationship is actually a perfect form of love, based on their personal preferences. But these preferences fail the test of the Good, because the Good transcends this kind of subjective judgement. It is universal, rather than just specific. And it is permanent, rather than ever-changing.

The Good also corresponds to virtue. For Plato, virtue is gained through knowledge. True knowledge has to be knowledge of the truth. And truth has to be unchanging. Therefore, the only permanent source of permanent knowledge has to be a "third place" beyond the changeable physical world and the changeable human mind — the Realm of Ideal Forms.

This leads us to one of the most controversial parts of Plato's already controversial concept. That is, the idea of *universals*.

As we just said, the reason that we call a triangle a triangle when we see one, or that we call a squirrel a squirrel, is because all triangles and squirrels share certain universal qualities.

For Plato, these universals didn't just apply to material objects, but also to concepts like beauty, love, and justice. These concepts have universal qualities too, just as triangles and squirrels do. And we recognize something like "love" or "beauty" by its universal qualities in the same way.

These universals are closely related to Plato's ideal forms. Think of it like this: If there is such a thing as a perfect triangle, then Plato believed it must exist in the Realm of Ideal Forms. That perfect triangle has all the qualities we associate with triangularity. It has three perfect sides, and its angles add up to a perfect 180 degrees.

Every triangle we encounter in the material world will fall short of perfection in some way. But every triangle we encounter *will* share these universal qualities, even if they're not perfect. And those universal qualities are what will help us to identify it as a triangle.

For most people, this concept of universals is common sense. You see a creature with four legs and a long, bushy tail, storing an acorn in a tree, and you call it a squirrel. You see a creature with long ears that barks at you as you walk past it, and you *don't* call it a squirrel.

This extends — or at least it used to extend — to abstract concepts as well. Most people would not choose "love" to describe a relationship in which one partner regularly cheats on the other, steals from them, and beats them senseless. That relationship seems to lack the universal qualities normally associated with the term love: affection, loyalty, attraction, respect, and so on.

Plato's belief that universals (as well as numbers) exist beyond the material world and beyond the human mind is usually called *realism*. Some people call it *Platonic realism*, to differentiate it from other related beliefs.

But as long as there have been human beings, there has been the realization that universals limit freedom. If there are universal qualities that define things like triangles and squirrels, men and women, and love and justice, then we humans *don't* get to define them.

And if we don't get to define things, then it means that some of the definitions we would *like* to apply to them might be wrong.

This was the substance of Plato's disagreement with the Sophists. There is either something absolute beyond man that offers a check on his behavior, or man is on his own, and rules are — like Heraclitus's constantly changing world — always in flux.

Peter Kreeft sums up Plato's ethics: "The Good measures man; man does not measure the Good."[94] The Good is eternal, unchanging, and perfect — a guide for how we should live.

8.

The metaphor Plato used to represent the Form of the Good is the sun. Sunlight reveals the truth, exposing shadows for what they are: just imperfect copies of the real objects they represent.

If this idea of the perfect Form of the Good sounds something like God, that's understandable. Plato didn't call it that specifically, though he did describe the Form of the Good as "the infinite."

94 Kreeft, *Socrates' Children*, vol. 1, 123.

He also believed that human beings had souls, which began in the Realm of Ideal Forms, and returned there after people died. These souls were the "ideal forms" of each individual. They didn't have any of the physical limitations that we all possess. They were the perfect versions of each of us, and they would, in theory, be infinite.

In fact, Plato believed that we all began life with prior (or *a priori*) knowledge of the Realm of Ideal Forms — thanks to our souls, which had already been there. This explained how we could know about the Realm of Ideal Forms in the first place: that information about it was with us all at birth. This is also why Plato famously said that "all learning is remembering," a process called *anamnesis*.

By this point, you might be thinking that Plato's beliefs seem to predict a lot of Christian ideas, even though Jesus Christ would not be born until nearly four hundred years later. And this is true. Some early Church leaders even insisted that Plato (and Socrates) "had been visited by the Holy Spirit."[95]

Some of the philosophers who would take up Plato's themes were, like him, not Christians. Others (including St. Augustine and St. Thomas Aquinas) became the greatest philosophers in the Christian tradition.

But not everyone, of course, agreed. Even in Plato's time, this set of beliefs threatened those who wanted to define reality on their own terms. Those included the Sophists, the descendants of Protagoras, who claimed that "man is the measure" of all things.

In Plato's dialogues, Socrates was usually able to vanquish the doubters who challenged him. In real life, they were harder to get rid of. The Skeptics, who offered a similar argument to the Sophists — that nothing could be known for certain — would eventually take over Plato's Academy.

But Plato had foreseen that his ideas might find a hostile audience. In the *Republic*, he imagined the fate of a man who had seen ultimate truth and wanted to show it to others. The fate of his old teacher, Socrates, was certainly on his mind as he concluded the Myth of the Cave.

95 Richard E. Rubenstein, *Aristotle's Children* (New York: Harvest Book/Harcourt, 2003), 53. In a footnote, Rubenstein adds that Justin Martyr, "an early Father of the Church, stated that Christ had been 'known in part even by Socrates.'"

9.

The man has returned to the cave, intent on sharing his knowledge of the world outside. He wants to tell the prisoners all about the sun, which illuminated the many truths he's learned.

Slowly, as he descends into the bowels of the earth, the man's pupils enlarge and his eyes began to adjust. When the familiar scent of smoke from the fires below drifts into his nostrils, he has to stop for a moment. It's overwhelming: if not for the one who freed him, he would still be here, staring at shadows.

The man shakes it off and continues his journey down, down, down. He thinks of the story of Prometheus, the fire-giver, who brought humans the gift of light. He'll soon learn that it's an omen he should have heeded.

The prisoners can't see him, of course: their necks are still chained to the wall. But they nod at his shadow in the firelight. Until he starts talking, that is.

They laugh. *They laugh at him — or at least, at his shadow — and they tell him he's ridiculous. The sights, the wonders, the truths he experienced. Preposterous! Impossible! Unbelievable!*

The more he talks, the more they snicker. Until they grow tired, and their necks ache from straining against the chains to laugh.

Finally, a slave speaks. His hair is matted, his skin blackened with years of soot. His back is bowed into a grotesque arch, and his voice grates from his throat.

"If you come back down here again with these stories," the slave grunts, "we'll have them catch you and kill you. Now go back wherever you came from, idiot, and leave us in peace." The slave spits on the cave floor, punctuating his statement, as the others murmur their assent.

Frightened, the man backs away from the fire and the captives, and slips into the shadows he once escaped. He'll never allow himself to be taken prisoner again. Because his real fear, he thinks, as he quietly begins his ascent to the surface, isn't being killed.

It's that if he were captured, he'd be forced to live. *Down here once more, far from the sun, and far from the truth. The horror of that thought overtakes him suddenly, and he begins to run.*

10.

In the *Republic,* Socrates ends this tale by explaining his metaphor to Glaucon — who, in real life, was Plato's brother.

"My opinion," Socrates says, "is that in the world of knowledge the idea of good appears last of all, and is seen only with an effort; and, when seen, is also inferred to be the universal author of all things beautiful and right, parent of light and of the lord of light in this visible world, and the immediate source of reason and truth in the intellectual."[96]

He adds that "this is the power upon which he who would act rationally either in public or private life must have his eye fixed."[97]

This points to perhaps the greatest paradox of Plato. Despite his reputation as a difficult, contradictory, and sometimes obtuse philosopher, a surprising amount of what he believed is taken for granted by a surprising number of people. You don't have to be a Christian, or even a member of an organized religion, to believe that ultimate truth lies beyond this world, and beyond human beings.

And it doesn't take a believer to acknowledge that some common features of life — like, say, numerical and geometrical concepts — point to a place beyond human experience.

But, as Peter Kreeft points out, "The easiest way to understand Plato is to Christianize him, and then, having understood this, to de-Christianize him again."[98]

11.

There are certainly ideas of Plato's that have come in for justifiable scrutiny. In the *Republic,* for example, he advocates for an ideal society that would include children raised by the government; "mating festivals" that would produce the optimal offspring; and no art except what is approved by the state.

96 Plato, *Republic.*

97 Plato, *Republic.*

98 Kreeft, *Socrates' Children,* vol. 1, 124.

As many observers have pointed out, the only way to achieve Plato's utopia seems to be through a totalitarian dictatorship. And his suggestions have echoed through nearly every awful would-be utopia since.

One of Plato's toughest critics was his star pupil at the Academy. We'll read about Aristotle, and how he tried to resolve those differences with his teacher, in the next chapter.

However, Plato enjoyed one of the greatest "second acts" of anyone in history. While it took him forty years to find his footing, he spent the next forty years as the head of the Academy, and produced a collection of written works that many would still argue are the most essential texts in Western philosophy.

The Academy would survive long past Plato's death. It remained open in various forms for almost a thousand years, until the Christian emperor Justinian closed it down in A.D. 529. But its influence, and Plato's, continued to spread.

Aristotle presented his own competing view of his teacher's philosophy. Neoplatonists like Plotinus and Christians like Origen adapted Plato's ideas, which spread throughout the Roman Empire. And a Catholic convert and bishop, St. Augustine, would reconcile Plato's thought with his rising new religion to become the first great Christian philosopher.

Yet, love him or despise him, no philosopher can ignore Plato. Neither can the rest of us.

That's because, as Edward Feser notes, "The core of Plato's theory is admitted even by many who are unsympathetic to his worldview to be highly plausible and defensible."[99]

And if Western philosophy really is the "series of footnotes" to Plato that Alfred North Whitehead contended, they're a set of footnotes that we've all read, whether we realize it or not.

12.

The man has finally emerged from the mouth of the cave. He stands now back in the daylight, hands on his knees.

He's breathing hard, and his heart still hammers against his ribs, but the warmth of the sun on his face consoles him.

[99] Feser, *The Last Superstition*, 39–40

So does this thought: there must be other prisoners somewhere, kept chained in the darkness, slaves to error and false belief.

He will find them. And somehow, he will show them the sun, the truth.

He begins to walk, purpose in every step. And in the glow of the rays from above, he smiles.

CHAPTER FOUR

THE PHILOSOPHER

1.

It's a beautiful spring morning in Athens, just outside the city walls, and class is about to begin. But this class, and this school, aren't like any that have ever existed.

Young men in togas recline on marble benches as the instructor clears his throat and begins to speak. They already know what the subject of today's lecture will be, because he's shared it with them beforehand. He also shows his students several pictures and charts throughout the lesson.[100]

That sounds a lot like any modern classroom. But before the founding of this school at the Lyceum, no one taught this way — not even the teacher's own instructor, Plato.

They sometimes call this place the "Peripatetic School." That's a reference to the Greek word peripatētikós, *which means "walking about." It's true that the instructor does sometime like to stroll around the tree-lined grounds while lecturing to his students, as Plato and other Greek teachers*

[100] This reconstruction of a typical day at the Lyceum comes primarily from two sources: John Patrick Lynch, *Aristotle's School: A Study of a Greek Educational Institution* (Berkeley: University of California Press, 1972); and Carlo Natali, *Aristotle: His Life and School.*

did. But a lot of the work here is actually done in the classroom, not on foot. There's less class discussion, too, but the lessons are more focused.

The students like it. Some of them remember going to hear one of Plato's talks about "The Good." They were "gaping with astonishment over the title,"[101] *and showed up eager to hear about how to get all the good things in life — wealth, health, power. Instead, they got a lecture about* math*! The students all went away grumbling and scratching their heads.*

One of these pupils will later say about his current teacher's carefully prepared lectures, "This kind of preparation is desirable."[102] *And after the teacher speaks for a while, he'll probably write down his notes and save them. Plato may have been a great writer, yet he never fully trusted the written word. This teacher is different. And while his writing doesn't have Plato's literary brilliance, it's also a completely different style: calm, clear, and factual.*

Soon, the teacher will add his notes to the library, which is housed in one of the other buildings on campus and which keeps growing. Among the holdings are constitutions from more than 150 Greek city-states. Today, we'd be surprised at a school without a library, but this one is the first of its kind.

To really get a sense of how different this school is, though, just step outside. There are botanical gardens, but they're not just for show. The teacher and students will examine the blossoms, stems, and leaves of these flowers and plants, trying to learn as much as possible about them.

And watch out for the animals! It's hard to tell what creatures you might find wandering the grounds. The teacher happens to be the former tutor of Alexander the Great, who is currently in the process of conquering much of the known world. Alexander hasn't forgotten his old tutor, though, and he occasionally sends back exotic species from India and Persia for the Lyceum's zoo.

101 Lynch, *Aristotle's School*, 91.
102 Lynch, *Aristotle's School*, 91.

Even if the animals don't survive the journey, they'll be put to good use. The teacher and students will dissect them. They've already learned from the inside out about several local species: how a chick develops in an egg, how an octopus discharges ink, and how a bee buzzes.

Here in the Lyceum, what's going on sounds a lot like science. The teacher, Aristotle, is known as one of the greatest philosophers in history. Centuries after his death, some will simply refer to him as The *Philosopher. But he's also the first great scientist.*

The nineteenth-century French naturalist Georges Cuvier will say, "Science seems to have sprung full-blown from the mind of Aristotle, like Minerva fully armed from the mind of Jupiter."[103] *Author Bryan Magee added, "Aristotle's desire to know about the world of experience was like an unslakable lust."*[104]

Aristotle made pioneering contributions to the fields of biology, botany, chemistry, psychology, and physics. He not only invented zoology: his research and animal classification system ensured that no one would surpass his work for two thousand years. Dozens of familiar terms — like "energy," "demonstration," substance," "essence," and "category" — were first found in Aristotle's writings.

He was also the father of formal logic, a master rhetorician and ethicist, and an influential political scientist. And all that is before we get to the philosophical works on which his fame really rests.

But you can't separate the scientist from the philosopher. It's Aristotle's commitment to the principles of science — observation, empirical data, trusting the evidence of our senses — that makes him so different from his mentor, Plato.

And separating Aristotle's common-sense scientific practices from philosophy, in fact, will cause philosophy incredible damage. That's a story we'll get to soon.

103 Georges Cuvier, *Cuvier's History of the Natural Sciences* (Paris: Publications scientifiques du Muséum, 2019), 221.

104 Magee, *The Story of Philosophy*, 32.

"As far as Aristotle was concerned," Bryan Magee wrote, "there is only one world that we can do any philosophizing about, and that is this world we live in and experience."[105] *Although Aristotle would live for just sixty-two years, and although most of his writings were lost for centuries, his ideas have always been with us — and they continue to shape our world.*

2.

Since he had such an eye for detail, it would be appropriate to give Aristotle the sort of precise biography he deserves. Unfortunately, as is the case with many ancient philosophers, large parts of his life are known only through questionable anecdotes or are shrouded in mystery. In his scrupulously researched 2013 book, *Aristotle: His Life and School,* Carlo Natali tried to demystify the historical record.

For starters, we know that Aristotle was born in 384 B.C. in Stagira, a small, coastal Greek city-state in Thrace. It was about six hundred miles to the northeast of Athens. As Natali points out, its history "is not illustrious."[106]

But it was close to Macedonia, a kingdom just to the north. Aristotle's father, Nicomachus, was a doctor, and some ancient sources say he was the court physician to the Macedonian king, Amyntus.

This connection to Macedonia influenced the course of Aristotle's entire life. As a boy, his playmate was probably the king's son, Philip. When he grew up, Philip II would declare himself the "Commander of the Greeks." And Philip's son, the even more ambitious Alexander the Great, would also play a major role in Aristotle's career.

But Aristotle's father died when his son was just ten or eleven years old. At some point soon afterward, Aristotle's mother, Phaestis, also died. So Aristotle was adopted and raised by his uncle, a man named Proxenus.

Proxenus's most significant contribution to history may be that he "handed over" the teenaged Aristotle to his friend Plato. But several ancient accounts suggest that Aristotle went through a rebellious stage first. One of them states,

> I am well aware that Epicurus, who was very devoted to truth, has said of him, in his letter *On Vocations,* that after he had devoured his father's inheritance he rushed into the army, and because he was bad at this, he

[105] Magee, *The Story of Philosophy,* 32.

[106] Natali, *Aristotle,* 6.

> got into selling drugs. Then, since the peripatos [school] of Plato was open to everybody . . . Aristotle presented himself and sat in on the lectures, not without talent, and gradually got out of that and into the theoretical [disposition].[107]

Are the references to drug sales a reference to Aristotle's father being a doctor? Or do they mean Aristotle was practicing medicine himself? Both points are uncertain. (And many people are skeptical of Epicurus as a source.)

What seems more sure is that sometime around the year 367 B.C., when he was seventeen or eighteen years old, Aristotle became a student at Plato's Academy. He would spend the next twenty years there, becoming Plato's star pupil. In his own famous words, Plato said that while his other students needed a whip, Aristotle needed a bridle.

The best student in the class often receives some perks, and it seems that Aristotle enjoyed a few. He was apparently a loner, and sometimes set his own course of study. "Aristotle is said to have frequently walked out on the discussions in the school to be by himself reading books," writes Carlo Natali, "and Plato found nothing to laugh at in that, though he tried courteously to involve the solitary young man in the school discussions."[108]

While Aristotle was studying abstract philosophy at the Academy, it also seems that he did research there in both astronomy and the natural sciences — two areas he would explore much further on his own.

There were major philosophical disagreements between Plato and Aristotle, as we'll soon see. And after twenty years, Aristotle decided to leave the Academy, following Plato's death in 347 B.C.

Some speculate that Aristotle departed because Plato's nephew, Speusippus, was chosen as the new head of the Academy. Did Aristotle want, or even expect, that he'd be given the job? Maybe. As author Richard E. Rubenstein speculates, "Being passed over for the directorship must have stung."[109]

Aristotle's criticisms of Plato's philosophy probably made it unlikely he'd be picked as the Academy's new leader. However, the popular idea that these criticisms led to bad feelings between Plato and Aristotle isn't supported by the evidence.

107 Natali, *Aristotle*, 9.

108 Natali, *Aristotle*, 20.

109 Rubenstein, *Aristotle's Children*, 31.

"From the text of Aristotle's works," Carlos Natali writes, "the clear conclusion to reach is that there were doctrinal differences between Aristotle and Plato, which however did not result in personal conflict." Aristotle even wrote a eulogy for Plato that praised his old teacher as a man "who alone, or first of mortals, clearly revealed by his own life and by the methods of his words, how to be happy is to be good."[110]

There's an even more familiar quote attributed to Aristotle that sums it all up: "Dear to me is Plato, but dearer still is truth."[111]

It could be that Aristotle left the Academy because he wasn't a fan of Speusippus's views. Speusippus went "much further" than his uncle Plato in his enthusiasm for numbers, and thought "that the only sure knowledge was the knowledge of mathematical relationships."[112] That wasn't going to sit well with the scientific-minded Aristotle.

And it could be that tensions with Macedonia convinced Aristotle to leave Athens for a while. The year Plato died, Philip II conquered the Greek city of Olynthus. That was a long way from Athens, but still too close for nervous Athenians.

Aristotle wasn't an Athenian citizen, and "his family's Macedonian connections were well known."[113] As Aristotle himself would say later, Athens could be a dangerous place for a foreigner. So, like Plato after the death of Socrates, he went into temporary exile.

3.

The next eight years are "the most obscure time in Aristotle's life."[114] He apparently spent part of the time in the court of Hermias, the ruler of Atarneus — a Greek city-state located in present-day Turkey.

Hermias is one of the most controversial figures in Aristotle's biography. A former slave and possibly a eunuch, he met Aristotle at Plato's Academy. His adopted daughter, Pythia, would become Aristotle's wife, and he also had close ties to the Macedonian king Philip II.

110 Natali, *Aristotle*, 21.
111 Magee, *The Story of Philosophy*, 32.
112 Rubenstein, *Aristotle's Children*, 31.
113 Rubenstein, *Aristotle's Children*, 32.
114 Natali, *Aristotle*, 32.

Hermias was known as a brave and refined leader, yet had a reputation for cruelty to his enemies. Aristotle evidently admired him enough to later write a poem, or hymn, in his honor, after Hermias was reportedly crucified by the king of Persia.

Not everyone who heard these verses approved. Some felt the poem was so over the top that it suggested Hermias was a god. There are also accounts that say Aristotle insisted on it being sung daily. Whether or not that's true, the poem would come back to haunt Aristotle years later.

At some point during this mysterious eight-year period in Aristotle's life, he became the tutor to Philip II's son Alexander. Because Philip "didn't have much faith in teachers of music or the general curriculum to provide [Alexander] with attentiveness and discipline," Philip "sent for the most well esteemed and well versed of the philosophers, Aristotle, and paid him a suitably handsome tuition."[115]

Alexander, then just thirteen, would soon become Alexander the Great, the ruler of most of the known world. So what did Aristotle teach him?

Some think that Aristotle tutored Alexander in his entire philosophy, from metaphysics to ethics to politics. Others believe the lessons were less comprehensive, centering on Greek culture, or maybe just the Socratic technique of dialectic, where two opposing viewpoints are examined to arrive at the truth.

The classes were held in the Macedonian fortress of Mieza, and Aristotle probably taught about thirty other students. But Aristotle must have taken his tutoring of the young prince seriously: he wrote two documents, "On Kingship" and "On Colonies," as guidebooks for Alexander.

Whatever the lessons included, they had ended by 335 B.C. That year, Aristotle returned to Athens to set up his own school.

The Lyceum was located to the east of Athens, just outside the city walls. It served as a temple to Apollo Lyceus, the wolf-god. But the site had been used for other purposes as well: as a gymnasium to train athletes; as a military training center; and as a venue for philosophical debates.

For the next thirteen years, it would be the home of Aristotle's classes. Because he wasn't an Athenian citizen, he had to rent space at the Lyceum instead of buying it. But he had plenty of money to do so.

After the site was unearthed by archeologists in 1996, it attracted visitors from around the world. Author Simon Critchley was struck by two major points of comparison between Aristotle's Lyceum and Plato's old school.

[115] Natali, *Aristotle*, 42.

> First, it is a direct copy of Plato's Academy. And second, it is much, much bigger. The relation between the Academy and the Lyceum is a little like that between a twee medieval Cambridge College and the monumental architecture of the University of Chicago.
>
> The reason Aristotle was able to do this was simple: money. If Plato was rich, then Aristotle was wealthier than Croesus, right up there with the Jeff Bezos-es of his day. He received the sum of 800 talents from his presumably grateful former student, Alexander, which was an enormous amount of money.[116]

This generous endowment allowed Aristotle "to build a huge research and teaching facility and amass the largest and most important library in the world." Under the leadership of Aristotle's successor, Theophrastus, the school's enrollment would grow to as many as two thousand students, "some of them sleeping in dormitories. The Lyceum was clearly the place to be, the educational destination of choice for the elites."[117]

What did the leader of this elite school look like? Most descriptions of him boil down to a single quote from the third-century scholar Diogenes Laërtius, who wrote, "He spoke with a lisp, as we learn from Timotheus the Athenian in his book *On Lives*; further, his calves were slender (so they say), his eyes small, and he was conspicuous by his attire, his rings, and the cut of his hair."[118]

Against that foppish portrait, Carlos Natali argues that "Aristotle was not a charismatic personality."[119] And based on the numerous other examples we have of his measured and down-to-earth philosophy, that assertion makes sense.

But Aristotle was doing more than just teaching. Like his mentor Plato, he was using this time to develop his own philosophy. The approximately fifty documents that we now call Aristotle's "works" are probably less than a third of his overall output. And even those documents are just lecture notes, rather than the finished works themselves.[120]

116 Simon Critchley, "Athens in Pieces: In Aristotle's Garden," *New York Times*, February 18, 2019, https://www.nytimes.com/2019/02/18/opinion/aristotle-lyceum.html.

117 Critchley, "Athens in Pieces."

118 Diogenes Laërtius, *Lives of the Eminent Philosophers*, ed. Robert Drew Hicks (Cambridge, MA: Harvard University Press, 1979), 525.

119 Natali, *Aristotle*, 65.

120 The estimation of Aristotle's total output comes from Richard Rubenstein, *Aristotle's Children*, 35. The great orator Cicero once called Aristotle's works a "river of gold,"

Yet even in this form, there is so much to discuss that we can only focus on the biggest ideas. And Aristotle's biggest ideas are among the largest in human thought.

4.

The most important of Aristotle's many important ideas — it's his equivalent to Plato's Realm of Ideal Forms — is his concept of the Four Causes.

We can explain everything in the world by answering four questions, Aristotle thought. Each of these questions corresponds to one of the Four Causes:

1. The *material cause*: From what is it made?
2. The *formal cause*: What is its form, or structure? (In other words, what do we call it?)
3. The *efficient cause*: How was it made?
4. The *final cause*: What is its purpose?

You wouldn't think, looking at this list, that it would be nearly as controversial an idea as Plato's Forms. And yet, it might be even more disputed.

The most debated are the second and fourth causes, because both of them have far-reaching implications. And like Plato's Forms, those implications suggest that man is *not* the measure of all things.

Imagine a regular old wooden pencil. It's easy to figure out its material cause: wood, a stick of lead, and a ring of metal that holds in place a rubber eraser.

It's also simple to figure out the pencil's efficient cause. It was almost certainly made in a factory. (Sometimes you can even tell where, if it's printed on the pencil.)

Those two causes are purely factual, and therefore impossible to debate. Now we get to the formal and final causes.

At first glance, these causes are just as easy to figure out. Everyone recognizes the form of a pencil — because we've all seen pencils before, and because this pencil shares the same set of qualities that we associate with other pencils. So we call this object a "pencil," and think nothing else about it.

And everyone also recognizes the final cause of a pencil. A pencil is a writing implement. Its purpose is to write on surfaces — primarily, paper.

---

compared to Plato's "silver" prose. Christopher Shields, "Aristotle," *Stanford Encyclopedia of Philosophy*, September 25, 2008, https://plato.stanford.edu/entries/aristotle/.

We know our descriptions of these two causes are accurate for another reason. Whether a pencil is brand-new and unsharpened, or whether its eraser is missing and it's been chewed on by a nervous student, we still call it a "pencil." Because in both cases, it has the *form* of a pencil.

But if the pencil is missing its lead, then we're probably going to throw it away. That's because it can no longer fulfill its final cause of writing — its *purpose*. We might even say the pencil is "no good" anymore, hurtful as that might be to the pencil.

Obviously, pencils are made by people. And, obviously, people are far more complex than pencils. But it's when we try to apply the four causes to things that *aren't* man-made that some begin to rebel.

5.

First, we have to talk about Aristotle's formal cause. This formal cause relates closely to *universals* — unchanging qualities shared by similar things, as we saw in the last chapter. But here we come to a major disagreement between Aristotle and Plato: about where these universals could be found.

Plato thought universals existed neither in the real world nor in our minds. He thought they could only be found in a third place: the Realm of Ideal Forms.

Aristotle, however, believed that there are no *universals* apart from *particulars*. He thought that universals are qualities that exist in actual things — not a separate category of thing themselves.

The form of a pencil, for example, or the form of a human being, is something we recognize when we see it in pencils, or in people, respectively.

This means that Aristotle did away with Plato's Realm of Ideal Forms. He didn't think it was necessary for there to be a perfect form of a pencil, existing in some other realm.[121]

His view was more practical: when we see a pencil, we observe its *individual* qualities. We see a thin yellow object with a pointed tip and a rubbery top. That is the evidence of our senses.

[121] For Aristotle, an object has a *substantial form* — the form that makes it what it is, such as a person or a pencil. It also has an *accidental form*, which refers to features of an object that don't change its essence — for example, the chewed-off eraser of an otherwise intact pencil.

And we then recognize, through our reason, the *universal* qualities it shares with all other pencils. We think about all the times we've experienced a similar object, and we remember instantly that it's called a pencil.

Aristotle's disagreement with Plato about universals highlights another major difference between the two men. Plato largely ignored the evidence we get from our senses. The physical world, he thought, is not the real world. The things we experience with our senses are just imperfect copies of ideal forms, which exist in another realm.

So Plato valued reason over the senses. We can at least *imagine* the Realm of Ideal Forms by using our minds, even if we can't truly access it that way.

But Aristotle held a different view of universals. He *didn't* discount the evidence we get from our senses. That sensory evidence is vital, he thought, since it's how we understand universals — by observing actual things.

That doesn't mean that Aristotle denied that universals exist, however. His view of universals, as existing first in things and then in our minds, rather than in some other realm, is known as *moderate realism*. It's a midpoint between the *realism* of Plato, and his Realm of Ideal Forms, and *nominalism*, a later concept which denies that universals exist at all. (We'll say much more about this soon.)

Aristotle was eminently practical: he saw that we can only understand universals, and the world around us, by using both our senses *and* our reason. This is what all of us do every single day — even when we're not thinking about it. And this is why many people think of Aristotle as the common-sense Greek philosopher.

6.

There's another important difference in the way Plato and Aristotle thought about forms. Plato believed that our souls were part of the Realm of Ideal Forms. They were trapped in our physical bodies, but would return to the Realm of Ideal Forms after our death.

This concept is called *dualism* — the idea that the mind (or the soul) and the body are separate from one another.

Aristotle, however, believed that the soul is just the *form* of a body. When we die, we lose our forms — and thus, our souls. (This seems to suggest that Aristotle did not believe humans have immortal souls, which would appear to be a deal-breaker for Christians. Aristotle's view, however, was somewhat more complicated. In *On the Soul,* he left the door open to the possibility that immaterial objects, like souls, could exist, by suggesting that there is such a thing as an "active mind" or "active intellect" that is "deathless and everlasting."[122])

The debate over dualism has kept reappearing throughout history. It still divides philosophers, as it divided Plato and Aristotle.

There's another big difference between Plato and Aristotle, as explained by author Arthur Herman:

> Plato's philosophy looks constantly backward, to what we were, or what we've lost, or to an original of which we are the pale imitation or copy. In that past original, Plato will say, we find the key that unlocks our future.
>
> Aristotle, by contrast, looks steadily forward, to what we can be rather than what we were. His outlook is by its nature optimistic: "The universe and everything in it is developing towards something continually better than what came before," including ourselves.[123]

But Aristotle also had a great deal in common with his teacher — something which often gets overlooked. Both he and Plato believed in universals — unlike some of the philosophers we'll read about soon. They both believed in the importance of forms. And they both thought that these concepts related to objective and eternal truths.

Universals aren't as controversial when they are applied to man-made objects like pencils. But when they're used to describe things that aren't man-made — like people, or like abstract qualities such as love, truth, and justice — then we don't get to set these definitions ourselves. So they inevitably restrict human freedom.

So does Aristotle's idea of a final cause. When we're talking about people, instead of man-made objects, the idea of having a final cause implies that we aren't just an accident: that we were made for some purpose.

[122] This idea of an eternal intellect remains a controversial idea — one that would be borrowed by several Jewish, Christian, and Muslim philosophers in the future. St. Thomas Aquinas finally reconciled this problem for Christians. He pointed out that the resurrection of the body allowed for Aristotle's idea that souls can be both part of our bodies *and* immortal. See Shields, "Aristotle."

[123] Arthur Herman, *The Cave and the Light: Plato versus Aristotle, and the Struggle for the Soul of Western Civilization* (New York: Random House, 2013), 52.

That reminds us of the possibility of something *beyond* man — a creator of some sort. Once again, that's a reminder that man's freedom is limited. And if your project is to expand human freedom — which we'll see was the project of most modern philosophers — then the idea of a final cause is going to be a problem that has to be eliminated.

7.

There's another way to think about Aristotle's Four Causes, and that is in groups of two. The final two causes — the efficient and the final cause — seem to naturally go together. It would be hard to imagine making a pencil if we didn't have some purpose in mind for it.

But once again, what's uncontroversial for pencils is problematic when it comes to people. If the efficient and final causes are linked, then that suggests people were also made for some purpose.[124]

Meanwhile, Aristotle believed the first two causes — the material and the formal cause — were inextricable. In his *Metaphysics,* he says that people

> who define a house as stones, bricks, and timbers are speaking of the potential house, for these are the matter; but those who propose 'a receptacle to shelter chattels and living beings,' or something of the sort, speak of the actuality. Those who combine both of these speak of the third kind of substance, which is composed of matter and form.[125]

This combination of matter and form, Aristotle called *hylomorphism* — *hyle* being the Greek word for "wood," which Aristotle borrowed to describe "matter," and *morphe,* which means "form."

You can see why it makes sense. At the most basic level, imagine matter without form. It's impossible to do. Even if we were able to observe a pile of

124 In the case of living things, and human beings in particular, the further away we get from our final cause, the worse off we will be. As Edward Feser points out, "behavioral and affective deviations from the essence are still deviations, whatever their cause and whether or not a creature which exhibits them has come to enjoy them. If a squirrel could be conditioned to want to eat nothing but toothpaste, it wouldn't follow that this is good for him." The squirrel should be gathering acorns, which is an important part of his final cause. Feser, *The Last Superstition,* 37.

125 Aristotle, *Metaphysics,* ed. W. D. Ross (Oxford: Clarendon Press, 1908).

protoplasmic matter, we would probably call it a "pile." Or we would call it *something*, and what we called it would be a reference to its form.

What about matter that can take on different forms? For example, what happens if we set a pencil on fire and it burns down to ashes?

Aristotle explained this in terms of *actuality* and *potentiality* — two terms that also have far-reaching implications.

A pencil as it actually exists has some obvious potentials. It can be used to write with, of course. It has the potential to erase writing, if it has an eraser. You could also use it as a back scratcher, or even a weapon.

It also has the potential to be set on fire — but only if that potential is unlocked by an outside agent: in this case, heat. The pencil can't actualize that potential itself. "And so, in so far as a thing is an organic unity, it cannot be acted on by itself," Aristotle writes in his *Metaphysics*, "for it is one and not two different things."[126]

And even an outside agent can't unlock a potential that the pencil doesn't already possess. A pencil can't be made to grow wings and fly, nor can it suddenly begin speaking.

Everything in the world, then, is a combination of *actuality* — what it is at this moment — and *potentiality* — all the things it could be. And Aristotle describes all change in terms of motion. Whether we're talking about a pencil burning to ashes or a person growing up, these changes involve motion.

How, then, did all this motion begin? For Aristotle, it logically had to start with a being that was *pure* actuality, that had no unrealized potential. Such a being would be unmovable, and therefore unchangeable and eternal.

"The first principle or primary being is not movable either in itself or accidentally, but produces the primary eternal and single movement," he wrote. "But since that which is moved must be moved by something . . . the first mover must be in itself unmovable."[127]

This "Unmoved Mover," Aristotle, very logically, called "God."

"And life also belongs to God," he wrote, "for the actuality of thought is life, and God is that actuality; and God's self-dependent actuality is life most good and eternal. We say therefore that God is a living being, eternal, most good, so that life and duration continuous and eternal belong to God; for this is God."[128]

[126] Aristotle, *Metaphysics*.
[127] Aristotle, *Metaphysics*.
[128] Aristotle, *Metaphysics*.

Of course, Aristotle's conception of God was not of the Christian God, since Christianity did not yet exist. It would take St. Thomas Aquinas, centuries later, to add that dimension to Aristotle's teachings.

Yet while Aristotle's Unmoved Mover is a long way from the personal God of Christianity, it's important not to lose the forest for the trees. Aristotle's God was, in his own words, "a living being, eternal, most good." The rest, you might say, is just details — controversial and divisive as those details would prove to be.[129]

8.

There's one final point in Aristotle's writing we should mention. It lacks the ripple effects of his Four Causes or his concepts of actuality and potentiality. But it does speak to both his personality and his idea of the final cause — the purpose — of human beings.

At some point while he was teaching at the Lyceum, Aristotle's wife, Pythia — who had given him a daughter named Pythia the Younger, died. Pythia had apparently helped Aristotle collect biological specimens during his travels, and probably doesn't get enough credit for her contributions to science.[130]

Aristotle then took up with a second female companion named Herpyllis. She was a native of Aristotle's hometown, Stagira, though whether she and Aristotle were married is unclear. It's also not certain whether Aristotle's son, Nicomachus, was born to Pythia or Herpyllis.[131]

129 Were Socrates, Plato, and Aristotle monotheists? It's a complicated question without an easy answer. Plato (and therefore, Socrates, the main character in many of his dialogues) goes back and forth in his writing between references to a "God" and "gods." However, Plato's idea of the Good as the highest of all things does suggest that he saw a single deity as the source of all goodness. Aristotle, meanwhile, got his own criticism for venerating humans as gods, as we've seen in this chapter. But his concept of the Unmoved Mover argues more conclusively than Plato or Socrates for a singular God — which is one reason St. Thomas Aquinas was able to "baptize" Aristotle's thought.

130 Aristotle was accused of making sacrifices to Pythia "the way the Athenians sacrifice to Demeter of Eleusis." Considering these and all the other rumors about Aristotle — that he was a drug dealer; that he venerated friends and family members like gods, etc. — author Carlo Natali observes, "There must have been something about Aristotle's character that excited such piquant fantasies; even in the Middle Ages great sport was made of scenes of the great thinker on all fours, straddled by a courtesan" (Natali, *Aristotle*, 14).

131 It's unclear whether Aristotle's companion Herpyllis was a free woman, a servant, or a slave. Some scholars "have found it inconvenient that a great thinker such as Aristotle had a companion out of wedlock, and they say that in the end the philosopher married her, or else affirm that Herpyllis was only Aristotle's 'housekeeper,'" writes Carlos Natali. However, Aristotle's will treated Herpyllis more generously than would be expected for a servant. "On the other hand, the fact that Aristotle wanted to be entombed close to

But we do know that Aristotle named his *Nichomachean Ethics,* one of the world's most famous writings about moral behavior, after his son. And in this book, we find one of Aristotle's most famous ethical concepts: the Golden Mean.

The idea that there's a desirable midpoint between two extremes of behavior had been around for some time. The Buddha had preached about the "Middle Way" as early as the sixth century B.C. And a century later, one of the moral sayings inscribed on the wall at the Temple of Apollo in Delphi was "Nothing to excess." Socrates, too, had given similar advice.

However, Aristotle developed this idea into a system that would guide people's actions. "In all the states of character we have mentioned, as in all other matters, there is a mark to which the man who has the rule looks, and heightens or relaxes his activity accordingly," he wrote. "And there is a standard which determines the mean states which we say are intermediate between excess and defect, being in accordance with the right rule."[132]

So, for example, if you have too much self-esteem, you're a braggart. If you have too little, you're falsely modest. The middle path is truthfulness: to give yourself the credit you deserve, and no more.

Or take shame. If you have too much, you'll be bashful. If you have too little, you'll be shameless. The Golden Mean is modesty.

This system is consistent with Aristotle's moderate personality. But it also calls to mind a larger question: why be moral in the first place? To answer, we return to Aristotle's idea of the final cause, or *telos*. What is the *telos* of human beings?

He defined it as another Greek word: *eudaemonia*. Sometimes this term is translated as "happiness," but the more precise definition is "human flourishing." (The two words are related: to be happy, for Aristotle, was to be a flourishing human being.)

But what is it that makes a human being flourish? Isn't that an impossibly subjective question? Not for Aristotle. Because man is the only creature gifted with reason, it followed for Aristotle that our highest purpose must be to use that reason to discover truth.

"Now if the function of man is an activity of soul which follows or implies a rational principle," he wrote, then "human good turns out to be activity of soul

---

Pythia . . . would lead us to think that Herpyllis enjoyed a status slightly inferior to that of his first wife" (Natali, *Aristotle*, 16).

132 Aristotle, *The Nicomachean Ethics of Aristotle*, ed. W. D. Ross (Oxford: Clarendon Press, 1908).

in accordance with virtue, and if there are more than one virtue, in accordance with the best and most complete."[133]

The equation can be put in a simpler form: human happiness = using reason to seek truth = virtue. If we're not seeking truth, then we're not virtuous. And if we're not virtuous, then we're not happy.

9.

Aristotle's Macedonian heritage may very well have put a premature end to his career at the Lyceum.

While he'd been teaching, his former pupil Alexander the Great had steadily extended his empire. By this point, it stretched across the Middle East, past the Persian Gulf and Caspian Sea, and to the Himalayas. This was an impossibly vast swath of territory. And the strain of keeping it together was beginning to show.

Reports made their way back to Athens about the thirty-year-old ruler's increasingly bizarre behavior. In a test of loyalty, he insisted that his men worship him as a god. Those who refused — including Aristotle's nephew, Callisthenes — were executed.

If that news chilled Aristotle, things were about to get worse. Three years later, Alexander died in the Babylonian palace of Nebuchadnezzar II. The cause of death was probably typhoid fever, although some insisted Alexander's wine had been poisoned.

When this news reached Athens, there was rejoicing by citizens who had never accepted Macedonian domination. There was also a regime change: Antipater, the city's ruler, was overthrown. And Aristotle was suddenly on the hot seat.

At issue was his connection to Alexander, and to Macedonia. And the "hymn" he'd written for his friend Hermias — a friend of the Macedonians — now looked suspicious, as well as strange. Why was Aristotle suggesting that Hermias be venerated like a god? Wasn't that exactly what Alexander had done?

The new regime was apparently planning to charge Aristotle with impiety. There were clear echoes of the fate of Socrates, and the famous quote attributed to Aristotle at the time was "I will not let the Athenians sin a second time against philosophy."[134]

[133] Aristotle, *Nicomachean Ethics.*

[134] Natali, *Aristotle,* 62.

Before a trial could happen, Aristotle gathered his slaves and household possessions, and set out for Chaclis, on the island of Euboea, about fifty miles north of Athens. His mother had left him some property there, and it's possible that he may also have started a new school.

If so, it didn't last long. Aristotle died, apparently of a stomach ailment, just a year later, at the age of sixty-two.

In his *Nicomachean Ethics,* Aristotle had written, "Though a man has lived happily up to old age and has had a death worthy of his life, many reverses may befall his descendants.... It would be odd, then, if the dead man were to share in these changes and become at one time happy, at another wretched; while it would also be odd if the fortunes of the descendants did not for some time have some effect on the happiness of their ancestors."[135]

The reverses that befell Aristotle's "descendants" — his writings — after his death make up one of the most amazing stories in history. It's a tale that extends beyond this chapter, but it begins not long after Aristotle's passing.

10.

The book collector of the first century B.C. isn't that much different than the book collector of today. He looks at the volumes that have recently been dragged up from a moldy basement, and sniffs.

Examining them with a skeptical eye, he sighs, and then makes an offer. The family members look at one another and shrug. It's generous, though still less than they were hoping. But on the other hand, what use are these crumbling, moth-eaten rolls of papyrus?

Does the wealthy book collector, Apellicon of Teos, realize what is in those rolls? Maybe. By the time he gets them back to Athens and examines them more closely, he'll certainly have figured it out.

For two centuries, these papyrus rolls have been buried in this cellar. The cellar sits beneath a modest home in Skepsis, a Greek colony located in present-day Turkey.

It was once owned by a man named Neleus. Neleus's uncle, Theophrastus, was once the head of the Lyceum in Athens, and left

[135] Aristotle, *Nicomachean Ethics.*

his nephew these manuscripts. Where had he gotten them? From the former scholarch and founder of the Lyceum — Aristotle.

Neleus's heirs weren't scholars, but they put the papyrus rolls under lock and key. They wanted to keep them safe from the country's military rulers, who would have seized them and added them to the library they were building in Pergamon — a library they hoped would be even greater than the famous one in Alexandria.

Then Apellicon got wind of what was in the basement, showed up, and made the family an offer they couldn't refuse.[136]

And this is how the works of Aristotle found their way back to Western civilization. Or at least, it was the first step of the journey.

Apellicon reportedly edits the scrolls, filling in parts that are missing due to damage. But he won't get to enjoy the books forever. When the Roman general Sulla invades Athens in 86 B.C., his soldiers go house to house. They find Apellicon hiding in his library, kill him, and tell the general what they've found. Sulla has the scrolls sent back to Rome.

Eventually, the books end up in the hands of Andronicus of Rhodes, who has taken over the leadership of the Lyceum. Andronicus sorts through the scrolls, makes copies, and ultimately publishes an edition of Aristotle's works that reintroduces him to a new generation of scholars.

"Once again," as Richard E. Rubenstein writes, "Aristotle's voice rang out across the Mediterranean world."[137]

11.

It's a great story, a real-life mashup of Indiana Jones and *National Treasure*. But is it too good to be true?

No one knows for sure. As Rubenstein states, other than the fact that Andronicus apparently did publish some of Aristotle's works, it's "anyone's guess" as to whether the rest of the tale is valid.

[136] The "basement" of Neleus's heirs was possibly no more than a trench, which was common in homes of this region at the time.

[137] Rubenstein, *Aristotle's Children*, 39.

The Stanford Encyclopedia of Philosophy notes that "it is not clear what Andronicus edited and how he did it." However, "what is clear is that Andronicus did not provide an authoritative text of Aristotle."[138] He *did* organize and catalog some of Aristotle's works, and that's as much as we can say for certain.

But if the details of Aristotle's revival are muddled, the broad outlines are not. Most of Aristotle's works really would go missing in the West for more than a thousand years after his death.

Their eventual recovery — and their even more surprising loss, once again — would mark perhaps the most consequential period in human history.

[138] Andrea Falcon, "Commentators on Aristotle: Andronicus of Rhodes," *Stanford Encyclopedia of Philosophy*, 2021. https://plato.stanford.edu/entries/aristotle-commentators/supplement.html.

CHAPTER FIVE

STUBBORN SPLINTERS

1.

The city of Corinth is abuzz on this sunny morning, sometime in 336 B.C. It's not every day that the most powerful man in Greece pays your town a visit — even if he's coming to demand your city's loyalty.

Of course, the leaders of Corinth are going to pledge that loyalty, however reluctantly. What Alexander the Great wants, Alexander the Great gets.

His father, the Macedonian king Philip II, has just been assassinated. So the twenty-year-old Alexander has inherited the throne. He's not truly great — not yet. But his sights are on conquests much greater than Greece. Within a decade, he will rule an empire that stretches from North Africa to Persia to India. This morning, however, he's looking for something much more modest.

Alexander and his soldiers make their way to a shadowy alley, near an open marketplace. There, a large clay burial urn rests against a building. Flies buzz around it, attracted by the scraps of food and other less savory items on the ground. The stench is unbelievable, and some of the soldiers bury their noses in their cloaks.

This is what Alexander has been seeking. Not the urn itself, but the old man who lives within it.

At the moment, the man is actually reclining on the ground next to his home, soaking up the sun. He isn't wearing any clothes; he often doesn't. That makes it easier for him to urinate and defecate whenever he wants. Those aren't his worst habits. He's also been known to masturbate in public. When someone objected once, he just shrugged. "I wish I could rub my stomach in the same way," he replied, "and so avoid hunger."

The food he does eat is scavenged from the trash, when he doesn't feel like begging for it. His only possession, besides a couple of soiled robes, is a lamp. He likes occasionally to wander around the marketplace, shining it in people's faces and telling them he's looking for just one human being. So far, he hasn't found one. But he doesn't seem too troubled. In fact, he doesn't seem too troubled by much of anything.

So why has Alexander the Great, soon to become the most powerful man in the world, sought out this filthy, penniless wretch? Because he had to see Diogenes of Sinope — the man Plato once called "Socrates gone mad" — for himself.

The contrast could hardly be more marked. Though he stands only five-and-a-half feet tall, the plume on Alexander's helmet, and his kingly posture, make him seem bigger.

Diogenes, meanwhile, is probably seventy years old, and years of hard living make him appear even older. But he just stares up at Alexander, bemused, stroking his matted beard.

The king clears his throat. "Diogenes of Sinope," he begins, "I am Alexander the Great."

Diogenes nods. "And I," he replies, "am Diogenes the Dog." As if on cue, a mangy canine appears from behind the urn and snaps up a rotting piece of meat.

Alexander blinks. "I have come to ask whether there is anything you desire," he says. After all, if anyone can make wishes come true, it's this brash new king.

There is a long pause, and then Diogenes nods again.

"Yes," he says. "I would like for you to move." He points up at the sky, and Alexander and his soldiers follow his finger. "You're blocking my sunlight."

For a moment, no one responds. Then the soldiers, outraged, begin to act. One spits on the urn; another curses Diogenes; another draws his sword. People have died for lesser insults to Alexander.

But the king simply holds up a hand, and the soldiers stand down. It almost looks like he's smiling.

Later, reflecting on the meeting, he will tell friends, "Truly, if I could not be Alexander, I would wish to be Diogenes."[139]

2.

The death of Aristotle was something like the disappearance of the last dinosaur.

Not in the sense that his philosophy was outdated. The reference, instead, is to the fact that there was no one in the Hellenistic period, after Socrates, Plato, and Aristotle, who was nearly as impressive and influential as the Big Three. The philosophers who followed were more like the early mammals: different and occasionally striking, but not at the same level as the giants before them.

The Hellenistic period actually begins with the death of Alexander the Great in 323 B.C., not with Aristotle's death a year later. And the Hellenistic period ends just before the birth of Christ, when Cleopatra and Mark Antony were defeated by Octavian in 31 B.C.

[139] Much of this opening section is reconstructed from *Lives of the Eminent Philosophers* by Diogenes Laërtius, as well as "An Encounter to Remember" by historian Laura Ford. Many historians believe the meeting took place in Corinth; others believe it actually happened in Athens. Diogenes Laërtius mentions the Craneum, a grove in Corinth, in his account, which is why this location was chosen. Diogenes Laërtius, *Lives of the Eminent Philosophers,* ed. Robert Drew Hicks (Cambridge, MA: Harvard University Press, 1979); Laura Ford, "An Encounter to Remember," Kosmos Society, February 2, 2016, https://kosmossociety.chs.harvard.edu/an-encounter-to-remember/.

It should be noted that Diogenes Laërtius had a reputation for inaccuracy — or just making thing up — so while his character judgments and anecdotes are colorful and often amusing, I've tried to be sparing with them. But as the primary source of information for many ancient philosophers, consulting him becomes almost inevitable. (And the Robert Drew Hicks translation seems to be the most colorful and amusing of those available.) So to some regrettable extent, *caveat emptor*.

This roughly three-hundred-year period saw Greek culture spread across the Mediterranean into North Africa and Asia. In the wake of Alexander the Great's conquests, it was natural that something like this would happen.

But there was no longer a philosopher with the stature of Socrates, Plato, or Aristotle. Instead, a variety of smaller splinter groups developed. All of these groups adapted the beliefs of the Big Three, which is why we consider them "splinters" from the main branches of philosophy. Some, however, also reached back further to the pre-Socratic philosophers. And some of them staked out daring new ground. Of these groups, four are noteworthy.

Only one of these four groups — the Stoics — was truly popular during this time. But all of them offered essentially ethical philosophies. And all of them tried to answer a single question: how can human beings be happy? The word for this happiness was *eudaemonia,* and each of these four groups tried to find its own way to achieve it.

Socrates, Plato, and Aristotle had all tried to answer that same question, of course. But these new splinter groups had far different solutions. These were practical philosophies, in a sense: they all started by identifying the *obstacles* to happiness, and then moved on to eliminating them.

This relates to a second Greek term, *ataraxia,* which means peace and freedom from fear and worry. All four groups saw fear as one of the great impediments to happiness. So their philosophies were, to a large extent, about banishing fear.

The philosophies these groups advanced only occasionally made reference to a higher power. They were really all about human beings, and not the gods. That makes these belief systems surprisingly modern. And all four philosophies still survive, in some form, to this day.

3.

The most radical of the four splinter groups was the Cynics. And the most radical of the Cynics was Diogenes of Sinope, whom we've already met.

"Cynics" here means something a little different than today's definition, which we use to describe someone who doesn't trust the motives of others. It's probably true that Diogenes *didn't* trust others — in fact, he spent a lot of his time making fun of their motives. However, these Cynics were more concerned with how human beings ought to live their lives. *Kyon* is the Greek word for "dog," and *kynikos* means "doglike." Which Diogenes certainly was.

In this case, Diogenes was following the Cynics' guide to happiness: "Live like a dog." This was to free themselves from their attachment to material things, which they believed make us *un*happy.

The idea of "imagining no possessions," of course, wasn't unique to the Cynics. In the sixth century B.C., the Buddha had taught that desire and attachment to things cause misery. Socrates, as we've already seen, was a fan of minimalism. (Jesus, meanwhile, would later preach a similar gospel to his disciples.)

But the leader of the Cynics was a more extreme example. There's a story about Diogenes—as you might guess, there are *a lot* of stories about Diogenes—watching a child drinking water in his cupped hands. Disgusted with himself, Diogenes threw away his cup: one more possession he didn't need.

The cup was more than just a possession, though. It was also a societal convention. And in his own lifestyle, Diogenes tried to show that rebelling against these conventions was a way to become free of all society's excesses, and live authentically.

Sometimes this rebellion took very basic forms. Diogenes reportedly had a habit of walking backward. Occasionally, it's said, he would attend a lecture or some other public event, but stare at the people instead of the performers.

And sometimes, the stunts were more pointed. Although he sometimes went to hear Plato speak at his Academy, Diogenes was no fan. In fact, he took particular delight in needling the great philosopher. One account claims that after Plato defined man as "an animal, biped and featherless," Diogenes plucked a chicken and brought it to Plato's next lecture. He waved it around and shouted, "This is Plato's man!"[140]

When Plato called him "Socrates gone mad," you can see what he meant. Socrates didn't mind making people uncomfortable; for Diogenes, it seemed to be a full-time job. He called himself a "cosmopolitan," which sounds funny until you remember its meaning. Diogenes really was a "citizen of the world," in the sense that he could go anywhere and feel equally at home.

Diogenes had grown up in Sinope, a coastal Ionian colony on the Black Sea. His father, Hicesias, was the colony's mintmaster, and Diogenes apparently had to leave Sinope under a cloud because he defaced official currency. The details are unclear—including whether his father was also involved—but some accounts tell us that Diogenes was exiled as punishment, and lost his possessions.

[140] Diogenes Laërtius, *Lives*, 43.

He wound up in Athens, where he met the philosopher Antisthenes, whom we might call the first Cynic. A former student of Socrates, he was far more conventional than Diogenes. But as Antisthenes grew older, he adopted a simple lifestyle, dressing like a laborer and lecturing against government, private property, and marriage.

He was also against having pupils, but Diogenes apparently wore him down. "Once when he stretched out his staff against him, the pupil offered his head with the words, 'Strike, for you will find no wood hard enough to keep me away from you, so long as I think you've something to say.' From that time forward he was his pupil, and, exile as he was, set out upon a simple life."[141]

But the student soon outdid the master. Diogenes modeled himself after a mouse he watched, which seemed to get along fine without a house or other "dainties." When he couldn't find a place to stay, he made his home in a burial urn. And when people insulted him — at one dinner, some guests threw him bones as a joke — he repaid them in kind, by lifting his leg and peeing on them like a dog.

Even in his waning years, when he was captured by pirates on a voyage to the Greek island of Aegina, Diogenes managed to get the last laugh. When he was put up for auction as a slave, he picked a Corinthian named Xeniades out of the crowd. "Sell me to this man," Diogenes said. "He needs a master."[142]

Apparently, that is just about how it worked. Xeniades brought Diogenes to Corinth, and had him run his household and tutor his children. He must have been satisfied with the results: "Xeniades used to go about saying, 'A good genius has entered my house.' "[143]

Diogenes may have lived to the age of ninety — some accounts say that he died on the same day as Alexander the Great in 323 B.C. And while none of his writings survive, his legend endures.

We don't know exactly how many followers Diogenes had. But while the appeal of his lifestyle may have been limited, the appeal of his philosophy remains obvious. Eudaemonia could be achieved if man lived naturally and authentically — not according to society's rules. This, Diogenes thought, was the only way to ensure true happiness.

In every age, this idea has its supporters. From the eighteenth-century Swiss philosopher Jean-Jacques Rousseau, who taught that civilization corrupts, to the

141 Diogenes Laërtius, *Lives*, 25.
142 Diogenes Laërtius, *Lives*, 77.
143 Diogenes Laërtius, *Lives*, 77.

hippies of the 1960s, who counseled tuning in, turning on, and dropping out, we can hear the echoes of Diogenes's anti-society message.

And when the high and mighty are skewered with a sense of humor, this philosophy becomes even more appealing. Diogenes must have known this, and he never passed up an opportunity to deliver a one-liner.

Like the time he passed by the house of a wealthy man, who had written over his door, "Let nothing evil enter." With, we must assume, a completely straight face, Diogenes innocently asked his followers, "How, then, is the master of the house to get in?"[144]

4.

If the Cynics were most likely the smallest of the four splinter groups, then the Stoics were undoubtedly the largest. As power in the West shifted from Greece to Rome, Stoicism would become something like the house philosophy of the Roman Empire. Some of its most prominent leaders were also believers.

It's also the philosophy, among these four splinter groups, that may be most familiar to us today — at least superficially. When you hear the word "stoic," you might be reminded of the old British saying about keeping "a stiff upper lip" when you're faced with hardships.

The founder of Stoicism, Zeno, was a native of Citium. This was a Greek city which also had many Phoenician residents and was located on the southeast coast of Cyprus.

Zeno apparently didn't become a philosopher until later in life: one story has it that he was visiting Athens when he learned that the ship in which he was supposed to return home had been wrecked. He responded, "It is well done of thee, Fortune, thus to drive me to philosophy"[145] — a completely Stoic reaction.

Zeno began his philosophical career by lecturing on a porch, or *stoa* — which is how his followers came to be called Stoics. And from the beginning, he apparently set the example we expect of a Stoic: "He showed the utmost endurance, and the greatest frugality; the food he used required no fire to dress, and the cloak he wore was thin."[146]

[144] Diogenes Laërtius, *Lives*, 41.

[145] Diogenes Laërtius, *Lives*, 115.

[146] Diogenes Laërtius, *Lives*, 139. Despite that description, Diogenes Laërtius did not present Zeno as the picture of health: he reportedly had "thick legs" and was "flabby and delicate." (He also enjoyed eating green figs and sunbathing.)

You could also sum up the Stoic philosophy by quoting an even more familiar source: the Serenity Prayer. It reads, "God grant me the serenity to accept the things I cannot change, courage to change the things I can, and the wisdom to know the difference."

The first dozen words are the important ones. Although there were definite links between Stoicism and the Christianity that would follow it, they weren't the same thing. A major reason is the Stoic conception of God.

Stoicism is essentially a *pantheistic* belief. That is, God is everywhere, and everything is God. This means we are all part of God, as well. And if this is the case, then there is no point in trying to change our fate — because it has already been determined.

Therefore, we should accept the things we can't change, and work instead on what we *can* change — our *reactions* to what happens to us. Unhappiness, the Stoics thought, would occur if we tried to alter fate. So to be happy, we should learn to be accepting of whatever comes our way.

Death was no exception. Because God is omnipresent in the world, when we die, we are simply returning to him. That meant death was not a thing to be controlled, nor to be worried about. And it also meant that suicide was a defensible — even honorable — option, if the pressures of life became too great.

Epictetus, a former slave who became the leading Stoic philosopher in the first century A.D., gave this advice on the subject to his followers: "Remember this: the door is open. Be not more timid than little children, but as they say when the thing does not please them, 'I will play no longer,' so do you, when things seem of such a kind, say, 'I will no longer play,' and be gone, but if you stay, do not complain."[147]

(Incidentally, Epictetus reportedly walked with a limp because while he was a slave, his master deliberately broke his leg — but Epictetus calmly refused to react. Now that's stoicism.)

The most famous Stoic philosophers were the Roman statesman Seneca, who was the chief advisor to the infamous emperor Nero in the first century A.D., and Marcus Aurelius, the emperor who ruled Rome between 161 and 180.

Seneca was most notable, as author Peter Kreeft points out, for his hypocrisy: he helped Nero kill his own mother, then covered it up in the Roman Senate. But Marcus Aurelius may be the only real example of Plato's elusive "philosopher

[147] Epictetus, *Discourses*, ed. George Long (New York: Appleton, 1904).

king." Respected as a leader, his book *Meditations*—a collection of Stoic wisdom—is still widely read, nearly two thousand years after it first appeared.

The advice in *Meditations* touched on all the classic Stoic tenets. Marcus Aurelius reminded us that even wicked people "possess a share of the divine," and that "those things which in this life are dearest unto us, and of most account, they are in themselves but vain, putrid, contemptible."[148]

Feelings, not fate, are what have to be controlled. Just imagine this advice being widely followed today: "Take away your opinion, and then there is taken away the complaint, 'I have been harmed.' Take away the complaint, 'I have been harmed,' and the harm is taken away."[149]

Stoicism remains attractive in theory, and difficult to practice. Yet it contained a great paradox: while they preached the importance of individual choices, Stoics also believed in a pantheistic universe without free will—where those choices ultimately meant little or nothing. This strange situation gives us the link to the third splinter group.

5.

The closest similarity between the Stoics and the Epicureans is the way both groups thought about death. Which is to say, they advised their followers not to think about it at all.

The catchphrase of the Epicureans comes from their founder, Epicurus, who said "Death is nothing to us."[150] The reason he felt this way, however, is quite different from the Stoic philosophy.

Epicurus was born on the island of Samos, located in the eastern Aegean Sea, around 341 B.C. His parents were Athenians, and after the death of Alexander the Great, Athenian citizens were expelled from the island. So the teenaged Epicurus moved around, teaching for a while in Mytilene, on the Greek island of Lesbos, before settling in Athens when he was in his mid-thirties.

He had studied philosophy, but he grew impatient with Plato (he reportedly called students at the Academy "the toadies of Dionysius") and Aristotle (whom he accused of wasting his inheritance and selling drugs). It wasn't until

148 Kreeft, *Socrates' Children*, vol. 1, 175.

149 Marcus Aurelius, *The Meditations*, ed. George Long (Mineola, NY: Dover Publications, 1997).

150 Diogenes Laërtius, *Lives*, 651.

he discovered the work of the pre-Socratic philosopher Democritus that his eyes were opened.

As we saw in chapter 1, Democritus believed the universe was made up of atoms and space. There was no God: atoms simply assembled, disassembled, and reassembled.

Epicurus saw the ethics implied by this metaphysical belief. If death just means that our atoms disperse, then how can we worry about it? That would be foolish, and a waste of time.

Instead, Epicurus believed, we should worry about using the short span of life we're given to the fullest. That meant pursuing pleasure, and avoiding pain.

This sounds like the embodiment of the acronym *YOLO* — "you only live once" — and would seem to be an anything-goes philosophy. But this was not the way Epicurus practiced it. The author Norman Wentworth DeWitt called him an "altruistic hedonist" instead.[151]

He set up a school called The Garden, named for its location in an actual garden that Epicurus owned. It was a relatively small group of like-minded individuals, brought together as much by lifestyle as by lessons. Epicurus's simple advice to them all was "live well." Women and slaves were welcome; marriage and children were frowned upon.

But Epicurus was determinedly moderate in his habits. In a letter to his friend Menoeceus, he advised, "Plain fare gives as much pleasure as a costly diet, when once the pain of want has been removed, while bread and water confer the highest possible pleasure when they are brought to hungry lips."[152] In an even fuller explanation of his philosophy, Epicurus added that pleasure is

> the absence of pain in the body and of trouble in the soul. It is not an unbroken succession of drinking-bouts and of revelry, not sexual love, not the enjoyment of the fish and other delicacies of a luxurious table, which produce a pleasant life; it is sober reasoning, searching out the grounds of every choice and avoidance, and banishing those beliefs through which the greatest tumults take possession of the soul.[153]

[151] Norman Wentworth Dewitt, *Epicurus and His Philosophy* (Minneapolis: University of Minnesota Press, 1954), 10.

[152] Diogenes Laërtius, *Lives*, 657.

[153] Diogenes Laërtius, *Lives*, 657.

Avoiding extremes, then — sort of like a version of Aristotle's Golden Mean — was the key to pleasure. So it's not surprising to learn that, while Epicurus admired the Cynic philosophy, he had no time for the outlandish behavior of Diogenes of Sinope (whom he may have met).[154]

And although there are similarities between the Epicurean and Stoic philosophies, Epicurus was sharing his beliefs long before Zeno climbed onto a porch in Athens.

When death did come for Epicurus, at age seventy-two, he reportedly faced it with courage. A blocked urinary tract caused him to suffer considerably. For relief, he climbed into a bronze tub filled with lukewarm water and drank some wine. But "the cheerfulness of my mind," he wrote, "which comes from the recollection of all my philosophical contemplation, counterbalances all these afflictions."[155]

For some time after his death, his legacy was considerable. Biographer Norman DeWitt called Epicurus "the most revered and the most reviled of all founders of thought in the Graeco-Roman world."

"His was the only creed that attained to the dimensions of a world philosophy," Dewitt wrote. "For the space of more than seven centuries, three before Christ and four afterward, it continued to command the devotion of multitudes of men."[156]

However, DeWitt also pointed out that "throughout these same seven centuries, no man was more ceaselessly reviled."[157] Epicureanism was, for obvious reasons, seen as contrary to Christian belief. And by the fifth century A.D., in the waning days of the Western Roman Empire, the great Christian philosopher St. Augustine could say confidently that "its ashes are so cold that not a single spark can be struck from them."[158]

[154] Perhaps Epicurus's advice about moderation is part of what biographer Norman Wentworth DeWitt called his "unacknowledged debt" to Aristotle. Dewitt, *Epicurus*, 10.

[155] Diogenes Laërtius, *The Lives and Opinions of Eminent Philosophers*, trans. C. D. Yonge (London: G. Bell and Sons, 1915), Project Gutenberg, https://www.gutenberg.org/files/57342/57342-h/57342-h.htm.

[156] Dewitt, *Epicurus*, 3.

[157] Dewitt, *Epicurus*, 3.

[158] Howard Jones, *The Epicurean Tradition* (New York: Routledge, 1989), 94. Epicurus did not deny the existence of gods, but his conception of them was, as Norman Wentworth Dewitt wrote, "astonishing." These gods were animate, human-like beings. Some were composed of the same atoms as humans, and they were not immortal — although they could remain incorrupt if they were vigilant. "Just as this vigilance ensures incorruptibility, so the assurance of incorruptibility ensures blissfulness. The happiness of the gods is perfect because the assurance of its perpetuity is perfect" (DeWitt, *Epicurus*, 249).

But Epicureanism was merely dormant, not dead. It would return with a vengeance in the modern era. Utilitarians like Jeremy Bentham would adopt his pleasure-and-pain calculus. Later in the nineteenth century, Karl Marx and Friedrich Nietzsche found much to admire in Epicurus's atomistic, live-for-today philosophy. More recently, supporters of abortion and euthanasia have used his views on the "nothingness" of death to validate their positions.

As long as there is death, then, there will be fear of death. And as long as there are people looking for a way to minimize or avoid that fear, Epicurus will live on.

6.

As we've seen, in fact, all three of the splinter groups mentioned so far in this chapter still survive. All promise happiness — or at least, a lessening of misery. Whether the fear is of death, of fate, or of societal expectations, the Epicureans, Stoics, and Cynics have a remedy.

But the most successful and influential of these splinter groups is the last one. And that's probably because its cure is the simplest of all.

The Skeptics identified unhappiness as man's quest for certainty. And the answer, they thought, was to abandon it entirely. Instead, "stop worrying and just go with the flow," as Bryan Magee put it, and "swim along with whatever customs and practices prevail in the circumstances we happen to find ourselves in."[159]

You could hardly find a better description of the rootless, valueless modern world than that. In fact, it's the blueprint for *relativism*, which argues that all truths are relative — and so we can't say that one is superior to another. But this philosophy actually started just before the Hellenistic Era.

The originator was Pyrrho, who was born around 365 B.C. in Elis, on the west coast of the Peloponnese peninsula in Greece. He was apparently a painter, but later turned to philosophy. The game-changing event in his life was when he traveled with Alexander the Great's conquering army, reportedly going as far abroad as India.

What he saw in his travels opened his eyes to different cultures and customs. Everyone, Pyrrho observed, seemed to believe what they believed with equal gusto — even when two beliefs were contradictory.

[159] Magee, *The Story of Philosophy*, 42.

As Diogenes Laërtius explained,

> Obviously the same thing is regarded by some as just and by others as unjust, or as good by some and bad by others. Persians think it not unnatural for a man to marry his daughter; to Greeks it is unlawful. The Massagetae ... have their wives in common; the Greeks have not. The Cilicians used to delight in piracy; not so the Greeks. Different people believe in different gods; some in providence, others not.... As to what is true, then, let suspension of judgement be our practice.[160]

The answer to this dilemma, then, was epistemological — related to what human beings can know. Pyrrho would let everyone off the hook: he insisted that humans didn't have the means to know the Truth with a capital *T*. And therefore, searching for it was futile — and destined to cause unhappiness.

This is an incredibly powerful and seductive idea, which has surfaced and resurfaced throughout human history. At its best, Pyhrro's belief can be used to promote tolerance and pluralism. In theory, it gives equal weight to opposing ideas. So it can create a live-and-let-live environment, where people agree to set aside differences for the sake of harmony.

At its worst, of course, it becomes an irresistible leveling agent. So it seems to lead inevitably to conflict. Some truth claims can't just be set aside. And when we give up the search for universal truth, then the only person who can judge those competing claims is man himself. Mistakes, of course, are likely, and eventually disputes don't get settled in court or with the ballot box but at the end of a club, or a gun.

If Skepticism sounds similar to Protagoras's "Man is the measure of all things" idea, that's because it was. The Sophists and the Skeptics weren't identical, but what they had in common was a disregard for universal truth. That disregard inevitably leads — either accidentally or on purpose — to man being the measurer of all claims.

To illustrate that connection, Pyrrho's main disciple, Timon of Philus, actually *was* a Sophist-turned-Skeptic. (He was also, apparently, a stage dancer before becoming a philosopher, and is said to have had only one eye. He must have had a sense of humor, at least: he referred to himself as a "cyclops."[161])

Timon's rhetorical trick was showing that "every argument or proof proceeded from premises which it did not itself establish."[162] Every time you make an

160 Diogenes Laërtius, *Lives*, 495–496.

161 Diogenes Laërtius, *Lives*, 523.

162 Magee, *The Story of Philosophy*, 42.

argument, you are relying on sources that *also* have to be verified. In this way, argument becomes impossible: it's just an endless cycle of verifying sources. It would be easier just to stop caring about what's true — which, of course, was the point.

The Skeptics would end up controlling Plato's Academy for nearly two hundred years. This must have been a bitter blow to Plato, up there in the Realm of Ideal Forms, since he had so often battled their ancestors, the Sophists.

When Timon's pupil, Arcesilaus, was the head of the Academy, he made a standing offer to debate any proposition his students cared to present. And his successor, Carneades, once got a lot of attention in Rome when he gave two lectures there. The first lecture powerfully supported the views of Plato and Aristotle; the second lecture attacked them with just as much vigor.

It was argument for the sake of argument — the Sophists all over again.

But the Skeptics' catchphrase — "There is nothing we can know for certain" — was a little like cherry-flavored battery acid. Once poured, it was impossibly corrosive. Yet philosophers — and the regular people who listened to them — would find it just as difficult to stop drinking.

7.

Although Greece was in decline and Rome was on the rise, there was one more great Greek philosopher to emerge. In a sense, he was also the leader of a splinter group, although a different type than the four we've just discussed. You could consider Plotinus a splinter from Plato's family tree.

He was also the last significant Greek philosopher in antiquity. That line had begun with Thales in the sixth century B.C., and ended when Plotinus died about nine hundred years later.

Plotinus[163] actually seems not to have been Greek (although he spoke it) but a native Egyptian instead. His early history is mysterious, and he wanted it to stay that way. "He never spoke of his family or home (Lycopolis, now Syout, in the Thebaid, in Egypt)," wrote his pupil and biographer, Porphyry. "He never would permit anybody to perpetuate him in a portrait or statue."[164]

[163] Plotinus's name is sometimes spelled "Plotinos."

[164] Plotinos and Porphyry, *Plotinos: Complete Works v. 1*, trans. Kenneth Sylvan Guthrie, Project Gutenberg, June 13, 2013, https://www.gutenberg.org/files/42930/42930-h/42930-h.htm.

This refusal, Porphyry tells us, was because Plotinus "seemed ashamed of having a body."[165] But that apparently wasn't because of any deformity or self-consciousness. Porphyry writes that several women were devoted to Plotinus, and that "he grew especially handsome in discussions; a light dew of perspiration appeared on his forehead, gentleness radiated in his countenance, he answered kindly, but satisfactorily."[166]

Plotinus's objection, instead, had to do with his philosophy. He was a devotee of Plato, who took Plato's conclusions about the material world to a far more extreme conclusion.

This adaptation came to be known as Neoplatonism (although no one used that term until centuries later). And it would have an enormous influence. Even though Plotinus was not a Christian himself, and apparently never mentioned Christianity in his writings, he became a kind of bridge between the ancient philosophers and the Christian thinkers to come.

Plotinus was twenty-eight and living in Alexandria when he decided to study philosophy. But he was "sad and discouraged" by the results, until he discovered a teacher named Ammonius. "This is the man I was looking for!" he exclaimed to his friends.[167]

Ammonius was best known for his commentaries on Aristotle. Yet it must have been his teaching about Plato that really resonated with Plotinus, who spent the next decade as his pupil. Plotinus later decided to follow the emperor Gordian's army to Persia so that he could study Persian and Hindu thought. Gordian was killed in Mesopotamia, however, and it took Plotinus no small amount of effort to escape.

He wound up in Rome, at age fifty, and taught a handful of students. By the time Porphyry encountered him nearly a decade later, he had also begun to write down his lessons. Plotinus would eventually write numerous books, which Porphyry edited into a series called the *Enneads*.[168]

The big takeaway from this work is Plotinus's concept of "The One." He based this idea on Plato's concept of "the Good" — the highest of all the Forms, and comparable to God.

[165] Plotinos and Porphyry, *Complete Works*.

[166] Plotinos and Porphyry, *Complete Works*.

[167] Plotinos and Porphyry, *Complete Works*.

[168] Porphyry noted, "Once Plotinos had written something, he could neither retouch, nor even re-read what he had done, because his weak eyesight made any reading very painful. His penmanship was poor." (Plotinos and Porphyry, *Complete Works*.)

Plotinus's "One" is such an awe-inspiring concept that it is impossible to describe, except in negatives. It is not finite. It doesn't have a name. It has no knowledge. As Peter Kreeft notes, we can't even say that it *exists* — since that would be too limiting a term.

"The One" seems to be a monistic concept — there is only one thing in the universe, and that is the One. But this mystical One is so transcendent that it's even trickier to grasp than Plato's rather abstract idea of the Good.

What's easier to understand is Plotinus's disdain for matter. This may be why he seemed ashamed to have a body. Plato had taught that our bodies are imperfect copies of Ideal Forms. And Aristotle had taught that bodies, and everything else in the world, are a composite of matter and form.

Plotinus agreed with both ideas, then upped the ante. The body is a combination of matter and form, he thought — but it's not in any way an equal partnership: "The human person is essentially a soul employing a body as an instrument of its temporary embodied life."[169]

For Plotinus, matter was ultimately an impediment to man's ultimate goal: unity with the One.

"That is the reason that it is right to say that 'the soul's welfare and beauty lie in assimilating herself to the divinity,'" he writes in the first *Ennead*, "because it is the principle of beauty and of the essences; or rather, being is beauty, while the other nature (non-being, matter), is ugliness. This is the First Evil, evil in itself."[170]

However, the term *evil* can be a little misleading. Even during the time of Plotinus, there were heretical Christian groups called Gnostics. While their beliefs varied widely, one thing that many agreed on was that the material world truly *was* corrupt and irredeemable.

Plotinus did not agree. In fact, the closest he came to addressing Christianity was a treatise called *Against the Gnostics; or, That the Creator and the World are Not Evil*. In this work, he used a metaphor to explain how his beliefs differed from the Gnostic view of matter.

"We may illustrate by two guests who dwelt together in a beautiful house," he wrote. "The first guest blamed the disposition of the plan, and the architect

[169] Lloyd Gerson, "Plotinus," *Stanford Encyclopedia of Philosophy*, June 30, 2003; revised June 28, 2018, https://plato.stanford.edu/entries/plotinus/#:~:text=The%20human%20person%20is%20essentiall.

[170] Plotinos and Porphyry, *Complete Works*.

who constructed it, but nevertheless remained within it."[171] These were the Gnostics, whose criticisms of the material world seemed, inevitably, like criticisms of God.

The other guest represented Plotinus, and those who agreed with him. "Instead of blaming the architect," this guest "praised his skill, and awaited the time when he might leave this house, when he should no longer need it."[172]

Plotinus's work was evidently well known to, and respected by, Roman leaders. So it's not surprising that, like Plato, he also nursed political dreams: while both men had their sights fixed on another world, they also had plans for this one. Plato's aspiration was a society ruled by "philosopher kings," while Plotinus fantasized about a city called "Platonopolis," where the only laws would be Plato's.

Plotinus's tribute to Plato never came to fruition. But his revisions of Plato, and insistence on the importance of the immortal soul, did eventually win him the approval of many Church authorities. Today, in the Vatican Museum, you can even see a sarcophagus in which Plotinus is believed to have been buried.[173]

Though not a Christian believer, Plotinus would have tremendous impact on the believers who followed—including one of the two greatest Christian philosophers in history. He is the subject of our next chapter.

✠ ✠ ✠

171 Plotinos and Porphyry, *Complete Works*.

172 Plotinos and Porphyry, *Complete Works*.

173 You can read more about the "so-called" Plotinus sarcophagus in the Vatican Museum here: http://saa.uaic.ro/articles/SAA.25.2.2019.465-482.pdf.

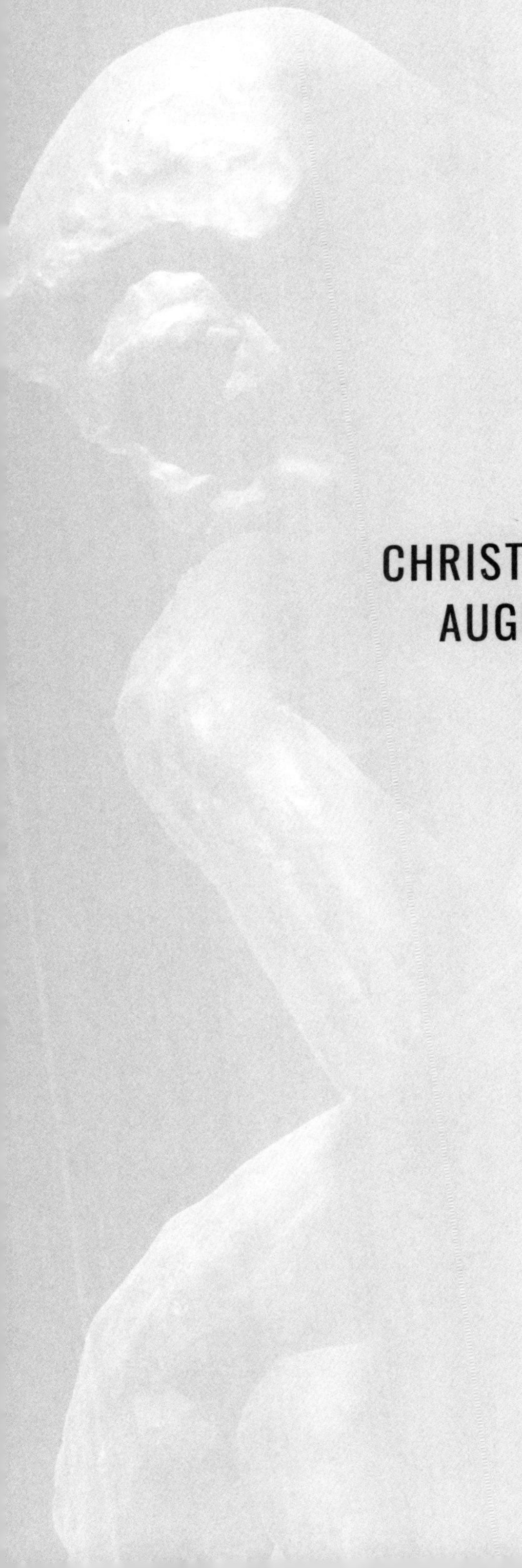

SECTION TWO

CHRISTIAN PHILOSOPHY: AUGUSTINE, AQUINAS, ABANDONMENT

Between the death of St. Augustine in A.D. 430 and the rise of St. Thomas Aquinas in the High Middle Ages, more than eight hundred years passed.

A good chunk of those years in Western Europe were spent in what is often called the "Dark Ages." This term became popular during the Enlightenment, the so-called "Age of Reason" that took place in the West during the seventeenth and eighteenth centuries.

The Enlightenment was a period of scientific, political, and philosophical upheavals, designed to liberate the individual. As you might guess from the name *Enlightenment*, its defenders believed they'd already proved their point about its value. They looked down their noses at the past generally, and the medieval period particularly.

One of them was the British historian Edward Gibbon, who wrote a six-volume series called *The History of the Decline and Fall of the Roman Empire*. These books argued that the Roman Empire fell because it adopted Christianity. That thesis harmonized perfectly with Enlightenment prejudices against religion, as we'll see later.

But later scholars, including Princeton professor Peter Brown, have shown that the term "Dark Ages" is far too reductive, for all sorts of reasons.

It focuses too much attention on the so-called "barbarian" hordes who overran Europe, and not enough on the advances that happened during this period, especially in agriculture. And it's especially silly when applied to the entire medieval period—as if the "Dark Ages" were only lightened by the Renaissance.

Some scholars now prefer calling the period between 500 and 1500 the medieval era, and then dividing it in half: 500 to 1000 is the early medieval period, and 1000 to 1500 is the late medieval period.

But whatever we call this time, one thing is certain. As the Goths and other tribes took over the Western Roman Empire in the sixth century, knowledge of the great Greek thinkers of the past was in danger of disappearing entirely. That was because fewer and fewer people could read Greek.[174]

"The loss of literacy in Greek was a potential catastrophe for Western society," writes Richard E. Rubenstein. "It would mean the simultaneous loss of philosophy, medicine, mathematics, engineering and science."[175]

So in the West, this eight-hundred-year period between Augustine and Aquinas was in large part about preservation — and sometimes, recovery — of past knowledge, rather than innovation.

The real advances were happening in the Arab world. Arab scholars had access to the "lost" works of Aristotle, and this gave them a huge leg up on European thinkers. Finally, in the early twelfth century, in the Spanish city of Toledo, a remarkable translation center was established. Arabic, Jewish, and Christian scholars worked side by side, figuring out how to reconcile the works of the ancient Greeks — especially Aristotle — with their own faiths.

This noble experiment prepared the way for the Scholastics, a group of Catholic theologians that included one of history's greatest thinkers. St. Thomas Aquinas "baptized" Aristotle, making his philosophy consistent with Christianity.

It was a monumental accomplishment — maybe the greatest moment in Western thought. But it didn't last.

It was Aquinas's fellow Catholics who first undercut his philosophy, insisting he assumed far too much about God and His creation. Few people today know the names of the Franciscan friars who helped undo Aquinas's work, but their impact on history was incalculable. They were the first to truly usher in the modern era — the era of the individual.

[174] Meanwhile, the Eastern Roman Empire — Byzantium — preserved ancient writings that would be rediscovered by the humanists of the Renaissance.

[175] Rubenstein, *Aristotle's Children*, 62.

CHAPTER SIX

CONFESSIONS AND CITIES

1.

Finally — finally — *after a night filled with tears, begging, prayers, and heart-rending revelations — the woman is asleep.*

She lies curled on the stone floor of the tiny shrine as dawn approaches. There is sand trapped in the folds of her robes: she was on her knees by the ocean earlier, pleading shamelessly with her son not to leave.

He tried to reason with her. He insisted he had to depart Carthage, the great port on the North African coast, for an even greater city. He's been offered a teaching opportunity in Rome, and this position is a clear step up, the path to a distinguished career. Isn't that what she wants, after all?

But his mother wouldn't listen. She knows that her son's teaching job is being offered by Manicheans, who want him to spread the Manichean gospel.

The Manicheans are a religious sect formed in Persia about a hundred years ago. Their leader, Mani, taught that life is struggle between good and evil. There is not one God, but two, and the eternal evil power is every bit the equal of the eternal good.

This evenly matched battle between light and darkness takes place within every human being. Light and the soul are goodness; the world of matter is evil. Mani revealed himself to his followers as the light-bringer, the successor of Buddha, Jesus, and the Persian prophet Zoroaster. The latest and last word in salvation, in other words.

This religion has caught on in a big way, but the weeping mother knows it directly contradicts her Christian beliefs. She's been heartsick since her son latched onto this faith.

Well, she's been heartsick about him for a long time, actually. Manicheanism is just the latest fad for this young man, who's been trying for years to figure out his place in the world. Mostly he's been sowing his wild oats: he loves drinking, and the company of women especially. He has a young son who was born out of wedlock, but that responsibility is the furthest thing from his mind on this night, in the fall of 383.

He's nearly thirty now, and he thinks this new religion might be the answer he's seeking. Even if it isn't, though, he knows he can't stay here in Carthage, just so that his nagging mother can keep after him about his bad habits, and the need to accept the Christian God. He's heard lots of good things about Rome — about the city, and of course, about the women there, and the chances he'll have for fun.

There's no way he's going to let his mother, well-intentioned as he knows she is, stand in the way of all that. For goodness' sake, she even swore there on the beach tonight, tears streaming down her face, that if he wouldn't come home, she would go with him to Italy. Imagine! He'd shuddered at the very thought.

So he did what any good, caring son would do: he lied through his teeth.

He gently removed his mother's clutching hands from his robes. Gently, he spoke to her — he's a convincing speaker, this charming young man — and told her that of course he wasn't going to leave Carthage tonight! The winds didn't look favorable, he said, scanning the reddening skies over the Mediterranean. And he certainly wouldn't put his friend, who owned a boat, in such danger.

Gently, he led his weeping mother to a small shrine nearby on the shore. It was built to honor St. Cyprian, a third-century bishop of Carthage. Cyprian was also a writer, and had been martyred by the Romans. The young man believed, sensibly and cynically enough, that spending time at this shrine would bring his mother comfort.

He was right. She left his side to kneel in front of the altar, offering prayers that were no doubt for him and his conversion. But finally, exhausted not just by the events of this evening but by at least fifteen years of similar worries, her head fell.

Gently, the young man helped her onto the stone floor. Half-asleep already, she did not resist. And soon enough, she fell into slumber, her occasional snores the only sound besides the waves lapping outside the open window.

If the woman had raised her head and looked beyond the chapel, she would have seen a shadowy figure stealing down the beach. She would have seen him hurriedly conferring with another man, and would have seen both of them getting into a small sailboat docked nearby. And she would have seen her son, under a full autumn moon, slipping away from the North African coastline and beginning his journey to destiny. To the eternal city, Rome.[176]

2.

As soon as the young man made it to Rome, he immediately fell deathly ill. Much later he would see this sickness as "loaded with all the past sins"[177] he had committed against God. But when he recovered, he began to doubt the Manichean worldview and started looking for a way to escape the cult.

History doesn't tell us exactly what his mother said when she ran down to the beach in Carthage the next morning and realized her son's deception. But we can guess. Most likely, she trudged back to the shrine of St. Cyprian and prayed. Again. No matter how many times her son let her down, she would never give up on him — or on God.

When a position opened up in Milan, for a teacher of rhetoric, the young man applied and got the job. His mother dutifully followed him there. She felt that her

[176] This opening section is based in large part on Augustine's own *Confessions*, pages 115–117.

[177] Saint Augustine, *The Confessions: With an Introduction and Contemporary Criticism*, trans. Maria Boulding, ed. David Vincent Meconi, S.J. (San Francisco: Ignatius Press, 2012), 117.

prayers were being answered when her son came under the guidance of the local bishop, Ambrose, who began to open the young man's eyes to Catholicism.

But the bishop, in turn, was even more impressed by the young man's mother. "When Ambrose saw me, he would often burst out in praise of her, telling me how lucky I was to have such a mother."[178]

This devoted mother and the fatherly bishop would both become saints. St. Monica is the patron saint of mothers — and, just as appropriately, the patron saint of patience and perseverance. Meanwhile, St. Ambrose is known as the patron saint of bees, a reference to his "honeyed tongue."

Both of these saints were instrumental in the formation of a third: the troubled young man, Aurelius Augustinus, who loved the pleasures of the flesh so much that he famously prayed, "Lord, make me chaste … but not yet!"[179]

From these uncertain and unpromising beginnings, he became one of the greatest figures in Christianity, literature — and philosophy: St. Augustine.

3.

Augustine wrote two books that are widely considered among the finest in world literature. His *Confessions* is the first true autobiography: an account of his gradual conversion to Christianity. *The City of God,* meanwhile, turns the focus to all of human history. Augustine interprets it by using the metaphor of two contrasting places: an earthly city and a heavenly one.

The teachings in those books and nearly ninety others, as well as his other writings, which include some eight thousand sermons, made Augustine the most important authority in Western Christianity. His period of dominance lasted for 1,500 years, only challenged in the nineteenth century.

Peter Kreeft makes an even broader claim about Augustine: "No one outside the Bible ever had more influence on Western civilization, except perhaps Socrates."[180]

Perhaps Augustine's single greatest accomplishment — and the thing that underpins his great written works — is his "baptism" of Plato. That is,

[178] St. Augustine, *The Confessions,* 133.

[179] Magee, *The Story of Philosophy,* 51.

[180] Peter Kreeft, *Socrates' Children,* vol. 2, *Medieval Philosophers* (South Bend, IN: St. Augustine Press, 2019), 25.

he was able to take the pre-Christian philosophy of Plato and adapt it for a Christian audience.

He was so successful, in fact, that many Christians "came to assume" that Plato's ideas, "although nowhere actually stated by Christ, had nevertheless somehow been originated by Christianity, and were to be thought of as a natural part of it."[181]

As we've already seen, Plato's beliefs translated relatively easily to Christian thought. A perfect realm that exists beyond the material world and beyond the human mind sounds a lot like Heaven. The highest of his forms, the Form of the Good, sounds something like God. The belief in immortal souls and in universals, likewise, lines up with standard Christian belief.

St. Thomas Aquinas, the medieval philosopher who would do a similar "baptizing" of Aristotle's work, said that "whenever Augustine, who was imbued with the doctrines of the Platonists, found in their writings anything consistent with the faith, he adopted it, and whatever he found contrary to the faith, he amended."[182]

Augustine reached that point through years of sin, soul-searching, and spiritual doubt. But it may be that he was so successful because, and not in spite of, his rocky path to belief. He was good at anticipating objections to his ideas — perhaps because he'd already considered many of those objections himself.

4.

To say that St. Augustine's life is one of the great conversion stories in history is only partially correct. It's actually a great *re*-conversion story.

He was born Catholic in Thagaste, a town in present-day Algeria. His parents were the fiercely devout Monica, and Patricius, who had a far different attitude. Patricius was a Roman decurion whose job was to collect taxes, and while he owned only a small amount of property (including some vineyards), he lived his own version of the good life.

Patricius was almost twenty years older than his wife. He verbally abused her and cheated on her openly. He was apparently a laissez-faire pagan, who grew especially hostile when Monica brought up the Christian Faith. No matter what he did, however, she refused to stop praying for his conversion.

181 Magee, *The Story of Philosophy*, 52.
182 Kreeft, *Socrates' Children*, vol. 2, 29.

Despite the example and urging of Monica, Augustine also began to drift away from Christianity at an early age. His parents spent lots of money on his education, sending him away to school. He was intelligent, but a poor student — he hated studying Greek, in particular. If he did finish a lesson, it was just to avoid being beaten. He had the gift of gab, but was only interested in using it to get attention.

A particular boyhood incident haunted him for the rest of his life. One night, he and some rowdy friends stole "enormous quantities" of pears from a neighbor's tree. The pears looked ugly and tasted even worse: Augustine and his buddies ended up throwing most of them to the pigs. That wasn't the point, however. "We derived pleasure from the deed," he remembered later, "simply because it was forbidden."[183]

As Augustine grew older, this lure of the forbidden led to his fascination with sex. His father only egged this on. Seeing his son naked in the baths one day, Patricius began speculating about having grandchildren — even bragging about their son to Monica, who must have been horrified.

Some of Augustine's exploits, he admitted, were invented to impress his friends: "I pretended to obscenities I had not committed," he wrote, "lest I might be thought less courageous for being more innocent."[184]

But he wasn't just a talker. At age eighteen, while studying in Carthage, he got a local girl pregnant. She had a son, whom they named Adeodatus,[185] and for the next fourteen years she was Augustine's common-law wife.

As he began to take more interest in his studies, Augustine soured on the Bible — he compared it unfavorably to the writing of the Roman orator Cicero — and became fascinated by the Manicheans instead.

Partly, this was because the doctrine of absolute good versus absolute evil was simple and appealing. But as Augustine would admit later, the Manichean philosophy also seemed to let him off the hook for his drinking and sexual escapades. If all evil is external, then his faults weren't truly his own.

Monica was at her wit's end with her son's behavior. She convinced him to break things off with his common-law wife, who returned to Africa after a tearful farewell. Monica's hope was that marriage would straighten out her wayward son.

183 St. Augustine, *The Confessions*, 41.

184 St. Augustine, *The Confessions*, 39.

185 Augustine's son, Adeodatus, was eventually baptized together with his father in Milan. However, he died just a little later, before reaching the age of eighteen, sometime around 390.

But the Italian girl to whom he was pledged was extremely young—too young for marriage. So he ended up taking another concubine while he waited.[186]

Still, Monica prayed. Occasionally she was consoled by a vision. One night, Monica dreamed that she was standing on a wooden ruler, joined by "a young man of radiant aspect,"[187] who seemed to be an angel. He asked why she was crying, and she told him her tears were for Augustine's ruin. The young man pointed, and there was her son, standing on the same ruler.

The dream, she was certain, was a sign that Augustine would eventually convert. When she told him about it the next day, he tried to reassure her with vague references about the future. She was insistent: the angel had told her, "Where you are, he will be."[188]

And she was right. But in the words of Augustine himself, not yet.

5.

Augustine finally managed to escape the Manicheans. But after breaking with this extreme philosophy, his next belief was no belief at all.

He became convinced that the Skeptics who had taken over Plato's Academy had the right idea; that we can't know anything for certain. It was a safe philosophy that asked even less of Augustine than Manicheanism.

But in his conversations with Bishop Ambrose of Milan, Augustine began to discover the work of the Neoplatonists. One was the Egyptian philosopher Plotinus, whom we read about in the last chapter.

Plotinus's concept of matter as inferior to the soul was familiar to Augustine, since the Manicheans had a similar idea. But Plotinus's belief in man's eternal soul, which is trying to return to its ultimate, omnipotent source, was a big improvement. Instead of a Manichean God who is *vulnerable* to evil, Plotinus's God *transcended* it.

186 The girl to whom Augustine was betrothed was perhaps as young as ten years old, since she was described as "two years below marriageable age," and that age in Italy was twelve at the time. Augustine was then over thirty, which may shock modern sensibilities. As the editors of the Ignatius critical edition of *The Confessions* point out, "Obviously the ways of ancient Rome are not ours today" (157). They also note that Monica was concerned that Augustine marry a girl who would help him rise up the social ladder.

187 St. Augustine, *The Confessions*, 70.

188 St. Augustine, *The Confessions*, 70–71.

This led Augustine to think deeply about evil and its source — especially how evil could exist in a world created by an omnipotent God.

He would come to realize that his hatred of material things, which he had learned from the Manicheans, was mistaken. So was the idea that evil was a thing itself. Augustine reasoned that evil was, instead, a *lack* of something. If everything that God created were inherently good, then evil would only arise when those good things were corrupted or destroyed. It was an absence, a *privatio boni,* or privation of the good. It has "no being at all,"[189] he concluded.

That idea, of course, has never satisfied all observers. Many still want to know how God could allow evil to occur in a world He created.

Our free will, Augustine realized, was part of the answer. To be fully rational beings, humans must have free will. And because we have free will, we can choose to do good or evil.

In short, Augustine concluded, "God is not the parent of evils."[190] By turning away from the good, man himself was that parent — through the use of his God-given free will. In fact, man had been evil's originator, ever since Adam and Eve were tempted in the Garden of Eden.

These theories about evil would one day come to be known as the "Augustinian theodicy." But thinking about the nature of evil inevitably forced Augustine to accept responsibility for his actions. The many times he had negated God's good now weighed heavily on him. And yet, he still resisted a full conversion. Like Jesus, he would have to suffer his own agony in a garden first.

6.

Anyone passing by this courtyard in Milan would do a double take at the sight that greets them.

One of the two men seated there is named Alypius. This little garden is right outside the house where he lives with Augustine. And right now, Alypius is sitting open-mouthed, sick with fear and worry for his friend.

That's because Augustine seems to be having a nervous breakdown. And perhaps that's exactly what's happening. As tears roll down his cheeks, he pulls out clumps of his own hair. He punches

[189] St. Augustine, *The Confessions*, 182.
[190] Buckingham, *The Philosophy Book*, 72.

himself in the face. He curls himself tightly into a ball, his knuckles white, then uncurls, murmuring and moaning all the while.

Augustine has become a fan of the Apostle Paul, who wrote to the Corinthians about how the body is made up of many parts, which work together as a unified whole. Augustine's spasms are like watching that idea get put to the test.

If Alypius could hear his friend's thoughts, he'd be even more disturbed. All of Augustine's past deeds have taken on human form. His drunken blackouts, his loveless hookups, his thefts and his vanity — they're all swirling around Augustine like demonic will-o-the-wisps, plucking and pinching him.

And they're whispering, taunting, and most of all, threatening. "Do you mean to get rid of us?" they ask. "Shall we never be your companions again after this moment … never … never again?"

They know that Augustine is here in the garden because he's determined, after years and years of backsliding and half-measures and outright failing, to commit himself to God. He's about to renounce all his worldly ambitions. His career. Fame. Sex. Even marriage.

And his past sins are equally determined to talk Augustine out of it. He might have renounced the Manichean idea that evil is a separate entity. But his demons now seem all too real.

Overwhelmed, Augustine retreats to a corner of the courtyard. He curls into the fetal position under a fig tree.

Then, at his lowest moment, he hears a voice drifting from an open window nearby. It's a child's voice, and it says, "Pick it up and read! Pick it up and read!"

Is this a line from a game? he wonders. Or is it a sign? He wipes the tears from his reddened face and walks back over to the bench where he and Alypius had been sitting. A copy of the New Testament is lying there. He'd brought it outside for spiritual reinforcement. Now he opens it.

His finger lands on a verse from Paul's letter to the Romans. "Not in dissipation or drunkenness, nor in debauchery or lewdness, nor in arguing or jealousy, but put on the Lord Jesus Christ, and make no provision for the flesh, or the gratification of your desires."

It can't get much clearer than that. Augustine is now calm, and tells his friend he has finally decided to follow Christ.

Alypius is delighted, but not nearly as much as the next person who will receive this news. The two friends go inside to share this miracle with Augustine's long-suffering mother, Monica.[191]

7.

Augustine was baptized by Bishop Ambrose the next Easter, at a Vigil Mass on April 24, 387. His son, Adeodatus, was baptized alongside him. And Augustine's mother, Monica, was there to witness the culmination of her years of prayer.

Monica had successfully converted her husband Patricius to the faith not long before his death in 370, and now she had done the same for their prodigal son. She was of course filled with joy. She was also emotionally and spiritually spent.

"For my part, my son, I find pleasure no longer in anything this life holds," she told Augustine. "What I am doing here still, or why I tarry, I do not know."[192]

Shortly afterward, Monica took to her bed with a fever, and died nine days later. She was fifty-six years old. Her last request of her son was to remember her at the altar of the Lord, "wherever you may be."[193]

Where he would be, eventually, was back home. Four years later, in the North African town of Hippo, near the mouth of the River Ubus, he became a priest. Four years after that, Augustine became the bishop of Hippo.

And not long after that, he began work on his autobiography. *Confessions* took three years to write, from 397 to 400, and told the story of his journey to Christ.

But these confessions also contained a good bit of Augustine's philosophy. One of the key sections of the book has to do with the concept of time.

Time, Augustine realized, played a critical role in figuring out the relationship between God and man. And he realized that the way humans break time

[191] This section is reconstructed from "Struggle in the Garden," from *The Confessions*, 214–225.

[192] St. Augustine, *The Confessions*, 253.

[193] St. Augustine, *The Confessions*, 254.

into three parts — past, present, and future — was something that simply could not apply to an eternal being.

"If nothing passed away, there would be no past time; if there was nothing still on its way, there would be no future time; and if nothing existed, there would be no present time," he wrote.[194]

Going a step further, Augustine explained that the past no longer exists; the future does not yet exist; and the present moment is just a way we mark the difference between those two extremes. In other words, he concluded, "we cannot really say that time exists."[195] It's a term we use to characterize experience — not a thing itself.

The implications are enormous. God is not subject to time: He exists in an "Eternal Now" that stands outside our human conception of time. So to ask what God was doing before He created Heaven and Earth, Augustine says, is a silly question. It assumes that there *was* a time "before." But if God *created* space and time, then the premise makes no sense.

The criticism that this theory is just the Church avoiding tough questions is also refuted by science:

> Modern physics arrived at essentially the same insight in the twentieth century. Whereas St. Augustine began with the notion that time is something created, modern physics starts with the notion that time — or space-time — is something physical. Einstein's theory of General Relativity (his theory of gravity) tells us that space-time is a dynamic entity: it can bend and have ripples in it.
>
> One of the most dramatic scientific breakthroughs of recent years was the detection of such "gravitational waves" by the LIGO experiment in 2015. These ripples of space-time carry energy and momentum just as other kinds of physical waves do. If space-time is an aspect or part of the physical universe, it follows that the beginning of the physical universe must have been the beginning of space and time itself. That means that one cannot meaningfully speak of a "time before the beginning of the physical universe."
>
> If, say, the universe is 13.8 billion years old (as in the simplest versions of the Big Bang theory), then it simply makes no sense to ask what was happening 20 billion years ago. It would be like asking what lies North

[194] St. Augustine, *The Confessions*, 344.

[195] St. Augustine, *The Confessions*, 344.

> of the North Pole. (It is not that there is "nothing there." It is that there is no such place as North of the North Pole. Nor is there such a time in the standard Big Bang theory as before the Big Bang.)[196]

There's an even deeper insight here that would be more fully explored by St. Thomas Aquinas. That is, if we think of God outside the bounds of time, we also have to rethink our idea of creation.

"Creation" suggests a timeframe: that God made the Heavens and the Earth, and then went about some other business. But if God exists instead in an Eternal Now, then He is *constantly* creating.

So everything that exists has not just been created and then abandoned by God: it's all dependent on Him to continue existing. As Aquinas would later note, creation is an "essentially ordered" series of causes and effects. In such a chain, nothing can exist without the first cause, which keeps the chain going.

Augustine's wrestling with the concept of time not only inspired many future philosophers — including Immanuel Kant and the atheist thinkers Arthur Schopenhauer and Bertrand Russell. It also gives the rest of us a way to understand one of the greatest mysteries of existence.

Augustine was able to find an easier solution to another vexing problem: the issue of universals. Here, he referred back to Plato's idea that universals exist in a third location — beyond the material world and the human mind.

Plato's third location was, as we've seen, the Realm of Ideal Forms. For Augustine, it seemed obvious that there was another name for this place where these universal qualities — like "redness" or "dogs" or "beauty" — could be found.

"Where are we to think these reasons exist," he asked, "if not in the mind of the creator?"[197] This idea of the Divine Mind as the source of things like universals and numbers was probably Augustine's neatest synthesis of his own thoughts and Plato's.

8.

Yet perhaps the best overall marriage of Augustine and Plato comes in *The City of God.* The book was written at a tipping point in Western civilization — when the fate of a particular city was on everyone's mind.

196 Stephen M. Barr, "St. Augustine's Relativistic Theory of Time," *Church Life Journal*, February 7, 2020. https://churchlifejournal.nd.edu/articles/augustines-push-against-the-limits-of-time/.

197 Saint Augustine, *Eighty-three Different Questions*, trans. David L. Mosher. (Washington, D.C.: Catholic University of America Press, 1982), 81.

At the end of the third century A.D., the Emperor Diocletian had decided that the Roman Empire was too large to be ruled as a single body. After a century of turmoil, in 395 — the same year Augustine became bishop of Hippo — this split was formalized. The empire was divided into Eastern and Western halves.

Rome had not been the capital of the Western Roman Empire for some time. Milan, where St. Ambrose was the bishop, became the capital city in A.D. 286, and it stayed that way for more than a hundred years. But Rome was still, in the minds of most people, the true center of the empire.

So when Rome was sacked by the Visigoths and their leader, Alaric, the invasion sent shock waves throughout Europe and beyond. Rome, the "eternal city," had been safe from foreign attacks for nearly a millennium.

The Goths had kept an uneasy peace with Rome for decades. But Alaric had become frustrated in his dealings with the increasingly unstable empire. On August 24, 410, his raiders entered the city and pillaged it for three days.

There wasn't a lot of actual damage, but the psychological blow was extreme. In the aftermath, there was plenty of blame to go around. Some thought Rome was being punished for abandoning pagan religion in favor of Christianity.

Following events from across the Mediterranean, Augustine wrote a book that was both a defense of the faith and a reminder that no earthly city could last forever. *The City of God* contains more than a thousand pages. But its premise is simple. The success the Roman Empire enjoyed, Augustine told his readers, was *because* of its devotion to the Christian God, not in *spite* of it.

A city, he reminded them, is "a community of rational beings united by a single agreement about that which they love."[198] As Peter Kreeft puts it, "Two loves have made two cities. Love of God to the refusal of self has made the City of God. Love of self to the refusal of God has made the city of the world."[199]

It's clear which path Rome had chosen. But while the fall of the Eternal City may seem like "the story to end all stories," it isn't: for faithful Christians, it's just "a nanosecond in eternity."[200]

Directly echoing Plato, Augustine noted that it's important for citizens everywhere to remember that they live in two cities simultaneously: an earthly city and a heavenly one.

[198] Kreeft, *Socrates' Children,* vol. 2, 36.

[199] Kreeft, *Socrates' Children,* vol. 2, 36.

[200] Rubenstein, *Aristotle's Children,* 48.

Citizens of the earthly city want peace, of course — but they want it by making their lives comfortable by earthly standards. But the heavenly city "lives like a captive and a stranger in the earthly city," and "it makes no scruple to obey the laws of the earthly city"[201] if those laws conflict with God's promise of eternal peace.

This idea of living "like a captive" on earth is a reminder of Plato's concept of souls trapped in material bodies, yearning for the Realm of Ideal Forms. The heavenly city, then, would be the earthly city in its perfect form.

Until citizens of the earthly city remember that earthly peace depends on the peace of heaven, Augustine concluded, peace will be impossible. Unfortunately, as storm clouds continued to mass over Europe, that's exactly how things went.

9.

The bishop is dying. And so, it seems, is the rest of civilization.

Behind the thick draperies in his bedroom, and beyond the city walls, in the countryside, there are occasional skirmishes: shouts, and the clang of swords. The troops defending Hippo are tiring against the onslaught of the Vandal army, led by King Genseric, that has laid siege to the city for the past two months.

The raiders, German tribes who sailed across the Mediterranean from Spain, have already ravaged much of the surrounding countryside. They've tortured and killed priests and nuns, and burned down churches. Only three in the region — in Carthage, Cirta, and this one in Hippo — have survived.

The bishop is saddened, but not surprised. He takes consolation in a thought that he quotes often to his fellow priests: "He is not to be thought great who thinks it strange that wood and stones should fall and mortals die."

In Hippo, they're trying to hang onto the wood and stones. Everyone has retreated behind the city walls. Outside, the Vandals have robbed the granaries and orchards for food. They've blockaded the port. Everything seems to be withering away, preparing the ground for a brutal new world.

[201] St. Augustine, *The City of God*, ed. Marcus Dods (Edinburgh: T. & T. Clark, 1871), 326.

But now, as July turns to August, the bishop is only vaguely aware of the turmoil outside his bedroom. He is seventy-six years old, and his thoughts are mostly on his own inner tumult.

He's asked that some of the Psalms of David be copied for him and hung on his walls. They're all short verses, and all are about the need for penance. The bishop knows he still needs to repent for a lot of things.

So he spends most of his days whispering the words of these psalms, and weeping freely. His condition isn't improving. When a local man recently visited with a sick relative, begging for healing, the bishop replied that if he had that power, he would use it on himself. Still, he laid hands on the sick man, who left smiling, seemingly cured.

Just yesterday, the bishop asked all the faithful residents of this house, including a fellow priest named Possidus, to stop checking in on him so much. He needs every moment, he tells them, for prayer. Because he knows there isn't much time left.

The bishop, Augustine, will die peacefully here in this bedroom, on August 28 of 430. He won't see the bravery of the Roman and Goth soldiers who fight under Boniface, the Count of Africa. They will manage to hold out against the Vandal siege for another whole year. Then they'll end up abandoning the city — which the Vandals will promptly burn to the ground.

Almost nothing will be spared — except for Augustine's cathedral and his library. The world is about to plunge into darkness. But Augustine and his writing will be one of the few beacons pointing the way back to the light of the earthly city — and ultimately, to the heavenly one as well.[202]

10.

That beacon would be the only real light in philosophy for quite some time. Many would agree with Bryan Magee when he suggested that Augustine "was

[202] This reconstruction of St. Augustine on his deathbed owes a great deal to Richard E. Rubenstein's vivid depiction in *Aristotle's Children*, pages 47–49.

the outstanding figure in philosophy between Aristotle and Aquinas, a period of some 1,600 years."[203]

Yet influential as he has been, and remains, there are some aspects of Augustine's philosophy that have come in for criticism.

For starters, although he moved far beyond the anti-materialistic philosophies of the Manicheans and of Neoplatonists like Plotinus, his thought still privileged the soul at the expense of the material world.

In the opinion of some observers, this thinking influenced Augustine's ideas about original sin and predestination. These views have been the source of a great deal of controversy over the centuries — although the latter idea, in particular, is sometimes misunderstood.[204]

It's not surprising that Augustine, for whom chastity had been such a struggle, saw sex as the original sin that had stained mankind since Adam. In his view, we're all born with the tendency to sin because we're all biologically related to Adam — and, therefore, all heirs of his original sin.

There's still an ongoing debate about whether Augustine, whose grasp of Greek was questionable, mistranslated Paul's letters — especially Romans 5 and 1 Corinthians 15 — to suggest that original sin was transmitted through sex.

Predestination is an even thornier issue. How could it be that God would decide in advance which souls are bound for Heaven? Doesn't this go against the concept of free will?

The concept of *double predestination* seems even more unforgiving. God chooses who is bound for Heaven, and also who is bound for Hell — and there's nothing either group can do to change their fate.

Augustine's writings are clear that God's grace is necessary for people to reach Heaven. But what about the people who don't accept or receive this grace?

Here is why Augustine's thoughts about time and God's eternal present are so important. If God is omnipotent, then He certainly knows who will accept His grace. But it doesn't follow that He would have *decided* who would accept it.

[203] Magee, *The Story of Philosophy*, 50.

[204] As Ralph Blumenau notes, predestination would become a key component of Protestantism in the future. "Unfortunately, [Martin] Luther and [John] Calvin were so seized of the omnipotence and inscrutability of God that they did teach that he not only foresees but also preordains the fate of individuals." Ralph Blumenau, "Free Will and Predestination," *Philosophy Now* (1998), https://philosophynow.org/issues/20/Free_will_and_Predestination.

To be able to accept or reject this grace is perhaps the most significant part of humans having free will.

"There is no *pre*-destination," as Peter Kreeft explains, "just destination."[205]

Things get trickier when we consider the case, for example, of a child who dies in infancy. What if a human being never gets to make the choice about accepting God's grace? Augustine stressed the importance of infant baptism; otherwise, these babies would still be tainted by original sin.

This seems too harsh to some observers. But here it's worth remembering Augustine's long-running debate with Pelagius, a Celtic monk who taught that there was no original sin, and that God's grace was not necessary for man's salvation. Man's free will, Pelagius taught, allows us to choose to follow God.

In 415, Augustine wrote a whole book, *On Nature and Grace,* which responded to what he saw as Pelagius's heresy. Some feel that "in the heat of the battle, Augustine came to lay more and more stress on the Predestinarian and less and less on the Free Will aspect of his earlier teaching."[206]

In the end, these controversies are outweighed by the continuing power and influence of Augustine's work. The clearest sign of this is what those who believed little of what Augustine had to say admitted about him.

For example, the twentieth-century British novelist Rebecca West was an outspoken feminist who had a tortured relationship with Christianity. She blamed God for the suffering of the world. And she was even fascinated by the Manicheanism that Augustine rejected.

But she admired Augustine enough to write his biography. In it, she called him "one of the greatest of all writers," whom no modern novelist had surpassed. "He reminds us of the immortal part of [Russian novelist Leo] Tolstoy," she wrote, "and transcends it."[207]

For Augustine, of course, there was only one immortal and transcendent part of any man — his soul. Like his inspiration, Plato, Augustine believed that these souls were trying to get back to a world beyond this one. And Augustine believed he had the map to get them there.

✠ ✠ ✠

205 Peter Kreeft, *Philosophy* (San Francisco: Ignatius Press, 2023), 146.

206 Blumenau, "Free Will and Predestination."

207 Rebecca West, *The Essential Rebecca West* (New York: Penguin, 1983), 166.

CHAPTER SEVEN

ARISTOTLE UNDERGROUND

1.

Once again, a philosopher is a prisoner.

This one, however, is not taking things as calmly as Socrates did in chapter 2. He's weeping openly in his tiny cell. And he has a lot to weep about.

His dungeon is at the bottom of Ager Calventianus, a dark, dank, Gothic fortress. The prisoner will end up being confined here, in what is now the northern Italian town of Pavia, for a year. He is sure he's going to die a grisly death, and he'll end up being right: he will be tortured until his eyes pop out, then bludgeoned to death with iron rods.

What makes it worse, the prisoner thinks as he slumps on the filthy stone floor and backhands his tears, is how far he's fallen. When he was twenty-five, the prisoner was already a Roman senator. When he was thirty-three, he became a consul. And the proudest day of his life happened just two years ago, when both his sons were appointed as consuls as well.

Yet the prisoner is not just a statesman, but a scholar. Although there aren't many works of Aristotle's that are known in the West, the prisoner set himself the job of translating them from Greek to Latin. He somehow did it, too, and wrote extensive commentaries on these and other great philosophical works.

So how, the prisoner thinks as he stares at the cold, dripping walls of his cell, did he get here*? He knows the answer, or at least some of it.*

He's spent the past two decades as the Master of Offices for Theodoric, the king of the Ostrogoths. And while Theodoric may, for all intents and purposes, be the head of what's left of the Western Roman Empire, he doesn't feel secure. After all, he's a Goth, not a Roman.

Theodoric also doesn't trust the new leaders in Constantinople, capital of the Eastern Roman Empire: Justin I and his ambitious nephew, Justinian. He's heard whispers that they may be plotting with some Roman senators and noblemen in his own kingdom — and maybe even with the pope! — to overthrow him.

So when some letters are intercepted that seem to reveal just such a plot between East and West, Theodoric is outraged. And when the prisoner tries to defend the honor of the Senate and claims the letters are forgeries, Theodoric throws his Master of Offices into prison too.

It doesn't matter that the illiterate Theodoric has always been in awe of the prisoner's wisdom. It doesn't matter that the prisoner has been, in many ways, a father figure to the great Goth leader.

Now there's nothing left to do but weep, and wait. Or so the prisoner thinks.

He suddenly sees a woman in his cell, standing directly over his head. Her face, he will write later, demands "absolute reverence: Her eyes glowed like fire, penetrating far beyond the common capability of mortals."[208]

She carries books in one hand, a scepter in the other, and her height confuses the prisoner: at some moments, it seems that her crown might pierce Heaven itself.

But she's not here to set him free. She is Lady Philosophy, and she's come to talk to the prisoner — a Roman named Anicius Manlius Severinus Boethius — about the consolations of philosophy.

[208] Joel C. Relihan, *The Prisoner's Philosophy: Life and Death in Boethius's* Consolation (South Bend, IN: University of Notre Dame Press, 2007), 2.

It's a conversation that will become his very last book,
and a bestseller for centuries after his execution.[209]

2.

The visit Lady Philosophy made to Boethius in his prison cell was imaginary. "His account of it," as Arthur Herman notes, "was not."[210]

The Consolation of Philosophy was written while Boethius was a captive. It was completed not long before his execution. And it became "one of the four most popular books in what was left of Western civilization for the next 1,000 years, together with the Bible and Augustine's *Confessions* and *The City of God*."[211]

Unlike those other three books, *Consolation* does not contain any direct reference to Christianity. Yet Boethius was by all accounts a devout Catholic, and hadn't lost his faith on death row. So why was his last work a seemingly secular one?

Arthur Herman explains:

> Boethius was four years old when the Roman Empire in the West ended. He grew up under the growing shadow of what we call the Dark Ages. He watched the spread of barbaric chaos, and the slow extinguishing of civilization, with deep alarm. He came to realize that Christian society *by itself* was not going to survive. The death of the Earthly City had led not to the creation of the Heavenly City, but to something far worse. To live in a dangerous world, people needed something more than the Bible and the Church Fathers — or the advice to simply turn the other cheek to our enemies.[212]

That something more, for Boethius, was the great Greek philosophers: "Boethius is the first Christian thinker to realize that Plato and Aristotle were still

[209] A number of sources were consulted for this opening section, including Arthur Herman's *The Cave and the Light* and Joel Relihan's *The Prisoner's Philosophy*.

[210] Herman, *The Cave and the Light*, 189.

[211] Kreeft, *Socrates' Children*, vol. 2, 42. Translator and biographer Joel Relihan makes the argument that *Consolations* is actually a work of Menippean satire, a style of Greek and Roman writing that is often in prose form. It usually makes fun of abstract ideas, rather than people. Relihan points out that the allegorical Lady Philosophy promised "consolation" and answers — but ultimately doesn't deliver them. This, he claims, makes the work a sendup of pagan philosophy, and an exploration of how Christian thought can replace it.

[212] Herman, *The Cave and the Light*, 190.

indispensable to Western civilization. They still provided an essential and rational framework for dealing with the real world — and also dying in it."[213]

And like Socrates — whom Boethius also thought was indispensable — he was also going to have to figure out the best way to die.

Facing death is a primary theme in *Consolation,* which is half prose and half poetry. In this dialogue between Lady Philosophy and Boethius, the condemned man comes to realize that despite the unfairness of his persecution, he might actually be luckier than his accusers.

"The good are always powerful, and the evil are always weak and futile," Lady Philosophy tells him. "Those who injure others are more unhappy than those whom they injure."[214]

Ultimately, Lady Philosophy shows Boethius "that all goodness comes from one source, the highest good, which is identified with God. Only by adhering to this good can a person be truly happy."[215]

This concept, of course, seems to relate closely to Plato's idea of the Good — the highest of the Ideal Forms. But throughout *Consolation,* Boethius also borrowed from Aristotle. He had translated all the works of Aristotle known at that time in the West: six books of logic, known as the *Organon*. So Boethius knew and appreciated both great philosophers.

Yet while *Consolation* leaned heavily on the Greeks, it also addressed a question that would be of growing importance in the centuries to come. That is, how far can pure reason take us — and how compatible is it with faith?

Boethius had made it his goal, in fact, to reconcile faith and reason. "To him, using reason did not mean demystifying the truths of faith, but building conceptual bridges between the worlds of secular and religious knowledge."[216]

One of those conceptual bridges comes in *Consolation,* when Boethius references St. Augustine's idea of the eternal present. Lady Philosophy uses this concept to explain how God can be omniscient, and human beings can still have free will.

[213] Herman, *The Cave and the Light,* 190.

[214] Kreeft, *Socrates' Children,* vol. 2, 44.

[215] John Marenbon, "Why We Should Read Boethius's *Consolation of Philosophy* Today," *Aeon,* October 9, 2020. https://aeon.co/essays/why-we-should-read-boethiuss-consolation-of-philosophy-today.

[216] Rubenstein, *Aristotle's Children,* 64.

But in the end, as he wrote what amounted to his last will and testament, Boethius may have realized that Lady Philosophy might not have all the answers.

In the view of author and professor John Marenbon, "Philosophy can indeed console even the condemned, Christian Boethius — but only to a certain extent. Purely rational, human speculation can grasp a good deal, but it can't achieve a fully coherent understanding of how the different elements in the divinely ordered universe fit together."[217]

The limitations of reason and the necessity of faith are recurring themes in the medieval period. Peter Kreeft, in fact, calls Boethius the last classical philosopher, and also the first medieval, or "scholastic," philosopher — that is, a thinker who sharply distinguished reason from faith.

Just three years after Boethius was put to death, another Christian left Rome for a hilltop monastery in Monte Cassino. To save Christianity, St. Benedict thought, believers needed to retreat from society and relearn their faith.

But it was in these monastic communities that Western thought, as well as Christianity, was preserved. Boethius had saved Greek philosophy — and now the monks were going to save both.

"It was only the relentless reproduction of Boethius's works, by generations of forgotten monks and scribes from Subiaco and Monte Cassino in Italy to Lindisfarne in Ireland, that allowed some fragments of that Greek legacy to enter the Western consciousness," says Arthur Herman.[218]

"From the age of Charlemagne to the Crusades," by the dim light of candles, these monks painstakingly "copied and recopied the manuscripts of Boethius, alongside St. Augustine, Cicero and Virgil, and St. Jerome's Latin Bible."[219]

"When writers talk about the monks of Ireland 'saving civilization,'" Herman adds, "this is what they mean."[220]

Although he didn't live in an Irish monastery — or even in Ireland — the next significant Western thinker did come originally from the Emerald Isle. And like Boethius, he was also keen to explore the boundaries between reason and faith.

217 Marenbon, "Why We Should Read Boethius's *Consolation of Philosophy* Today."
218 Herman, *The Cave and the Light*, 193.
219 Herman, *The Cave and the Light*, 193.
220 Herman, *The Cave and the Light*, 193.

3.

In his book *A History of Western Philosophy*, Bertrand Russell called John Scotus[221] Erigena "the most astonishing person of the ninth century; he would have been less surprising if he had lived in the fifth or the fifteenth century."[222]

In other words, Erigena was one of the only bright spots in Western philosophy during the "Dark Ages." He was clearly an independent thinker at a time when those were in short supply.

Bertrand Russell was impressed that although Erigena "spent much of his life under the patronage of Charles the Bald, king of France, and though he was certainly far from orthodox ... so far as we know, he escaped persecution."[223]

But an even more surprising thing about Erigena was his expertise in Greek, a language that had mostly disappeared in Western Europe by this time. He was able to translate *On the Divine Names*, a work by Pseudo-Dionysius the Areopagite. When it was sent to Pope Nicholas for approval, the pope's librarian "was astonished that a man from a remote and barbarous country could have possessed such a profound knowledge of Greek."[224]

This translation of Pseudo-Dionysius had widespread influence during the medieval period. It drew a line between faith and reason by insisting that we can only know what God is *not*—not what he truly *is*. (Dionysius did say that we can know what God is *like*—but our analogies fall short, since the "goodness" of God is not the same as human goodness.)

Erigena's personal contribution to philosophy had a more modest effect. As Peter Kreeft puts it, Erigena's book *The Division of Nature* does the reverse of what St. Augustine had accomplished. Augustine had Christianized Neoplatonism; Erigena, on the other hand, tried to Neoplatonize Christianity.

221 "Scotus" is short for "Scots," which meant "Irish" at the time.

222 Bertrand Russell, *A History of Western Philosophy, and Its Connection with Political and Social Circumstances from the Earliest Times to the Present Day* (New York: Simon and Schuster, 1945), 400.

223 Russell, *A History of Western Philosophy*, 400.

224 Russell, *A History of Western Philosophy*, 404. Pseudo-Dionysius the Areopagite was "an early sixth-century monk who pretended to be the first-century disciple of St. Paul mentioned" in Acts 17:34. This alias-taking was "a literary device common in ancient times." Peter Kreeft, who lists him as one of the one hundred greatest philosophers, notes that no less an authority than St. Thomas Aquinas quoted Pseudo-Dionysius 1,700 times (Kreeft, *Socrates' Children*, vol. 2, 46).

Like Plotinus, Erigena sees God as beyond being—as a "One" that can't be perceived or defined. Even to call God "Good" or "Being" would be too limiting.

This directly contradicted Aristotle, who believed God *was* being. For Erigena, as for Plotinus, God was *above* being.

To further explain, Erigena divides nature into four categories:

1. Nature which creates and is not created. In other words, God.
2. Nature which is created, and also creates. These are the forms of Plato—or universals—which exist in the mind of God.
3. Nature which is created, but does not create. This is the material universe—Plato's imperfect copies.
4. Nature which is not created and does not create. This is God, as the end and purpose of all things.

Categories two and three are essentially Plato, bookended in categories one and four by God, the Alpha and the Omega. This is perhaps the best example of Erigena's "Neoplatonization" of Christianity, and it was his Big Idea.

But his is a difficult philosophy to grasp overall. Parts of it were condemned as heretical—for example, the idea that sin created biological sex. More understandably—though still controversially—Erigena was apparently an animal lover. Perhaps alone among medieval thinkers, he argued that animals (and plants) also had immortal souls.

As Peter Kreeft notes, Erigena's ideas didn't catch on. However, in the West at this time, his ambition and erudition made him a remarkable man indeed.

4.

The Christian West during the first part of the medieval era was, as we've seen, not a hotbed of philosophy. But things were much different in the Arab world.

It all started, however, because of a Christian controversy in the fifth century. This dispute involved Nestorius, the patriarch of Constantinople.

Nestorius rejected the idea that God, through Jesus Christ, had been born of the Virgin Mary. Instead, he claimed, Christ had two separate natures: one human and one divine.

This belief was condemned by the Catholic Church in 431 at the Council of Ephesus, in present-day Turkey. Cyril, the patriarch of Alexandria, led the charge against Nestorius.[225] The council affirmed that Christ had a single, unified nature. Otherwise, Cyril argued, Christ's presence in the Eucharist would be meaningless.

Defeated and stripped of his title, Nestorius retreated. He wound up exiled in a monastery in Upper Egypt. But he retained some followers. They were branded as heretics, but they included many great linguists.

Some of them took refuge in the university at Nisibis, in Persia — a school regarded as the best in Asia. There, they set to work translating great Greek books into Persian. These included many of Aristotle's writings that had been lost for centuries in the West.

In the seventh century, following the death of the prophet Muhammed, the new religion of Islam spread quickly, through conquest and conversion. When Islam reached Persia, the Nestorian scholars re-translated the Greek books into Arabic.

So by the ninth and tenth centuries, Islamic scholars had access to such works of Aristotle's as *Physics, Metaphysics,* and *On the Soul.* And they began figuring out how to incorporate these teachings of Aristotle into the framework of Islam.

It was a gigantic challenge. "Greek philosophy in the Islamic world, suggestively translated by the term *falsafa* to emphasize its Greek origins, was frequently the object of controversy and persecution," writes Oliver Leaman.[226]

We'll see several examples of that in this chapter. Yet the greatest of the philosophers from this era — most of them Arabic, one of them a Jew — found ways to reconcile Aristotle's beliefs with their own.

In the end, it would be the Christian world that would benefit most from their work. But it could never have happened without the men we'll meet next.

5.

One of the earliest Muslim philosophers was al-Fârâbî, a Persian Sufi mystic who was active at the turn of the tenth century.

He continued the project of Western philosophers like Boethius — reconciling the works of Plato and Aristotle. In fact, he wrote a book titled *On the*

[225] Richard Rubenstein gives more background on other controversies involving Cyril, including the Nestorian heresy, and the murder in 415 of the great female thinker Hypatia, the daughter of an Alexandrian mathematician. She was accused of spreading pagan philosophy — an incendiary charge after the recent Arian heresy. "Cyril vehemently denied any connection with the crime," Rubinstein writes, "but nobody was ever punished for it" (Rubenstein, *Aristotle's Children,* 72).

[226] Oliver Leaman, *Moses Maimonides* (New York: Routledge, 2013), 23.

Harmonization of the Opinions of the Two Sages: The Divine Plato and Aristotle.[227] But he had a lot more of Aristotle's writing to work with than Boethius did.

Al-Fârâbî made one crucial distinction that would play a huge role in medieval thought: between *essence* and *existence.* This is a subject that will be discussed more later — especially in the section about St. Thomas Aquinas — but al-Fârâbî is generally credited with starting the discussion.

It relates, in part, to a major problem that Aristotle, in particular, presented for Muslims — and would also present for Christians and Jews. That is, his belief that the universe has always existed. This seems to contradict biblical teaching, which states that God created creation.[228]

For al-Fârâbî, the key was a statement made by Aristotle: "That the idea of *what* a thing is does not include *that* it is."[229]

We can imagine very clearly a unicorn, or the fictional character Harry Potter. We can describe them both in great detail. But because we know their *essences* doesn't mean that they actually *exist.*

Likewise, people and animals who have died also have essences, even though they no longer have existence. So just because something has an essence does not mean it also has — or has *ever* had — an existence.

For something to actually exist, then, there must be something that *makes* it exist. It can't be the thing itself, or else the essence of Harry Potter could create a real Harry Potter — which we know makes no sense.

If you imagine that everything in the universe — including the universe itself — is a combination of essence and existence, then "in that case, the universe must have a cause outside itself."[230]

That First Cause, for al-Fârâbî, was God — who is necessarily existent. Everything else in creation is an "accident," in the sense that it didn't *have* to exist.

[227] There is some academic controversy over the authorship of *On the Harmonization of the Opinions of the Two Sages.* Some scholars claim al-Fârâbî could not have been the author, since some of the views in the book don't seem to harmonize with his own thought.

[228] Plato's view of the universe was different from Aristotle's idea that it has always existed. Plato's concept of a "Demiurge" creating the cosmos out of chaos, like many of his other beliefs, was easier to reconcile with Christian (and monotheistic) teaching. However, he didn't address the source of the chaos.

[229] Kreeft, *Socrates' Children,* vol. 2, 66.

[230] Feser, *The Last Superstition,* 107.

The rest of al-Fârâbî's conception of God (or Allah) sounds a lot like the Neoplatonic version: a perfect "One" that we can try to define, but which exceeds our vocabulary.

But his Big Idea started with a seemingly stray remark by Aristotle, which he expanded to its logical end. That was how al-Fârâbî was able to begin reconciling the seemingly irreconcilable differences between the monotheistic religions and Aristotle.[231]

6.

Imagine yourself awakening for the first time. You possess the intelligence you have right now, yet this is your introduction to the world.

You are blindfolded, so you can't see anything. Your arms and legs are outstretched, and they don't touch each other.

They don't touch anything else, either: you are suspended, completely still, in midair. There is nothing, no sensation at all, to indicate that you have a body, or any physical being at all.

You simply float there, sightless and motionless, in a perfect vacuum, in complete silence.

Do you exist? If so, how do you know it?

You think hard about this question. All you can do is think, after all. And then it hits you.

You can think. *You're aware of your self, even if you experience no physical sensations — even if you can't prove you have a body at all.*

You are self-aware, in other words. And if you're self-aware, then you must also be a self.

You do exist. And your own reason has just proved it.

[231] For more information about al-Fârâbî, consult Jon McGinnis and David C. Reisman's *Classical Arabic Philosophy: An Anthology of Sources* (Indianapolis: Hackett, 2007), 81–94.

7.

This is one of the most famous thought experiments in history. Most people refer to it as the "Flying Man," although some would say that the "Floating Man" is a better description.

Whatever you call it, it comes to us from the eleventh-century Persian philosopher Ibn Sînâ — otherwise known as Avicenna.

Avicenna is generally acknowledged as the most important of the Muslim thinkers of the Islamic "Golden Era." He was something like an Arabic version of Aristotle: a scientist, physician, geographer, astronomer, poet, and philosopher.

He wrote an estimated 450 books, though less than half survive. These include a five-volume medical encyclopedia that remained state of the art for centuries afterward.

And he famously said that he preferred a life that was short and wide to one that was narrow and long. "God, Who is exalted, has been generous concerning my external and internal faculties," he once wrote, "so I use every faculty as it should be used."[232]

This may be why he apparently died in 1037 from too much food, too many herbal remedies (including opium), and too much sex.

"Evidently, Avicenna learned a great deal from Aristotle," one writer wryly notes, "save for the patently Aristotelian virtue of moderation."[233]

It's true, though, that Avicenna was one of the key Muslim synthesizers of Aristotle's philosophy. And even when Aristotle's views clashed with Islamic belief, Avicenna had an answer.

Both philosophy and religion relate the same truth, he believed. But religion relates it symbolically, while philosophy relates it literally. Implied in this belief is a dangerous assertion, however: that reason operates at a higher level than faith.

This way of thinking would eventually get Avicenna accused of heresy by Muslims and Christians alike. But that was a risk he was willing to take to achieve his goal. Like his predecessor al-Fârâbî, he wanted to reconcile Aristotle and Islam.

232 Michael Marder, "The Philosopher's Plant 6.0: Avicenna's Celery," *Project Syndicate*, April 4, 2013. https://www.project-syndicate.org/blog/the-philosopher-s-plant-6-0--avicenna-s-celery.

233 Marder, "The Philosopher's Plant 6.0."

One way that Avicenna did this was to continue al-Fârâbî's separation of existence and essence. But another way was more ambitious, and original.

"Avicenna's method, in a word, was to spiritualize Aristotle at certain key points by reading Platonic ideas into his thinking," writes Richard Rubenstein. "If the Philosopher's this-worldly system could be 'corrected' by incorporating in it the notion that the material universe is a reflection of eternal Spirit, it might be made acceptable to orthodox monotheists."[234]

The single biggest Platonic idea that Avicenna incorporated was mind-body dualism. And the way he did it became his own Big Idea: the concept of the "Flying Man."

The Flying Man thought experiment appeared in Avicenna's *Book of Healing*, which was published in 1027. It sounds a lot like what modern people experience when they enter a sensory deprivation tank.

As we've already seen, Avicenna's experiment suggests that the mind and body are separate, though the mind is ultimately superior. The mind may be trapped in the body. But when the body's senses fail, the mind can still use reason to recognize that it exists.

"It follows from this that the human self—what I am—is distinct from my body, or anything physical," the editors of *The Philosophy Book* write. "The Flying Man experiment, says Avicenna, is a way of alerting and reminding oneself of the existence of the mind as something other than, and distinct from, the body."[235]

This idea seemed to affirm that humans could have immortal souls, separate from their bodies. However, Avicenna's theory also contradicted traditional Islamic belief about the complete resurrection of human beings—both body and mind.

This was one of the reasons Avicenna was later attacked by the twelfth-century philosopher al-Ghazâlî. He wrote the book *The Incoherence of the Philosophers* about what he saw as the incoherence of one philosopher in particular: Avicenna.

Avicenna's ideas would end up being greeted more warmly in the Christian world. Medieval philosophers "liked the way his interpretations of Aristotle's texts made them easily compatible with the idea of an immortal soul." And the Flying Man laid the groundwork for an even more famous philosophical experiment.

[234] Rubenstein, *Aristotle's Children*, 81–83.

[235] Buckingham, *The Philosophy Book*, 78.

That came in 1637, when the French philosopher René Descartes officially reopened the mind-body problem. We'll read about that experiment soon, and the shockwaves it sent throughout philosophy and Western culture. But that earthquake really began with Avicenna.

8.

Avicenna wasn't the only Muslim philosopher attacked for heresy. But the next thinker on our list was even more bold.

Ibn Rushd was born in Córdoba, which was part of Muslim Spain, in 1126. He was, like several of his predecessors, a polymath, who wrote about a variety of scientific and theological subjects. He was so prolific a writer that he earned the nickname "The Commentator."

Like his father and grandfather, he was an Islamic judge (a *qâdî*). He worked for the Almohads, one of the most orthodox Muslim regimes of his era, and he was close to the powerful caliph. (Later, he would even become the caliph's personal physician.)

But after hours, Rushd — better known by his Latin name, Averroës — was also an Aristotelian scholar. In fact, he was devoted to the works of "The Master of Those Who Know."

"Let us praise God," Averroës wrote, "who set this man apart from all others in perfection, and made him approach very near to the highest dignity humanity can attain."[236]

Averroës was determined to harmonize Aristotle with Islamic belief. But he wasn't interested in using Plato's work to make Aristotle more "spiritual." As Richard Rubenstein writes,

> Although a faithful monotheist himself, Averroës insisted on "de-Platonizing" Aristotle — on reaffirming his focus on individual substances rather than timeless Ideas, and defending his contention that the natural universe is governed by natural laws, not by the whimsical or mysterious decisions of a miracle-making God.... An Aristotelian philosopher could be a convinced monotheist, but he could not believe in a simple-minded way in doctrines like divine miracles, the resurrection of the body, or the immortality of the individual soul. Either these doctrines

[236] Herman, *The Cave and the Light*, 227.

> were true in a way that was unprovable by reason, or they were true in ways more complex than what was generally understood.[237]

Here, Averroës borrowed from Avicenna's idea that philosophy and religion teach the same truth different ways. Averroës distinguished between three sorts of minds.

The first, and highest, type of mind belongs to "men of demonstration," who are the philosophers. They use reason to prove their beliefs.

The second type of mind belongs to theologians, "dialectical men." They value faith and reason — but their emphasis is on faith, and their reason is not fully developed.

And the third type of mind belongs to the "men of exhortation" — the masses. Their reason is barely developed, so they respond to preaching that speaks to their imagination.[238]

All three groups believe in the same truths, and are pursuing the same goals, Averroës thought. But the philosophers have the most sophisticated understanding of these truths.

This idea of the "double truth" was, of course, a hazardous game. It suggested that religion wasn't literally true, but was only "a Santa Claus story to make those who are intellectually childlike happy and good."[239]

There was more. In his uncompromising adaptation of Aristotle, Averroës reiterated the beliefs that the universe had always existed and that when men die their souls go with them. More precisely, they're absorbed into the universal intelligence, he thought, "like a drop of water returning to the ocean."[240]

These insights "earned Averroës an admiration equaled by no other living non-Christian," writes Arthur Herman. "For the first time, scholars saw in Aristotle a great thinker who did not see the world of the senses as an illusion or a vale of sin and suffering or even a complex forest of symbols."

"Here was a thinker, one undeniably of the highest order, who seemed unaware of the need for a Savior and Redeemer or of a better, more perfect world to come. Aristotle's universe is whole and complete."[241]

[237] Rubenstein, *Aristotle's Children*, 81–82.

[238] The descriptions of these three types of men are from Peter Kreeft, *Socrates' Children*, vol. 2, 74.

[239] Kreeft, *Socrates' Children*, vol. 2, 75.

[240] Herman, *The Cave and the Light*, 229.

[241] Herman, *The Cave and the Light*, 228.

That view was not, however, shared by either Muslim thinkers or the Catholic Church. In 1195, Averroës was banished from Córdoba, and his books were burned. Though he later regained favor and rejoined the royal court, his exile was a reminder that his unorthodox views had powerful Islamic enemies.

The University of Paris, meanwhile, issued its own, Church-backed condemnation of Averroës in 1210. And "for good measure, it extended the ban to the works of Aristotle."[242]

Like Averroës's punishment by the royal authorities, this banishment also turned out to be temporary. Very soon, a Catholic philosopher would be born who would harmonize Church teaching and Aristotle more completely than any other thinker.

Yet the enemies of Averroës in both the Islamic and Christian worlds were a sign of things to come. Trying to square Aristotle and religious belief was risky business. And if these efforts got a philosopher placed on a blacklist, then Aristotle was probably going to join him there.

9.

Speaking of blacklists, that's where the greatest Jewish thinker of the medieval era ended up as well.

The Guide to the Perplexed, by Moses Maimonides, was even more radical than the philosophy of Averroës. And it met with disapproval from the rabbis, just as Averroës had been censored by Muslim authorities.

The similarities between those two philosophers are striking. Like Averroës, Moses ben Maimon was born in Córdoba, Spain. Like Averroës, his father was a judge, and like Averroës, he would later become a judge himself, as well as a royal physician.

But when the strict Islamic regime of the Almohads took power in Córdoba, things worked out very differently for these two men.

While Averroës, a Muslim, rose to prominence in Córdoba, conditions there became hostile for Christians and Jews. The new rulers abolished the *jizya* — a tax that non-Muslims could pay to ensure their protection. Now their only choices were conversion to Islam, death, or exile.

[242] Herman, *The Cave and the Light,* 229.

So, because "there was no longer a place there for Jews living openly,"[243] Moses Maimonides's family fled the city. After a decade of wandering, they finally settled in Cairo, Egypt.

There, Maimonides became the personal doctor of the sultan, Saladin. He also applied his highly organized mind to the law.

Between 1168 and 1178, Maimonides created *The Mishneh Torah*, which was "a complete restatement of Jewish Oral Law." He wrote it "in plain Hebrew so that 'young and old' could know and understand all the Jewish observances."[244]

His philosophy, meanwhile, owed a lot to Aristotle, and very little to Plato. Like Averroës, whose work he admired, he wasn't interested in using Plato to soften Aristotle's sharp edges.

"The works of Aristotle are the roots and foundations of all works on the sciences," Maimonides wrote. Plato, meanwhile, "is said to have written in parables and not really contributed anything which is not to be found in Aristotle."[245]

This desire for precise language is one reason that Maimonides had no patience for humanizing God. As he put it in one exasperated passage:

> The negation of the doctrine of the corporeality of God and the denial of His having a likeness to created things and of His being subject to affections are matters that ought to be made clear and explained to everyone according to his capacity, and ought to be inculcated in virtue of traditional authority upon children, women, stupid ones, and those of defective natural disposition, just as they adopt the notion that God is one.[246]

As other philosophers — from Aristotle to Averroës — had argued, God was a concept that resisted definition. For Maimonides, this needed to be explained, even to the "stupid" and "defective" people who preferred the image of God as a white-haired old man.

[243] Leaman, *Moses Maimonides*, 32.

[244] Buckingham, *The Philosophy Book*, 85.

[245] Leaman, *Moses Maimonides*, 39.

[246] Moses Maimonides, *The Guide of the Perplexed*, vol. 1 (Chicago: University of Chicago Press, 1963), 81.

God, he argued, can only be understood in the negative — by what he is not. This was a philosophy proposed by the sixth-century Christian thinker Pseudo-Dionysius the Areopagite, and Maimonides expanded on it.

"No positive predicates at all can be applied to God," Oliver Leaman explains. "We can talk about God's actions and the effects of those actions, but we cannot move from language about the existence of things to any definite language about the nature of God's existence."[247]

"This is a very radical doctrine," Leaman points out.[248] Even the uncompromising Averroës had acknowledged that while the language non-philosophers used to describe God wasn't *technically* accurate, it was at least pointing to the same truth.

But for the legal scholar Maimonides, that wasn't good enough. *The Guide to the Perplexed,* published in 1197, was dedicated to one of his students who was confused about how to reconcile Jewish law, science, and Aristotle.

In trying to solve the confusion, Maimonides

> quite clearly implies that there are problems in knowing whom we believe in if we believe in God. When we pray we do not produce any effect on God, we can establish no sort of connection with him. God cannot even notice the fact that people pray to him given his complete independence from any connection with the world of corruption and generation. The idea of God possessing an attitude of care and concern for "his" creatures so prevalent in the liturgy of both Islam and Judaism is accordingly inappropriate and empty.[249]

The only real compromise Maimonides was willing to make was this: "He rather grudgingly accepts that it is slightly more appropriate to talk of God's actions as compared with his qualities."[250] If we talk about God as a creator, we're talking about what He *does,* not who He *is.*[251]

Maimonides had a similarly impersonal view of the afterlife. *Something* survives after we die, he thought — but it's not individual souls. Instead, it's just

[247] Leaman, *Moses Maimonides,* 73–74.

[248] Leaman, *Moses Maimonides,* 79.

[249] Leaman, *Moses Maimonides,* 78–79.

[250] Leaman, *Moses Maimonides,* 87.

[251] Maimonides *did* also admit that anthropomorphic depictions of God could sometimes be useful — to show people what they ought to do.

ideas, with "nothing to distinguish between one possessor of ideas and another. The perfected intellects all contain the same collection of ideas and so are identical to each other."[252]

All this was unlikely to find favor among the Jewish authorities — especially those in Europe. When *A Guide to the Perplexed* was translated into Hebrew from Arabic, there were calls for it to be banned and burned — from both Jewish and Christian officials.[253]

Nearly overlooked was a key concession that Maimonides had made to religion. It was the one place where he took serious issue with Aristotle, and it would influence the greatest of the medieval Christian philosophers, St. Thomas Aquinas.

This was the question of whether the world had always existed. Aristotle, as we've seen, argued that it had. Many of the medieval Muslim philosophers, like Avicenna, had agreed with him, even though that seemed to contradict sacred scripture.

But Maimonides argued that it was actually *scripture*, not Aristotle, that was more reasonable on this point. A God like Aristotle's Unmoved Mover, or like Avicenna's conception of God, could only know *universals*: for example, the universal concept of man, rather than individual men.

The problem with this idea, Maimonides thought, was "that God then seems to become ignorant of great amounts of potential knowledge which is particular and yet important. For example, most of the Bible deals with particular events and their consequences, and it can hardly be acceptable to assert that God does not know that Moses left Egypt or that Abraham made a covenant with him."[254]

A God who knew *both* universals and specifics — the God of the Bible — was superior. This was the kind of God Maimonides preferred.

By showing that Aristotle's more limited idea of God is inferior to the biblical God, Maimonides is able to claim something else: that Aristotle's view of an eternal universe might *also* be flawed.

"If we accept the eternity of the universe as taught by Aristotle," he wrote,

> that everything in the universe is the result of fixed laws, that nature does not change and that there is nothing supernatural, we should necessarily be in opposition to the foundation of our religion, we should disbelieve

252 Leaman, *Moses Maimonides*, 269.

253 As Oliver Leaman notes, some rabbis wanted *A Guide to the Perplexed* banned because it closed the door "on ijtihād (innovation) within the context of Jewish law." (Leaman, *Moses Maimonides*, 34.)

254 Leaman, *Moses Maimonides*, 239–240.

> all miracles and signs, and certainly reject all hopes and fear derived from scripture, unless miracles are to be explained figuratively.[255]

This is a difficult needle to thread, and even today, it remains controversial. But the exception that Maimonides carved out — that "Aristotle's analysis of natural events is taken to be valid in so far as it goes, but it goes awry if it seeks to explain the origination and the passing away of those events as a whole"[256] — had a lasting effect.

Specifically, it would allow other philosophers—notably, Thomas Aquinas—to downplay this issue in favor of more pressing ones. The question for them would not be how the universe began — but what keeps it going.

10.

The era of *falsafah* would essentially come to an end after the death of Averroës in 1198. The backlash to Muslim philosophers who tried to bring Aristotle in line with Islam had become too fierce.

Traditionalists like the Persian mystic al-Ghazâlî, a Sunni Muslim, wanted to bring the new breed to heel. His book *The Incoherence of the Philosophers* attacked both Aristotle and Avicenna. This prompted another member of the new breed, Averroës, to write his own reply to al-Ghazâlî. It was sarcastically titled *The Incoherence of Incoherence*.

That was a clever name, and the volume was an equally clever defense of philosophy. But al-Ghazâlî's book would have the greater influence. It "broke the back of rationalistic philosophy" in the Islamic world, "and in fact brought the career of philosophy … to an end in the Arabic part of the Islamic world."

"Since philosophy in those days included much of what we call science," Richard Rubenstein observes, "this did not bode well for the future of scientific inquiry in the Islamic world."[257] And in the decades and centuries to come, that inquiry largely ceased. In this battle of faith and reason, faith had triumphed.

Meanwhile, in Judaism — like Islam — most philosophers had secular day jobs. This gave thinkers like Moses Maimonides the chance to propose ideas that ran counter to religious belief. But "this very freedom made them a danger

255 Leaman, *Moses Maimonides*, 168.

256 Leaman, *Moses Maimonides*, 173.

257 Rubenstein, *Aristotle's Children*, 85.

in the eyes of the orthodox religious teachers, at least when they moved from fields like law and medicine to metaphysics, theology, and politics."[258]

That left Christianity as the last of the Big Three monotheistic religions where philosophy might continue to flourish. Its advantage was its vast organization. The structure of the Catholic Church had helped hold Europe together during the challenging first half of the medieval era.

"With its high degree of centralization, its vast number of priests and nuns in orders, its properties, its armies, and its monopoly of education, the Church was the dominant force in European intellectual culture — an institution without parallel in any other society."[259]

If it proved open to Aristotelian thought — in a way that Judaism and Islam had not been — then "European thinking would be transformed from the top down. A rationalist, scientific approach to nature and society would inevitably become part of the Western worldview."[260]

The miracle is that it actually happened. The tragedy is that it didn't last. And the subsequent tragedy is that so few people today know about any of it.

[258] Rubenstein, *Aristotle's Children*, 86.

[259] Rubenstein, *Aristotle's Children*, 87.

[260] Rubenstein, *Aristotle's Children*, 87.

CHAPTER EIGHT

GETTING SCHOOLED

1.

This room is, for all intents and purposes, a library. The manuscripts spread out across the dark wooden tables make that clear. And in the flickering candlelight, men pore over the texts, nodding as they make notes.

But this isn't a quiet library, by any means. Discussions are going on here, on many subjects, and in many languages. Some of the men wear turbans and speak in Arabic. Others are Sephardic Jews, who stroke their beards while making their arguments in Spanish. And others, with rough brown robes and bald scalps, are Christian monks.

Most of these monks are members of the Benedictine order — like you. You've had a seat at this table for just a couple of months, and you don't speak much yet. You just listen, and read. That's enough for now, because there's so much to absorb here.

The former Archbishop of Toledo, Francis Raymond de Sauvetât, was also a Benedictine. He set up this translation center nearly a hundred years ago, in the early twelfth century.

Raymond recruited great scholars from across Europe, and — more importantly — from across faiths. The Crusades are more than a hundred years old at this point, early in the 1200s. They won't be concluded for almost a hundred years more.

But here in Toledo, religious differences are secondary to the work at hand. You and your colleagues are working to translate some of the greatest philosophical works in history. The goal is to make these treasures, many of them lost for centuries in the West, more accessible.

And it's also to puzzle over the contradictions that these works reveal. No works are more problematic — and more exciting — than Aristotle's.

One of your fellow Christian scholars, seated at the other end of this long table, is a middle-aged monk with bright eyes and a quick wit. They call him Michael the Scot, because he was born in Scotland. Other people whisper that he might be a wizard: he knows alchemy and astrology, as well as languages.

Whether he has magical powers or not, he's definitely a whiz when it comes to translations. He and another brilliant linguist, with the rhyming nickname of "Herman the German,"[261] *are working right now on a Latin version of* Aristotle's History of Animals. *They're translating the Arabic text into Latin. Included in the bargain is an accompanying commentary by the great Muslim philosopher, Averroës.*

You gaze above the candlelight, up the high stone walls and into the shadows on the ceiling, and shake your head. This is an incredible place, but sometimes it's all a bit overwhelming.

The translation center is located in the Cathedral of Toledo, in the very center of the city. It's a structure that reminds you, and everyone, of the delicate balance between faiths.

This building is on the site of an earlier Catholic church. When Muslims overtook Toledo in the early eighth century, that church was torn down and an Islamic mosque was built in its place.

[261] "Herman the German" (in Latin, *Hermannus Alemannus*) worked at the translation center from about 1240 to 1256. He seems to have later become the bishop of Astorga in the Spanish province of León.

Then, in 1085, Alfonso VI of León reconquered the city. There was less resistance than expected from the Muslim citizens, perhaps because the new ruler agreed to preserve much of what the Muslims had built in Toledo.

And in Toledo, "scholarship flourished as in some dream of ancient Athens or Alexandria."[262] *The center of that scholarship is where you are right now: in the hall of the former mosque, which has been reconsecrated as a Christian church.*

Toledo might be a beacon of religious tolerance, but as you turn your attention back to the scrolls on the table, it's hard not to feel conflicted.

For one thing, there are signs that this era of cooperation might be drawing to a close. It won't be long before the Church will condemn both Averroës and Aristotle. And in just a few years, Jews and Muslims will be required to wear distinctive clothing — in some cases, a yellow badge — to distinguish them from Christians.

For another, what you've read of Aristotle so far has convinced you of this: his way of looking at the world makes a lot of sense. You've also seen the problems with Aristotle's philosophy — the ones that conflict with Christian teaching. Yet even those problems, you think, might represent an opportunity. "The Arab commentators had disagreed with him on certain points, and even dared to update and correct him. Why should Christian scholars be more diffident?"[263]

Why? Maybe because it's already obvious that the Jewish and Muslim authorities aren't going to go along with some of these ideas from the Greeks: they're already pushing back.

Will the same thing happen to you, if you follow in their footsteps? You listen to the murmuring of the conversations around you, the sputtering of the candles. You absently touch the wooden rosary beads in your lap. And you wonder.

[262] Rubenstein, *Aristotle's Children*, 14.

[263] Rubenstein, *Aristotle's Children*, 80. This entire scene owes a great deal to Rubenstein's book, the best treatment of this little-understood yet critical period in history.

2.

Christians were the last major religious group to grapple with the mysteries of Aristotle. That struggle would be the defining event of the Scholastic era, of the entire medieval era, and — this book will argue — of all of human history.

The Scholastics — or "Schoolmen" — were a group of Christian philosophers who were defined by how they undertook that struggle. The main tool at their disposal was the use of logic — which is sometimes described as *dialectical reasoning.*

Dialectical reasoning is a form of argument that has three parts. Someone makes an argument, called a *thesis*. Then someone makes a counterargument, or *antithesis.*

When the thesis and antithesis collide, the goal is to reach a conclusion, or *synthesis,* of both arguments, that answers the question or solves the contradiction.

Using this type of rational argument, the Scholastic philosophers hoped, they would be able to use *reason* to prove the things they believed through their *faith.* It wasn't always successful, but when it worked, it managed to ground Christian belief in the science and logic of Aristotle.

Three men are generally credited as being the founders of Scholasticism. We'll read about two of them in this chapter. The third, Lanfranc, was a former archbishop of Canterbury who famously defended the doctrine of transubstantiation — that Christ is actually present in the bread and wine of the Eucharist — against Bernard of Tours during the 1050s.

The *first* great Scholastic was actually Lanfranc's successor as archbishop of Canterbury. He was a Benedictine monk from Burgundy, an area that is now part of Italy. His name was Anselmo d'Aosta.

Today we know him as St. Anselm, and we know him primarily for what Peter Kreeft calls "the most famous argument in the history of human thought."[264] It was Anselm's attempt to use the Scholastic principles of logic to "reason through" a problem. And the problem he picked was, perhaps, the most vexing question to face humanity: Does God exist?

[264] Kreeft, *Socrates' Children,* vol. 2, 54.

The answer that Anselm came up with goes like this:

> Imagine the most perfect being it's possible to imagine. Now imagine that this being is perfect in every conceivable way — except this being does not exist.

To Anselm, this was illogical. If a being is perfect, but doesn't exist, then it can't be perfect. "And assuredly that, than which nothing greater can be conceived, cannot exist in the understanding alone," he wrote.[265]

In other words, the greatest possible being *has* to exist — or it can't be the greatest possible being. And how could we even imagine such a being, unless it were possible for such a being to exist?

This argument appeared in Anselm's *Proslogion,* a short meditation published in 1078 that dealt with God's seemingly contradictory qualities. It's a simple premise, but as Peter Kreeft notes, probably no other argument has gotten more philosophers to give their two cents about it.

Several of the famous philosophers who disagreed with it were also devout Christians, including Thomas Aquinas. In the eighteenth century, Immanuel Kant — who usually gets credit for calling it the "ontological argument," meaning an argument about the nature of being — also rejected it.

Despite the controversies it generated, the ontological argument remains compelling. Many would probably agree with Bryan Magee, who wrote, "Most reflective people feel that this argument will not do, but ... it is disconcertingly difficult to show what is wrong with it."[266]

Even in his own day, Anselm's argument was attacked. One of the fiercest criticisms came from Gaunilo, a French monk from Tours. Gaunilo called Anselm's thesis nothing more than wordplay, centered around the definition of the word *perfect.*[267]

[265] Kenneth Himma, "Anselm: Ontological Argument for God's Existence," *Internet Encyclopedia of Philosophy,* https://iep.utm.edu/anselm-ontological-argument/.

[266] Magee, *The Story of Philosophy,* 57

[267] Gaunilo's argument centered around the idea of a perfect island. Just because we can imagine it, he wrote, doesn't mean it exists. Anslem replied that the idea of a perfect God is necessarily different than the idea of a perfect island. The concept of a perfect God *requires* a maximum amount of goodness, omnipotence, and omniscience. The concept of a perfect island does not.

But Anslem didn't get angry with his critic. Instead, he "published Gaunilo's blunt criticism as an addendum to his essay," and then defended his position "point by point."[268]

"It did not matter that Gaunilo was a person of lower status and lesser reputation than he. What mattered was the quest for truth."[269] Building criticism into their arguments would become a hallmark of the Scholastics.

So was finding the difficult balance between faith and reason — which had undone some of the finest scholars in the Jewish and Muslim worlds.[270] Anselm would try to explain this balance in a quote that became one of the most famous of the age.

"I do not seek to understand so that I may believe," he said, "but I believe so that I may understand."[271] It was a reference to the book of Isaiah, where the prophet reminds Ahaz, the king of Judah, of the importance of belief in God. It was also similar to a phrase that St. Augustine had used from time to time.

In short, it means that without belief, there can be no true understanding. Faith is the *context* for understanding — not the result of it.

"He was not devaluing reason or logic: just the opposite," writes Arthur Herman. "He was simply reminding readers of where his, and their, priorities needed to be."[272]

The next Scholastic founder, by contrast, faced far more serious struggles with priorities. Those struggles would cost him a great deal personally — and they would have a powerful ripple effect throughout Western thought.

3.

"If Aristotle had had a younger son," Arthur Herman imagines, "he might have wanted him to be like Peter Abelard."[273]

[268] Rubenstein, *Aristotle's Children*, 103–104.

[269] Rubenstein, *Aristotle's Children*, 103–104.

[270] Regarding the balance between faith and reason, the 1870 document *Dei Filius*, the incipit of the dogmatic constitution of the First Vatican Council, states: "Even if faith is above reason, there can never be any real disagreement between faith and reason: since the same God who reveals mysteries and instills faith has given the human mind the light of reason; But God cannot deny himself, nor can he ever contradict the truth." Dogmatic Constitution *Dei Filius* (April 24, 1870), www.vatican.va. 1870. https://www.vatican.va/content/pius-ix/la/documents/constitutio-dogmatica-dei-filius-24-aprilis-1870.html.

[271] Kreeft, *Socrates' Children*, vol. 2, 54.

[272] Herman, *The Cave and the Light*, 198.

[273] Herman, *The Cave and the Light*, 198.

That may be true. Born Pierre le Pallett in Brittany, Peter Abelard was a brilliant scholar, and an even better teacher. He was so popular, in fact, that students followed him around — not just from school to school, but from city to city.

As a student himself, Abelard had been a prodigy — and a royal pain in the ass. While he was a schoolboy at the Cloister School of Notre Dame in Paris, he delighted in sparring with the master, William of Champeux.

William was a devotee of Plato, and one of the best logicians in France. But he was no match for the young man who was already wielding his knowledge of Aristotle "like a sword."

Frustrated, William expelled his headstrong young adversary. Unfazed, Abelard started his own school — taking with him some of William's best pupils.

"I began to think of myself," Abelard would later remember, "as the only philosopher in the world."[274]

Abelard would later debate publicly with William, and with another former teacher, Roscelin de Compiégne. But these were more than just rhetorical showcases.

At issue was the big controversy of the day, one that dated back to the time of the Greeks. Were there such things as universals? And if there were, where did these universals exist?

William followed the line of Plato. He defended the realist position that universals exist in another realm, beyond both the material world and the mind. Roscelin took the extreme opposite stance. He was a nominalist, who denied that universals exist at all. (In fact, he called universals a *flatus vocis* — a "fart of the voice.")[275]

If there were no universals at all, the consequences would be enormous. For one thing, there would be no such thing as a universal human nature, or universal truths. Every time we referred to qualities that seemed to apply to a group — whether that was the redness of apples or the characteristics of men and women — we'd just be kidding ourselves that these statements had any basis in reality. They'd just be words, without anything to back them up.

It was a radical theory. So Abelard vanquished both his opponents by proposing a middle ground between realism and nominalism. He suggested that universals *do* exist — but only in the mind, and only as concepts. These universals don't exist in the material world.

[274] Kreeft, *Socrates' Children*, vol. 2, 56.
[275] Kreeft, *Socrates' Children*, vol. 2, 57.

These universals are more than just words, as nominalists like Roscelin thought. But they also don't exist in some other place, as realists like William thought. This was a brilliant sleight-of-hand. Abelard's middle ground became known as *conceptualism*, and for a while, it seemed to solve the problem of universals.

It really didn't, however. Abelard was a disciple of Aristotle. But conceptualism is different from Aristotle's idea of universals existing *first* in individual things, and *then* in our minds.

If universals are *only* concepts found in individual minds, then we have to trust that we're all talking about the same thing when we call an apple "red." But we have no real way of knowing that this is so — because how can we *really* know what's happening in someone else's mind?

Bruce Aune, a nominalist and widely published scholar, makes a similar point in his book *Metaphysics: The Elements.* Abelard's view

> that we can form an abstract idea of what is common to similar things ... does not stand up to criticism if it is granted that, strictly speaking, similar things do not have any "thing" in common.... Thus, Abailard's [sic] view, carefully thought out, is in danger of collapsing into nominalism, the view that universals can be nothing but general terms.[276]

Conceptualism, then, undermines the possibility of universals, even while it claims to defend them.

But at the time, Abelard was the toast of Paris. His Big Idea spoke to an even larger development that was happening all across Europe. The so-called "Dark Ages" were long past, and civilization was beginning to speed up.

That meant changes were afoot everywhere — even in Christianity. And the debate over universals was more than just theory and wordplay.

The Christian tradition had, in one sense, elevated the individual. Christ's sacrifice had made every person's life important in a way that it never had been in pagan religions. However, Christianity also imposed restrictions that limited individual freedom.

Meanwhile, the social system in Europe had traditionally grouped people by their class, rather than seeing them as individuals. But people were beginning to chafe at these restrictions.

[276] Bruce Aune, *Metaphysics* (Minneapolis: University of Minnesota Press, 1985), 54–55.

> Most people might still be defined by their membership in large hereditary groups, but some were becoming mobile. Wandering scholars and troubadours, traders and Crusaders, itinerant preachers and country folk moving to the city — all were developing a new sense that, no matter what universal class they belonged to, their individuality mattered.[277]

Abelard was the hero of these emerging individuals, who were tired of being confined by universal rules. He was also the hero of his students, and no wonder. He spoke to them in the same liberating way. It was up to *them* to interpret the work of the philosophers, apostles, and Church Fathers, he told his eager classes. After all, "man's reason was what made him the image of God. 'In fact,' Abelard once told his class, 'you are gods!' The students yelled and cheered. Then they hoisted Abelard on their shoulders and carried him through the streets."[278]

"Some worried about where all this was heading," Arthur Herman notes, "but not Abelard."[279] His hubris would soon catch up with him — in a particularly gruesome fashion.

4.

Peter Abelard wasn't just a groundbreaking philosopher. He was also part of one of the great love stories in history, one that people sometimes call a real-life *Romeo and Juliet*. It began when Abelard, then nearing forty, started tutoring a beautiful sixteen-year-old student named Heloise.

Her uncle Fulbert, the canon of the cathedral at Notre Dame, knew his niece was brilliant and needed the best education possible. And Heloise was a dream pupil, mastering every subject — from Greek and Latin to theology and philosophy.

Maybe it was inevitable that she and her tall, handsome instructor would become lovers. In Fulbert's upstairs library, "under the cloak of study, we freely practiced love," Abelard admitted later.[280] Maybe it was equally inevitable that Heloise would become pregnant.

Abelard helped Heloise escape to his sister's house, where she had their child — a son they named Astrolabe. Abelard proposed marriage; Heloise at

277 Rubenstein, *Aristotle's Children*, 114.

278 Herman, *The Cave and the Light*, 200.

279 Herman, *The Cave and the Light*, 200.

280 Herman, *The Cave and the Light*, 201.

first refused, arguing that marriage would compromise his work as a philosopher. She insisted "it would be far sweeter for her to be called my mistress than to be known as my wife."[281]

But Abelard eventually wore her down. They were married early one morning, and even Heloise's uncle grudgingly attended. The marriage was supposed to stay a secret. However, Uncle Fulbert, still angry about the deception, began to threaten his niece with punishment. So Abelard sent Heloise to a nearby convent to hide.

When her uncle discovered this, he believed Abelard was trying to get rid of Heloise and became enraged. He sent a group of friends and relatives to Abelard's lodgings to get revenge.

In the dead of night, the posse broke in and castrated Abelard. As he put it later, "They cut off those parts of my body with which I had done that which was the cause of their sorrow."[282] In disgrace, he withdrew to a monastery in Saint-Denis — though he and Heloise exchanged love letters for the rest of his life.

Abelard eventually returned to teaching, at various locations throughout France. He kept writing, too. Sometime in the 1130s, he published his autobiography, *The History of My Calamities*. It was inspired by St. Augustine's *Confessions*, and recounted his affair with Heloise.

He might have suffered greatly, but Abelard remained famous — and, to some extent, unrepentant. His book of ethics, *Scito Teipsum* ("Know Thyself"), argued that it's our *intentions*, not our *actions*, that determine morality.

As Peter Kreeft observes, denying the connection between intention and action fits neatly into Abelard's position on universals. "If there are no essences, no universal natures," he writes, "then a human act cannot be judged as right or wrong because it is an act of this or that nature."[283]

Abelard would finally be called to account by Bernard of Clairvaux, a Benedictine abbot who was one of the most powerful figures in Christianity. In 1139, Bernard denounced Abelard's writings as heretical, and asked Pope Innocent II to intervene.

[281] Peter Abelard, *Historia Calamitatum: The Story of My Misfortunes*, trans. Henry Adams Bellows (New York: Macmillan, 1922), Medieval Sourcebook, Fordham University, https://sourcebooks.fordham.edu/basis/abelard-histcal.asp.

[282] Abelard, *Historia Calamitatum.*

[283] Kreeft, *Socrates' Children*, vol. 2, 58.

"His books have wings,"[284] Bernard warned the pope. Abelard's influence, especially on young and impressionable students, amounted to a "new gospel."[285] The sixty-two-year-old Abelard responded by asking for a public debate in Paris with Bernard, in front of a gathering of bishops and nobles.

This debate was supposed to occur on the morning of June 3, 1140. But instead of dazzling the audience on the biggest stage of his career, Abelard abruptly withdrew.

He never explained why. It's possible he felt "the deck had been stacked against him."[286] The assembled bishops began the proceedings by reading a list of heresy charges against Abelard, and he may have realized that whatever he said would make no difference. Or his poor health may have been to blame: he would die just two years later.

"I will never be a philosopher," he wrote near the end of his life, "if this is to speak against Saint Paul; I would not be an Aristotle, if this were to separate me from Christ."[287] But what Abelard did, and did most effectively, was to separate universals from any grounding in reality.

It's ironic in one sense: that the admirer of Aristotle would help undo Aristotle's view of universals. But the way Abelard championed the individual over the universal would become hugely influential in the centuries to follow.

"Abelard," as Peter Kreeft observes wryly, "is a very up-to-date thinker."[288]

[284] Rubenstein, *Aristotle's Children*, 122.

[285] Rubenstein, *Aristotle's Children*, 122.

[286] Rubenstein, *Aristotle's Children*, 124.

[287] Herman, *The Cave and the Light*, 203.

[288] Kreeft, *Socrates' Children*, vol. 2, 58.

CHAPTER NINE

UNCOMMON COMMON SENSE

1.

Sunlight filters into the classroom through the iron bars and the panes of leaded glass, as the young man trudges in to take his seat. He sits, every day, in the same place: at the very end of one of the two long, wooden rows of desks. His books perch on the rail; he perches on a bench.

Actually, "perches" is the wrong word — it's too dainty to describe this young man. He's big. *So big that you can't miss him: he's tall, and probably weighs at least three hundred pounds. When he takes his seat at the end of the bench each morning, it groans under his bulk.*

The other thing you can't miss is that the young man almost never speaks. Sometimes, it seems like he's not just silent, but in some other world entirely. Later in life, this distracted quality will show itself in other ways. He'll sometimes forget to eat. Sometimes he won't remember he's holding a candle, until the wax finally splatters onto his thick fingers and burns them.

The teacher of this class has noticed these things about the large young man at the end of the bench. He's noticed a lot *of things about this unusual student. And one of them is that the young man, while he seems slow, has a mind that is anything but. That's why the teacher has made him the Master of Students — responsible for taking notes on the teacher's lectures.*

This teacher is the Chair of Theology at the College of St. James, here at the University of Paris. He's a German by birth, and a Dominican friar. They call him Doctor Universalis because of the breadth of his knowledge; after his death, he'll be known as Albertus Magnus — "the great."

He's an expert on, among other things, the writings of Aristotle. This is an interest he shares with the young student he's now observing closely.

Or rather, he's observing the other pupils in the class. He can see that, as usual, they're laughing at the Master of Students, who — as usual — doesn't seem to notice. A couple of students are whispering behind the sleeves of their robes, and the teacher registers a phrase he's heard them use before to mock the strange young man: "dumb ox."

The teacher steps down from the carved wooden chair where he's been seated, at the head of the class. He's nowhere near as large as his Master of Students, but he's an imposing figure nonetheless. The pupils who were whispering straighten their robes and their posture, but it's too late now. The teacher has heard enough.

He doesn't reprimand the whisperers, however. Instead, he calls out the name of the Master of Students and asks him to speak. He wants to know the young man's opinion about a passage from Aristotle the class has been reading.

All eyes turn to the student at the end of the bench. He shifts his bulk and begins to speak. He talks slowly, unhurriedly — in just the way you'd expect if you saw him.

But what you wouldn't *expect is the effect of his words. The young man is clear and convincing. The passage he's speaking about is difficult, but he makes it understandable. His explanation is as simple as it can possibly be — but not simpler.*

When he's finished, the young man lapses back into stillness. The teacher nods and surveys the rest of the class.

"You call him the Dumb Ox!" he thunders. "I tell you that this Dumb Ox" — here he thrusts a finger toward the young man at the end of the bench — "shall bellow so loud that his bellowings will fill the world!"[289]

The students, their eyes downcast, are now silent. So is the young man, who barely seems to have heard his teacher defend him. It's almost as if he's determined to prove his peers are correct.

But St. Albert the Great has spoken. And history will prove that he was more right than anyone could have guessed about his strange, wonderful student — who will come to be known throughout the world as St. Thomas Aquinas.

2.

This is perhaps the most famous story told about St. Thomas Aquinas, the "dumb ox" who became, in the view of many, the greatest Christian philosopher in history.

There are a few other familiar tales about St. Thomas. How he was born near present-day Lazio, Italy, in 1225, the son of a knight and nobleman named Landulf of Aquino. How he studied for a decade with the Benedictine monks, then stunned his parents by deciding to join the Dominican order instead.

How his parents — aghast that their youngest son would want to join this poor, ragtag gang of monks instead of the far wealthier and more prestigious Benedictines — kidnapped him and kept him prisoner in the family castle for a year.

How his brothers tried to break down his resolve by sending a naked prostitute into his room, and how Thomas chased the terrified girl out with a flaming brand from the fireplace. How he used the brand to make the sign

[289] The famous "dumb ox" quote from St. Albert the Great has been told and retold for centuries. It shows up in this form in G. K. Chesterton's charming biography of Aquinas.

Speaking of famous quotes, the one about an explanation being "as simple as it can possibly be — but not simpler" is often attributed to Albert Einstein. Alice Calaprice, the editor of the 2011 book *The Ultimate Quotable Einstein*, believes it might be "a compressed version of lines from a 1933 lecture by Einstein." That version goes, "It can scarcely be denied that the supreme goal of all theory is to make the irreducible basic elements as simple and as few as possible without having to surrender the adequate representation of a single datum of experience." Not quite as catchy, for certain. Andrew Robinson, "Did Einstein Really Say That?" *Nature* 557 (April 2018): 30, https://doi.org/10.1038/d41586-018-05004-4. 2018.

of the cross on his door. How two angels appeared to him that night to give him the gift of perfect chastity — marked by a girdle that he wore for the rest of his days.[290]

How his mother finally allowed him to escape through an open window one night. How he was transported first to Rome, and then to Paris, to begin his studies.

And how he became the star pupil of Albertus Magnus, who recognized greatness in the unusual young man. We're told, in fact, that "Aquinas was to Albert what Aristotle was to Plato."[291]

There are other stories about St. Thomas, yet there really isn't a great biography of this remarkable saint. Perhaps the best one was written by Yale professor Denys Turner, who confesses up front how hard it was to write about such an "impossible man."

> The man indeed was a saint. But he made it his business to ensure that you would not get to know about it.... He prayed, for sure, early in the day and long, but most of the time he taught, and when not teaching he read and he wrote, often late into the night. Otherwise he traveled frequently within and between Italy, Germany, and France, fulfilling conventional duties as a Dominican friar, and apart from the fact that he often forgot to eat and was somewhat overweight, that was pretty much it.... [T]heological genius he may have been. But there is not a lot of material on the record making for an exciting hagiographical read.[292]

Aquinas was, in a lot of ways, the opposite of his predecessor, St. Augustine. Where Augustine was personal and confessional, Aquinas was bland and inscrutable. "His life," Denys Turner explains, "is a sort of hoax, the hoax of the genuinely humble who will not make a fuss even out of persuading people that he is not worth making a fuss of. He just disappears, unannounced, and his texts appear, as if authorless."[293]

In those texts, we see another major difference: one of Aquinas's greatest achievements was to "baptize" the work of Aristotle, in the same way that Augustine had "baptized" the work of Plato.

[290] A girdle that purports to be the Aquinas original is now a relic that belongs to the Prato Cathedral in Tuscany, Italy. It has a reputation for helping pregnant women who venerate it.

[291] Renn Dickson Hampden, *The Life of Thomas Aquinas* (London: John J. Griffin, 1848), 30.

[292] Denys Turner, *Thomas Aquinas: A Portrait* (New Haven, CT: Yale University Press, 2013), 3.

[293] Turner, *Thomas Aquinas*, 4.

There's no doubt that of the two, Aquinas had the more difficult job. But while it's true that he did more than anyone else to make Aristotle's work compatible with Christianity, that still sells his accomplishments short.

"In all his works, however, Aquinas refused to simply recycle Aristotle, as the Averröists had," Arthur Herman writes. "He pointed Aristotle in entirely new directions and raised him to a higher, more relevant level for the Western future."[294]

The result was "a vast synthesis of all that had been best argued in Western thought by this time," which he showed "to be compatible with Christian belief."[295] Aquinas drew not just on the work of the Greeks and the Christians, but also the writings of the greatest Islamic and Jewish philosophers.

> What he had understood better than any other, was that philosophy necessarily forms the central framework of the whole edifice of the sciences, and that Christendom did not yet possess a philosophy which would be the expression of its particular culture and the reply to its peculiar needs. Having seen that, he took it as his personal mission to form one, and then to rethink all the theological problems with the aid of this philosophy. And this is what he accomplished in the space of fifteen years, from 1255 to 1270.[296]

We now call this philosophy "Thomist." How influential has it been, and is it still? As Peter Kreeft notes, "There have been more Thomists than Platonists, Aristotelians, Augustinians, Cartesians, Humeans, Kantians, Nietzscheans, Marxists, Heideggerians, or anything else in the history of philosophy. His philosophy has staying power."[297]

Slow and steady, as they say, wins the race. Aquinas might have appeared sluggish, but he was a scholar's scholar. He once told some friends, while looking at Paris from a hillside, that he would rather own one missing page of a manuscript than all the majestic lands that lay before them. And when he was asked for what he thanked God most, his answer was, "I have understood every page I ever read."[298]

[294] Herman, *The Cave and the Light*, 239.

[295] Magee, *The Story of Philosophy*, 59.

[296] Fernand Van Steenberghen, *The Philosophical Movement in the Thirteenth Century* (Edinburgh: Nelson, 1955), 97.

[297] Kreeft, *Socrates' Children*, vol. 2, 79.

[298] G. K. Chesterton, *St. Thomas Aquinas: The Dumb Ox* (Mansfield Centre, CT: Martino Publishing, 2011), 14.

Aquinas crafted his own philosophy while presenting, and then responding to, his opponents' most convincing arguments. He was "judicious and moderate, careful and patient to avoid opposite extremes and oversimplifications," says Peter Kreeft, who compares Aquinas's philosophy to "a Gothic cathedral, built up over centuries into a rich and complex variety in unity — like the universe itself."[299]

It's a telling metaphor. Unlike most philosophers, it's in Aquinas's ideas where we find splendor: not in his "invisible" biography, and not even in his deliberately unflashy prose.

Those ideas, to an unprecedented degree, accomplished what philosophers had tried to do for centuries: reconciling religion and reason. And Aquinas did this by being "scrupulous about maintaining the distinction between philosophy and religion."[300]

Aquinas was determined not just to keep the two separate, but to not waste time arguing about things that could never be proven. He once received a letter from someone who wanted to know whether "the names of all the blessed were written on a scroll exhibited in heaven."

"He wrote back with untiring calm; 'So far as I can see, this is not the case; but there is no harm in saying so.' "[301]

Aquinas identified three major things that he believed could only be known by faith: "the creation of the universe from nothing, God's nature as a Trinity, and Jesus Christ's role in man's salvation."[302]

As we've already seen, these were hugely divisive issues. For example, Aristotle's belief that the universe had always existed had made his teaching a big problem for religious believers.

Aquinas simply asserted that there was no way to prove anything conclusive about this. He believed, through faith, that the universe had been created by God. But that wasn't really the issue, as he saw it.

"Even if the universe had no beginning in time," there would still have to be a God of some sort "keeping it going."[303] So there was really no contradiction between what Aristotle had written and what Christians — or Jews, or Muslims — believed.

[299] Kreeft, *Socrates' Children*, vol. 2, 80.
[300] Magee, *The Story of Philosophy*, 59.
[301] Chesterton, *St. Thomas Aquinas*, 102.
[302] Rubenstein, *Aristotle's Children*, 198.
[303] Feser, *The Last Superstition*, 100.

What was far more important to Aquinas was what *could* be proven about God and His creation by human reason. According to his view, that was what might seem a surprising amount of information. But it wasn't a surprise to Aquinas: "It was the very life of the Thomist teaching that Reason can be trusted."[304]

That was because God had given us senses that we could trust—so we could use them to see His presence in creation. Unlike Plato's idea that the senses were deceptive, Aquinas sided with Aristotle: the senses are our primary means of knowing the world, and therefore, of knowing God as well.

3.

St. Thomas Aquinas wrote more than eight million words of philosophy. Most are contained in two magisterial works: the *Summa contra Gentiles* and the unfinished *Summa Theologica*. In these books, Aquinas laid out a clear, considered doctrine. It refined the ideas of his predecessors and made them consistent with Christian teaching.

The most significant piece of this doctrine centered on the concepts of *essence* and *existence*. As we saw in chapter 7, the tenth-century Muslim philosopher al-Fârâbî had introduced this concept. He based it on a statement made by Aristotle: "That the idea of *what* a thing is does not include *that* it is."[305]

So if something has an *essence*, that doesn't mean that it *exists*. People who have died, for example, still have an essence—but they no longer have an existence.

But if you consider that everything that has existed also had an essence, and you logically trace that chain backwards, then you reach the conclusion that what must have *started* this process is a being of *pure existence*.

This is similar to another distinction that also comes from Aristotle, which you may remember from chapter 4: the difference between *actuality* and *potentiality*—otherwise thought of as "change."

Aristotle had come up with his concept of the Unmoved Mover by using these distinctions. Everything in the world, Aristotle had said, is a combination of actuality—what it *really* is—and potentiality—what it *could* be, if it were changed.

[304] Chesterton, *St. Thomas Aquinas*, 24.

[305] Kreeft, *Socrates' Children*, vol. 2, 66.

Tracing that chain back to the beginning, Aristotle said, we would inevitably reach a being that was *pure actuality,* that had *no* unrealized potential. That being, he called the Unmoved Mover. And Aquinas called that same being God.

If you accept that conclusion, then there are several others that follow. First of all, as Edward Feser points out, there can only be *one* being of pure actuality.

That being would have to be immaterial, "since to be a material thing entails being changeable in various ways, which a purely actual being cannot be." As Feser continues,

> The Unmoved Mover is in any event that to which every motion or change in the material universe — not just moving stones, but melting glaciers, orbiting moons, budding flowers, growing boys and girls, and so on through all of nature — traces back. Being the common first member of all the various essentially ordered causal series that result in these instances of change, the Unmoved Mover is outside and distinct from them all, as that which sustains the entire world in motion from instant to instant.[306]

This, Feser points out, is far different than the usual way opponents characterize this argument. Aquinas is *not* arguing that "everything has a cause," because this inevitably leads to the response, "So what causes God?" Instead, as Feser notes,

> His aim is to show that given that there are in fact some causes of various sorts, the nature of cause and effect entails that God is necessary as an uncaused cause of the universe, even if we assume that the universe has always existed and thus had no beginning.
>
> The argument is not that the world wouldn't have got started if God hadn't knocked down the first domino at some point in the distant past; it is that it wouldn't exist here and now, or undergo change or exhibit final causes here and now, unless God were here and now, and at every moment, sustaining it in being, change, and goal-directedness.[307]

The way to think of the world, in Aquinas's philosophy, was something like a musician playing music. Feser uses this analogy: God is the musician, and the

[306] Feser, *The Last Superstition*, 98.
[307] Feser, *The Last Superstition*, 86.

world is the music. If the musician stops playing, there is no more music. In other words, God is the *first* cause of the world — but He's also the *continuous* cause, as well.

4.

The First Cause debate is actually part of a larger argument. We can't know God's true nature, Aquinas believed. But it *is* possible to make a rational case for His existence.

At the beginning of *Summa contra Gentiles,* Aquinas outlined five possible reasons for a rational belief in God. These "Five Ways" take up only a couple of pages of the massive *Summa,* but they've generated untold amounts of controversy since.

We've already seen three of these Five Ways. The First Way, the "Argument from Motion" is related to the idea of the Unmoved Mover, and the concept of actuality and potentiality.

As Aquinas wrote, "Whatever is moved must be moved by another."[308] That is, motion — call it "change" — has to be initiated by something unmoving and unchanging. Or something that is all act, and no potential.

The Second Way, the "Nature of Efficient Cause," is related to the idea of God as the First Cause — and as the *sustaining* cause. To understand this better, we have to separate two kinds of causal chains: *accidentally ordered* and *essentially ordered.*

In an *accidentally ordered* chain of events, the events don't necessarily depend on the first cause. For example, if a father has a son, the son can have sons of his own without the father's involvement. The chain of sons can continue, even if the father dies. The sons have the ability to continue the chain, independent of the father who started it.[309]

But in an *essentially ordered* chain of events, everything depends on the first cause. If we imagine a hand holding a stick and pushing a stone, then this simultaneous chain would stop if the hand stopped holding the stick. And since something *else* caused the hand to hold the stick, we can keep tracing the chain backwards.

Eventually, Aquinas thought, we would end up with a "First Efficient Cause," which would be God. And since the world is full of essentially ordered

308 Steven M. Cahn, ed., *Classics of Western Philosophy,* 4th ed. (Indianapolis: Hackett, 1995), 424.

309 The examples here of fathers and sons and the hand and the stick are borrowed from Edward Feser's *The Last Superstition.* His book is particularly effective in explaining these chains of cause.

chains of events, this First Efficient Cause is necessary — not just to *start* them, but to *sustain* them.

The difference between accidentally and essentially ordered chains of events is why Aquinas wasn't concerned about proving that the universe had always existed. That chain of events is accidentally ordered, and in theory, could go on forever — even though Aquinas didn't believe that it does.

Aquinas's Third Way relates to the concept of existence and essence. If everything in the world is a *combination* of existence and essence, then it stands to reason that none of these things are strictly *necessary*. That is, they all can, and will, go out of existence eventually.

So, "there must exist something the existence of which is necessary."[310] In other words, something that is *pure* existence or being, something that *cannot* go out of existence. Again, Aquinas says, "This all men speak of as God."[311]

These first three arguments are all facets of the *cosmological argument* for God. Whether we refer to motion and change, efficient cause, or essence and existence, we're talking about tracing back chains to a logical source.

Earlier philosophers developed their own versions of the cosmological argument. These include Aristotle, of course, but also Muslim philosophers like Averröes and the Jewish thinker Maimonides. So Aquinas's refinement of the cosmological argument followed a long tradition.

His Fourth and Fifth Ways were somewhat different. In the Fourth Way, often called "The Argument from Degree," Aquinas drew as much on Plato as he did on Aristotle.

The Fourth Way argued that terms like *good, true,* and *noble* only make sense when they are applied to "something which is the maximum ... so that there is something which is truest, something best," and so on. This something "which is to all beings the cause of their being, goodness, and every other possible perfection,"[312] is God.

That sounds something like Plato's Ideal Forms — especially his idea of the Good as the highest of all possible forms. Aquinas even called God "the highest good," and cited St. Augustine when he mentioned that, because God has "infinite goodness," He can even allow evil to exist, and make something good out of it.

310 Cahn, *Classics of Western Philosophy*, 424.
311 Cahn, *Classics of Western Philosophy*, 425.
312 Cahn, *Classics of Western Philosophy*, 425.

Aquinas's Fifth Way, the "Argument from Design," is perhaps the most commonly misunderstood. He pointed out that the world is full of "natural bodies" that "move towards an end," such as plants growing or the stars moving across the sky. These processes can, and do, "exist in the natural world, even apart from conscious awareness"[313] — which was exactly what Aristotle had noticed.

How can these processes happen automatically? Aquinas believed that "some intelligent being exists by whom all natural things are directed to their end; and this being we call God."[314]

This idea is sometimes misinterpreted as a version of Intelligent Design. Intelligent Design is a much later theory which suggests that the complexity we observe in nature couldn't occur without an Intelligent Designer — God.

However, this wasn't what Aquinas was suggesting. His Fifth Way was based instead on Aristotle, and his Four Causes. Specifically, the last cause — the final cause.

The final cause, you may remember from chapter 4, tells us the *purpose* of a thing. A pencil's purpose is to be used for writing. A heart's purpose is to pump blood. And so on.

All things, then, have some purpose, some goal — not a *conscious* goal, in most cases, but some reason to exist. And in nature, many of these goals seem to be pursued unconsciously. A heart doesn't think about pumping blood, any more than a pencil thinks about writing.

Aquinas believed that this consciousness, which directs things toward their natural ends, has to come from somewhere. Therefore, he proposed a supreme intelligence — God as a universal mind.

This was an idea that could be traced back to Plato. More directly, it was cited by St. Augustine, who thought that this divine intelligence was where things like universals and numbers existed.

This Fifth Way is sometimes referred to as the *teleological argument* for God's existence. That's a reference to *telos*, the Greek world for "purpose." God, in the teleological argument, is the consciousness that supplies the purpose for actions that seem unconscious.

Besides the cosmological and teleological arguments, there's a third common argument for God's existence, which we saw in chapter 8. That is the

313 Feser, *The Last Superstition*, 115.
314 Cahn, *Classics of Western Philosophy*, 425.

ontological argument proposed by St. Anselm — the idea that if you can imagine a perfect being, it follows that this perfect being also has to exist.

Aquinas did not support this argument. The reason has to do with the concept of essence and existence. He believed that the ontological argument used the *essence* of God to prove his *existence*.

This, to Aquinas, wasn't logical. We can't start with the *definition* of God: we have to start with evidence of His existence, instead.

Aquinas also wasn't afraid to take issue with the beliefs of another priest who would become, like him, a future saint. That was St. Bonaventure.

Born Giovanni di Fidanza in a part of Italy then known as the Papal States, St. Bonaventure was a close contemporary of Aquinas. Bonaventure was four years older, and he became the minister-general of the new Franciscan Order, which he helped build. But he was also known for his humble nature: "When someone came to the convent to find the great man, they had trouble picking him out amongst his brethren, washing dishes."[315]

Despite the differences that would divide the Franciscans and Aquinas's own order, the Dominicans, the two men were close friends. But that didn't stop Aquinas from taking issue with Bonaventure on occasion.

Bonaventure was familiar with Aristotle's work, but he was more comfortable with the philosophy of Plato, as expressed by St. Augustine. This difference Peter Kreeft notes, was something like the difference between heart and head. Bonaventure emphasized knowing God through the experience of His *love* — as opposed to Aquinas's emphasis on knowing Him through the *intellect*.

Like many medieval Christian philosophers, Bonaventure took issue with Aristotle's idea that the universe had always existed. He also had a problem with Aristotle's Four Causes: he felt they excluded God from natural processes like the growth of a tree.

And, like Plato, he imagined the soul existing independent of the body. But like Aristotle, he believed that everything is a combination of matter and form. So Bonaventure split the difference: he proposed that souls (and angels) were made of a "special, spiritual matter"[316] created by God.

Compromises like this, the attorney and scholar Richard Rubenstein explains, were an attempt to make Aristotle more palatable to Christian skeptics:

[315] John Paul Meenan, "The Seraphic Doctor: Saint Bonaventure," *Catholic Insight*, July 15, 2023. https://catholicinsight.com/the-seraphic-bonaventure/.

[316] Sir Anthony Kenny, *Aquinas on Mind* (New York: Routledge, 1994), 139.

"Bonaventure and his English student John Peckham believed that by making philosophical sense of Franciscan beliefs, they could forge a conservative consensus that would take a more cautious approach to Aristotle and avoid a dangerous split between religion and science."[317]

The older, more judicious Bonaventure saw that if Aristotle ran afoul of Christian authorities, there could be serious ripple effects. He created, instead, an "eclectic and Neoplatonic Aristotelianism, subordinated to an Augustinian theology."[318]

But Aquinas thought this controversy was overblown, and doubled down on his endorsement of Aristotle. According to Rubenstein, St. Thomas thought "the measures proposed by the Franciscans made for bad religion and bad science."

> Aristotle's view of nature was perfectly adequate as far as it went, Thomas insisted, and should not be tampered with by spiritualizing matter, adding supernatural to natural causes, or anything of the sort. Where the Philosopher fell short — seriously short — was in failing to recognize that all created things, with their built-in tendencies to behave or develop according to their natures, owe their entire being to God. God did not create things once upon a time and then step back while nature took over. Creation is constant.
>
> As Boethius, Augustine, and Bonaventure himself recognized, it does not take place in time at all. There is simply no inconsistency between God's eternal sovereignty over the entire universe and the potency of natural causes in time. One can therefore study nature as a "pure" scientist while remaining entirely within the tradition of Christian faith.[319]

That, at least, was the goal. Aquinas was building what he saw as a "natural theology" that made science and belief compatible. The natural laws that defined his theology, he thought, complemented, rather than conflicted with, divine law.

"Grace does not destroy nature, but perfects it," he wrote in the beginning of the *Summa Theologica*. "And natural reason should minister to faith as the natural bent of the will ministers to charity."[320]

317 Rubenstein, *Aristotle's Children*, 197.
318 Van Steenberghen, *The Philosophical Movement*, 61.
319 Rubenstein, *Aristotle's Children*, 197–198.
320 Cahn, *Classics of Western Philosophy*, 417.

So "there can be no conflict between religion and natural science, between loving the Creator and understanding his creation, so long as one correctly defines and demarcates both realms of thought."[321]

Therefore, there was no need, Aquinas thought, to radically revise Aristotle. "Bonaventure meant well, but he did not understand that undermining the autonomy of nature also undermines the autonomy of natural reason."[322]

But many people still believed that Thomas Aquinas was a radical. And Bonaventure's fears would prove well founded. While he remained friends with Aquinas until death, the most serious and lasting challenge to Aquinas — and Aristotle — would come from within Bonaventure's own order, the Franciscans.

5.

At the University of Paris, where Aquinas had studied with Albert the Great, the work of Aristotle had sometimes run afoul of the authorities. During the first half of the thirteenth century, his writings, and the writings of his Arab translators, were sometimes prohibited.

But like many book bans, these rules were difficult to enforce. "By 1255, all of Aristotle's works were being taught at the University of Paris," writes Christopher Beckwith. "The new translations were officially approved (with the exception of a few specific arguments considered heretical), and were assigned as the new 'liberal arts' curriculum — most of which consisted of logic and 'natural philosophy' — that was required of all bachelor's level university students in Western Europe."[323]

There was still uneasiness about several of Aristotle's teachings — especially his belief that the universe had always existed. But a new generation of scholars were eagerly studying, commenting on, and — in the case of Aquinas, in particular — correcting the errors they saw in Aristotle.

Between 1258 and 1264, Aquinas produced his *Summa contra Gentiles* — "The Contents of God and His Creatures." This four-volume collection walked skeptics and unbelievers through the Christian faith, step by step.

[321] Rubenstein, *Aristotle's Children*, 198.

[322] Rubenstein, *Aristotle's Children*, 199.

[323] Christopher I. Beckwith, *Warriors of the Cloisters: The Central Asian Origins of Science in the Medieval World* (Princeton, NJ: Princeton University Press, 2012), 108.

It first addressed general questions about God and nature. Aquinas gradually narrowed the focus to monotheism, and then Christianity specifically. The first three books, however, concern the things we can know based on our reason rather than our faith.

It was, in many ways, the high point of Western thought: a consistent and balanced blend of philosophy, science, and theology. It drew on Aristotle's observations about nature and its limits to argue for a system of natural law that both kept man in check and pointed him to his final cause. But Bonaventure's student, John Peckham, was not convinced.

"If you reflect on this slow growth of Aristotelianism in the course of the thirteenth century and its consequences for culture," wrote Fernand van Steenberghen, "you soon see that it was fraught with very real danger for Christianity."[324]

Part of that danger was embodied by Siger de Brabant, a teacher at the University of Paris and leader of a radical group of arts masters and students. Siger was not just a disciple of Aristotle — he was also a fan of Aristotle's Muslim interpreter, Averröes.

One of the doctrines Siger and his allies embraced was the idea that souls don't retain their individuality after death. Instead, Averröes had taught, they are absorbed back into God. Siger borrowed this idea, and proposed that our souls become part of a single intellect when we die.

This doctrine, as we've already seen, had created big problems for Averröes in the Islamic world. It contradicted the idea of individual souls rejoining with their bodies after death. And this idea was now going to create issues for Siger in the Christian world as well.

But it didn't just make problems for Siger. "Powerful figures at the university, not only the Franciscans but also secular masters and even a few Dominicans, were saying that Siger de Brabant was merely spelling out the unorthodox implications of Aquinas's own theology."[325]

Aquinas had left the University of Paris by this time and had moved to Rome, where he was at work on the *Summa Theologica*. But in 1270, he was summoned back to Paris, and refuted Siger's beliefs in a document called *On There Being Only One Intellect.*

[324] Van Steenberghen, *The Philosophical Movement*, 79.

[325] Rubenstein, *Aristotle's Children*, 219.

Ever since he had arrived at the University of Paris, Aquinas had met teachers and students who were Averröes enthusiasts. But he disagreed with many of the great Islamic thinker's beliefs — including his teaching of the "double truth." That is, the idea that there are two kinds of truths: one for philosophers and one for believers. As Arthur Herman describes it:

> The message of revealed religion contained in the Bible and church doctrine was meant for everyone, not just the rednecks among us. Likewise, every human being deserved to know the whole truth, not just a chosen elite. To fall for the notion of a "double truth" and argue there was one set of truths for reason and another for faith and never the two shall meet made nonsense of the idea of truth itself.[326]

Averröes "was not so much an Aristotelian as a corruptor of Aristotelian philosophy,"[327] Aquinas wrote. And his argument against Siger was so convincing that Siger himself recanted his position.

But that wasn't convincing enough for John Peckham and the conservatives at the university. Aquinas's whole philosophy was too heavily invested in Aristotle for their liking.

> Aquinas pretended to oppose Siger and his cohorts as vigorously as they did, but when one looked under the surface, weren't he and the radicals really saying the same thing? Nature was governed by natural laws that worked without God's intervention. Men and women could be happy in this life, despite their fallen state. The soul received its individuality from the body. And ... at least as a theoretical possibility, the material world could be co-eternal with God.[328]

As Peckham put it, Thomism "despises the doctrines of the Fathers and bases itself almost completely on the doctrines of philosophers, so that the house of God is filled with idols."[329]

In other words, Aquinas was too much of a materialist for the Augustinians. To agree with Aristotle, for example, that everything is a combination of

[326] Herman, *The Cave and the Light*, 233.
[327] Van Steenberghen, *The Philosophical Movement*, 83.
[328] Rubenstein, *Aristotle's Children*, 226.
[329] Van Steenberghen, *The Philosophical Movement*, 104.

matter and form — to say that "even God ... cannot create anything that isn't something"[330] — was too limiting an idea.

This struggle between these two schools of thought, which erupted in 1270, would continue until the end of the century. It started at the University of Paris, and later spread to Oxford.

The controversy reached a high (or low) point in 1277. The newly elected pope, John XXI, had heard about Siger's heresies and demanded a report. The bishop of Paris, Stephen Tempier, did better than that: he banned 219 propositions being taught at the university.

Many of the propositions were Aristotelian teachings. And many of them had to do with the natural world. Inevitably, this brought the work of Aquinas under the microscope as well.

"This resounding condemnation can be considered the most important of the Middle Ages, as much by its historical significance as by its prolonged repercussions on the movement of ideas," wrote Fernand van Steenberghen. "It is the central event around which the whole history of philosophy during the last third of the thirteenth century can be grouped."[331]

But the man who was central to so many of these controversies would not be around to see them play out.

6.

The friar hurries down the hall. The grey morning has only darkened since dawn. Sleet pelts against the windows of San Domenico Maggiore.

He stops and raps at the door of a cell. There is a murmur from within, and he enters.

The friar sits down at a table covered with sheets of vellum. He rubs his hands together, blows into them, and looks up expectantly.

Father Thomas Aquinas broods in the light of two flickering candles. He's looking in the friar's direction, but past him, at some unseen object.

The friar, Reginald of Piperno, isn't surprised. He was once Thomas's student. For the past year, he's been a fellow teacher here, at the monastery

[330] Turner, *Thomas Aquinas*, 50.

[331] Van Steenberghen, *The Philosophical Movement*, 94.

in Naples. He's also Thomas's secretary, the man to whom the great writer dictates his work. And for most of the past decade, he's been Thomas's confessor. So if anyone is used to these distracted silences, it's Reginald.

It's Dec. 6, 1273 — the feast of St. Nicholas. Thomas said this morning's Mass, then returned to his cell, and Reginald followed shortly thereafter, as is their custom. They're working on what will become the Summa Theologica, *a book intended for theology students. They're midway through a section on the seven sacraments.*

Reginald picks up a quill from the table, and searches for the inkwell. Then Thomas finally speaks.

"I can write no more."

Only a little surprised, Reginald nods. The past few years have been hard ones for Thomas. The recent controversies at the University of Paris would have taken a tremendous toll on any normal man. And Thomas is as far from a normal man as Reginald can imagine.

Over the past five years, Thomas has produced the equivalent of what, centuries later, would be two or three novels — each month. *If he needs a day off — well, he's earned it, hasn't he?*

"Tomorrow, then …" Reginald begins. Thomas cuts him off.

"I can write no more," he repeats. "Ever."

Now Reginald meets his steady gaze. Thomas is no longer drifting. He's laser-focused.

"I adjure you by the living almighty God, and by the faith you have in our order, and by charity that you strictly promise me you will never reveal in my lifetime what I tell you," he says. Reginald nods his head dumbly.

"Everything that I have written seems like straw to me," says Thomas, "compared to those things that I have seen and have been revealed to me."

There is silence again between the two men. The sleet rattles more insistently outside, and the candles gutter in a draft.

In his lifetime, Thomas Aquinas has written some eight million words. But he's going to let God have the last one.[332]

7.

That revelation, whatever it was, seems to have been the greatest of several mystical experiences Aquinas underwent in the last years of his life.

Before he left Paris, he had written a difficult essay on the Blessed Sacrament. When he finished,

> he threw down his thesis at the foot of the crucifix on the altar, and left it lying there; as if awaiting judgment. Then … the other Friars … declared afterwards that the figure of Christ had come down from the cross before their mortal eyes; and stood upon the scroll, saying, "Thomas, thou hast written well concerning the Sacrament of My Body."[333]

The astonished priests then watched Thomas rise several feet in the air.

And in Naples, late one night "in the stillness of the church of St. Dominic … a voice spoke from the carven Christ, and told the kneeling Friar that he had written rightly, and offered him the choice of a reward among all the things of the world."

Aquinas's response was, "I will have Thyself."[334]

In February 1274, the pope himself had requested that Aquinas attend a general council of the Church in Lyon, France. Undoubtedly, he would have preferred to stay in Italy, but he and Reginald dutifully set out for the journey. It did not last long.[335]

332 The text of Aquinas's conversation with Reginald comes from Fred Sanders, "Thomas Aquinas' Big Pile of Straw," Scriptorium Daily, December 6, 2010, https://scriptoriumdaily.com/thomas-aquinas-big-pile-of-straw/.

Aquinas's cell at San Domenico Maggiore was restored in 2020. You can see photos of this famous site at the Friends of Naples website: https://www.friendsofnaples.org/en/basilica-of-san-domenico-maggiore-cell-of-san-tommaso-daquino/.

333 Chesterton, *St. Thomas Aquinas*, 109.

334 Chesterton, *St. Thomas Aquinas*, 107.

335 Jacques Maritain, *St. Thomas Aquinas*, 1958. https://www3.nd.edu/~maritain/jmc/etext/thomas1.htm. There are a number of retellings of Aquinas's final journey, not all of which agree on details. I have tried to collate several different versions — including those from Hampden, Chesterton, Maritain, and Turner — to create this one.

One of the points unclear in the retellings of Aquinas's death is who, exactly, heard St. Thomas's final confession. It would make sense that one of the Cistercians, who

While riding his donkey, Aquinas was struck in the head, perhaps by a falling branch. He stopped at his niece's house, just north of Naples, but collapsed when he arrived.

He was taken to the nearby Cistercian monastery at Fossanuova, where he spent the next month. "This is my rest for ever and ever," he said when he arrived. "Here will I dwell, for I have chosen it."

Growing weaker, "he asked to have The Song of Solomon read through to him from beginning to end."[336] He also made a final confession that astounded his confessor. The priest "ran forth as if in fear, and whispered that his confession had been that of a child of five."[337]

Thomas Aquinas was just forty-nine years old when he died. G. K. Chesterton speculated that Aquinas was broken by the battles over his philosophy that occurred at the end of his life. Specifically, his enemies' attempt to link him with the heresies of Siger and Averröes.

"He never recovered from the shock," Chesterton wrote. "He won his battle, because he was the best brain of his time, but he could not forget such an inversion of the whole idea and purpose of his life."[338]

But as biographer Denys Turner points out, Aquinas had always believed deeply in the power of keeping still. His final silence was, perhaps, a kind of statement.

Theology, Aquinas thought, emerges from silence. "And, all those words *end* in silence because, as he said, it is through the Son who is the Word that we enter into the silence of the Father, the Godhead itself, which is utterly beyond our comprehension."[339]

In the years that followed his death, however, it seemed as though Aquinas's own words had achieved a philosophical victory.

The controversies of the 1270s had divided the Dominicans, who mostly defended Aquinas, and the Franciscans, who mostly opposed him. But by 1323, less than fifty years after his death, Aquinas was canonized as a saint.

---

did not know him, would have been shocked by the innocence of his sins, yet some stories insist that Reginald, his faithful secretary and confessor, was the priest on hand.

336 Chesterton, *St. Thomas Aquinas,* 114.

337 Chesterton, *St. Thomas Aquinas,* 114.

338 Chesterton, *St. Thomas Aquinas,* 113.

339 Turner, *Thomas Aquinas,* 42.

And two years later, "in a most unusual document, the bishop of Paris retracted the Parisian condemnations that 'concerned or are claimed to concern the doctrine of Blessed Thomas.' "[340] Even more tellingly,

> the notable fact is that the condemnations had so little effect, even in the short run, on the development of Thomist theology, rationalist thinking, or scholarly interest in natural science. Even in the flood tide of repression there was no attempt to revive the ban on Aristotle's works.
>
> The Philosopher's natural philosophy, along with the works of Averroës, Avicenna, and other controversial commentators, remained the core of the European liberal arts curriculum. Theologians continued to debate the major issues raised by the Aristotelian worldview, from the doctrine of secondary causes to the eternity of the world and the nature of the soul.
>
> And Thomism, which had been struck a "glancing blow," recovered its status as a respectable blend of philosophy and theology. Several centuries later, it would become the preferred philosophy of the Roman Catholic Church.[341]

It seemed that the world had come to agree with something G. K. Chesterton would write centuries later: "The fact that Thomism is the philosophy of common sense is itself a matter of common sense."[342]

But the enemies of Aquinas had not disappeared. They would remerge, and this time — without Aquinas around to defend his views — they would do far more damage.

A contemporary of Aquinas once said, "He could alone restore all philosophy, if it had been burnt by fire."[343] The fire that was coming, it seemed, would attempt to do just that.

✠ ✠ ✠

[340] Rubenstein, *Aristotle's Children*, 236–237.

[341] Rubenstein, *Aristotle's Children*, 236–237.

[342] Chesterton, *St. Thomas Aquinas*, 116.

[343] Chesterton, *St. Thomas Aquinas*, 110.

CHAPTER TEN

THE RAZOR'S EDGE

1.

You wake up alone, in darkness.

The sun, you think, will probably rise soon. You don't know this for sure, of course. You won't be able to know until you see the sun lighting up the sky and feel its heat.

Correction: what you believe *to be its light and heat. You don't really know for sure that these things come from the object above you, the one you hope is going to appear soon — though you can't really know that's going to happen, either. Not until it actually happens.*

Your dog pushes his way into the bedroom. At least, you call *it a dog. You've heard other people call objects that look similar "dogs," so you call yours a dog as well. You can't be 100 percent certain that you're talking about the same thing as other people are when they talk about their dogs, but it saves time to just agree and not think too deeply about it. These doubts get exhausting, and the day hasn't even started yet.*

The dog nuzzles your hand. His nose — or at least what you call *his nose — is cold and damp — or at least, what you* think of *as the feelings of "coldness" and "dampness."*

This bedroom is filled with sensory data to analyze. The dog's nose, and the warmth of the bedsheets. The smell of flowers outside, carried on the breeze drifting in through the open window. The sounds of a garbage truck clattering along from down the street. The sour taste of morning breath, and the dark shapes of your desk and chair, just visible in the gloom.

Or at least, what you call *a bedroom, and bedsheets, and flowers, and breeze, and on and on and on. You know these things as individual objects, though the words you use to describe bedrooms and bedsheets and flowers are only words. And you suppose that these objects create certain effects — the breeze stirring curtains; the truck rumbling from house to house — though you can't really prove any of it.*

What you do *believe is that God created the world, and that God is good. You have faith that this is so — strong faith, in fact. But that's as far as things go. What the link really is between God and this world of objects you live in, you have no idea. Nor will you ever. That's not for you to discover. It is, as the saying goes, well above your pay grade.*

Welcome to the wonderful, inscrutable world of William of Ockham — the world that his philosophy helped create.

It's a world of ultimate simplicity — and ultimate perplexity. It created modern science — and logically invalidated it, too.

That might be the most influential paradox in history — just like William of Ockham might be the most influential philosopher.

2.

Some will argue, of course, that calling a somewhat obscure British friar "the most influential philosopher in history" is a ridiculous overstatement.

What about Socrates, they might ask? What about Plato? What about Aristotle? What about Augustine and Aquinas, or some of the more modern philosophers we haven't talked about yet?

All defensible points. Yet it's equally defensible to state that this medieval Franciscan monk demolished the work of all the ancient and medieval philosophers — and made possible the work of all the modern ones.

In that sense, William of Ockham was not just the first modern *philosopher*. He was the first modernist, period.

Name a view that we now think of as "enlightened," and chances are that William of Ockham proposed or endorsed it. Separation of church and state? The empirical method? The social contract? Limited government? Check to all of the above.

In addition, Ockham was an activist who consistently challenged authority—particularly within the Catholic Church. He criticized Church leaders, especially the materialistic and property-owning ones. He denied papal infallibility. And, perhaps not surprisingly, he was eventually excommunicated.

That was in part because during the turbulent fourteenth century, Ockham denounced Pope John XXII as a heretic. He allied himself with King Ludwig of Bavaria, who essentially appointed his own alternate pope.[344]

Ockham never took the ultimate step of breaking from the Church: that wouldn't happen for another two hundred years, when Martin Luther helped kick off the Protestant Revolution. But it's easy to see why some consider Ockham a "proto-Protestant," whose complaints about the Church paved the way for its breakup.

Yet it's through his philosophy that Ockham would have the greatest effect on the Catholic Church—and eventually, on all of Christianity.

[344] While Ockham declared himself the enemy of a pope he considered heretical, this didn't necessarily prove he was against the papacy. British historian Brian Tierney, a Catholic, made the case that Ockham was in fact a *supporter* of papal infallibility—and claimed Ockham wanted to use it, and the Inquisitions of the time, to root out his own personal foes:

> Ockham wanted to see all his enemies punished as heretics. For him the main point of having the true faith defined authentically by a true pope was to facilitate the crushing of dissent by the Inquisition. There was no grain of tolerance in him; he was filled with odium theologicum; he raged incessantly against his enemies. The abusive words "heresy," "heretics," "heretical depravity" are scattered over almost every page of his polemical treatises.... [I]f by some twist of fate Ockham himself had ever become pope his enemies would have trembled before the severity of his judgments.
>
> In the end Ockham's conclusions were simply perverse. He wanted the institutional church to crush error while denying that any church institution could certainly define the truth. He offers us only dogma without order, anarchy without freedom, subjectivism without tolerance. And in a real sense it was Ockham's obsession with the idea of infallibility that drove him to such conclusions.

Brian Tierney, *Origins of Papal Infallibility, 1150–1350: A Study on the Concepts of Infallibility, Sovereignty and Tradition in the Middle Ages* (Leiden, Netherlands: E.J. Brill, 1972), 235–236.

"Even now," writes Richard Rubenstein, "reading William of Ockham is like watching a high-wire artist operate without a safety net.... [T]he abyss that yawns beneath him is a permanent divorce between faith and reason."[345]

It would be impossible for Ockham, for his Church, and for the rest of the world, to stay balanced on that tightrope forever.

3.

Most of what we know about Ockham, we learn from his writing. His early biographical details are extremely scarce.

He was apparently born around 1288 in the English village of Ockham (which means "Oak Hamlet"), located near Surrey. When he was a boy — perhaps as young as seven or eight — he entered the Order of Friars Minor, the Franciscans. He was educated first at the Greyfriars convent in London, then at Oxford.

In both places, he received excellent schooling. At Greyfriars, "most of the leading English Franciscan theologians of this period would have visited London on business of the order."[346] And in one place or another — or even, perhaps, in Paris, where advanced students at Oxford sometimes had the chance to study — it's possible that Ockham had as a teacher John Duns Scotus.

The "Scots" in Duns Scotus referred to his Scottish heritage. "Duns" was his hometown, a village just north of the English border. He was a member of the Franciscans, and in his philosophy, he was an Aristotelian — like Thomas Aquinas.

But Duns Scotus believed Aquinas had made a big mistake in the way he tried to reconcile Aristotle and Christianity. This synthesis of faith and reason, Duns Scotus thought, was an overreach.

"Aquinas, in Scotus's estimation, makes God and His actions too comprehensible, too rational, too open to our puny philosophical investigations," writes Edward Feser. "So radically free is God's will, in Scotus's view, that we simply cannot deduce from the natural order either His intentions or any necessary features of the things He created, since He might have created them in any number of ways, as His inscrutable will directed."[347]

[345] Rubenstein, *Aristotle's Children*, 258.

[346] Spade, *The Cambridge Companion to Ockham*, 19.

[347] Feser, *The Last Superstition*, 168.

The problem, as Duns Scotus saw it, was that Aquinas's ideas were *limiting* God. "God is absolutely free to do as he wishes, Duns Scotus insisted ... and he is not bound in the slightest by the natural laws that humans discover.

"If he wished, God could retroactively unmake everything that he has made, as well as make a human embryo develop into a fish or a flower." Therefore, "everything that science discovers must be provisional. God's absolute freedom makes the laws of nature merely probable rather than certain."[348]

This was a philosophy that appeared conservative at first glance. Duns Scotus seemed to be joining other critics who argued that Aquinas was claiming to know too much about God.

Yet Duns Scotus's criticism also contained a radical undercurrent. It called into question the whole idea that faith and reason *needed* to be reconciled.

Duns Scotus, who "was not a rebel by temperament,"[349] would not be the man to take these suggestions to their logical conclusion. That would instead be his student, William of Ockham.

In 1321, Ockham had returned to London from Oxford, to teach and write at Greyfriars. Here, he developed many of his most significant ideas. Even at Greyfriars, Ockham's views were controversial. Soon enough, those ideas would attract the notice of Church authorities, and Ockham would be forced to choose exile or compromise.

But he didn't mind walking that tightrope. In fact, he seemed to welcome the danger.

4.

The one thing for which Ockham[350] is best known — the principle of Ockham's Razor — is, in the view of many people, a myth.

A myth, in the sense that Ockham didn't invent it — and he certainly didn't name it.

Ockham's Razor can be easily restated: the simplest answer to a problem is often the best. The more complicated an explanation is, the more chances there are for mistakes.

348 Rubenstein, *Aristotle's Children*, 250.

349 Rubenstein, *Aristotle's Children*, 248.

350 "Ockham" is also commonly spelled "Occam."

Aristotle was probably the first to state this principle. Several other Aristotelian philosophers, including the medieval Jewish thinker Moses Maimonides, made similar observations. Another was St. Thomas Aquinas. Even Ockham's own teacher, Duns Scotus, repeated this advice. So why does Ockham get credit for it?[351]

Probably because Ockham wielded this razor more viciously than any of his predecessors. He used it to "cut to shreds everything that was left of Plato's Forms and Neoplatonism's metaphysics." He sliced up the concept of essence and existence, and with it the idea that the essence of a thing reveals its purpose.

"Once Ockham's razor got started, in fact," Arthur Herman notes, "not much was left standing."[352] That included the link between faith and reason. For centuries, philosophers had tried to discover this link, to make it visible, to reinforce it.

Now, with a few swipes of Ockham's razor, the link would be cut. And thanks to the series of events it would help inspire, the connection would soon seem irreparable.

5.

According to his absolute power, God could have chosen to save people in ways that seem absurd and even blasphemous. For example, he could have incarnated himself in a stone or an ass rather than in a man.[353]

[351] "The Myth of Ockham's Razor" is a 1918 paper by William Thorburn, published in the magazine *Mind*, which argues that the idea of Ockham's Razor "is a modern myth" which dates from the 1600s. "The Metaphysical (or Methodological) Law of Parcimony (or Logical Frugality), indicated but not very distinctly expressed by Aristotle . . . was fully established, not by Ockham (+1347), but by his teacher Duns Scotus (+1308): the greatest mind of the Later Middle Ages," Thorburn said.

In his *Posterior Analytics*, Aristotle wrote, "We may assume the superiority ceteris paribus [other things being equal] of the demonstration which derives from fewer postulates or hypotheses — in short, from fewer premises, for, given that all these are equally well known, where they are fewer, knowledge will be more speedily acquired, and that is a desideratum" (Alan Baker, "Simplicity," *Stanford Encyclopedia of Philosophy*, October 29, 2004; revised May 16, 2022, https://plato.stanford.edu/entries/simplicity/).

Meanwhile, in his second objection to God's existence in the *Summa Theologica*, Thomas Aquinas observed, "it is superfluous to suppose that what can be accounted for by a few principles has been produced by many" (Cahn, *Classics of Western Philosophy*, 423).

While the idea has clearly been around for a while, it's also true that none of these thinkers put it in precisely its familiar form. And it was apparently not until the rather late date of 1852 that Sir William Hamilton used the term "Occam's Razor" in his *Discussions*.

[352] Herman, *The Cave and the Light*, 247.

[353] Spade, *The Cambridge Companion to Ockham*, 230.

As you might guess, this is the sort of idea that got Ockham in hot water. And as author Steven Ozment points out, statements like this have been interpreted as "sheer, destructive mischief on Ockham's part."[354]

To be fair, Ockham was apparently trying here to defend the subsistence theory of the Incarnation: that Christ was a single being, a human who subsisted in the eternal Word of God. What Ockham was really saying was that other theories of the Incarnation were *as silly as* claiming that God would have chosen to become a stone or a donkey, instead of a man.

In fact, the subsistence theory was one that Thomas Aquinas and many other theologians had also supported. But as usual, Ockham felt he had to shock people to show them that God's power has no limits.

There's more than just shock value, however, in Ockham's ethics. He returned to an idea that an earlier Scholastic, Peter Abelard, had proposed: that we must judge a person's actions by intentions.

That's because, Ockham wrote, we might start doing something for what seems to be a good reason — and then end up doing it for a bad reason. For example, we might go to church intending to praise God. But along the way, we might change our view and end up in church just to make ourselves look good. The act, Ockham argued, could be both good *and* bad, depending on our intent: "Goodness is only a name or a connotative concept, principally signifying the act itself as neutral and connoting an act of the will that is perfectly virtuous and the right reason it is elicited in conformity with. Hence such an act is called 'virtuous' by an extrinsic denomination."[355]

Therefore," scholar Peter King observes, "acts have no intrinsic moral qualities at all."[356] This would come to be known as *voluntarism*: the idea that the will takes precedence over the intellect. And *theological voluntarism* holds that an act isn't good because we're trying to do God's will; it's good because God *wills* it to be good.

This, of course, poses a question: How can we know what God wills? Ultimately, Ockham thought, we *can't* — because we can have no knowledge of God. So "it seems as though God could command any given act or type of act to

[354] Steven Ozment, *The Age of Reform, 1250–1550* (New Haven, CT: Yale University Press, 1980), 38.

[355] Spade, *The Cambridge Companion to Ockham*, 230.

[356] Spade, *The Cambridge Companion to Ockham*, 230.

be obligatory or prohibited, and indeed that his command would be constitutive of the rightness or wrongness of these acts."[357]

To his credit, Ockham anticipated this objection — and then, as usual, came up with an example guaranteed to outrage. God could, he said, make us hate Him, for example. But if we obeyed, we would actually be showing our love for God anyway. So the command would cancel itself out.

That may seem like convoluted logic, but Ockham was determined to follow his reasoning to the end of the line, even if — and perhaps, *because* — it upset his critics. And even if that reasoning seemed to undermine morality itself.

When it came to the question of universals, Ockham once again borrowed from Peter Abelard. Though he, like Abelard, is often called a nominalist — someone who denies that universals exist in anything but name — it's more accurate to call Ockham a conceptualist instead.

Ockham did believe that universals exist — but only as "thought objects in the mind." As we saw in chapter 8, this is less of a distinction than it seems.

Conceptualism really does the same job as nominalism. Whether you think universals are just names or that they exist only in our minds, both beliefs make it impossible to assume that things have shared essences or that one thing causes another.

For Ockham, this was a *feature* of conceptualism, not a bug. It was just another reminder of God's supreme power and our inability to understand that power in the world around us. To think that we have this capability — as Aquinas had taught — was arrogant. And it was a mistake that went all the way back to Aristotle.

"Though the Philosopher has made, with God's help, many great discoveries," Ockham wrote, "he has, nevertheless, mingled errors with the truth."[358]

One of those errors, Ockham thought, was the last of Aristotle's Four Causes. To think we could know the final cause of something was, once again, trespassing on God's domain.

"Someone who is just following natural reason would claim that the question 'why?' is inappropriate in the case of natural actions," he wrote. "For he

[357] Spade, *The Cambridge Companion to Ockham*, 239.

[358] William of Ockham, *Philosophical Writings*, trans. Philotheus Boehner (Indianapolis: Bobbs-Merrill, 1964), 3.

would maintain that it is no real question to ask something like, 'For what reason is fire generated?' "[359]

This philosophy undoubtedly, as Richard Rubenstein and others point out, gave birth to modern empirical science. "For the natural relationships that people can describe using their powers of observation and reason are not unreal in the sense of being illusory or meaningless. Not at all. They are simply probable rather than certain, 'contingent' rather than necessary, limited to explaining natural processes rather than capable of explaining God."[360]

It is, however, a *limited* science — not just one that can't reach any definitive conclusions, but one where causes and effects are always suspect. And, as Edward Feser points out, it's a science that carries the seeds of its own destruction.

"Skepticism about the possibility of our knowing objective causal connections between things," he writes, "notoriously threatens not only cosmological arguments for God's existence, but the very possibility of science."[361]

The thing that backstopped Ockham's entire system was one "supreme ethical rule": doing the will of God.[362] But there was no rational way to know what that will *was* — as Ockham's provocative examples pointed out.

"Because of the arbitrary nature of reality, man cannot know the essential nature of sin and grace," writes author Carl Olson. "Thus, he has no way of knowing his state before God — outside of intuition and inner experience."[363]

Everything, in other words, rested on faith — and faith of an individual nature. "Intuition and inner experience" were personal, subjective qualities. And that idea complemented the growing desire, across Europe, to liberate the individual. Peter Abelard had seen this coming, some three hundred years earlier, and the desire was picking up steam.

This new individualism was not, in itself, a bad thing — as long as it stayed "subordinat[e] to the standards of truth, goodness, and beauty," instead of becoming a mere "negotiation of power."[364] But as people began inhaling the

359 William of Ockham, *Quodlibetal Questions*, trans. Alfred J. Freddoso and Francis E. Kelley (New Haven, CT: Yale University Press, 1998), 246–249.

360 Rubenstein, *Aristotle's Children*, 254.

361 Feser, *The Last Superstition*, 169.

362 William of Ockham, *Philosophical Writings*, xlix.

363 Carl Olson, "The Error of Nominalism," *Catholic Answers*, October 1, 2005. https://www.catholic.com/magazine/print-edition/whats-in-a-name-2.

364 D. C. Schindler, *Freedom from Reality: The Diabolical Character of Modern Liberty* (South Bend, IN: University of Notre Dame Press, 2019), 271.

intoxicating scent of freedom, that would become less and less likely. Liberation would become *liberalism*: a rival philosophy of Christianity that "turns out to destroy infinitely more than it pretends to preserve."[365]

Meanwhile, since God was impossible to know or understand, he also became more distant — and therefore, less significant. He was "no longer Pure Being, pervading and sustaining the world at every moment, but merely a superhuman external spectator, arranging things from outside."[366]

These were developments that Duns Scotus and Ockham could not have predicted. They were being faithful, as they saw it, to the Franciscans' view of faith's importance.

But what would happen when these became liberated from a belief in God? The secular version of the concept "that morality derives from arbitrary divine commands" would turn into "the notion that all law rests ultimately on the sheer will of a sovereign, rather than in a rationally ascertainable natural order."[367]

The fourteenth century was filled with omens of this shift. It started with the humiliating capture of Pope Boniface VIII in the papal palace by soldiers of the French king, Philip IV. It included the Great Western Schism, where multiple popes were elected and battled for legitimacy; the continuation of Inquisitions to root out heretics; and the start of the Hundred Years' War between England and France.

Might, then, was becoming more important than right. Especially because might seemed easier to understand than God's now-inscrutable will, and his now-unknowable creation.

6.

The authorities, of course, knew enough already about the troublemaking William of Ockham.

In 1323, Ockham was ordered to appear before a papal commission in Avignon, France. Like so many philosophers before him, he was charged with heresy.

Richard Rubenstein suggests this dispute wasn't solely about doctrine. Members of the Franciscan order had, for years, taken issue with the teachings

[365] Schindler, *Freedom from Reality*, 271.
[366] Feser, *The Last Superstition*, 170.
[367] Feser, *The Last Superstition*, 170.

of the Dominican, Thomas Aquinas. Now his allies "saw their chance to even the score."[368]

For the next four years, Ockham waited at the Franciscan monastery in Avignon to hear the result of the charges. He stayed busy, writing his *Summary of Logic* and finishing several other projects. He also made a new friend: Michael of Cessna, the Franciscans' Minister General.

Michael had been called to Avignon to answer his own charges of heresy. At issue was the Franciscans' belief about owning property. Michael believed the Franciscans were following the example of Jesus and the disciples, who had practiced "apostolic poverty," as well as the order's founder, St. Francis, who believed that poverty meant living without property.

But Pope John XXII insisted that property ownership could actually be a virtue. In this belief, he had defenders — including the late Thomas Aquinas, who had argued that private ownership encourages stewardship and order.

Ockham was naturally sympathetic to Michael's view. And it was this dispute, rather than his own controversial writings, that got him kicked out of the Church.

At Michael's request, Ockham studied the pope's previous statements on this subject. He concluded that John XXII was a heretic: he had been shown the truth about apostolic poverty, Ockham contended, and refused to budge. Therefore, he should be removed from office.

That was clearly going to make staying as the guest of a papal commission awkward. So late on the evening of May 26, 1328, Ockham, Michael, and a few other Franciscans escaped on horseback from the monastery at Avignon.[369]

King Ludwig of Bavaria, who had just become Holy Roman Emperor, offered them sanctuary. Ludwig was in the middle of his own dispute with John XXII. In fact, he had just engineered the election of his own, alternate pope. Therefore, he welcomed the dissidents and took them with him to Munich for protection.

Ockham was excommunicated that June. He would never return to his native England. But he allegedly promised Ludwig, "Defend me with your sword, and I will defend you with my pen."[370]

"For the rest of his life, William of Ockham would devote himself to defending not only the emperor's autonomy but every other secular ruler's from the

368 Rubenstein, *Aristotle's Children*, 258.

369 In fact, Ockham's official excommunication occurred on June 6, 1328, a couple of weeks after he left Avignon without papal permission.

370 Herman, *The Cave and the Light*, 251.

presumptions of Saint Peter's successors," writes Arthur Herman. "He found an eager audience."[371]

Ockham's "power to the people" approach suggested that it was the members of the Church who were responsible for its leaders — not the other way around. "This was why if a pope was a notorious heretic, 'a general council can be summoned without the authority of the pope to judge and depose' him."[372] This view would come to be known as *conciliarism.*

In the short term, these ideas did not take root. Early in the fifteenth century, Church authorities finally resolved the multiple-pope schism by upholding the authority of the pontiff. It seemed that things had finally gone back to normal.

But down the line, it was a different story. Ockham's ideas had once again foreseen the desire of people to be liberated from authority. "Over time, the idea slowly took root that 'governments are instituted among men deriving their just powers from the consent of the governed.' "[373]

That idea would, of course, lead to revolutions around the globe — most significantly, an uprising in a New World that was barely known at the time.

By then, Ockham would be long dead, and largely forgotten. He was about sixty when he passed away in April of 1347 — possibly from the Black Death, which had began sweeping across Europe the previous year.

When the American Revolution occurred, medieval thinkers had already been dismissed for centuries as irrelevant. Scholasticism was a relic of a dark and backwards era. The Enlightenment was the latest, the brightest, and the greatest hope for humanity — just as every subsequent modern movement has billed itself. But all of them owe something to William of Ockham.

[371] Herman, *The Cave and the Light,* 251.

[372] Herman, *The Cave and the Light,* 254.

[373] Herman, *The Cave and the Light,* 256. St. Robert Bellarmine, one of history's most underrated political theorists, further developed Ockham's ideas early in the seventeenth century. Bellarmine argued against the idea of the divine right of kings, and even contended that the pope only had indirect control over worldly governments.

This was a view that some considered borderline heretical. However, it was well within established Catholic tradition: Bellarmine opposed the absolute temporal power of the pope, but acknowledged that occasionally — for example, ecclesiastical matters like the Investiture Crisis of the eleventh and twelfth centuries, when royal governments wanted to choose bishops — the pope would have to exercise that temporal power. Nevertheless, Bellarmine's views clearly anticipated the political revolutions that would follow in the next century — especially in the American colonies.

7.

Of course, to give William of Ockham full credit — or blame — for this seismic shift in Western history is a bit overstated.

"Although it is true that he contributed to, and was part of, the intellectual and social transformations taking place in fourteenth-century Europe," the editors of *The Cambridge Companion to Ockham* point out, "he did not originate them, cannot bear sole responsibility for them ... and did not even approve of all of them."[374]

That hasn't stopped Ockham from becoming the villain in some versions of this tale. University of Chicago professor Richard Weaver, in his 1954 book *Ideas have Consequences,* called Ockham "the best representative of a change which came over man's conception of reality at this historic juncture."[375]

Ockham's denial of universals, Weaver thought, was "decisive for one's view of the nature and destiny of humankind.... With this change in the affirmation of what is real, the whole orientation of culture takes a turn, and we are on the road to modern empiricism."

But in the foreword to the 2013 edition of *Ideas Have Consequences,* Roger Kimball admitted there was something "comical" about making a medieval philosopher "the source of our present difficulties."[376]

"If William of Occam is responsible for what's wrong with the world," Kimball wrote, "there's not much we can do about it."[377]

For others, Ockham was a visionary. The late atheist Christopher Hitchens praised Ockham for not being "afraid to follow his own logic wherever it might take him" and for anticipating "the coming of true science."[378]

He did more, in fact, than just anticipate it. That "true science" was already being developed in Ockham's own time. In a fascinating section of his book *Aristotle's Children,* Richard Rubenstein tells the story of two Ockhamites who taught at the University of Paris in the mid-thirteenth century.

374 Spade, *The Cambridge Companion to Ockham,* 4.

375 Richard M. Weaver, *Ideas Have Consequences* (Chicago: University of Chicago Press, 2013), 36–37.

376 Roger Kimball, foreword to Weaver, *Ideas Have Consequences,* 20.

377 Kimball, foreword to Weaver, *Ideas Have Consequences,* 20.

378 Christopher Hitchens, *God Is Not Great* (New York: Twelve, 2007), 26.

Jean Buridan and his pupil, Nicole Oresme, developed theories that directly contradicted Aristotle.[379] Buridan used Ockham's razor to show that Aristotle's idea about motion could be simplified. Once an object is set in motion, Buridan discovered, it stays in motion unless it meets resistance.

And Oresme dared to contradict both Aristotle *and* the Church. He pointed out that if the earth rotated, then explanations of movement in the heavens would get a lot easier.

Oresme hedged his bet by saying that the scriptural interpretation of events — that the earth stands still — was still the one he endorsed. But "when Oresme allowed the earth to rotate, it was only a matter of time (and further cultural change) before someone else would allow it to revolve."[380]

In Paris, "something new was being born: a science increasingly alienated from religion, and a faith seeking a foothold in 'a mechanical world of lifeless matter, local motion, and random collision.' "[381]

These Ockhamite scientists were not the only Catholics making big discoveries during the medieval period. The Franciscan empiricist Roger Bacon, for example, had been proposing what would eventually become the scientific method, and speculating about flying machines, before Ockham was born.

But the true legacy of Ockham's razor was its slashing of the link between reason and faith.

"The intimate connection between God and nature, and God and reason, had finally, decisively been severed."[382] Where did that leave man? More liberated than ever before, explains Arthur Herman: "Freed of the burden of trying to reconcile faith with reason, we can plunge into the world with a new optimism and gusto — but also with the sense that we have been left pretty much to ourselves."[383]

8.

A standard argument of modern historians is that by the fourteenth century it had become necessary for science to break with religion — and with Aristotle.

[379] The Islamic philosopher Avicenna is often credited as advancing an even earlier refutation of Aristotle's theory of motion.

[380] Rubenstein, *Aristotle's Children*, 278.

[381] Rubenstein, *Aristotle's Children*, 279.

[382] Herman, *The Cave and the Light*, 247.

[383] Herman, *The Cave and the Light*, 247.

As the examples of Buridan and Oresme show, Aristotle had been wrong about a lot of things. The list of mistakes is long, if understandable.

He thought heavenly bodies were embedded in crystal spheres and rotated in perfect circles. He thought heavy objects fell faster than lighter ones, though later discoveries showed that objects fall at the same speed, regardless of their weight. (These were two errors that Buridan and Oresme challenged.)

Aristotle thought earth was the center of the universe, which of course would become a major historical controversy. He thought the brain was for refrigerating blood, not for thinking. He didn't believe in atoms or in empty space.

Focusing on those errors, critics ignored the many, many things Aristotle got right. But this also obscures an even more critical point.

Modern science would refute many of Aristotle's conclusions. It would not, however, refute his *ideas* — such as hylomorphism and the Four Causes. After all, writes Edward Feser, "it is not as if the subsequent findings of modern science cannot be incorporated within an Aristotelian framework."[384]

So why, then, were the new scientists and philosophers who followed Ockham so eager to throw out Aristotle's entire system? And why did so many people have such hostility to Aristotle's beliefs?

As just one example, in his 1517 *Disputation Against Scholastic Theology*, Martin Luther wrote, "Virtually the entire *Ethics* of Aristotle is the worst enemy of grace," and, "It is an error to say that no man can become a theologian without Aristotle.... Indeed, no one can become a theologian unless he becomes one without Aristotle." He added that "the whole Aristotle is to theology as darkness is to light."[385]

That document was written earlier in the same year that Luther posted his 95 Theses on the door of the Castle Church in Wittenberg, Germany, and began the Protestant Reformation.

As the title of his "disputation" shows, Luther's problem wasn't just with Aristotle. It was with the Scholastics who had adopted, and adapted, Aristotle — including Thomas Aquinas. And of course, Luther had a larger dispute with the Church in general.

[384] Feser, *The Last Superstition*, 180.

[385] Martin Luther, "Martin Luther's 1517 Disputation against Scholastic Theology," William Roach, August 21, 2017, https://williamroach.org/2017/08/20/martin-luthers-1517-disputation-against-scholastic-theology/.

"Aristotle was discredited, in part, because the Catholic Church had used his ideas to maintain its cultural hegemony in Europe — a supremacy that many Westerners considered oppressive, and that was now obsolete," writes Richard Rubenstein.[386]

But that "oppression" was about more than just pompous feudal lords or property-owning popes. It was, simply, that people now wanted to be free to do as they wished. And Aristotle, Aquinas, and the Catholic Church were standing in their way.

Some of those people were kings, like Henry VIII, who wanted to divorce and take a new wife. Some were religious leaders like Luther, who wanted to make belief — and salvation — personal, and like John Calvin, who wanted to remove the stigma of Christians owning property and acquiring wealth. Some were merchants, who rubbed their hands in anticipation as Europe's markets opened up before them. And most were just regular people tempted by a world where they, too, could do their own thing at last.

The opponents of those exciting new possibilities needed to be dealt with. The easiest way to do this was to focus on the demonstrable errors that Aristotle had made. These errors could be used to neutralize Aquinas and the Scholastics, who had endorsed Aristotle, and, in turn, the Catholic Church, which had finally endorsed the Scholastics.

In his book *An Intellectual History of Liberalism*, the French philosopher Pierre Manent summarizes:

> In order to escape decisively from the power of the singular religious institution of the Church, one had to renounce thinking about human life in terms of its good or end, which would always be vulnerable to the Church's "trump." Since, therefore, power in the body politic can no longer be considered the power of the good that orders what it gives (the Augustinian definition of grace), man can understand himself only by creating himself.
>
> The idea of man's self-creation characterizes the so-called Promethean ambition of modern man, who wants to be the offspring of his own works. Religious minds have unfailingly reprimanded this modern man for his "presumption," which claims to usurp divine attributes.[387]

[386] Rubenstein, *Aristotle's Children*, 290.

[387] Pierre Manent, *An Intellectual History of Liberalism* (Princeton, NJ: Princeton University Press, 1995), 114.

In short, modern man wanted God's power of creation, to create himself. Aristotle, Aquinas, and the Catholic Church were the enemies of this craving.

"To a very great extent it was a desire to further the project, and not an actual refutation of Aristotle, that moved modern thinkers away from his metaphysics," notes Edward Feser. "The agenda determined the arguments, rather than the other way around."[388]

It's also fair to acknowledge a criticism of the Aristotelian and Scholastic model of knowledge: that as it grew increasingly analytical, it lost touch with a necessary sense of wonder.

The Scholastics were mocked for supposedly trying to figure out the answer to pointless inquiries such as "How many angels can dance on the head of a pin?" That question seems to have been the invention of later writers: there's no evidence that Aquinas, Duns Scotus, or any of the usual suspects actually posed it.[389]

However, the joke does indicate a real problem. The twentieth-century Catholic convert Marshall McLuhan, famous for declaring that "The medium is the message," distinguished between *concept* and *percept* in religion.

"To a Catholic, faith is not simply an act of the mind, that is, a matter of ideology or thought (*con*cepts)," his son Eric wrote, in an introduction to McLuhan's religious writings. "Faith is a mode of *per*ception, a sense like sight or hearing or touch.... As a way of *knowing*, faith operates in the realm of percepts, not concepts."[390]

"I don't think concepts have any relevance in religion," McLuhan himself said. McLuhan was a Thomist, "for whom the sensory order resonates with the Divine Logos."[391] He believed that Aquinas had recognized this himself, that experience — not mere reasoning — is what gives religion its enchantment.

388 Feser, *The Last Superstition*, 175.

389 Aquinas, sometimes known as the "Angelic Doctor," did try to establish the existence of angels at some length in his writings — which is perhaps why this phrase about angels dancing on the head of a pin has become attributed to him. For Aquinas, angels were incorporeal beings of pure spirit and intellect; for other medieval thinkers, such as St. Bonaventure, angels did have a sort of spiritual matter.

390 Marshall McLuhan, Eric McLuhan, and Jacek Szlarek, *The Medium and the Light: Reflections on Religion* (Eugene, OR: Wipf & Stock, 2010), xv. Author Rod Dreher wrote about this "direct experience of the holy" and Marshall McLuhan's thoughts about it in his June 12, 2023 Substack newsletter, "Everybody Has Become Porous." https://roddreher.substack.com/p/everybody-has-become-porous.

391 McLuhan, McLuhan, and Szlarek, *The Medium and the Light*, xv.

But other Scholastics had not acknowledged this truth. The desire for a personal relationship with God was also, in some sense, a desire for a "direct experience of the holy" — which academic Scholasticism was no longer providing.

It's worth remembering that Scholasticism hadn't been intended for a general audience. Although it had become common in the universities, the rise in literacy and the birth of the printing press created the desire for a simpler, more accessible faith. And once again, this would be a faith that would privilege the individual.

So in the end, out went a series of beliefs. No more talk of seeing God in nature, or that things have any purpose. No more talk of logically tracing back causes to their origin, or of any definite causes at all. No more talk of obligations, and no more talk of limitations.

To make the break complete, the whole medieval period would have to be downgraded. It couldn't be seen as a time when a group of brilliant scholars from a variety of faiths rediscovered one of the world's greatest thinkers, worked to balance his views with their own religions, and began practicing science.

Instead, the entire period would become known as the "Dark Ages," a time of bleak prospects and blind faith. Even the most intelligent thinkers of this time would be insulted. (It's one reason we call people "dunces": the term came to describe followers of John Duns Scotus.)

In recent years, that simplistic view of the medieval era has been challenged. But it still holds a lot of sway. Consider these comments from prominent atheist author Sam Harris, in his book *The End of Faith: Religion, Terror, and the Future of Reason*:

> Imagine that we could revive a well-educated Christian of the fourteenth century. The man would prove to be a total ignoramus, except on matters of faith. His beliefs about geography, astronomy, and medicine would embarrass even a child, but he would know more or less everything there is to know about God.[392]

The irony of this statement, of course, is twofold. The first is that a well-educated Christian of the fourteenth century — let's use Nicole Oresme as an example — was capable of making groundbreaking scientific discoveries.

[392] Sam Harris, *The End of Faith: Religion, Terror, and the Future of Reason* (New York: W. W. Norton, 2005), 21.

Born a peasant, Oresme became not just a great astronomer but also a significant economist (he was an early defender of the natural right of property ownership), mathematician (he wrote the first proof for the divergence of the harmonic series), and psychologist (he helped develop the idea of the unconscious mind).

Yet even though he was also a Catholic bishop, Orseme would never have claimed "to know more or less everything there is to know about God." In fact, as a Scholastic, he would have argued just the opposite.

The second irony is that the "geography, astronomy, and medicine" Harris reveres — in fact, all the so-called "hard sciences" — all got their liberating spark from the well-educated Christian "ignoramuses" he mocks.

William of Ockham, and the razor he wielded, cut away assumptions of all types. That razor cleared the path for a radical empiricism, where nothing can be taken for granted and every belief is subject to constant experiments. And, increasingly, it cut Christians off from the ability to defend their beliefs using reason.

While the Catholic Reformation of the sixteenth and seventeenth centuries saw priests — especially Jesuits — continue to use reason in their apologetics, personal faith would become more and more important in the Protestant Reformation. Ockham had been excommunicated from the Catholic Church — but his influence loomed large outside it.

Whether you think of him as a conscious liberator or as the accidental opener of Pandora's box, Ockham and his influence remain undeniable — and inescapable.

9.

Several philosophers who followed the Scholastics made their break with Aristotle the old-fashioned way: they turned to his teacher, Plato.

Or, more accurately, they turned to the Neoplatonists — like Plotinus, Pseudo-Dionysius and John Scotus Erigena. Plato had trusted the mind over the material world, and the Neoplatonists had followed suit.

The Scholastics had seemingly reconciled the split between the mind and the body. But like an old wound, it was about to be opened back up.

The three philosophers in this section were a reflection of the desire for *per*cept over *con*cept. Though they were all brilliant scholars, they each appealed to holy mystery, to simplicity, and to ignorance.

One early example was the German Dominican Meister (Johannes) Eckhart. Eckhart's conception of God is similar to Plotinus's idea of "the One" — a transcendent and mysterious entity that he compared at various times to a desert or wilderness.

Eckhart described this "One" as the "Godhead," which was the source of everything — even of the three Persons of the Trinity. Achieving unity with this primal source was the goal for Eckhart, just as it had been for Plotinus.

To do so, man must "live without why" and detach himself from everything. Detachment is the ultimate goal of Eckhart's philosophy, "for to realize detachment is to realize for oneself the nature of God. To be full of creatures is to be empty of God; and to be empty of creatures is to be full of God," Eckhart tells us.[393]

He described this in terms of mystical experience, the "breaking-through": "But in my breaking through, where I stand free of my own will, of God's will, of all His works, and of God himself, then I am above all creatures and am neither God nor creature, but I am that which I was and shall remain for evermore."[394]

This philosophy was not without controversy. Some believed it to be pantheistic — that Eckhart was saying existence was equivalent to God. And his belief in an entity above the Trinity was bound to arouse comment.

In 1329, the year after Eckhart's death, Pope John XXII condemned seventeen of his sayings as heretical, and classified another eleven as "having a very bad sound and suspect of heresy."[395]

Not surprisingly, in the first group was Eckhart's assertion that "we are fully transformed and converted into God; in the same way as in the sacrament the bread is converted into the body of Christ, so I am converted into Him, so that He converts me into His being as one, not as *like*. By the living God it is true that there is no difference."

Another notable German thinker of this era was Nicolaus of Cusa, a fifteenth-century theologian. Nicolaus admired Eckhart's work, and he pursued a similar path away from Aristotle and the Scholastics.

393 "Introduction to Meister Eckhart," *Esoterica*, n.d., accessed September 3, 2023. http://esoteric.msu.edu/REL275/EckhartIntroduction.html.

394 Meister Eckhart, *The Complete Mystical Works of Meister Eckhart*, trans. and ed. Maurice O'C. Walshe (New York: Crossroad Publishing, 2009), 424.

395 Eckhart, *The Complete Mystical Works of Meister Eckhart*, 28.

For inspiration, however, Nicolaus went back not to Plato but to Socrates. His idea that the only thing we can really know is our own ignorance, Nicolaus thought, was appropriate when trying to understand God.

Reason, he taught, was inadequate for this job. "Our reason seeks finitude, absolute reference points, and non-contradiction. The universe, imaging God as it does, refuses to provide us with these things."

As an example, in his book *On Learned Ignorance*, Nicolaus made an observation that had startling implications — not just for theology, but for science: "The earth is not fixed in place at some given point because nothing is utterly at rest; nor can it be the exact physical center of the natural universe, even if it seems nearer the center than 'the fixed stars'.... The universe is therefore 'infinite,' in the sense of physically unbounded."[396]

Only God can determine "the exact center and circumference of the created universe. What we take to be center and outer limits depends on our viewpoint."[397]

At least seventy years before Copernicus would propose his heliocentric theory about the earth circling the sun, Nicolaus's "ontological relativity" cast doubt on the comforting certainty that our world was the center of everything.

For Nicolaus, reality — like its Creator — was infinite. The universe was filled with contradictions and paradoxes, and Aristotle and the Scholastics couldn't help us decode them. Only "leaned ignorance," Nicolaus thought, was the answer.

That belief in the value of ignorance was the guiding principle of Desiderius Erasmus, who turned it into a series of bestselling books.

In fact, Erasmus, a Dutch Catholic theologian of the fifteenth and sixteenth centuries, was "the first writer to earn a living with his pen." (This, as Arthur Herman points out, was "no mean feat, since his books were all written in Latin."[398] It was also the result of Erasmus joining forces with the Italian publisher Aldus Manutius, who used the still-novel printing press to distribute Erasmus's work.)

396 Clyde Lee Miller, "Cusanus, Nicolaus [Nicolas of Cusa]," *Stanford Encyclopedia of Philosophy*, July 10, 2009; revised November 9, 2021, https://plato.stanford.edu/entries/cusanus/.

397 Miller, "Cusanus, Nicolaus."

398 Herman, *The Cave and the Light*, 312.

The most popular of his books by far was published in 1509. It was titled *In Praise of Folly,* and it poked fun at corruption within the Catholic Church.

The main character is the goddess Folly, who takes aim at priests who haven't read the Bible and "say they have sufficiently discharged their offices if they but anyhow mumble over a few odd prayers, which, so help me, Hercules! I wonder if any god either hear or understand, since they do neither themselves."[399]

Bishops, cardinals, and even popes — "the most diligent of all others in gathering in the harvest of money"[400] — are mocked. The Church's practice of granting indulgences — forgiveness of punishment due to sin — in return for monetary payment is criticized, more than a decade before Martin Luther made it one of his primary complaints.

But the ultimate message was a defense of folly — that is, remaining naïve and ignorant. Erasmus thought this was "an essential part of being human, and is what ultimately brings us the most happiness and contentment."[401]

Knowledge, on the other hand, is the name of the mountain where Lucifer lives. "That great Architect of the World, God, gave man an injunction against his eating of the Tree of Knowledge," Folly says, "as if knowledge were the bane of happiness."[402]

Like Eckhart before him, and like Luther who followed, Erasmus proposed a personal relationship with God. Simplicity and humility were the keys. Everything else — the knowledge of the Scholastics in particular — just gets in the way.

"Erasmus never goes after Aristotle directly," Arthur Herman notes, "but for the rest — 'realists, nominalists, Thomists, Albertists, Occamists and Scotists' — he accuses them of poisoning the true message of Christianity with 'their syllogisms, major and minor, conclusions, corollaries, idiotic hypotheses, and further scholastic rubbish.' "[403]

This message hit home at a time when higher education and religion were both in a rut. "Like the Church itself, by 1500 Europe's universities had become

399 Desiderius Erasmus, *In Praise of Folly,* ed. John Wilson (Mineola, NY: Dover Publications, 2012), 58.

400 Erasmus, *In Praise of Folly,* 58.

401 Buckingham, *The Philosophy Book,* 97.

402 Erasmus, *In Praise of Folly,* 67.

403 Herman, *The Cave and the Light,* 313.

victims of their own success. They had become degree factories, and quality control suffered as a result.

"Just as there were priests who didn't know the Mass or drank or kept mistresses, so there were philosophy professors who invoked the name of Aristotle without having read a single one of his works, and theology professors who had never turned a page of the *Summa* or *The City of God* — or the letters of Saint Paul."[404]

The wider availability of books was one way to combat this malaise. Erasmus's goal was to focus attention on the Bible — the one text he felt everyone needed to read. To do this properly, however, it made sense to learn Greek and Latin.

Other European scholars of the fifteenth century were also rediscovering classical sources. This movement, called *humanism* — a reference to the humanities, such as grammar, rhetoric, and poetry — gained influence, both within and outside the Catholic Church. This period is sometimes called "Renaissance humanism," because it both anticipated the wider Renaissance, in Italy and Western Europe, and existed alongside it.

Paradoxically, Erasmus's desire to return to simplicity and ignorance helped start an entirely new educational trend. But as he surveyed the landscape he'd helped create, he was satisfied.

"The world is coming to its senses as if awakening out of a deep sleep," he wrote in 1519.[405] It was two years before Pope Leo X excommunicated Martin Luther, and the Renaissance was spreading across Europe. "Everywhere the arts and sciences are reborn."

Whether that optimism was warranted depended — as the Copernican revolution would soon make clear — a great deal on one's perspective.

✠ ✠ ✠

[404] Herman, *The Cave and the Light*, 314.

[405] Herman, *The Cave and the Light*, 317.

SECTION THREE

THIS IS THE MODERN WORLD: BREAKING FREE AND FREE FALLING

AT THIS POINT, EARLY in the sixteenth century, everything changes.

Philosophy is now increasingly divorced from science. So, in many cases, it ceases to propose answers to problems. Instead, it *creates* problems — many of which it is unable to solve.

One of these problems is the split between man's reason and his senses. Aristotle and Aquinas had balanced each of these ways of knowing the world. But that balance is gone now. So the chasm between *rationalists* — those who value the evidence of reason — and *empiricists* — those who value the evidence of the senses — will yawn wider and wider.

In a distant third place is theology. Religion is becoming increasingly irrelevant to both philosophy and science — especially the Catholic faith.

But it's science, not philosophy, that will now claim to become the problem-solving discipline. Freed from Aristotle and the Scholastics — freed from any obligation to higher purpose, or to any purpose at all — science can concern itself with two major issues.

Understanding nature — knowledge for the sake of knowledge, an idea that went all the way back to the Greeks — is no longer the mission. The goals instead are the *prediction* and *control* of nature.

Nature, we might remember, also includes people. They'll be eventually downgraded to the most intelligent animals of the bunch, and their animalistic tendencies will be noted and accounted for.

This far more focused field of study will yield astounding results. From medicine to travel, from factories dedicated to heavy industry to labor-saving devices for the home, science will now be dedicated to making man's life as long, and as pleasant, as possible — at least in the abstract.

Politics will become a science, too. The philosophers of this modern era will begin liberating man politically. In theory, he'll have more freedom than ever before. And he'll gradually owe less and less to anyone or anything. Not to his family, not to his community, not to his church, not to his God.

Here, once again, it was necessary to make a break with Aristotle. *The* Philosopher had equated politics with virtue. The goal of the state is to develop virtue in citizens, Aristotle had said, so that they can live virtuous lives. But that old-fashioned view asks far too much of people. They just want safety and comfort and *stuff*, after all.

This is all what will come to be known as the Enlightenment. It will conquer the Western world, though it will be a conquest to which most people will assent. Even if they disagree with certain parts of it, it will allow them to do things that would have been forbidden before. Deep down, they'll admit that the trade seems to be worth it. That is, if they think about it at all. Many won't — since they'll have no control over these massive changes anyway.

Many people's lives will, of course, get much worse as a result of this liberation of science and politics. Those who labor on behalf of the new technology won't always see their lot improve. Some — miners, factory workers, child laborers, slaves — will live short, harsh lives in service to industry and "progress." There will be winners and losers in this new world, just as there were in the old.

And liberation won't always be easy. Sometimes it will require revolutions, often bloody ones. In Europe, especially, lots of people will die — among them women, children, and the elderly. But defenders of the Enlightenment will say that's just the price of progress.

The promise of comfort, and of freedom — from the expectations and obligations of the Church, and of the natural laws it upheld — will distract attention from the downside. At least, that will be the hope.

What's striking, then, is that three of the first modernist philosophers were so clear about the true costs of this new era. Two were what we'd today call political scientists, and the other usually gets credit for being the first modern scientist.

All three of these men faced questions about their faith. The conclusions they reached about human nature, in many cases, seemed at odds with Christianity. Being an atheist in this era usually meant having unorthodox beliefs about God, rather than no belief at all. And the views of all three men were, in the eyes of their peers, decidedly suspect.

All three, in short, were brilliant observers of their fellow men, and of the world. Their foresight is often more admirable than their conclusions.

CHAPTER ELEVEN

FEAR AND LOVE IN FLORENCE

1.

The prisoner is shoved forward. He stumbles; his hands are bound roughly behind his back. But he doesn't fall.

Instead, he stares, transfixed, at the rope and makeshift pulley before him.

He'd thought things were bad the night before, here in the Bargello prison in the Republic of Florence. In the cell where he was held, the walls were "full of lice so big and fat they seem like butterflies," and the stench of human waste was unbearable.

And he'd known this moment was coming. He'd heard the cries from other prisoners: "Too high from the ground!"

They were talking about the pulley, to which his arms are now fastened. The rope is looped over a beam in the ceiling. At the other end are two burly jailers. One of them smirks as they begin tugging on the rope.

Slowly, agonizingly, the prisoner is lifted toward the ceiling. He instinctively curls his legs up to his chest to try balancing his weight. But it doesn't really help.

This isn't the worst part, however. That comes next. The jailers nod at one another, and then abruptly the rope goes slack. For one glorious second, the pressure on the prisoner's arms vanishes.

Then the jailers tug the rope again, before his body can hit the stone floor. The sensation is indescribable. His arms feel as though they're being ripped out of their sockets. And that's more or less what's happening.

This is a form of torture known as the strappado. *It comes from the Italian word for "pull":* strappare. *One drop from the ceiling is usually enough to make a prisoner talk. Three or four should permanently dislocate both of his shoulders.*

This prisoner will allow himself to be dropped six *times. And he still won't talk.*

What his captors want is information about a plot to overthrow the Medici, the ruling family of Florence. The prisoner is the likeliest of suspects.

Last summer, he'd led a makeshift militia to defend the city from a group of Spanish mercenaries. The mercenaries had been hired to restore the Medici family to power. The prisoner, however, was inspired by Aristotle's idea of a citizen army, men who would defend their homeland to the death.

In practice, that's not how it happened. The professional army of Spaniards overran the citizen militia, most of which deserted. The Medici were restored, and the prisoner was lucky to escape with just a fine. But they began watching him at every turn. And now the Medici family wants to know what he *knows about the latest threat to their rule.*

Why the jailers stop at half a dozen drops is a mystery. Maybe they believe the prisoner when he says he doesn't know anything. Perhaps they're impressed: this unassuming little man is evidently tougher than he looks.

But probably they know they'll have another shot at him, tomorrow, or the next day. For now, they'll let him think about what's just happened.

And that's what he does. Back in his filthy cell, the prisoner assesses his unpromising situation. He has a thin face that some describe as fox-like, and it looks especially crafty now, as he hits on an idea.

Though the slightest movement sends agonizing pains down both arms, the prisoner requests a pen and some paper. He's going to write a letter to Giuliano de' Medici.

Giuliano is the youngest son of Lorenzo the Magnificent, the head of the Medici. They are a family of great power and influence. Giuliano's older brother Giovanni will soon become Pope Leo X. [406]

But it's Giuliano to whom the prisoner chooses to write. Giuliano will not only be the next ruler of Florence, but he has a reputation for kindness, and for appreciating the arts. So the prisoner decides to write him a sonnet.

"Giuliano, I have a pair of shackles on my legs and six drops of the strappado on my back," he begins. "My other misfortunes I shall not tell, since that is the way they treat poets."

It's a funny line. But of course, he also humbly begs for mercy. And the prisoner's strategy apparently works. He is soon released,[407] *as the city turns its attention to celebrating Giovanni's election as the new pope. Spring is in the air, and the prisoner is hopeful.*

"He had plunged deep into that abyss," his biographer will write centuries later, "and now he had recovered from the fall, he wanted to try to climb up the slope again."

This time, he will climb up clear-eyed. He'll write to Guiliano again, but this time, he will give him advice. One of the things he'll suggest is the importance of being like a fox.

That's because while a fox is not the strongest animal, its gift is its cleverness: it knows how to avoid traps and snares. "He who has known best how to employ the fox," the prisoner will write, "has succeeded best."

Nobody knows this better, after all, than the prisoner himself.[408]

406 Giulio Medici, the future Pope Clement VII, was actually Giovanni Medici's cousin.

407 It's possible that Machiavelli was freed not on his own merits, but because of a general amnesty declared in Florence after hometown boy Giovanni Medici was elected pope.

408 This sequence of Machiavelli's gruesome torture in prison is based on a number of accounts, including Italian author Roberto Ridolfi's 1953 biography *The Life of Niccoló Macchiavelli*. The quotes from Machiavelli's letter come from this book, pages 137–138.

2.

Niccolò Machiavelli was not, as one chronicler points out, an "armchair strategist."[409]

His political theories were the result of years spent in politics — and years seeing the worst sides of human nature. He was, of course, the prisoner in our first section — who realized that one of the first rules of politics is telling people what you know they want to hear.

But he also realized that telling the truth can be equally important — especially when *nobody* wants to hear it. "Since it is my intention to write something of use to those who will understand, I deem it best to stick to the practical truth of things rather than to fancies," he wrote.[410]

He had seen firsthand the machinations of powerful people. Before the Medici returned to power, Machiavelli had spent years as the Florentine Secretary. He was the right-hand man of Piero Soderini, the city's ruler.

In that job, he'd traveled to the courts of King Louis XII of France, Pope Julius II, and Maximillian, the Holy Roman Emperor. He watched and he listened, fascinated by the different strategies these rulers used to get and keep power.

One man, in particular, made a lasting impression on Machiavelli. That was Cesare Borgia.

Borgia was a Spaniard, the illegitimate son of Pope Alexander VI. As a teenager, he'd been made a bishop, and then a cardinal. But he resigned to pursue his other interest, conquest: of both women and territory. He was successful on both counts. By the time Machiavelli met him, Borgia had bedded numerous women, and ruled a big chunk of central Italy.

Handsome, daring, and dressed all in black, Borgia seemed like the kind of man Florence needed. After their meeting in 1502, Machiavelli "wrote excitedly to his bosses in the Palazzo della Signoria of the lessons offered by this majestic enemy.

"In the ruthless young warrior he saw a potential hero: a leader strong enough to expel the foreign armies and transform Italy from a poetic entity into a real one."[411]

[409] Herman, *The Cave and the Light*, 273.

[410] Niccolò Machiavelli, *The Prince*, trans. Daniel John Donno (New York: Bantam Classics, 1985), 56.

[411] Claudia Roth Pierpont, "The Florentine," *New Yorker*, September 8, 2008. https://www.newyorker.com/magazine/2008/09/15/the-florentine.

Machiavelli's subsequent attempt at creating a militia to defend Florence hadn't gone so well, of course. He was no Borgia. But perhaps he could help train one instead.

After his release from prison, Machiavelli first tried to explain why his own attempt at rallying the citizens of Florence had failed. His *Discourses* took a realistic look at the downfall of great societies, from the Roman Empire to sixteenth-century Italy.

The conclusion he reached was that "every free society is doomed from the start."[412] The more free a society becomes, he reasoned, "the more prosperous and more arrogant it becomes as well. Like ancient Rome or Renaissance Florence, it sows the seeds of its own servitude. Although self-government and liberty are the highest forms of political life, Machiavelli revealed that human nature also makes them the most unstable."[413]

If freedom didn't work, then how could a society possibly survive? The answer was a leader willing to use brute force — as well as cunning, deception, and ruthlessness, when necessary.

Those observations might seem shocking to people who were used to hearing about what a leader *ought* to do. But successful worldly rulers, Machiavelli had seen, didn't look anything like Plato's benevolent philosopher kings. They were more like Cesare Borgia and Borgia's father, the equally amoral Pope Alexander VI.

"A man who strives after goodness in all his acts is sure to come to ruin," Machiavelli wrote, "since there are so many men who are not good. Hence it is necessary that a prince who is interested in his survival learn to be other than good, making use of this capacity or refraining from it according to need."[414]

Now Machiavelli was interested in turning these reflections into an instruction manual of sorts: a guide for rulers. He called it *The Prince,* and he hoped it would get him into the good graces of the Medici — and perhaps win him a government job again.

He would first dedicate this guide to Giuliano Medici. But in 1516, Giuliano died young, at age thirty-seven. In keeping with the practical instructions in his book, Machiavelli revised the dedication — since Giuliano could no longer help him.

412 Herman, *The Cave and the Light,* 276.

413 Herman, *The Cave and the Light,* 276.

414 Machiavelli, *The Prince,* 56.

Instead, Machiavelli dedicated the book to Giuliano's nephew, Lorenzo II, the new ruler of Florence. He suggested it would help Lorenzo avoid the mistakes that had plagued past leaders — especially, and somewhat ironically, the leaders of Florence before the Medici regained control.

"Never at any time does Machiavelli base an argument on whatever it is people are supposed to do, still less on any Christian or biblical exhortation," wrote Bryan Magee. "What he provides is an accurately observed and superbly written account of what actually happens."[415]

The book was filled with reminders of what Machiavelli had seen with his own eyes, and recorded in his *Discourses*: freedom means nothing unless a ruler has the will to restrict it when necessary.

One of the most famous questions posed in *The Prince* is whether a ruler should try to be loved or feared. A ruler should attempt to be both, Machiavelli wrote — but since that's usually impossible, rulers "will find greater security in being feared than being loved."[416]

Rulers should not be gratuitously cruel, of course — but they shouldn't mind having that reputation, either. "Cesare Borgia was considered cruel,"[417] Machiavelli noted. Yet Borgia's cruelty made him far more effective than the past leaders of Florence.

"A prince, therefore, must be indifferent to the charge of cruelty.... Having set an example once or twice, he may thereafter act far more mercifully than the princes who, through excessive kindness, allow disorders to arise from which murder and rapine ensue."[418]

Tyranny, Machiavelli suggested, is preferable to anarchy. This is an idea that would resonate throughout the centuries.

If this meant a ruler had to look to the animal kingdom, to the fox and the lion, for examples, then so be it — "since at times he will be forced to act like a beast as well as a human being."[419]

There was also genteel advice. A ruler should be a patron of the arts — like the Medici family, who supported such Renaissance geniuses as Donatello, Botticelli,

[415] Magee, *The Story of Philosophy*, 72.

[416] Machiavelli, *The Prince*, 60.

[417] Machiavelli, *The Prince*, 59.

[418] Machiavelli, *The Prince*, 59.

[419] Herman, *The Cave and the Light*, 278.

and Michelangelo. And he ought to encourage citizens to pursue their trades peaceably, and "keep the people occupied with festivals and spectacles."[420]

But Machiavelli's suggestion that it was "useful" for a prince to *appear* "merciful, faithful, humane, religious, upright" raised eyebrows, especially among Christians. So did what followed: if the prince is required *not* to be these things, then he should "be able and know how to change to the opposite."

Machiavelli ended *The Prince* with a rousing call for a liberator — someone who could free Italy from foreign conquerors. "Let your illustrious house take up this task," he wrote to Lorenzo, "with that boldness and with that hope which is reserved to just enterprises, so that this nation may be ennobled under your banner."[421]

That's not the way it worked for any of the key players in *The Prince*. As a reminder of how quickly things could turn sour for a leader, Cesare Borgia had been ambushed in northern Spain by a group of enemy knights in 1507. His assailants stripped him of his fine clothes, and even the leather mask he wore to cover his scars from syphilis. Borgia's corpse was left naked, with just one concession to modesty: his enemies covered his genitals with a stone. He was just thirty-one years old.

The Medici, meanwhile, would be expelled from Florence again in 1527. That followed the sack of Rome by mutinous soldiers of the Holy Roman Emperor, Charles V. The Medici were too wealthy and influential not to return to Florence, and eventually they would. But the dog-eat-dog world Machiavelli had described applied to everyone.

And Machiavelli himself never regained his government post. The best he managed was a commission to write a history of Florence, the city he had loved and defended, and where he'd learned so many hard lessons. He died in June of 1527, not long after the Medici lost power. There's no evidence, meanwhile, that Giuliano or Lorenzo ever read *The Prince*.

Yet the book would go on to much wider acclaim than even Machiavelli had imagined. It remains the best-known guide for acquiring and keeping power. Tyrants around the world have taken his advice, and so have the elected leaders of free nations. It's been borrowed as well by modern authors — like Robert

[420] Machiavelli, *The Prince*, 79.
[421] Machiavelli, *The Prince*, 90.

Greene, who based his own "amoral, cunning, ruthless" bestseller *The 48 Laws of Power* on Machiavelli.[422]

"So universal and valid are the best of these insights," Bryan Magee observed, "that one sees them confirmed wherever human beings jockey for place and preferment, not only in politics but in professional associations of any kind."[423]

Yet the book seems so extreme that some have claimed it wasn't intended to be serious. Was *The Prince* meant to be satirical, mocking the corruption of leaders like Cesare Borgia? Was Machiavelli actually having a laugh at the expense of the Medici family?

After all, at around the same time in Britain, the Catholic philosopher and statesman Thomas More released his own misunderstood masterpiece. Published in 1516, *Utopia* was the story of a fictional island in the New World that boasted a perfect society.

More coined the term *utopia,* which could be interpreted two ways. The Greek word for "a perfect place" is eu-*topos*. But the word for "no place" is the similar sounding ou-*topos*.

Some saw More's made-up "Utopia" as a serious plea for social reform. After all, his island paradise has abolished private property, has free health care and full employment, and enjoys religious tolerance (except for atheists).

Others pointed out that More was unlikely to be serious in endorsing female priests, sun and moon worship, and slavery, which popes had been condemning since the previous century. After all, More would later be executed for opposing Henry VIII's split with the Catholic Church — and was made a saint for his martyrdom.

The fact that the narrator was More himself blurred the issue further. Was this a biting critique of Catholicism, on the eve of the Protestant Reformation? Or was it a tongue-in-cheek reminder that ever since Plato, every plan for a perfect society had been doomed to failure?

Most readers believed Niccolò Machiavelli's own plan was, in fact, genuine. *The Prince* was a long way from the Greeks and the Scholastics, who believed that being good inevitably meant being virtuous. But in this practical new world of might-makes-right, the old rules no longer seemed to apply.

422 "Amoral, cunning, ruthless" — from the book description at the publisher's website: https://sites.prh.com/robertgreenebooks?ref=PRH932BAC1760EB&aid=48045&linkid=PRH932BAC1760EB.

423 Magee, *The Story of Philosophy*, 73.

"If men wanted to be free and to realize their highest nature," observes Arthur Herman, "they were going to have to look somewhere other than politics."[424]

3.

And hereupon it was my Mother Dear
Did bring forth Twins at once, both Me, and Fear.[425]

Thomas Hobbes wrote this verse when he was eighty-four years old. He had decided to set down his autobiography, in Latin elegiac couplets.

The reference here is to his birth, in April 1588. It was apparently a premature delivery, because Hobbes's mother — like many English citizens — was so frightened by the coming of the Spanish Armada that summer.

The mighty Armada was on its way to invade England. Its goal was to overthrow the Protestant ruler of Britain, Queen Elizabeth I, and restore Catholic rule. And it seemed likely to succeed.

It didn't, and not just because of the bravery of British naval hero Sir Francis Drake. Unexpected and powerful west winds off the coast of Scotland and Ireland sank many of the Spanish ships, and the invasion was foiled. Grateful English citizens displayed medals that read "God blew, and they were scattered" to commemorate the victory.[426]

Thomas Hobbes would probably not have worn such a medal. His belief in God, in fact, was something many questioned. But his belief in fear was long-lasting and sincere.

As Hobbes wrote, fear was his "twin" when he was born — and he never escaped that feeling. He lived through the English Civil War and its bloody aftermath, when Oliver Cromwell became the country's military leader. Hobbes became convinced that man's greatest fear is of a violent death — and that we would do just about anything to avoid one.

424 Herman, *The Cave and the Light*, 279.

425 Thomas Hobbes, *The Life of Mr. Thomas Hobbes of Malmesbury Written by Himself in a Latine Poem, and Now Translated into English*, 1680 (Ann Arbor: Text Creation Partnership), https://quod.lib.umich.edu/e/eebo/A44004.0001.001/1:2?rgn=div1.

426 You can see pictures of the "God blew and they were scattered" medals at the Library of Congress website: https://www.loc.gov/collections/sir-francis-drake/articles-and-essays/drake-biography/armada/.

From his experiences, Hobbes developed a political philosophy that owed something to Machiavelli: it was better to plan based on what man *is*, rather than what he *should be*.

And what Hobbes thought man was, in his state of nature — without any laws to govern him — was an ugly thing indeed. He was constantly fighting the war "of every man against every man."[427] In this state of nature, he would forcibly take another man's wife, children, cattle, and land, if he could.

Hobbes imagined a barbaric and blood-soaked landscape, where no possessions could be secure, where no one would enjoy a moment's peace, and where armed conflicts would be the only way to determine society's victors.

The life of man in such a world, Hobbes concluded, would be "solitary, poor, nasty, brutish, and short."[428]

That may be the most famous line from Hobbes's writing. It comes from his 1651 book *Leviathan*. The subtitle is *The Matter, Forme and Power of a Commonwealth Ecclesiasticall and Civil*. But most people just call it "Leviathan," because the title relates so closely to what Hobbes proposed.

In the Bible, Leviathan is a gigantic sea monster. Hobbes chose this creature as a metaphor for his preferred form of government. It might be big, and it might be frightening. But it's better than the alternative: anarchy and violent death.[429]

To avoid these outcomes, man makes a deal. This deal would come to be known as a *social contract*, and Hobbes is generally credited as the philosopher who originated it.

The deal is this: to avoid anarchy and to protect their life and property, men agree to give up their freedom to a sovereign — a ruler. Making a covenant with God, Hobbes thought, was impossible. But an earthly sovereign would agree to protect his subjects, in exchange for their loyalty.

So men give up their right to act however they please. They give up the "war of all against all." In exchange, they get security and protection from a leader whose power is permanent and complete. "For the sovereign is absolute … or else there is no sovereignty at all."[430]

[427] Cahn, *Classics of Western Philosophy*, 490.

[428] Cahn, *Classics of Western Philosophy*, 490.

[429] Abraham Bosse's original frontispiece for Thomas Hobbes's *Leviathan* is an anamorphic depiction of his idea: a gigantic ruler composed of the bodies of his subjects.

[430] Cahn, *Classics of Western Philosophy*, 524.

And if the sovereign turns out to be a tyrant? Well, "the estate of man can never be without some incommodity or another."[431] Some fates, we should remember, are worse than others. After all, even under a harsh ruler, we can enjoy a civil society, rather than the "miseries and horrible calamities that accompany a civil war."[432]

It was a severe philosophy for a severe era. But it was based not just on cynical calculations about politics — but on the views Hobbes had of the universe, as well.

4.

While his political ideas — and even his most famous, frowning portrait — might make him seem like a curmudgeonly grouch, Thomas Hobbes actually had a number of friends.[433] Two of them were the French mathematician Pierre Gassendi and the British scientist Francis Bacon.

Hobbes corresponded with these people and often visited them, as well. And on a trip to Italy in 1636, one of his acquaintances — the astronomer Galileo Galilei — showed him something that opened his eyes.

At the time of this visit, Galileo was under house arrest at his villa in Arcetri. This was the result of his dispute with the Catholic Church over the theory that the earth revolved around the sun.

Galileo had insisted that the experiments he conducted, looking through a telescope in the garden behind his house, proved the Copernican system. Church officials had not agreed

Cardinal Robert Bellarmine cautioned that

> if there were a real proof that the Sun is in the centre of the universe ... then we should have to proceed with great circumspection in explaining passages of Scripture which appear to teach the contrary, and we should rather have to say that we did not understand

[431] Cahn, *Classics of Western Philosophy*, 515.

[432] Cahn, *Classics of Western Philosophy*, 515.

[433] The most famous picture of Hobbes is in the National Portrait Gallery. It was painted by John Michael Wright between 1669 and 1670, when Hobbes was eighty-two years old. His biographer, A. P. Martinich, writes that Hobbes "was above average in height, about six feet tall. In youth, his black hair had earned him the nickname 'Crow'. As he aged, it turned from reddish-white to white. He kept his hair at shoulder length even when the top of his head became bald in the characteristic male pattern. He had a full moustache but only a tuft of whiskers beneath his lower lip." A. P. Martinich, *Thomas Hobbes* (New York: St. Martin's Press, 1997), 7–8.

> them than declare an opinion to be false which is proved to be true. But I do not think there is any such proof since none has been shown to me.[434]

In this respect, Bellarmine was correct: Galileo had *not* proven his assertion, even though it later turned out to be right.

Galileo recanted the idea, and was indignant that he had not been pardoned. God, he wrote, "knows that in this cause for which I suffer, though many might have spoken with more learning, none, not even the ancient Fathers, has spoken with more piety or with greater zeal for the Church than I."[435]

The great astronomer was nearing the end of his life. He was in pain and losing his eyesight, but he had not given up his experiments. And Hobbes was fascinated by Galileo's insistence that all physical bodies were perpetually in motion.

This was a theory that the Catholic philosophers and scientists Jean Buridan and Nicole Oresme had proposed back in the fourteenth century. Galileo would refine this contradiction of Aristotle's belief. But Hobbes, who was haunted by the idea, saw in it something more.

Galileo's universe of perpetual motion, Hobbes thought, could explain more than just heavenly bodies. It could also account for *everything* that occurs in our world.

In short, only material — matter — exists. Man is therefore a kind of machine, and so is his mind. "All mental processes," Hobbes believed, "were to be understood as movements of matter inside an individual's skull."[436]

The pre-Socratic philosophers Democritus and Leucippus had proposed a universe made up of atoms and void. And Epicurus, the founder of the Epicureans, had insisted that "Death is nothing to us," because all it means is that our atoms separate.

But Hobbes went further than these thinkers. He proposed a mechanistic universe, one where Aristotle's Four Causes could be whittled down to just two.

[434] Cardinal Bellarmine's letter to Galileo can be read here: http://law2.umkc.edu/faculty/projects/ftrials/galileo/letterbellarmine.html.

[435] William R, Shea and Mariano Artigas, *Galileo in Rome: The Rise and Fall of a Troublesome Genius* (Oxford: Oxford University Press, 2004), 199.

[436] Magee, *The Story of Philosophy*, 79.

> For him, there are only two kinds of causes, efficient and material causes.... [And] [t]here are two kinds of efficient causes: those that push and those that pull. In pushing motion, the efficient cause is the body that pushes; the material cause is the body pushed. There are no formal or final causes at all; such ideas are not science but myth.[437]

Hobbes had no time for Aristotle, in fact. He considered The Philosopher's *Metaphysics* "absurd," his *Politics* "repugnant," and his *Ethics* "ignorant."[438] These beliefs owed a great deal to Hobbes's view of existence as purely material.

Any talk about "incorporeal substances," Hobbes thought, was a contradiction—whether these were thoughts, or angels, or spirits. The angels and demons of the Bible, he contended, had to be material beings, or else they couldn't exist.

And like many of the philosophers we've seen so far—Christian and otherwise—Hobbes thought that "the nature of God is incomprehensible; that is to say, we understand nothing of What He Is, but only That He Is."[439]

Statements like these—and Hobbes's dim view of human nature—led people to wonder about his religious beliefs. In the village of Westport, where Hobbes grew up, his father had served as a minister in the Church of England—"but not an exemplary one."[440] He once fell asleep during a service after playing cards all Saturday night, fought with another minister outside the church, and finally ran off to London, abandoning his family.

But Hobbes had the support of his uncle Francis, a glover, who helped pay for his education at Oxford. There, he became a tutor to William Cavendish, a future earl of Devonshire. The Cavendish connection allowed Hobbes access to the family's extensive library, as well as to some of the philosophers and scientists he later befriended.

Many of these eminent people were believers. Was Hobbes? Or was he an atheist, as many people have contended?

[437] Martinich, *Thomas Hobbes*, 86.

[438] Rubenstein, *Aristotle's Childen*, 285.

[439] Thomas Hobbes, *Leviathan* (1651), Early English Books Online, https://quod.lib.umich.edu/cgi/t/text/text-idx?c=eebo.

[440] Martinich, *Thomas Hobbes*, 4.

This view was challenged by people who knew Hobbes personally — as well as by Hobbes himself. Others called him a *deist* — someone who believes in a God who does not intervene in the world after creating it.[441]

It would have been unwise for Hobbes to publicly profess atheism, so we'll probably never know the answer for certain. What we can say, however, is that his view of a mechanistic universe led to such questions — and to another troubling consequence.

5.

Does man have free will? It's one of the oldest and most difficult philosophical dilemmas.

The issue was debated intensely after the Big Three philosophers in Greece. The Stoics thought we could not change our fate, which seemed to argue against free will. Epicurus believed in an atomistic universe, which seemed to cast doubt on the idea. But he also said that atoms could sometimes "swerve" unexpectedly, giving us the possibility of choice.

St. Augustine, meanwhile, wrote a lot about free will. He eventually reached the conclusion that we have it — but we need God's grace to fully access it.

The concept of a purely material universe, on the other hand, has a powerful effect on the concept of free will. If every event is caused by a previous event, then everything "becomes part of the meaningless, purposeless chains of efficient causation between material elements recognized by the Mechanical Philosophy."[442]

Aristotle's Four Causes had allowed for free will because they included formal, and especially, final causes. For example, a person could decide, on the spur of the moment, to create a different sort of final cause for an action than the one he originally planned. He might suddenly decide to open a piece of mail and read it, rather than ripping it in half and throwing it in the trash.

[441] While most observers are understandably skeptical about Hobbes's belief in God, A. P. Martinich notes that when Hobbes became seriously ill in 1647, his friend, the French Catholic priest Marin Mersenne, "tried to convert him to Roman Catholicism, but Hobbes remained firmly committed to the Church of England. He gratefully received the Eucharist from an Anglican churchman, John Cosin, and confessed to another Anglican, John Pierson" (Martinich, *Thomas Hobbes*, 13).

[442] Feser, *The Last Superstition*, 209.

But Hobbes's philosophy seemed to eliminate that possibility. It was a kind of *determinism*, "the doctrine that every event has a cause."

> His determinism is consonant with his commitment to the ideal of modern science, according to which all explanations are mechanistic, that is, given in terms of the shapes, sizes and motions of bodies. Non-material entities and final causes are excluded from being acceptable principles of explanation.[443]

Of course, this meant that the "choices" that Hobbes spoke of in books like *Leviathan* were suspect, too. After all, aren't people ultimately going to make predetermined decisions about electing a sovereign — and won't a sovereign also make predetermined decisions about how he'll enforce his rule?

Even in his own lifetime, Hobbes tried to answer this objection. He proposed an idea that would come to be called *compatibilism*: that free will and determinism are actually compatible, and that one does not rule out the other.

In a 1645 debate with John Bramhall, Hobbes argued that "acting freely is compatible with acting of necessity." "People act according to their will; and they would not act if they did not will; but, from these propositions, it neither follows that people can will something other than what they actually will, nor that they can 'will to will.' "[444]

Clearly, it's a complex theory. And classical compatibilists would argue that it offers "a rich picture of freedom"[445] — that it accounts not just for the actions a person performs, but for the actions they *don't* perform, and also for the actions they could never *hope* to perform.

Not surprisingly, as the *Stanford Encyclopedia of Philosophy* notes, it also "failed decisively."[446] It strikes many people as an attempt to have your cake and eat it too: arguing on the one hand that everything is mechanical and predictable, but also trying to preserve the free will that almost everyone believes we have.

Except, perhaps, Hobbes. In *Leviathan,* he had addressed the subject far more directly:

443 Martinich, *Thomas Hobbes*, 198.

444 Martinich, *Thomas Hobbes*, 109.

445 Michael McKenna and Justin D. Coates, "Compatibilism," *Stanford Encyclopedia of Philosophy*, April 26, 2004; revised November 26, 2019, https://plato.stanford.edu/entries/compatibilism/.

446 McKenna and Coates, "Compatibilism."

> And therefore if a man should talk to me of a Round Quadrangle; or Accidents Of Bread In Cheese; or Immaterial Substances; or of A Free Subject; A Free Will; or any Free, but free from being hindred by opposition, I should not say he were in an Errour; but that his words were without meaning; that is to say, Absurd.[447]

6.

Hobbes had actually written *Leviathan* during political exile in France, while England's civil war had raged. He returned home in 1651, at the war's conclusion, as the Lord Protector, Oliver Cromwell, came to power and England temporarily became a republic. *Leviathan* was released that same year, into a turbulent and suspicion-filled environment.

The initial reaction was not so much negative as uneasy. Hobbes quoted Scripture extensively, yet "for all the talk of God, He seems to drop out of the picture."[448] His defense of an absolute sovereign could apply equally to a king, or a military leader like Cromwell.

Brian Duppa, a bishop and advisor to the recently executed King Charles I, wrote, "There are strange mixtures in the book; many things said so well that I could embrace him for it, and many things so wildly and unchristianly, that I could scarce have so much charity for him, as to think he was ever Christian."[449]

Was Hobbes a royalist or a republican? Was he a Christian or an atheist? It was difficult to tell — which was one of the most brilliant things about his book, in such a bitterly divided time. "*Leviathan* seduces its reader with familiar or attractive positions, but in swallowing down the argument, one internalises a set of Hobbesian relationships."[450]

Undoubtedly, many people despised Hobbes and *Leviathan,* but "it solidified his reputation as a philosopher."[451] And that reputation would last to the end of his extremely long life — he reached the age of ninety-one — and survives to this day.

[447] Hobbes, *Leviathan.*

[448] Patricia Springborg, *The Cambridge Companion to Hobbes's* Leviathan, ed. Tom Sorrell (Cambridge: Cambridge University Press, 2007), 442.

[449] Springborg, *The Cambridge Companion to Hobbes's* Leviathan, 442–443.

[450] Springborg, *The Cambridge Companion to Hobbes's* Leviathan, 444.

[451] Martinich, *Thomas Hobbes,* 15.

In the poem that served as his autobiography, Hobbes insisted that "My Life and Writings speak one Congruous Sense." And the final couplet, appropriately enough, references the two concepts that inspired those controversial writings:

I've now Compleated my Eighty fourth year,
And Death approaching, prompts me not to fear.[452]

7.

One of the people who appreciated both Machiavelli and Hobbes was the man people call the Godfather of Science.

Sir Francis Bacon served as the Lord Chancellor of England during the reign of James I, in the early years of the seventeenth century. But he became much better known for his experiments, and for his philosophy. Great scientists from Sir Isaac Newton to Charles Darwin have acknowledged their debt to him.

So did Thomas Hobbes, Bacon's private secretary. Hobbes shared Bacon's empiricism — his belief that we have to depend solely on the evidence of our senses. And he admired the philosophy Bacon constructed out of this belief. It was epitomized by his catchphrase: "Knowledge is power."

But not just a vague power — the power of knowledge for its own sake, like the ancients and Scholastics had believed. Bacon saw knowledge instead as the *practical* power to improve human life.

By adopting the new science Bacon was helping bring about, "there cannot but follow an improvement in man's estate and an enlargement of his power over nature."[453] After Adam and Eve, man had lost both his faith and his dominion over the world. But he could get at least some of it back: "the former by religion and faith, the latter by arts and sciences."[454]

This was a clear distinction: faith and reason should stay in their respective lanes, and religion should let science get on with science. It reflected Bacon's optimism, too. Unlike Machiavelli and Hobbes, he didn't think the worst of his fellow man. And unencumbered by superstition, man's scientific future looked bright.

452 Hobbes, *The Life of Mr. Thomas Hobbes.*

453 Francis Bacon, *The Works of Francis Bacon,* ed. James Spedding, Robert Leslie Ellis, and Douglas Denon Heath (Cambridge: Cambridge University Press, 2011), 247.

454 Bacon, *The Works of Francis Bacon,* 248.

"It would be an unsound fancy and self-contradictory to expect that things which have never yet been done can be done," Bacon wrote in his 1620 book *Novum Organum,* "except by means which have never yet been tried."[455]

To try that which had never been tried, Bacon came up with what we now call the scientific method. It was the "New Instrument" referenced by the book's title.

The first step was to get rid of things that distort our perception. Bacon called these "idols." For example, "idols of the tribe" are weaknesses we have as human beings, like our feelings and prejudices. "Idols of the market place" are the distortions that can be caused by imprecise language.

Our understanding needs to be "thoroughly freed and cleansed"[456] — a mental blank slate. Then we're ready for step two: the collection of data.

We can use the data we gather to make educated guesses about wider similarities in nature. This is the process known as *induction*: coming up with general observations based on specific facts. The database grows as we collect more data and keep testing it.

How will we know that the conclusions, or "axioms," that we get from our data are correct? Because they'll "supply practice with its instruments."[457] In other words, they'll lead to new discoveries. And if we just keep gathering and building, progress will be inevitable.

Bacon saw this method as a replacement for Aristotle's "tainted and corrupted" natural philosophy. Besides, he argued, Aristotle's beliefs were never as popular as they seemed; people were simply peer pressured into accepting them.

Bacon proposed instead a thoroughly secular system that didn't challenge Christianity directly: it just made it irrelevant. "The tendency was, more and more, to limit theology to the comparatively restricted sphere of faith and morals."[458]

This was the inevitable consequence of Duns Scotus and Ockham's insistence that we could only know God by faith alone. It opened the door for

455 Bacon, *The Works of Francis Bacon,* 49.

456 Bacon, *The Works of Francis Bacon,* 70.

457 Bacon, *The Works of Francis Bacon,* 70.

458 George H. Smith, "Freethought and Freedom: Francis Bacon and the Rise of Secularism," Libertarianism.org, May 15, 2015, https://www.libertarianism.org/columns/freethought-freedom-francis-bacon-rise-secularism.

Bacon's empirical science, where turning hard data into new inventions was what mattered.[459]

Bacon's beliefs have led to some historical myths. He never said, as many have claimed, that nature should be "put on the rack" and forced to give up her secrets. In fact, he makes a special point, in *Novum Organum*, to address the fears of those who believe science will "shake the authority of religion."[460]

"If the matter be truly considered," he wrote earnestly, "natural philosophy is, after the word of God, at once the surest medicine against superstition and the most approved nourishment for faith, and therefore she is rightly given to religion as her most faithful handmaid, since the one displays the will of God, the other his power."[461]

But just as it was inevitable that Duns Scotus and Ockham would lead to Bacon, it was also inevitable that Bacon would inspire other scientists who had far less reason to worry about God — now relegated to the margins — and His power.

The cosmos of Machiavelli, Hobbes, and Bacon was, increasingly, "governed by impersonal mechanical laws"[462] — which we could now discover, record, and use to predict and control nature. Faith was affirmed by all three men — but also marginalized. In their view, it had stood in the way of progress long enough.

[459] The famous cautionary tale about Bacon's fetish for new inventions is the one about him stuffing a chicken with snow in an effort to preserve it—and then catching his death of pneumonia in 1626. However, the story, which was spread by Bacon's former secretary Thomas Hobbes, is probably apocryphal.

[460] Bacon, *The Works of Francis Bacon*, 88.

[461] Bacon, *The Works of Francis Bacon*, 89.

[462] Herman, *The Cave and the Light*, 344.

CHAPTER TWELVE

THINGS THINKING THINGS

1.

It's late, and you're drowsing by the fireside.

Steam rises from a cup of tea on the table. Logs crackle on the grate, and sparks leap against the screen.

Woodsmoke carries the faint scent of apples to your nostrils. The heat drifts in waves, from the hearth to the comfortable armchair where you sit. You can feel the warmth on your bare legs, just below your fluffy bathrobe, and you sigh in contentment.

This is just about as good as it gets. Isn't it?

Not if this is just a dream. Which, of course, it could be. You have dreams like this all the time, and then wake up to find yourself in a cold bed, shivering and disappointed. It all felt so real! *But you know your senses can sometimes deceive you.*

That is, if it's your senses *deceiving you, and not someone — or something — else. Think about it: you've seen* The Matrix *a bunch of times. The people in that film weren't just dreaming innocently. They were being* made *to dream by a malevolent power, to keep them ignorant of reality.*

So what if that's what this is all about? What if this dream is the work of an evil genius — a demon! — whose job is to trick you into thinking the reality you dream is real?

What if, in fact, you don't even have a body? Your hands, your eyes, your flesh, your blood — what if it's all an illusion the demon has conjured up?

This is getting really bad. Just like in the film The Matrix, *you'd like to take the blue pill now and go back to sleep, to your dreams — to forget you ever started having these doubts. But you can't. It's too late. You've swallowed the red pill instead. And now you have to see the reality it reveals.*

That reality is pretty bleak. You have no way of knowing whether this is all a simulation, no way of knowing whether it's the work of a demon trying to trick you, and no way of knowing whether you have any physical presence at all.

You are deep, deep, deep in a pit of philosophical despair. Isn't there anything *at all you can hang on to?*

You think. You think some more. And then you realize that there is one thing — one thing only.

You think. *And therefore, you are a "thinking thing." A "thing that thinks."*

It's not much. But it's certain, at least. And it is the light that may, eventually, lead you out of this pit at last.

2.

That's a version of the most famous thought experiment in history. Some people simply call it "Descartes's Demon."

It's the basis of *Discourse on the Method,* a 1637 essay by the French philosopher René Descartes.[463] For many people, it marked the real beginning of modern philosophy, the decisive break with Aristotle and the Scholastics.

[463] Four years after publishing *Discourse on the Method,* Descartes included a reworked version of the argument in his *Meditations on First Philosophy*. The issues in *Discourse,* he wrote, "seemed to me to be so important that I judged they ought to be dealt with more than once" (Cahn, *Classics of Western Philosophy,* 432).

It's one of the most readable and engaging works in Western thought. Like too few philosophers, Descartes was a gifted writer, whose only equals are Plato and St. Augustine. In *Discourse*, he speaks in the first person, inviting the reader into his rooms to experience his dilemma with him. It's easy to like this narrator.

Descartes, like Francis Bacon, had no use for Aristotle, the Scholastics, and their natural philosophy. "The best way of proving the falsity of Aristotle's principles," he wrote, "is to point out that they have not enabled any progress to be made in all the many centuries in which they have been followed."[464]

This was, of course, an absurd statement, which ignored hundreds of years of progress made by Aristotelian thinkers — most of them fellow Catholics. But Descartes was well known for his arrogance. As one of his biographers admits, he was "a self-centered, vainglorious, vindictive man."[465]

But it's also true that "philosophy was in a sorry state in 1637."[466] The pioneering Scholastics were long gone, and their descendants were arguing over minutiae. Humanism and mysticism appealed to increasingly small audiences. The really exciting work seemed either cold-bloodedly cynical (Machiavelli), or more about science than true philosophy (Bacon).

Yet while his ideas were far different than Bacon's, Descartes agreed with him wholeheartedly about the need to get beyond Aristotle for the sake of progress. Both men were after the same *sort* of progress, too: the kind that would make men "the lords and possessors of nature."[467]

Surprisingly, however, *Discourse* doesn't really advance a bold new set of ideas. Instead, it sets out to demolish just about every old idea instead. The cheerful and engaging tone of the essay obscures this fact: the main thing Descartes has to offer is doubt. The title of the Descartes section in Bryan Magee's *The Story of Thought* says it best: his philosophy is "Back to Square One."[468]

The goal, for Descartes, was both simple and daunting. The son of a lawyer and magistrate, Descartes had been educated by the Jesuits. He was a natural

464 René Descartes, *The Philosophical Writings of Descartes*, vol. 1, John Cottingham, Robert Stoothoff, and Dugald Murdoch (Cambridge: Cambridge University Press, 1985), 189.

465 Russell Shorto, *Descartes' Bones. A Skeletal History of the Conflict between Faith and Reason* (New York: Vintage Books, 2008), 33.

466 Peter Kreeft, *Socrates' Children*, vol. 3, *Modern Philosophers* (Elk Grove Village, IL: Word on Fire, 2022, e-book), ch. 55.

467 Descartes, *The Philosophical Writings of Descartes*, vol. 1, 142–143.

468 Magee, *The Story of Philosophy*, 84.

mathematician — not quite as advanced as his contemporary Sir Isaac Newton, but brilliant enough to one day invent analytic geometry, which is sometimes called Cartesian geometry in his honor. At college, he studied law, according to his father's wishes.

But he was frustrated by what he saw as a lack of certainty in most sorts of knowledge. In math, answers were dependable and precise. How could he apply those principles to other fields of study?

So after graduation, Descartes "entirely abandoned the study of letters, and resolved no longer to seek any other science than the knowledge of myself, or of the great book of the world."[469] He traveled widely, joined the Dutch army, and became a military engineer.

One bitterly cold night in November 1619, while stationed in Germany, Descartes shut himself in a small room with a ceramic furnace. Dozing in the warmth, he had three dreams. Some argue they were likely hallucinations, but Descartes believed he'd been visited by a divine presence.

He emerged the next day with two ideas developing. One was of a type of geometry based on a coordinate system, which would later become analytic geometry. The other was a way to apply this mathematical system to philosophy.

To do this, he employed a tactic similar to the first step of Francis Bacon's scientific method. He resolved to cleanse his palate: he would strip away every bit of knowledge that he couldn't verify.

"My design was singly to find ground of assurance," he explained, "and cast aside the loose earth and sand, that I might reach the rock or the clay."[470] Descartes would descend, in stages, into this philosophical pit that he dug.

The first step down took him in the opposite direction of Bacon. Descartes quickly eliminated the evidence of his senses, which, he noted, can "sometimes deceive us."[471] Far from being an unbiased source of information, sensory evidence is filled with errors: optical illusions, misheard sounds, tricks of the touch and tongue.

In the second step, Descartes acknowledged that dreams can often seem more lifelike than real life. So he couldn't be sure that what he thought was reality was actually happening.

And third, and worst of all, Descartes had to admit that if he were dreaming his life, it was also possible that this dream was being created by "an evil genius,

[469] Descartes, *The Philosophical Writings of Descartes*, vol. 1, 115.

[470] Descartes, *The Philosophical Writings of Descartes*, vol. 1, 124–125.

[471] Descartes, *The Philosophical Writings of Descartes*, vol. 1, 172.

supremely powerful and clever, who has directed his entire effort at deceiving me."[472] Things seemed hopeless.

Then Descartes hit bedrock. He realized that even if everything he was experiencing was a lie, he was still capable of thought. The familiar phrase in Latin is *Cogito ergo sum* — usually translated as "I think, therefore I am."

That he was a "thinking thing" was such a solid idea "that all the most extravagant suppositions of the sceptics" couldn't shake it. So Descartes believed he could "accept it without scruple as the first principle of the philosophy I was seeking."[473]

This gave Descartes a basis upon which to build his new system of knowledge. However, it didn't get him out of the pit he'd dug for himself. To escape, he was going to have to call on an old friend for help.

3.

As we saw in chapter 8, the medieval philosopher St. Anselm had proposed the ontological argument for God's existence. If we can imagine a perfect being, but it doesn't exist, then it isn't perfect — so it must exist.

This attempt to use reason to show that God is real had been rejected by other philosophers, including St. Thomas Aquinas. But Descartes turned to it now to get himself out of the hole.

There had to be "some other, more perfect being on which I depended," Descartes reasoned, "and from which I had acquired all that I possessed."[474] He used math to emphasize this point: "Thus I concluded that it is at least as certain as any geometrical proof that God, who is this perfect being, is or exists."[475]

Now Descartes began to ascend the steps of the ladder. If God is a perfect being, then He wouldn't deceive me. Therefore, I can trust that I am real, and therefore, that the material world is real. Finally, daylight.

The immediate problem was solved, but several others now remained. Descartes acknowledged one of them: that without this belief in God, we're stuck back at the bottom of the pit, knowing only that we are "thinking things."

"For in the first place, what I took just now as a rule, namely that everything we conceive very clearly and very distinctly is true, is assured only for

472 Cahn, *Classics of Western Philosophy*, 439.

473 Descartes, *The Philosophical Writings of Descartes*, vol. 1, 126–127.

474 Descartes, *The Philosophical Writings of Descartes*, vol. 1, 128.

475 Descartes, *The Philosophical Writings of Descartes*, vol. 1, 129.

the reasons that God is or exists, that he is a perfect being, and that everything in us comes from him," he wrote.[476]

This, as Edward Feser notes, was ironic. The modern philosophers' effort to separate faith from reason now "made a direct appeal to God *more* necessary than it had been in the Scholastic view."[477]

And while we could trust our senses enough to conduct experiments in the material world, we still couldn't *know* that world in any meaningful way. Descartes had divided the world into two categories: mind and matter. But what the link between those two worlds was — and how individual minds could actually communicate — remained unclear.

This has become known as a "mind-body problem." Since Descartes was the one who reopened the gap between the mind and the body — a gap that Plato had famously opened, and which Aristotle and the Scholastics had closed — credit for it is often given to him.

"Cartesian dualism" is a dilemma that has haunted philosophy — and humanity — ever since. As Russell Sholto points out, "The problem is so elemental and yet so sweeping that attempts to solve it today run across many disciplines, from computer science to neuroscience to psychology."[478]

"Haunted" is an appropriate term. The twentieth-century British philosopher Gilbert Ryle invented the phrase "the ghost in the machine"[479] to describe Descartes's dualism. "The mind is its own place," Ryle wrote of Descartes and his beliefs, "and in his inner life each of us lives the life of a ghostly Robinson Crusoe."[480]

This was the cost of having a mechanistic universe, where matter obeyed mathematical laws and could be manipulated as we chose. Ryle described the dilemma of a religious believer like Descartes. He wanted to believe that the physical

[476] Descartes, *The Philosophical Writings of Descartes*, vol. 1, 130.

[477] Feser, *The Last Superstition*, 198.

[478] Shorto, *Descartes' Bones*, 178.

[479] Gilbert Ryle, *The Concept of Mind* (New York: Barnes & Noble, 1949), 13.

[480] Ryle, *The Concept of Mind*, 12. Ryle's point in "Descartes' Myth," the first chapter of his book *The Concept of Mind*, was that Descartes had made a "category mistake" in claiming mind and body are separate. "These expressions do not indicate two different species of existence," Ryle wrote. Instead, "they indicate two different senses of 'exist.'" Ryle used the example of someone who visits a university, sees all the different buildings, offices, and playing fields, and then asks, "But where's the *university*?" The person made a category mistake by looking for another building, rather than the collective that all the grounds represent (Ryle, *The Concept of Mind*, 17).

world is mechanical, for the sake of science, yet couldn't accept the "discouraging rider to those claims": that the mind also works like clockwork.[481]

So Descartes preserved the mind's independence by splitting it from the body. Since then, the mind has served many scientists and philosophers as a "rug." Anything "that doesn't fit the mechanistic model" can be conveniently swept under it and "treated as a mere projection."[482]

The opponents of Descartes saw what was likely to happen: materialism would win out by default. This solution to the mind-body problem was to eliminate it entirely—by claiming that *everything* in the world, including the mind, is material.

Thomas Hobbes, who was no fan of Descartes, proposed this very idea of pure materialism. Others would follow. It was just too tempting: it completely cleared the way for modern science, by eliminating not just faith but reason as well. Now there would be no opponents at all to stand in the way of progress.

It wasn't that simple, of course: the mind is "notoriously resistant to scientific explanation."[483] And Descartes, of course, did not agree with pure materialism. But he struggled for the rest of his life to find an answer to the mind-body problem.

At one point, he proposed that the pineal gland, located in the center of the brain, was the missing link. And in his final book, Descartes suggested that the answer was a sort of "connective tissue" between mind and body—which might be defined as "passion," or perhaps "heart."

But "the hard fact of modernity is that from the time Descartes separated the two, nobody has yet come up with a definitive, universally satisfying way to solder mind and body together again."[484]

However, Descartes was definitely successful in one way. He turned the focus of philosophy to the branch called *epistemology*—what can we know, and how can we know it? Many who followed him, in fact, "came to think of philosophy as, essentially, epistemology."[485]

And the mind-body problem didn't stop Descartes from attracting followers. In fact, as Cartesian thought grew in popularity, Descartes was sometimes

[481] Ryle, *The Concept of Mind*, 15.

[482] Feser, *The Last Superstition*, 193.

[483] Feser, *The Last Superstition*, 191.

[484] Shorto, *Descartes' Bones*, 179.

[485] Magee, *The Story of Philosophy*, 89.

accused of atheism. His most prominent opponent was the Dutch Calvinist theologian Gysbert Voetius, the rector of the university at Utrecht.

Voetius was dismayed by the rise of Cartesianism in Utrecht, and attacked it—and its founder. Descartes responded in kind, and soon a bitter personal battle ensued that would take up much of the last decade of Descartes's life. His philosophy was banned in Utrecht, and he was charged with libel.

Machiavelli, Hobbes, and Bacon had all been called atheists for abandoning Scholasticism. But Descartes was apparently the most sincere believer of the quartet, so that criticism must have stung.

"Descartes himself was so devout in his faith yet so certain of the legitimacy of reason-based investigations of the natural world," Russell Shorto writes, "that the division of reality into two distinct halves seemed the only logical conclusion."[486]

Of all the invented problems of modern philosophy, it was this one—proposed by a believing Catholic intent on "building a wall around the fortress of faith"[487]—that would likely do the most damage to belief.

4.

It's always dangerous to apply biography to philosophy. And yet, some of the events of Descartes's life are hard to separate from his work.

While he may have favored the mind over matter, Descartes was a serious empirical scientist. He treated the body as a machine—and therefore, the answers to bodily problems were there in the body, just waiting to be found.

He performed hundreds of dissections—of everything from rabbits and cows to dogs and eels. While living in Amsterdam, he visited a local butcher and brought home freshly killed animals for his experiments. Descartes opened up their heads, hoping to unlock the secrets of memory and imagination—and perhaps even to find the connection between mind and body.

But there was an even holier grail he was searching for: the secret of eternal life. He had become convinced that "he could crack the body's code and extend the human lifespan to as much as a thousand years."[488] Being Descartes, he boldly shared this hope, and other philosophers and European royals waited anxiously for news of his progress.

[486] Shorto, *Descartes' Bones*, 62.
[487] Shorto, *Descartes' Bones*, 62.
[488] Shorto, *Descartes' Bones*, 32.

Descartes had been a sickly child, so his preoccupation with bodily health made sense. Throughout most of his life, he also kept his distance from most people. He had, as far as historians can tell, only one intimate relationship.

That was with Helena Jans, the maid of an Amsterdam friend of Descartes. In October 1634, she became pregnant with the philosopher's child. The girl, named Francine, was born the next year. While Descartes couldn't officially claim paternity, he did live with mother and child. The family stayed undercover: Jans posed as his servant and Francine as his niece.

When Francine was five, however, tragedy struck: she contracted scarlet fever. Descartes reportedly returned home from a trip just in time to hold his daughter as she died. For this proud yet solitary man, the loss was devastating. "He mourned her with a tenderness that made him feel that true philosophy cannot suppress nature. He declared that her death had left him with the greatest regret he had ever felt in his life."[489]

Perhaps his lingering grief was what helped convince him, in 1649, to accept a post in Sweden, as a sort of philosophical tutor to Queen Christina. It didn't go well. He hated the cold, as well as the 5 a.m. start time that Christina demanded for her lessons. And the mercurial queen quickly grew bored with her new instructor. Descartes felt isolated, frustrated, and feared his childhood sickliness would return.

The following year, it did. Descartes stubbornly refused to see the doctor, and by the time he finally gave in, the illness could not be treated. The man who hoped to unlock the secret of longevity was dead at age fifty-three.

But he still commanded a fiercely loyal following. In fact, the battle for Descartes's remains would span countries and centuries — a story expertly told in Russell Shorto's 2006 book *Descartes' Bones.*

And one of the philosopher's followers appears to have been the source of a truly bizarre story that began circulating after Descartes's death.

The tale goes like this. On a voyage at sea, a curious captain hears noises coming from a large trunk belonging to Descartes. The captain is horrified at what he finds when he opens it: a mechanical girl that suddenly sits up in the trunk. Believing it's a demon, the captain throws the offensive object into the ocean.

[489] Minsoo Kang, "The Mechanical Daughter of René Descartes," *Modern Intellectual History* 14, no. 3 (2016): 633–660. https://doi.org/10.1017/s147924431600024x.

In some versions of the story, the robot girl is actually named Francine. But the connection to Descartes's illegitimate daughter is already clear enough. So is the link to the mechanistic philosophy of Descartes. It's the perfect metaphor for his idea that the body is just a machine.

It turns out that the source of this fable may have been a Carthusian monk named Bonaventure d'Argonne, who recounted the story in a 1699 book. He was a supporter of Descartes. And the only thing stranger than the story itself is that Argonne was apparently using it to protect the philosopher's reputation.

The *robot,* Argonne suggested, had been real. The actual "tall tale," he told his readers, was that Descartes had a daughter out of wedlock. People who saw the robot, he explained, had nastily inferred that Descartes had a human daughter. "So Descartes's moral failing is covered up with a respectable explanation of his mechanical creation."[490]

Although Descartes was interested in automatons and mentions them in his writing, it's extremely doubtful any such robot existed. But it's not hard to understand how someone who'd read Descartes describe the human body as "a machine made by the hands of God"[491] might believe such a fantastic story.

There's also something desperately sad about this legend. It's been appropriated numerous times over the centuries, and has become more and more popular in recent years. The most modern versions sometimes take on grotesque characteristics: the doll, it's suggested, was not just a robot but a kind of sex surrogate as well.

A new image of Descartes has emerged: one that "not only depicts the thinker primarily as a significant contributor to the Scientific Revolution, but also anachronistically as a proto-cybernetic theorist who can be imagined as a maker of a beautiful and uncanny automaton."[492]

Yet that sci-fi reboot obscures the private tragedy of a man who spent his last years mourning the loss of his very real daughter — a man who was attacked repeatedly for his beliefs, and who died alone in a foreign land.

[490] As Minsoo Kang writes regarding the fable of Descartes' mechanical daughter, "It is impossible to know whether this storyteller actually existed, or if Argonne fabricated the tale himself, using the literary convention of a heard tale, or how seriously it is meant to be taken. While Argonne supported Cartesian ideas, his characterization of the narrator as *'un Cartesian fort zélé'* seems to indicate that we are supposed to take the story with a grain of salt, as nothing more than an amusing anecdote." (Kang, "The Mechanical Daughter of René Descartes.")

[491] Descartes, *The Philosophical Writings of Descartes,* vol. 1, 99.

[492] Kang, "The Mechanical Daughter of René Descartes."

The mind-body problem has taunted philosophers ever since it was reopened in 1637. But in the end, there's no one it may have been a bigger problem for than René Descartes himself.

5.

There would be several other noteworthy rationalist philosophers during the seventeenth century. Most of them could be found on the European continent — in France, Holland, and Germany. Like Descartes, many of them were also great mathematicians.

Ever since the days of Pythagoras, the certainty of numbers had fascinated philosophers, including Plato. And the connection between math and rationalism — which both valued reason rather than the senses — is direct.

An exception to this rule was the rationalist Dutch thinker Baruch Spinoza. He made his living grinding lenses for glasses — and also for new scientific devices like microscopes and telescopes. Spinoza could have been a professor of philosophy at the University of Heidelberg, but he turned the job down: he was more interested in "philosophizing 'in accordance with his own mind.'"[493]

Following his own mind ensured that Spinoza remained a solitary figure. Born in 1632 in Amsterdam to a Portuguese family, he was given an orthodox Jewish upbringing and education. But at age twenty-four he was expelled from the Jewish community for his "abominable heresies" and "monstrous deeds."[494]

This expulsion took place during a solemn ceremony punctuated by the blowing of a great horn and the gradual extinguishing of candles. The elders intoned that Spinoza should be "accursed by day, and accursed by night."[495] The Lord should never pardon him, and his name should be blotted out from the sky.

Perhaps in keeping with this last direction, Spinoza took the Latin name *Benedict* after his expulsion. But the "extraordinary harshness"[496] of his ostracism — called a writ of *herem* — was noteworthy. Why did the community react so strongly?

[493] Magee, *The Story of Philosophy*, 90.

[494] Steven M. Nadler, *Spinoza and Medieval Jewish Philosophy* (Cambridge: Cambridge University Press, 2014), 3.

[495] Kreeft, *Socrates' Children*, vol. 3, ch. 57.

[496] Nadler, *Spinoza and Medieval Jewish Philosophy*, 3.

Spinoza's biographer Stephen Nadler believes it was the result of the "bold philosophical, theological, and religious views that Spinoza would begin expressing in his written works within a couple of years."[497]

These views were a long way from Cartesian dualism. In fact, Spinoza's conception of God denied that there was any separation between mind and matter — or that there was any separation in the universe at all.

In his *Ethics*, published posthumously in 1677, Spinoza defined God as "a being absolutely infinite — that is, a substance consisting in infinite attributes, of which each expresses eternal and infinite essentiality."[498]

This belief, in the view of many, was *pantheism* — the idea that God and the universe are one and the same thing. It was a view that Parmenides had suggested, back in the pre-Socratic days and which the Stoics had later held. It was also similar to the Hindu belief, in the Upanishads, that human beings are drops of water in a great ocean — and that our mistake comes when we think of ourselves as separate from that ocean instead of at one with it.

This view had been rejected by the monotheistic religions. It seemed to take away the idea that God had created the world — since He *was* the world. And it led inevitably to another question: In a world where everything is really just a *single* thing, how can free will be possible?

According to Spinoza, it couldn't be. "In the mind there is no absolute or free will; but the mind is determined to wish this or that by a cause, which has also been determined by another cause, and this last by another cause, and so on to infinity," he wrote.[499]

If we think we have free will, it's understandable — but mistaken. "Experience teaches us no less clearly than reason, that men believe themselves to be free, simply because they are conscious of their actions," Spinoza wrote, "and unconscious of the causes whereby those actions are determined."[500]

These views probably won Spinoza no friends among the Jewish community. Neither, it seems, did his thoughts on the immortality of the soul. He believed that the mind survives death — but not necessarily in an individual form. In this respect, his beliefs resemble those of the medieval Jewish

[497] Nadler, *Spinoza and Medieval Jewish Philosophy*, 13.

[498] Benedict de Spinoza. *The Ethics*, Project Gutenberg, last updated December 11, 2017, https://www.gutenberg.org/files/3800/3800-h/3800-h.htm.

[499] Spinoza, *The Ethics*.

[500] Spinoza, *The Ethics*.

philosopher Moses Maimonides, who imagined our consciousness being absorbed back into a single entity after death.

Simply put, "God is the cause of all things, which are in him."[501] Whether man has free will depends on whether he accepts this truth. If he does, "he will be more completely conscious of himself and of God; in other words, he will be more perfect and blessed."[502] We shouldn't be afraid, because what will happen, will happen regardless. Only by resisting can we make ourselves unhappy.

"If the way which I have pointed out as leading to this result seems exceedingly hard, it may nevertheless be discovered," Spinoza concluded. But "all things excellent are as difficult as they are rare."

One person who apparently overcame those difficulties was the twentieth-century scientist Albert Einstein. "I believe in Spinoza's God who reveals himself in the orderly harmony of what exists," Einstein once said when asked about his religious beliefs, "not in a God who concerns himself with fates and actions of human beings."[503]

Spinoza died young, at age forty-four — most likely because of years of breathing in dust from grinding lenses. Apparently, he lived up to his own stoic, determinist philosophy. "On the last day of his life he was entirely calm, not exalted, like Socrates in the *Phaedo*, but conversing, as he would on any other day, about matters of interest to his interlocutor."[504]

Did his belief that the world is how it has to be, and that nothing can change it, finally offer him comfort or despair? That's a question even more challenging than Spinoza's deterministic philosophy.

6.

The opposite of Spinoza, personality-wise, would probably be Gottfried Leibniz.

Leibniz got, and deserved, notoriety. He was an intellectual prodigy, a true polymath. And like Descartes, he was a pioneering mathematician. Not only did he invent differential and integral calculus independently of Sir Isaac Newton, he actually published his version first. (Consequently, Leibniz was accused of

501 Buckingham, *The Philosophy Book*, 126.

502 Spinoza, *The Ethics*.

503 Albert Einstein, *The Ultimate Quotable Einstein*, ed. Alice Calaprice (Princeton, NJ: Princeton University Press, 2013), 325.

504 Russell, *A History of Western Philosophy*, 574.

plagiarism. While the charge was probably false, the damage to his reputation was permanent.)

If he'd also bothered to publish his version of mathematical logic, it might have sped up developments in that field by a century or more. This bothered Bertrand Russell, who was one of the people who ended up developing the system Leibniz abandoned.

Russell believed Leibniz had frittered away his gifts trying to publish work "designed to win the approbation of princes and princesses"—like Princess Caroline of Ansbach, whom Leibniz tutored.[505]

The book in question was Leibniz's *Theodicy*, which was published in 1710. It was the only volume of his work to appear in his lifetime—though he published many essays and articles, such as those that contained his calculus—and it suggested that we are living in the best of all possible worlds. Russell was one of many who disagreed.

"The consequence is that there are two systems of philosophy which may be regarded as representing Leibniz," complained Russell. The first, his published work, "was optimistic, orthodox, fantastic, and shallow; the other, which has been slowly unearthed from his manuscripts ... was profound, coherent, largely Spinozistic, and amazingly logical."[506]

Leibniz recognized his own lack of discipline. He once described the chaos of his note-keeping, and how it was often faster for him just to do the work over again than to search through his unindexed papers. So it's perhaps amazing that any of his writing reached us at all.

But he was also, as Russell suggested, an optimist. "Leibniz's goal was not modest; it was to synthesize philosophy and science within a Christian moral framework."[507] And by doing so, he believed—like all the modernist philosophers—that we could improve the human condition.

Born in Leipzig, Germany, in 1646, Leibniz established his genius early. His father was a professor of moral theology at Leipzig University. And from boyhood, he had the run of his father's extensive library.

505 Russell, *A History of Western Philosophy*, 581.

506 Russell, *A History of Western Philosophy*, 581.

507 Marc E. Bobro, "The Optimistic Science of Leibniz," *New Atlantis* (2014). https://www.thenewatlantis.com/publications/the-optimistic-science-of-leibniz.

At age fourteen, he enrolled at the university. At seventeen, he earned his master's degree in philosophy, and at eighteen, his law degree. (He wanted to get his doctorate in law but was refused because he was too young.)

No matter. By nineteen, Leibniz had published his first book. And at age twenty-one, he was offered a university professorship, but turned it down.

Instead, he wound up working for the royal House of Hanover, as a courier, diplomat, historian, librarian, and court adviser — while developing a series of mathematical discoveries in his spare time. He also perfected a "calculating machine" and laid the theoretical groundwork for today's computers.

It's not surprising, then, that the philosophy Leibniz developed was so indebted to math and logic. As his *Discourse on Metaphysics* puts it, "God Does Nothing Which Is Not Orderly and It Is Not Even Possible to Imagine Events That Are Not Regular."[508]

The philosophy that Bertrand Russell criticized — the work that won Leibniz his fame — actually contains one of the most forward-looking concepts of the seventeenth century. In the same way that Descartes anticipated fields like robotics and artificial intelligence, Leibniz foresaw today's fascination with alternate reality.

His main idea begins with logic. There are two kinds of truths: *truths of reason* and *truths of fact*. A truth of reason is impossible to contradict. For example, if we say, "Triangles always have three sides," we don't have to examine this statement further. It is a *necessary* truth.

But a truth of fact, on the other hand, *does* need to be verified. It is a *contingent* truth, because it might have been otherwise. If someone says, "My neighbor has three children," then we would have to confirm this fact. It doesn't *have* to be true. The neighbor could have one child, or two children, or no children at all.

Leibniz insisted that every contingent truth — every truth that depends on something else to be true — is subject to what he called the "Principle of Sufficient Reason." And each contingent truth has a cause. There must be a *reason* why the neighbor has three children, instead of one, two, or none.

But God, as an all-powerful being, can already see *all* those other possible worlds — the ones where my neighbor had one child, or two, or none. Imagine all the contingent truths in the world, and now imagine separate realities where each of these things could be true. It's an almost limitless multiverse.

[508] Cahn, *Classics of Western Philosophy*, 605.

However, Leibniz pointed out, God *didn't* create any of those alternate realities. He created this one instead.

So, because "in the Ideas of God there is an infinite number of possible universes, and as only one of them can be actual, there must be a sufficient reason for the choice of God, which leads Him to decide upon one rather than another." Therefore, our reason tells us that we must live in the best of all possible worlds — because God's "goodness makes Him choose it, and His power makes Him produce it."[509]

This idea of "the best of all possible worlds" was the subject of Leibniz's *Theodicy*. He coined the term himself — a combination of the Greek words *theos* (god) and *dikē* (justice). The book was really an attempt to solve the problem of evil: How can a perfect God allow evil to exist?

Leibniz's answer drew on St. Augustine's belief that God is not the cause of evil, and that out of evil God can create a greater good. The twist was casting God in the role of ultimate mathematician. Imagine Dr. Strange, at the end of the Marvel Comics film *Avengers: Infinity War*, precisely calculating all future possibilities and probabilities of the battle with the villain Thanos.

Being able to view every possible alternate reality, God chose this one. And whatever evil is in it — even the evil of Judas, who betrayed Christ — "the sequence of things in which that sinner is included is the most perfect among all possible sequences."[510]

This view, however, was mocked by other philosophers, most notably the prolific French author and public intellectual Voltaire. He turned Leibniz into the character of Dr. Pangloss in his satirical 1759 novel *Candide*.

As increasingly terrible things happen to the innocent Candide and his tutor Pangloss, the doctor holds fast to his belief that "it's impossible that things would not be as they in fact are. Because everything is for the best."[511]

Even when Pangloss becomes a filthy beggar, his face horribly scarred by syphilis, he remains upbeat. He tells Candide that syphilis was originally

[509] Gottfried Leibniz, "Monadology" (1714), Oliver Knill, Harvard University, January 7, 2017, https://people.math.harvard.edu/~knill/various/monadology/index.html#:~:text=known%20in%20another.

[510] Cahn, *Classics of Western Philosophy*, 624.

[511] Voltaire, *Candide, Or, Optimism*, trans. Burton Raffel (New Haven, CT: Yale University Press, 2005), 17.

brought back from the New World. And he's grateful — because if Columbus had never traveled there, Europeans would have never discovered chocolate!

The most famous dig at Leibniz comes when Candide — "horror-stricken, overcome, covered with blood, shaking, said to himself — 'If this is the best of all possible worlds, what are the others like?' "[512]

It was easy for skeptics to make fun of this part of Leibniz's philosophy. His concept of monads was harder to lampoon. In fact, it was simply harder to *understand*. Read a dozen different philosophy books, and you'll find a dozen different descriptions.

The term *monad* is based on the Greek word *monas*, which means "unit." For Leibniz, *monads* were the building blocks of reality. They are the simplest substance possible.

In his book *Monadology*, Leibniz described monads this way: "Now where there are no parts, neither extension, nor shape, nor divisibility is possible. And these monads are the true atoms of nature and, in a word, the elements of things."[513]

Monads may sound like atoms, but they aren't, because they have no shape, size, or physical presence. Furthermore, they can't interact with one another: they "have no windows through which anything could enter them or depart from them."[514] And each monad is completely unique.

To make things even more complicated, Leibniz thought that people and animals have one dominant monad that controls the others in their bodies. This dominant monad is similar to the idea of a soul.

Each monad is like a "mirror of the universe."[515] It contains not just perceptions of the entire universe, but every possibility from all the alternate realities out there. In this way, all monads are essentially the same: what makes each monad different is "the point of view from which it expresses the universe."[516]

The most controversial aspect of Leibniz's monad theory is the idea that each monad is programmed by God to perform its intended function.

This was a concept Leibniz described as "pre-established harmony."[517] It was his answer to the mind-body problem Descartes had reintroduced. How do

512 Voltaire, *Candide*, 19.
513 Leibniz, "Monadology."
514 Leibniz, "Monadology."
515 Leibniz, "Monadology."
516 Cahn, *Classics of Western Philosophy*, 600.
517 Leibniz, "Monadology."

the mind and body interact? They don't, because monads can't interact with one another. God's programming just makes it seem like they're doing so.

"Pre-established harmony" would seem to suggest that Leibniz didn't really believe in free will. He argued that he did, but his argument sounds a lot like Spinoza's: we have freedom ... to accept that we don't really have free will.

Leibniz's vision of a perfectly orderly universe didn't get as much attention as it might have, in part because of his disorderly writing habits.[518] *Monadology* didn't appear until after his death in 1716, and the cataloging of his scattered work — which includes some fifteen thousand letters — has been such a monumental job that it has stretched into the present day.

During his lifetime, Leibniz's reputation was also suspect. Besides the accusations that he'd plagiarized Newton's work, his religious faith — like that of every other modern philosopher we've seen so far — was questioned. In Hanover, he was accused of being a *Löwenix* — someone who "believes nothing." Despite his royal connections and epistolary friendships, there were few guests at his funeral.

But perhaps more than any other modern philosopher, Leibniz believed sincerely in the idea of progress. Even if that progress is preordained, his view that things can and will get better — compared to the doubt of Descartes and the resignation of Spinoza — might make him seem an appealing alternative.

7.

The men in the coach are laughing about the money they lost last night.

This is a frequent conversation. Gambling is a favorite pastime, and cards and dice keep things interesting on this trip.

518 Leibniz's harmonious universe also sounds a little like the one proposed by his mathematical rival, Sir Isaac Newton. Newton's laws of gravity seemed to explain all physical phenomena, and in the view of some, turned God into a sort of cosmic watchmaker. But Leibniz criticized this idea. He felt Newton's laws of gravity didn't give God enough credit.

According to [this] doctrine, God Almighty wants to wind up his watch from time to time: otherwise it would cease to move. He had not, it seems, sufficient foresight to make it a perpetual motion.

The problem with the Newtonian picture, according to Leibniz, is not, as a contemporary reader might assume, that God becomes a detached watchmaker, indifferent to the details of his creation. Rather, according to Leibniz, Newton's watchmaker-God is too directly involved in his creation because his creation is imperfect.

In other words, having God perform miracles — winding his watch "to supply the wants of nature" — implied an imperfect creator. And that, Leibniz felt, was unacceptable (Bobro, "The Optimistic Science of Leibniz").

Artus Gouffier, the Duke de Roannez, is the host. Just twenty-five years old, he's the governor of Poitou, a province in the west of France. His coach is traveling through the region so the duke can survey the lands he oversees.

Another young gambler in the coach is Damien Mitton, a financier. His wife is seven months pregnant, yet he's made it clear he'd rather be on this pleasure trip than at home with her. But the conversation is dominated by the oldest, most cynical member of the party.

This is Antoine Gombaud, who calls himself the chevalier de Méré. He adopted the title "chevalier" for his writing — he's an amateur poet — and, partly through his own insistence, it stuck. He's loud, boisterous, and seems to know something about everything. It's obvious he loves an audience, and the younger men in the coach seem to be eating it up.

Now in his forties, de Méré is a former soldier who's trying to recast himself as an intellectual. One of his hobbies is math; his other, even more passionate pursuit, is gambling. He lost the most money last night, and he's trying to work out why.

Finally, he turns to the fourth man in the carriage, who's been silent so far.

"Maybe Pascal can tell us the answer," de Méré says with a smirk.

Everyone looks at Blaise Pascal, the one person in this coach who doesn't belong. He's short and pale, with a high forehead and wispy mustache. He's been sickly since he was a boy, and at this moment, the cancer that will kill him before he's forty years old is probably beginning to eat its way through his stomach.

The duke was a friend of Pascal's as a child, when they were neighbors in Paris, and treats him kindly. But de Méré and Mitton have been teasing Pascal throughout the trip. While they play dice, Pascal sits hunched over, scribbling on strips of paper. And when he does want to talk — surprisingly loudly for such a slight man — it's always about math.

True, de Méré considers himself a mathematician too. But it's boring to drone on and on about numbers at the gaming tables. Now, however, this odd little man might be able to solve a problem that's been bothering the chevalier.

"Here's the thing," he begins with a smile. Mitton watches de Méré closely, to see if this is a jest, and if he's supposed to laugh. "How many times would I have to throw a pair of dice to make it worth my while to bet on throwing two sixes?"

This is no joke. The chevalier has realized that when he bets on throwing a six in four tosses of a single dice, his odds are favorable. But when he bets on throwing two *sixes with a* pair *of dice, over* eight *tosses, the odds seem to get worse — much worse than he thinks they should. And therefore, he's been losing money. Why?*

Pascal calculates for a few moments, then responds. The mistake de Méré has been making is a small one, but it has major ramifications.

When two dice are rolled instead of one, de Méré's odds of success drop from just above 50 percent — which is how he's been winning when he bets on single dice — to just below 50 percent — which is why he's been losing. The two dice would have to be thrown at least twenty-five times, Pascal explains, to raise the odds above 50 percent again, and make it worthwhile for de Méré to bet.

The older man smiles. He'll use this information the next time he's at the table.

And Blaise Pascal smiles, too. Over the next year of 1654, in a series of letters with another great mathematician, Pierre de Fermat, he'll expand this question into an entirely new science. Probability will change the way the world manages risk — not just in gambling, but in every profession.

More importantly, he'll soon have an answer for another problem of de Méré's. This will happen a few months later, when Pascal visits his friend the duke again.

When Pascal arrives, the duke is laughing over a letter he's just received from de Méré. The worldly chevalier is poking fun at all the dull Christians he knows. "Would God really want such narrow people to spend eternity in Heaven with him?" de Méré asks.

Life, he continues, is just a game to be played well, like dice or cards. Trying to learn more about God, de Méré says, seems pointless.

Blaise Pascal will have none of this. As much as talking about math animates him, makes him seem bigger and stronger, he now seems to be on fire.

"You must wager!" he tells the duke. "It is not optional."

The duke drops the letter in surprise. "I-I don't understand."

"Your faith is a wager," Pascal repeats, "and you're already playing this game by being alive. So what will you choose?"

"I've attended church all my life," the duke objects, "but I've never known if God is there. How can you prove that God is real?"

Pascal shakes his head. "I can't. If there is a God, He is infinitely incomprehensible. Reason can decide nothing here."

The duke, normally good-natured, explodes. "How can you ask me to choose, then?"

The mathematician holds up his hands. "Even if you fail to choose, you're making a choice. So let's weigh the gain and the loss in wagering that God exists. If you gain, you gain all; if you lose, you lose nothing. Wager, then, without hesitation that He is."

"Fine." The duke shrugs. "So I'll just say that I believe, even if I don't."

"That won't work." Pascal stubbornly folds his arms across his narrow chest. "You have to be sincere. If you act like you believe, then belief will follow."

Now the duke is shaking his head. "That's what I'm afraid of. Spending all that time, giving up all the things I enjoy. And for what?" He looks pointedly at Pascal. "What if I do all that, and waste my whole life — and it turns out to be for nothing?"

Pascal has been expecting this. His expression softens, and he puts his hand on the duke's shoulder.

"Artus, what harm will befall you in taking this side?" he asks. "You'll be faithful, honest, humble, grateful, generous, a sincere friend, truthful. Yes, you'll give up the pleasures of glory and luxury; but won't you have others?"

The duke is silent, looking closely at his old friend.

"If you make this bet," Pascal says firmly, "you'll realize that you have wagered for something certain and infinite. For which," he adds, gently wagging a finger, "you have given nothing."[519]

8.

René Descartes had his demon. Baruch Spinoza had his pantheistic God. And Gottfried Leibniz had his monads.

But Blaise Pascal may have had the most rational rationalist philosophy of all.

"Pascal's Wager" is the name given to his thought experiment about why it makes sense to believe in God. It convinced the Duke of Roannez, and it's won over untold numbers of other converts over the centuries.

Pascal was, like most of the other rationalists, a mathematician of uncommon genius. He was so devoted to geometry that his overprotective father, Etienne, wouldn't let him study it until he was twelve — and only then because he had figured out much of it himself. Later, Pascal would say, "What is beyond geometry is beyond us."[520]

But Pascal's Wager is different from the other philosophies in this chapter. It doesn't depend on using reason to determine the *existence* of God.

Instead, it uses the science of probability — which Pascal helped create — to argue that the odds of belief are better than unbelief. And it was a wager Pascal developed while watching gamblers try to outwit one another at the gaming tables.

He was always more natural in the role of observer than player. Almost from birth, Pascal was ill, with frequent headaches. His mother died not long afterward, and his father raised the boy and his two sisters alone. Blaise quickly made a name for himself as a math prodigy, presenting his first paper on conic sections when he was just sixteen.

[519] This scene of Pascal in the duke's carriage is based on several accounts, including James A. Connor's *Pascal's Wager: The Man Who Played Dice with God*; and Joyce McPherson's *A Piece of the Mountain: The Story of Blaise Pascal*. Much of Pascal's dialogue, meanwhile, is adapted from his *Pensées*, pages 67–69.

[520] Herman, *The Cave and the Light*, 345.

Despite pains in his legs that sometimes made it impossible for him to walk, when he was nineteen he invented a machine to help his father compute tax debts. Named the Pascaline, it was the first modern calculator.[521]

Three years later, Pascal made an even more celebrated discovery. The old saying, attributed to Aristotle, was that "nature abhors a vacuum"—in other words, that a vacuum can't exist. But Pascal was determined to show otherwise.

He was far too weak to do the fieldwork for this experiment. So in September 1648, he convinced his brother-in-law, Florin Perier, to climb the Puy de Dôme, the tallest mountain in central France. Perier carried a bowl filled with mercury and some long glass tubes. As he climbed, the mercury level in the tubes fell, thanks to the pressure from the air.

Today we call this barometric pressure. At the time, it was revolutionary proof that vacuums do exist, and that air has weight. This experiment opened the door for modern physics and hydraulics, as well as dozens of inventions, from pressure gauges to hypodermic needles.

At that moment, it seemed Pascal's fortunes were rising faster than quicksilver. But a series of events turned him away from a career in science. His father died in 1651. The following year, his sister, Jacqueline, entered a convent at Port Royal, leaving him alone for the first time.

Port Royal was the center of the Jansenist movement in France, and Jacqueline was a convert. The Jansenists were a Catholic sect which taught that man is corrupt and irredeemable, and has no free will. God decides the elect, and only they can receive His grace.

The Jansenists believed they were following the teachings of St. Augustine. Most people disagreed. The sect was strongly opposed by the Jesuit order, and five of their propositions were condemned in 1653 by Pope Innocent X.

Pascal at first fought Jacqueline's vocation—partly because she wanted to donate her third of the family inheritance to the convent. But he, too, was won over, and would eventually spend most of his time and energy defending the Jansenists.

His *Provincial Letters,* written under a pseudonym in 1656 and 1657, targeted the Jesuits. These letters were "one of the greatest and nastiest works of the modern age ... a book of satire that Voltaire kept by his bedside every night

[521] Gottfried Leibniz would improve Pascal's calculator by adding to it multiplication and division functions.

and used as a model."[522] It's a measure of Pascal's skill as a writer that he managed to win public support for the Jansenists and their bleak worldview.

But something in that uncompromising outlook appealed to Pascal. One November night in 1654, he'd had a mystical visitation "from about half past ten at night until about half past midnight." He described it as a "night of fire."[523]

Pascal never spoke of it to anyone. The only record of that experience was a short document he wrote and kept pinned inside his jacket, next to his heart. It was discovered inside his coat a decade after his death.

"Righteous Father, the world has not known you," the document reads, "but I have known you."[524] In an effort to deepen that knowledge, and prevent the sin of pride, Pascal also began wearing a belt with iron spikes "in order to supercharge his penance. Any time he had a prideful thought, or felt pulled toward some diversion, he pushed on the girdle with his elbow, driving the points into his flesh, sharply reminding himself what his life was about."[525]

Pascal's last work was intended to be a comprehensive defense of the Christian faith, but he didn't have the strength to finish. It wouldn't appear until nearly a decade after his death in 1662.

The *Pensées* — French for "Thoughts" — ended up just a collection of fragments, yet it's still considered a masterpiece. The book contains his famous wager, still the most famous of all his groundbreaking ideas.

Like the other three rationalists in this chapter, Pascal's philosophy brought him into conflict with his faith. But Pascal's Wager was the most orthodox Christian notion to emerge from the rationalist movement. Biographer James Connor notes that this bet depends heavily on the notion of choice — which the Jansenists denied.

"Buried in his argument is the notion that people can decide on their own beliefs, that they have the power to choose the good and to change their lives," Connor writes.[526] So perhaps Pascal made his wager on free will after all.

[522] James A. Connor, *Pascal's Wager* (New York: Harper Collins, 2009), 5.

[523] Connor, *Pascal's Wager*, 147.

[524] Connor, *Pascal's Wager*, 148.

[525] Connor, *Pascal's Wager*, 198.

[526] Connor, *Pascal's Wager*, 187.

CHAPTER THIRTEEN

ENLIGHTENED SKEPTICISM

1.

Everything is going into the flames.

It's late August here in Somerset, in the southwestern English countryside, but the man feeding papers into the fireplace still feels a chill. Three days from now, he'll be fifty-one years old. But he plans, by his birthday, to be well on his way out of his native country.

He's been staying with an old friend here in Somerset, where he was born. But now it's too dangerous to remain. Spies have been tracking his movements all summer. One of them is the Rev. Humphrey Prideux, the librarian of Christ Church, who's been keeping a close eye on him for years. Another spy recently observed him taking "several hand baskets of papers" from his rooms at Oxford.[527]

These are the documents he's now tossing onto the grate. The firelight flickers on his thin, anxious face. There hasn't been time to set his affairs in order, nor even to pack his clothes. As his papers burn, he'll scribble down detailed instructions for his friend Edward Clarke: what to keep, what to sell, whom to pay.

[527] Maurice Cranston, *Locke* (New York: Macmillan, 1957), 228.

But he'll also acknowledge that he may not make it out of England. The roads are being watched, and it's possible he'll be stopped before he can reach the coast. If he's captured, he knows his destination will be the Tower of London.

There he'll join Algernon Sydney, who was recently arrested for his part in an alleged plot against King Charles II. Just a month ago, another friend, the Earl of Essex, Lord William Russell, was beheaded for his involvement. Two decades after the monarchy was restored in England, Catholics and Protestants still view one another warily.

Charles has proposed religious tolerance. But fears of a "Popish plot" that will see him succeeded by his brother, the Catholic Duke of York, are rampant. One of the people who fanned those flames was the Earl of Shaftesbury. There were suspicions he'd been secretly organizing a rebellion — to drive Charles II off the throne before a Catholic succession could happen.

The earl died in exile earlier this year. But talk about the "Rye House Plot" — a foiled plan to assassinate Charles II and the duke on their way back from the horse races — has kept the country abuzz. Suspected conspirators are now being rounded up.

The man in front of the fireplace is one of the earl's longtime friends. So although there's little evidence to prove it, he's believed to be part of the Rye House scheme. And he doesn't expect mercy if he's taken into custody.

"Upon consideration," he writes hurriedly to Edward Clarke, "I have thought it best to make a will which you will find amongst the other papers, by which you may be legally entitled to whatsoever I leave."[528]

He tosses the last packet of documents, bound in twine, into the fireplace. He's burned nearly everything — everything except one single manuscript. This batch of papers he will take with him as he slips into the dusk, into the deep green countryside.

[528] Cranston, *Locke*, 230.

It's a huge risk, because of the ideas contained in that packet. But in less than two weeks' time, the manuscript will make it safely to Rotterdam, Holland — along with its author.

The world won't read these words for another seven years. By that time, a so-called Glorious Revolution will have taken place in England. The Protestant rulers William and Mary will have ended fears of a Catholic succession to the throne. And the author of this manuscript will finally have returned to his home country as well.

Two Treatises on Government *will be one of three major works published by John Locke between 1689 and 1690. The other two are* A Letter Concerning Toleration *and* An Essay Concerning Human Understanding. *All three have been years in the making, and all three will reshape the world.*

Locke's ideas about government — the views in that packet of papers he smuggled out of the English countryside one desperate August — may prove his most influential work.

Absolute monarchy, he writes, is no form of government at all. Citizens don't have the ability to renounce their God-given rights to liberty. But they do *have the power to remove a government that acts against their interests.*

It's a view that will spark multiple revolutions — including the one that will shrink Locke's own British Empire. And it will lead to unprecedented freedom for mankind — for both good and ill.[529]

2.

There may be no better example of the pros and cons of modern philosophy than John Locke.

More than any other thinker, Locke is the architect of liberalism. His writings on politics played a major role in bringing freedom to people in England, in Europe, and especially in America. The Founding Fathers — Thomas Jefferson

529 This sequence of John Locke preparing to flee England owes a great deal to Arthur Herman's compelling reimagining in *The Cave and the Light*, 354–355. Maurice Cranston's 1957 biography of Locke also supplied important details.

in particular — were inspired by his view that people have the right to get rid of their leaders when those leaders no longer serve the will of the public.

In addition, Locke is famous for his views on tolerance — especially religious tolerance. *A Letter Concerning Toleration* imagines a society where all believers can practice their faith in peace. "No Man by nature is bound unto any particular Church or Sect," Locke observed, "but every one joins himself voluntarily to that Society in which he believes he has found that Profession and Worship which is truly acceptable unto God."[530]

And unlike the work of the rationalists elsewhere in Europe, such as René Descartes, Locke's natural philosophy is built on a solid Aristotelian base. God also plays a major role: He grants us the power of reason, which helps us interpret His plans.

Most people who have lived in the West for the past three hundred years have lived in the world John Locke played a large role in creating. The benefits of that world have been many, including unprecedented freedom and unprecedented prosperity.

Yet for all his optimism and common sense, storm clouds loom over Locke's work. His promise of religious liberty probably didn't include Catholics. In an effort to maximize man's freedom, his views of nature featured some astonishing conclusions about the disabled, human consciousness, and identity.

Meanwhile, his break with Aristotle on the question of universals would inevitably lead to a radical skepticism about the material world. This is one of philosophy's greatest ironies: in an effort to make the world safe for science, Locke helped cut the legs out from under science — and the world itself.

And while Locke's philosophy has helped create the freest societies in history, his views also contain the seeds of those societies' downfall. This is one of the great lessons of human nature, realized by Niccolò Machiavelli more than 150 years before Locke: liberation from one sort of tyranny will eventually lead to another.

Locke believed that "the law works to increase liberty, by which he means our liberation from the constraints of the natural world," notes Notre Dame

[530] John Locke, *The Works, vol. 5, Four Letters Concerning Toleration* (1685), Online Library of Liberty, https://oll.libertyfund.org/title/locke-the-works-vol-5-four-letters-concerning-toleration.

professor Patrick Deneen. "Thus one of the liberal state's main roles becomes the active liberation of individuals from any limiting conditions."[531]

"At the forefront of liberal theory is the liberation from natural limitations on the achievement of our desires." Those goals, Deneen adds, were not just life, liberty, and health, but also "indolency of the body."[532]

Once again, when it counted, Locke sided against Aristotle, and not with him. Locke's ideal government had little to do with virtue — and everything to do with tolerance.

John Locke was, more than any other thinker, the philosopher who toppled kings. Whether those kings' former subjects deserve the crown Locke awarded them remains an open question.

3.

The philosopher to whom John Locke is most often compared is his countryman, Thomas Hobbes. The two had radically different political views, yet they were both shaped by the same conflict: the English Civil War.

Locke was some forty years younger than Hobbes. He was just a boy in Belluton, a village in Somerset, when the war began in 1642. Locke's father, Nicholas, was a lawyer who served in the Parliamentary Army, which opposed the forces of King Charles I. It seems a safe bet that Locke grew up no fan of monarchs.

His father sent him to London's Westminster School, where he become a King's Scholar. At age twenty, he was enrolled at Christ Church, the largest college at the University of Oxford. He would remain affiliated with Oxford, off and on, for the next three decades, as a student and teacher.

In 1666, Locke met the tiny man who would have a profoundly large effect on his life. Lord Anthony Ashley Cooper was barely five feet tall, but he made an impression on all who met him. Later he became a peer, the first Earl of Shaftesbury — and the leader of a new political party called the Whigs, which opposed the king.

The future earl invited Locke into his home, as his aide and personal physician. That was a wise decision. Although he didn't yet have a medical degree,

[531] Patrick J. Deneen, *Why Liberalism Failed* (New Haven, CT: Yale University Press, 2018), 49.

[532] Deneen, *Why Liberalism Failed*, 50.

Locke soon oversaw a risky but successful operation that drained an abscessed cyst in Cooper's liver. Cooper would always believe he owed his life to Locke.

From Cooper, Locke got numerous connections — and a very practical view of religious liberty. Cooper, like many Protestants in England at the time, was staunchly anti-Catholic. But he publicly opposed religious persecution "because religious persecution divided a nation, drove many of its most industrious citizens to emigrate, and generally impeded commercial development. He saw more clearly than most Englishmen of his time how colonial expansion and international trade could be made to bring enormous fortunes to investors like himself and at the same time increase the wealth and power of the country as a whole."[533]

In short, toleration wasn't about religious freedom; it was about *economic* freedom, instead.

While working for the earl, Locke conducted medical research at the Royal Society. He'd read Descartes by this time, and he agreed with the need for a new way of approaching science. But as an aspiring doctor, he could never agree to disregard the evidence of the senses. Descartes was a rationalist; Locke would always be an empiricist.

He eventually received his bachelor of medicine degree from Oxford in 1675. But by that time, the Earl of Shaftesbury had fallen out of favor with King Charles II. The earl was now in danger — and so was Locke, who was increasingly seen as his right-hand man. Locke went to France: the reason given was his health, but he spent the next four years abroad while things cooled down.

While Locke was in Paris, he was disturbed by the public worship of King Louis XIV, "the Sun King." Louis XIV was a devout Catholic who had nevertheless set himself, not God, at the center of his own "heliocentric universe." And he ruled it "as absolutely as the actual sun dominated Copernicus's and Galileo's solar system," with no room for religious dissent.[534]

It was this government that people like the Earl of Shaftesbury feared, and met with their own anti-Catholic bias. And as Locke watched in disgust, his "one goal in life was to make sure the same thing never happened in England. But whereas others tried to fight for freedom with guns or plots or revolutions, Locke would fight for it with ideas."[535]

533 Cranston, *Locke,* 107.

534 Herman, *The Cave and the Light,* 351.

535 Herman, *The Cave and the Light,* 355.

Locke returned from France in 1679, then had to flee the country again four years later. By then, Shaftesbury had died an exile in Holland. But as we saw in the opening segment of this chapter, the royal authorities were rounding up his friends and collaborators.

The actual threat from the Rye House Plot remains unknown. However, the danger to Locke was real: Lord William Russell and Algernon Sydney were both executed, and Locke very well might have shared their fate.

He returned home when William of Orange and his wife and first cousin, Mary — the daughter of King James II — took power in England in 1689. It was a "Glorious Revolution" for Protestants: William had fought for years against King Louis XIV of France. The invasion of England was fast and nearly bloodless; James II abdicated the throne, and fears of a Catholic succession to the British monarchy were put to rest.

Locke's three great works reached the public shortly after his return to England. In each book, he advanced ideas that seemed like a breath of pure, fresh air. Tolerance, practical science, freedom, and common sense — these were the hallmarks of Locke's thought. The full consequences would take longer to materialize.

4.

Locke began his *Essay Concerning Human Understanding* simply enough. He insisted on the senses as the source of all our information, and denied that innate knowledge exists.

For Locke, the mind was a "tabula rasa" — a blank slate. There is nothing in the mind that is not first in the senses, as his famous saying goes. The material world gives us sensation, while the mind, he said, supplies us with reflection — our perception of "the operations of our own minds." He called these two sources of information "sense" and "internal sense."[536]

However, he also denied the possibility of universals. Locke took the conceptualist position: universals are nothing more than "men making abstract ideas, and settling them into their minds with names annexed to them."[537]

[536] John Locke, *The Works, vol. 1 An Essay Concerning Human Understanding Part 1* (1689), Online Library of Liberty, https://oll.libertyfund.org/title/locke-the-works-vol-1-an-essay-concerning-human-understanding-part-1.

[537] Locke, *Essay Concerning Human Understanding.*

This makes life — and science — more convenient, but it means that deeper knowledge is impossible. "Men can have no ideas of Real Essences," he insisted.[538]

So what *can* we know about the world around us? Locke separated the qualities of physical objects. *Primary qualities* we can measure objectively. For example, we can record an object's weight, shape, and number — how many objects there are. *Secondary qualities* can vary from person to person. These include an object's color, sound, odor, and taste.

Where do we find these secondary qualities, which are sometimes referred to as *qualia*? According to Locke, they exist in the mind — which is why one person may think that a bucket of lukewarm water is hot, and another will think it's cold.

"Intrinsically, the material world is just a vast system of colorless, odorless, tasteless, soundless particles," Edward Feser observes. "It is our minds that classify certain clusters of these particles into kinds of substances sharing a certain form, and it is our minds which perceive them, falsely, as if they really possessed features resembling our ideas of secondary qualities."[539]

But what *is* the object, really, underneath all those primary and secondary qualities? Here, Locke was stumped. He admitted that it was a "something, I know not what."[540]

And therefore, he concluded, the whole idea of "substance" is meaningless. Locke did not go further with this idea, but other philosophers followed it to its natural conclusion, as we'll soon see.

However, Locke did make some truly unexpected leaps. He noted the "frequent production of monsters" and "changelings"[541] in all species of animals, including people. Here he was speaking — using the language of the time — about the physically and mentally disabled.

Locke brought them up to argue against Aristotle's ideas of universals and forms. He thought these "monsters" and "changelings" were so unlike regular human beings that they either needed to belong to a completely new classification — or no classification at all.

[538] Cahn, *Classics of Western Philosophy*, 701.

[539] Feser, *The Last Superstition*, 83.

[540] Locke's famous phrase about the mystery of understanding matter actually came in the form of a parable about an "Indian" who insisted that the world was supported by an elephant, which stood on the back of a tortoise. When asked what the tortoise was standing on, the Indian replied, "*Something, he knew not what*" (Cahn, *Classics of Western Philosophy*, 677).

[541] Locke, *Essay Concerning Human Understanding*.

"We find that some of these monstrous productions have few or none of those qualities which are supposed to result from, and accompany, the essence of that species from whence they derive their originals," he wrote.

As Edward Feser points out in his book *Locke*, the reasoning here is easily refuted. Consider human beings who lack the ability for rational thought, either because they were not born with it, or have lost it in an accident. These people are still human beings, as Aristotle, the Scholastics, and most of us would argue. Not instantiating the form of man perfectly "does not mean that [someone] fails to instantiate it at all."[542]

This train of thought begs several questions. For example, should we consider a person who is missing an arm or a leg a human being? And it leads, potentially, to a much darker place: the idea that someone who lost, or never had, the ability to think rationally, has forfeited the right to be considered human — and thus, to live.

This relates to another surprising conclusion of Locke's, one that continues to have a major influence in the world. That is his idea that identity depends on consciousness. Specifically, *continuous* consciousness.

"For it is by the consciousness it has of its present thoughts and actions" that a person "is *self to itself* now." And that consciousness's recollection of the past, and thoughts about the future, unites "those distant actions into the same person."[543]

In other words, if we could transplant our consciousness into our little finger, and then cut off that finger, then "it is evident the little finger would be the person, the same person; and self would have nothing to do with the rest of the body."[544]

This concept presents further problems. To cite just one example:

> We can imagine that the brain of a person with perfectly accurate memories is divided into two, after which each of the two halves are surgically transplanted into one of two bodies cloned from the body of the original person. Each new person is equally physically continuous with the original, and let us suppose that each also has exactly the same memories of being the original person. So it seems that the quasi-Lockean sort of theory we've been discussing would entail that each of them is the same person as the original person.[545]

[542] Feser, *The Last Superstition*, 130.
[543] Locke, *Essay Concerning Human Understanding*.
[544] Locke, *Essay Concerning Human Understanding*.
[545] Edward Feser, *Locke* (New York: Oneworld Publications, 2013), 73.

This seems impossible, though some have tried to defend it — occasionally by arguing that it proves there's no such thing as "persons" after all.

Once again, we see the consequences of a modern philosopher determined to break from the past. Locke was trying to come up with an idea about identity that would avoid Aristotle and the Scholastics, who argued that a person's identity is determined by *form*, and rationalists like Plato and Descartes, who believed identity is *innate*.

"He wants to show that personal immortality, and in particular the resurrection at Judgment Day, is possible even if one rejects both Aristotelian substantial forms and Cartesian immaterial substances."[546] But not only did Locke fail to do this, his theory about continuous consciousness — like his idea about "monsters" and "changelings" — can lead to more ominous conclusions.

For example, "those who take a more or less Lockean view of personal identity are likely to defend the moral legitimacy of abortion and euthanasia," Edward Feser explains, "for they are more likely to take the view that fetuses and patients in 'persistent vegetative states,' lacking as they do the rich conscious lives of normal adults, do not count as persons."[547]

Locke, as Feser notes, might well have disagreed with those conclusions. But they're easy to reach following his guidelines.

Meanwhile, Locke's *Two Treatises on Government* is best known for how different it seems to be from the work of Thomas Hobbes. In *Leviathan*, Hobbes had suggested that man in his state of nature was engaged in a "war of all against all." He would, and should, accept a tyrant as a ruler, if that guaranteed his safety and property.

Locke argued that man isn't nearly that bad. Even in his state of nature, he has the gift of God-given reason. And that state of nature "has a law of nature to govern it, which obliges everyone; and Reason, which is that law, teaches all mankind, who will but consult it."[548]

Because we're all God's property, Locke argued, we have to use the reason he gave us to choose the right leaders. We don't need a repressive government. Instead, we want — because God wants us to have — a government that makes us free.

[546] Feser, *Locke*, 66.
[547] Feser, *Locke*, 71.
[548] Herman, *The Cave and the Light*, 359.

And we're also obligated to emulate God, the ultimate property owner. "Nowhere are we closer to God than when we create property from our own handiwork, just as man is the handiwork of his Lord God."[549]

The influence of Locke's business-minded patron, the Earl of Shaftesbury, is distinct. The American Founders may have changed Locke's fundamental rights of "life, liberty, and property" to the more high-minded and vague "life, liberty, and the pursuit of happiness." But economic growth was always part of Locke's plan.

This is where Locke and Hobbes intersect. What many people don't realize is the deep connection between the two philosophers. Locke had actually borrowed heavily from Hobbes in an early essay, agreeing that man should give absolute power to a monarch. He would later change this view,

> but at no time in his life would Locke admit his debt to Hobbes.[550] He even came to pretend he had never read Hobbes properly. Partly, perhaps, this pretence was the repudiation of a former master; it may also have been due to the fact that the word "Hobbist" came to be a pejorative one in all but a very few quarters, and Locke was forever anxious to avoid a bad name.[551]

Some important similarities would persist. "Hobbes and Locke both — for all their differences — begin by conceiving natural humans not as parts of wholes but as wholes apart. We are by nature 'free and independent,' naturally ungoverned and even nonrelational."[552]

This meant that for Locke, all our relationships — not just our relationships with our rulers, but also our marriages and family relationships — are essentially voluntary. There are no strings attached, and we get to decide whether they're worth continuing. Even a child "must ultimately subject his inheritance to the logic of consent."[553]

And ultimately, Locke's political project concludes in paradox. "Its ideal of liberty can be realized only through a powerful state," writes Patrick Deneen. "If

[549] Herman, *The Cave and the Light*, 360.

[550] As Maurice Cranston observed, "Locke never acknowledged what he owed to [French philosopher Pierre] Gassendi, but at least he did not deny it as he denied his debt to Hobbes" (Cranston, *Locke*, 103).

[551] Cranston, *Locke*, 62–63.

[552] Deneen, *Why Liberalism Failed*, 48.

[553] Deneen, *Why Liberalism Failed*, 33.

the expansion of freedom is secured by law, then the opposite also holds true in practice: increasing freedom requires the expansion of law."[554]

Even if those laws dissolve the bonds between husbands and wives, or between parents and children, the liberty of the individual must be protected. For Locke, man's obligations to God, at least, were clear. Others who adopted his thinking would disagree on this point.

"I find no difficulty to suppose the freedom of mankind," Locke wrote.[555] The difficulty would lie with his descendants.

5.

The sacred principle of Locke's *Letter Concerning Toleration* is the separation of church and state. Of all his commonsense conclusions, this one seems to be the most commonsensical to modern readers.

Locke argued that belief cannot, and should not, be coerced by the state. "The care of souls is not committed to the civil magistrate," he wrote, "because it appears not that God has ever given any such authority to one man over another as to compel anyone to his religion."[556]

The church, meanwhile, is a voluntary association of men, who choose — or don't choose — to accept the beliefs of their religion. And as long as those beliefs don't hurt anyone else, or infringe on their liberty, then the state should remain neutral.

Locke provided two examples. When Catholics insist that Christ's body is present in the Eucharist, or when Jews deny the divinity of Christ, no one else is being harmed. "I readily grant that these opinions are false and absurd," he wrote. "But the business of laws is not to provide for the truth of opinions, but for the safety and security of the commonwealth and of every particular man's goods and person."[557]

There are, of course, exceptions to this religious freedom. Behavior like drunkenness and debauchery, for instance, is unacceptable. So is a church whose members receive "the protection and service of another prince"[558] — a

554 Deneen, *Why Liberalism Failed*, 49.

555 John Locke, *The Two Treatises of Civil Government (Hollis Ed.)* (1689), Online Library of Liberty, https://oll.libertyfund.org/title/hollis-the-two-treatises-of-civil-government-hollis-ed.

556 Locke, *Four Letters Concerning Toleration*.

557 Locke, *Four Letters Concerning Toleration*.

558 Locke, *Four Letters Concerning Toleration*.

thinly veiled reference to the claim that Catholics owe their allegiance to the pope. And so is atheism, which is "not at all to be tolerated."[559]

As Edward Feser points out, this defense of toleration is "a religious one, not a secular one."[560] It rests on a belief in God — which is why atheists are excluded. But Locke does stack the deck in favor of Protestantism. As one example, he "emphasizes the importance of personal moral behavior over doctrine and ceremony, insinuating, contrary to the Catholic view, that doctrine and ceremony are inessential to authentic Christianity."[561]

Most tellingly, Locke found "toleration to be the chief characteristic mark of the true Church."[562] This single line would echo through subsequent battles over religious freedom. Doctrine was insignificant, and certainly no business of the state. Toleration, writes Feser, placed "all conflicting creedal claims on an equally low epistemic footing."[563]

The result would eventually be that it doesn't matter what you believe — or *if* you believe — as long as you tolerate the beliefs of others. Unless, of course, your beliefs conflict with an individual's freedom — which must be enforced by the state.

That idea would inevitably create a religious — and irreligious — landscape that Locke could hardly have imagined in his wildest dreams. But in religion, as in politics and natural science, that lack of imagination would lead to a brave new world.

6.

Locke spent his final years quietly, in the Essex home of Lady Damaris Masham. She was the daughter of Ralph Cudworth, a theologian and philosopher who had been a great influence on Locke. She was also a feminist who agreed with Locke on the need for education — especially for women.

Lady Masham was married to Sir Francis Masham, but in her younger years, she and Locke had exchanged love letters. The relationship had cooled over the years into friendship. At her estate in the fall of 1704, the two studied together the letters of St. Paul. Near the end of October, Locke's health began to fail, and Lady Masham read to him from the Psalms as he died.

559 Locke, *Four Letters Concerning Toleration.*
560 Feser, *Locke*, 155.
561 Feser, *Locke*, 156.
562 Locke, *Four Letters Concerning Toleration.*
563 Feser, *The Last Supersition*, 175.

Few of the American leaders who would use his ideas to liberate their nation were even born at the time. And as Locke's biographer, Maurice Cranston, wrote in 1957, "Only an historian of European thought with a panoramic vision, could judge his stature. But this at least one can say here: Locke did not merely enlarge men's knowledge, he changed their ways of thinking."[564]

The first of those changes, in fact, would soon arrive.

7.

One of the great ironies of modern philosophy, as we've already stated, is that the more independent of God it tried to be, the more God became necessary for it to make any sense.

This is where George Berkeley enters the picture. Berkeley is responsible for just one major idea, but even today, it has the power to surprise.

We've already met a strict materialist — Thomas Hobbes, who insisted that everything in the world, even the mind, is just matter. Berkeley would take the opposite tack: he denied that *any* matter existed. He was, as he called himself, an *im*materialist.

If it's true that "generations of hapless Philosophy 101 students have come to think that philosophy is fundamentally about wondering whether the table in front of you really exists,"[565] then we can trace that idea back to George Berkeley. But we can't really *blame* it on him — because all he was doing was exposing the holes in John Locke's philosophy. Berkeley was, as Bryan Magee called him, "The Consistent Empiricist."[566]

Born in 1685, Berkeley was an Irishman who was educated at Trinity College in Dublin and later became the Anglican bishop of Coyne. He was "a typical Enlightenment figure, fascinated by the new science and eager to experiment."[567]

He wasn't afraid to put himself in harm's way for the sake of science. While he was still in college, Berkeley watched a public execution. He came home curious about what it would feel like to be hung, and he convinced a friend that they should try it and see.

[564] Cranston, *Locke*, 482.

[565] Feser, *The Last Supersition*, 201.

[566] Magee, *The Story of Philosophy*, 110.

[567] Kreeft, *Socrates' Children*, vol. 3, ch. 60.

Berkeley went first, but his friend "waited a little too long for the signal agreed upon." When Berkeley was finally cut down, "he fell, senseless and motionless, upon the floor."[568] But when he revived, he was cheerful enough: his only complaint was that his shirt was rumpled. (His friend, however, declined to take his turn in the experiment.)

Later, Berkeley traveled to Italy and got an extremely close-up view of Mount Vesuvius as it erupted in 1717. "Imagine a vast torrent of liquid fire rolling from the top down the side of the mountain," he later wrote, "and with irresistible fury bearing down and consuming vines, olives, fig-trees, houses; in a word, every thing that stood in its way."[569]

Berkeley would apply the same fearlessness to his reading of John Locke's philosophy. In 1710, when he was just twenty-five years old, he published *A Treatise Concerning the Principles of Human Knowledge*. This book took aim at several claims made by Locke about the world and how we understand it.

Locke had said that all we can know about the objects around us are their primary and secondary qualities. And those secondary qualities — things like color, taste, and smell — exist only in our minds, not in the objects themselves.

What's underneath all those primary and secondary qualities? Locke admitted we can't know — it's just a "something, I know not what." This, he explained, made talking about substance meaningless — since we can't know anything about it.

Berkeley seized on this point. If we can't know anything about substance, he asked, then how do we even know it *exists*? That was "conceptual nonsense." Magee explains Berkeley's objection: "In asserting the existence of something beyond the bounds of all possible experience, Locke was breaking the fundamental principle of empiricism."[570]

We know that we have experiences, Berkeley said. However,

> we could never possess corresponding grounds for believing that these experiences are attached to objects that are not us. Therefore, said Berkeley, a consistent empiricism leads us to the conclusion that what

568 Tom Jones, *George Berkeley: A Philosophical Life* (Princeton, NJ: Princeton University Press, 2021), 452.

569 Jones, *George Berkeley*, 256.

570 Magee, *The Story of Philosophy*, 111.

> exists are minds and their contents, or subjects and their experiences. There are no grounds for believing in the existence of anything else.[571]

In short, all we have are our perceptions. And this leads us to the truly startling byproduct of Berkeley's philosophy.

Berkeley did not, as some believe, pose the old question, "If a tree falls in the forest, and no one is around to hear it, does it make a sound?" But in his *Treatise*, he did ask something related.

"The objects of sense exist only when they are perceived,"[572] he wrote. So why is it, then, that objects — like the trees in some distant forest, or the room that you just left — don't go out of existence when no one is around to perceive them?

The answer, Berkeley said, was that those trees, and that room — and every other object in the world, including us — are constantly being perceived by God. Therefore, objects in the world exist in our minds when we perceive them, or in *God's* mind at *all* times. God, once again, becomes the ultimate backstop of reality.

This was an acceptable outcome for Berkeley. After all, he wanted to remind his readers "that the Eyes of the LORD are in every place beholding the Evil and the Good; that he is with us and keepeth us in all places whither we go ... and that we have a most absolute and immediate dependence on him."[573]

But it's also true that "far from supplying us with empirical certainty ... Berkeley leaves us depending for our knowledge of the world, and of the existence of other minds, upon our faith in a God that would never deceive us."[574]

So even though John Locke set out to refute the rationalism of René Descartes, his conclusions helped us end up at exactly the same place, a little more than two decades later. Without a God who would never deceive us, where would we be?

In just a few years, David Hume would help the world find out.

8.

> "Some men just want to watch the world burn."
>
> — *Michael Caine as Alfred Pennyworth, The Dark Knight*

[571] Magee, *The Story of Philosophy*, 111.

[572] George Berkeley, *A Treatise Concerning the Principles of Human Knowledge* (New York: Barnes & Noble, 2006), 18.

[573] Berkeley, *A Treatise Concerning the Principles of Human Knowledge*, 78.

[574] Buckingham, *The Philosophy Book*, 141.

David Hume was not, we should point out, a supervillain, like Batman's arch-nemesis, the Joker. He *was*, however, a good-humored Scotsman with "a ruddy Complexion & a chearful [sic] Countenance."[575] And he *did* once say, " 'Tis not contrary for me to prefer the destruction of the whole world to the scratching of my finger."[576]

But Hume's philosophy was deadly serious. He was "the most formidable, challenging, and difficult-to-refute skeptic in the history of human thought."[577] He relentlessly attacked the weaknesses of others' arguments — especially the empiricists who came before him.

Unlike the Joker, Hume didn't want to watch the world burn. Instead, he denied we could know that there *was* a world to watch burn — or even that there was actually a David Hume who could watch it.

There had been doubters in philosophy before: Protagoras had insisted we all have our individual truths, and the Skeptics had denied the possibility of objective truth. But Hume's philosophy went further. It denied the material world, morality, cause and effect, and even the possibility of self.

It was such a radical break with everything that had come before that it even overwhelmed Hume, when he sat down and thought about it.

> Where am I, or what? From what causes do I derive my existence, and to what condition shall I return? Whose favour shall I court, and whose anger must I dread? What beings surround me? and on whom have I any influence, or who have any influence on me? I am confounded with all these questions, and begin to fancy myself in the most deplorable condition imaginable, inviron'd with the deepest darkness, and utterly depriv'd of the use of every member and faculty.[578]

So he had to distract himself, to forget about this "deplorable condition" that his philosophy had created:

[575] Dennis C. Rasmussen, *The Infidel and the Professor: David Hume, Adam Smith, and the Friendship That Shaped Modern Thought* (Princeton, NJ: Princeton University Press, 2017), 21.

[576] David Hume, *A Treatise of Human Nature: Being an Attempt to Introduce the Experimental Method of Reasoning into Moral Subjects*, 415–416. The citations from David Hume in this section come from the "Hume Texts Online" database at davidhume.org. His books are attractively displayed and searchable, and the resource is invaluable—every philosopher should have such a tribute!

[577] Kreeft, *Socrates' Children*, vol. 3, ch. 62.

[578] Hume, *A Treatise of Human Nature*, 268–269.

> Most fortunately it happens, that since reason is incapable of dispelling these clouds, nature herself suffices to that purpose, and cures me of this philosophical melancholy and delirium, either by relaxing this bent of mind, or by some avocation, and lively impression of my senses, which obliterate all these chimeras. I dine, I play a game of back-gammon, I converse, and am merry with my friends; and when after three or four hour's amusement, I wou'd return to these speculations, they appear so cold, and strain'd, and ridiculous, that I cannot find in my heart to enter into them any farther.[579]

But distraction could not undo what Hume had already undone. The modern philosophers had been trying to liberate the world from what they thought held it back: the outdated ideas of the Greeks (especially Aristotle) and the Scholastics (especially Aquinas).

Now Hume was about to liberate philosophy not just from those ideas — but from *all* ideas. Even the modern rationalists, like Descartes, and the modern empiricists, like Locke, would be swept away in the tide of his doubt.

It was the true victory of Ockham's Razor, which had been steadily slicing away at the possibility of human knowledge since the medieval era. The more philosophers had tried to discover certainty, the less they found. "Finally, with Hume, we will reach a point of nearly nothing."[580]

In most history books, the Enlightenment covers the entire eighteenth century. But by the time of Hume's death in 1776, it was already, effectively, over.

9.

There's a funny story that was told about David Hume in his hometown of Edinburgh. One of the city's lochs was being drained so that a bridge could be built, and while he was on a walk, Hume slipped and fell into a patch of mud. He was a large man, and he quickly sank up to his knees. He couldn't get himself unstuck and had to cry out for help.

An old woman heard him and came to investigate. She was religious, and she knew Hume's reputation. Most people in town believed he was an atheist, and he would come to be known as "The Great Infidel."

[579] Hume, *A Treatise of Human Nature*, 269.
[580] Kreeft, *Socrates' Children*, vol. 3, ch. 62.

She fixed Hume with a stare, and told him "the mishap ... was a just judgement from Heaven, for his ungodliness and infidelity."[581] Hume insisted that he believed in God and begged for help, but she refused.

Finally, the old woman agreed to help him up — on one condition. He had to recite the Lord's Prayer and the Apostle's Creed.

Hume promptly "doff'd his hat, and devoutly rais[ed] his eyes and hands to Heaven, audibly and emphatically pronounced the Lord's Prayer and Creed."[582] Hearing this, the woman gave him her hand and pulled him from the mud.

As we've already seen, there have been suspected atheists throughout the history of philosophy. From Democritus and Leucippus and their godless universe of atoms to the accusations that dogged most of the modern philosophers, a belief in God has always been optional in this field.

But beginning with David Hume, belief would become less and less likely. Being a nonbeliever could still get you into trouble — as the anecdote above shows. Yet Hume was remarkably forthright about his lack of faith and the ways it affected his thinking. This, too, would have a significant effect on future philosophers.

He was born in 1711 to a Presbyterian family in Ninewalls, just south of Edinburgh. His father was a successful farmer, but he died when Hume was young. So he was raised by his mother, the daughter of Sir David Falconer, the Lord President of the College of Justice.

Beginning at age ten, Hume spent four years at Edinburgh University. But academia was not for him: he would later say that "there is nothing to be learnt from a Professor, which is not to be met with in Books."[583] So he was largely self-educated, reading classics like Cicero and Virgil and current philosophers like John Locke.

It was Locke, in fact, who helped Hume lose his faith. Not long before he died, Hume admitted to James Boswell, the famous biographer of Samuel Johnson, that he had "never had entertained any belief in Religion"[584] since he encountered the work of Locke and the clergyman and philosopher Samuel Clarke.

[581] Geri Walton, "David Hume Anecdotes Related to Him," GeriWalton.com, April 27, 2015, https://www.geriwalton.com/anecdotes-of-david-hume/.

[582] Walton, "David Hume: Anecdotes."

[583] Rasmussen, *The Infidel and the Professor*, 19.

[584] Rasmussen, *The Infidel and the Professor*, 20.

Hume compared religious beliefs to "robbers" who "chaced from the open country . . . fly into the forest, and lie in wait to break in upon every unguarded avenue of the mind, and overwhelm it with religious fears and prejudices." A true philosopher, he thought, should resist, and bring "the war into the most secret recesses of the enemy."[585]

He would take his own advice, and made his own philosophy a war against belief of all kinds. After spending several years in France, he published *A Treatise of Human Nature* in 1739.

The book was not a success at the time, but its influence steadily grew and spread. Today it's not only considered Hume's finest work, but one of the most important books of philosophy in history. In part, that's because Hume — like Plato and Descartes — was a witty and entertaining writer. His conclusions may be unpleasant, but his prose makes them go down more easily than you'd think.

For those who knew him, his personality did the same trick. "In general he was open, kindly, and cheerful, so much so that even those who were scandalized by his writings . . . were often disarmed when they met him in person."[586]

Beneath the smile and the thick Scottish burr, however, lurked the negation of just about every previous philosophical principle.

10.

While Hume admired George Berkeley's radical break with Locke, he felt Berkeley hadn't gone far enough. So he set out to do the job himself.

Hume distinguished between two kinds of perceptions: *impressions* and *ideas.* Impressions are "all our more lively perceptions, when we hear, or see, or feel, or love, or hate, or desire, or will."[587] Ideas, meanwhile, are mental *copies* of impressions. This is what happens when we think about something we've experienced with our senses.

Hume's goal was to eliminate all doubt about knowledge. To do this, he dramatically shrank the field of possible knowledge first.

> When we entertain, therefore, any suspicion, that a philosophical term is employed without any meaning or idea (as is but too frequent), we need but enquire, from what impression is that supposed idea derived? And if

[585] David Hume, *An Enquiry Concerning Human Understanding.*
[586] Rasmussen, *The Infidel and the Professor,* 46.
[587] Hume, *An Enquiry Concerning Human Understanding,* 18.

> it be impossible to assign any, this will serve to confirm our suspicion. By bringing ideas into so clear a light, we may reasonably hope to remove all dispute, which may arise, concerning their nature and reality.[588]

This means that if we can't show the "impression" — the sensory evidence — from which an "idea" is derived, then it doesn't count. So "all ideas that are *not* copied from impressions, including God, the soul, the self, immortality, substance, moral good and evil, and causality . . . are not merely false but meaningless."[589]

According to John Locke, continuous consciousness is what gives us our identity. But Hume wasn't willing to go even that far. He recognized the experience of different impressions — heat, cold, love, hatred, and so on. But that's all he claimed he could know for sure.

"I never can catch *myself* at any time without a perception, and never can observe any thing but the perception," he wrote.[590] René Descartes had claimed thinking proved his existence. Hume thought it just proved thinking.

Someone else "may, perhaps, perceive something simple and continu'd, which he calls himself; tho' I am certain there is no such principle in me."[591] Certainly, this meant there could be no soul, and no life after death — which Hume found a "gloomy" prospect anyway.[592]

Hume followed all this up in 1748 with *An Enquiry Concerning Human Understanding,* which employed a system of logic similar to the ones used by rationalist philosophers like Leibniz. In this book, Hume distinguished between two kinds of statements: *Relations of Ideas* and *Matters of Fact.*

Relations of Ideas are statements that don't need to be verified, like mathematical equations and geometrical principles. Matters of Fact, meanwhile, are statements that do have to be verified, like "The sun will come up tomorrow."

[588] Hume, *An Enquiry Concerning Human Understanding,* 21–22.

[589] Kreeft, *Socrates' Children,* vol. 3, ch. 62.

[590] Hume, *A Treatise of Human Nature,* 252.

[591] Hume, *A Treatise of Human Nature,* 252.

[592] Samuel Johnson's famous biographer, James Boswell, interviewed Hume in 1776, shortly before Hume's death. Not one to lob softball questions, Boswell asked Hume about the prospect of life after death, "saying that a future state was surely a pleasing idea. He said no, for that it was always seen through a gloomy medium; there was always a Phlegethon or a hell." James Boswell, "Death and David Hume," Scotland's Pages — Timeline — 1776, National Library of Scotland, https://digital.nls.uk/scotlandspages/timeline/17762.html.

But here Hume introduced a twist that "demolishes all claims for meaningful knowledge of objective reality, not just in religion and metaphysical philosophy but also in common sense and even in science."[593] He wrote:

> All reasonings concerning matter of fact seem to be founded on the relation of Cause and Effect. By means of that relation alone we can go beyond the evidence of our memory and senses.... A man finding a watch or any other machine in a desert island, would conclude that there had once been men in that island. All our reasonings concerning fact are of the same nature. And here it is constantly supposed that there is a connexion between the present fact and that which is inferred from it.[594]

Hume insisted that this "connexion" between events is something we can never know for sure. What we think is cause and effect — to use his famous example, when one billiard ball knocks into another, and makes the second ball move — is just conjecture.

"All events seem entirely loose and separate," he wrote. "One event follows another; but we never can observe any tie between them. They seem conjoined, but never connected."[595]

Therefore, "it is impossible to give any just definition of cause. From causes which appear *similar* we expect similar effects. This is the sum of all our experimental conclusions."[596]

No knowledge of Matters of Fact, then, can ever be certain. The best we can do, Hume believed, is make educated guesses, based on our experience.

"Custom, then, is the great guide of human life," he explained. "It is that principle alone which renders our experience useful to us, and makes us expect, for the future, a similar train of events with those which have appeared in the past."[597]

So if someone were to "throw himself out at the window, and meet with no obstruction," Hume was sure "he will not remain a moment suspended in the air."[598] But there's always the next time. And we can't know that until it happens.

[593] Kreeft, *Socrates' Children*, vol. 3, ch. 62.

[594] Hume, *A Treatise of Human Nature*, 84.

[595] Hume, *An Enquiry Concerning Human Understanding*, 73–74.

[596] Hume, *An Enquiry Concerning Human Understanding*, 76–77.

[597] Hume, *An Enquiry Concerning Human Understanding*, 44–45.

[598] Hume, *An Enquiry Concerning Human Understanding*, 91.

Hume did pretend that his philosophy could actually help "our most holy religion" by reminding people that reason is unsuitable for understanding Christianity. "It is a sure method of exposing it to put it to such a trial as it is, by no means, fitted to endure."[599]

It's an entirely unconvincing argument, which Hume certainly realized. But it's the inevitable result of medieval philosophers like Scotus and Ockham, who made the same claim for the sincere reasons. It was only a matter of time before someone as clever as Hume turned that view against them.

Hume showed his cards by taking particular delight in trying to expose miracles and prophecies as false. These events fall so far outside our everyday "custom and experience" that they're completely improbable. If you choose to believe in them, that's miraculous itself. So is a belief in Christianity, which "even at this day cannot be believed by any reasonable person" without a miracle.[600]

You can almost imagine Hume smiling as he wrote these words. Yet irony is abundant in modern philosophy, and here we have one of the greatest examples. Having eliminated certainty of every kind, Hume left us with … faith.

It's faith in "custom and experience," and not faith in God, specifically. But some four hundred years after the medieval philosophers made their break with Aquinas, we were left knowing even less than we thought. It was a strange sort of progress indeed.

11.

It would almost make sense to end the story of Western thought right here, since it's hard to see how anyone could go further than Hume.

Some tried. Or at least, they attempted to address the problems Hume posed. One was the Prussian philosopher Immanuel Kant, whom we'll meet in the next chapter. But Hume was also a great influence on the thought of Georg Hegel, Kant's main descendant.

How much effect Hume had on his Edinburgh friend Adam Smith, the father of capitalism, is still debated. But in his book *The Infidel and the Professor* — a portrait of the friendship between Hume and Smith — Dennis

[599] Hume, *An Enquiry Concerning Human Understanding*, 129–130.
[600] Hume, *An Enquiry Concerning Human Understanding*, 130–131.

Rasmussen points out the many striking similarities in their thinking, even on the subject of religion.[601]

Smith is best known as the economist who came up with the idea of the "invisible hand." This is, for many, the optimistic view of capitalism. When people participate in an economy, and produce some value, everyone wins.

The principle beneath this concept is more pragmatic. Smith's "invisible hand" can only distribute wealth to everyone because of man's self-interest.

That is, people work to benefit themselves. The secondary effect is that others happen to benefit as well. As Smith pointed out in his 1776 masterpiece *An Inquiry into the Nature and Causes of the Wealth of Nations,* "I have never known much good done by those who affected to trade for the publick good."[602]

Man, Smith thought, is merely an animal that makes bargains: "Give me that which I want, and you shall have this which you want."[603] As he dryly noted, "Nobody ever saw a dog make a fair and deliberate exchange of one bone with another dog."[604]

Smith's primary innovation was his belief in the division of labor. He gave the example of a pin-maker, who, in the old days, could only make one pin a day by himself. But when the labor is divided among several people, the business can make thousands of pins a day.

Productivity increases, wealth increases, and the economy grows. Smith also contended that the quality of the product improves with specialization. And not insignificantly, freedom also grows. People are no longer bound to the towns and villages where they were born. Their labor can take them where they want to go.

601 Rasmussen points out that while Smith was nominally a believer, when Smith ventures onto religious terrain his writing is frequently evasive or equivocal; as one scholar observes, his references to a providential God are often "attended with circumlocutions, indirect speech, and frequent use of the verb 'to seem.' " Moreover, these references have the appearance of a supplement or addendum to a self-standing moral theory. As has often been noted, the basic framework of Smith's theory — according to which morality develops from human sentiments and the ultimate standard of right and wrong is determined by the sentiments of an impartial spectator — does not rely in any way on religious premises or a divine will (*The Infidel and the Professor*, 106).

602 Adam Smith, *An Inquiry into the Nature and Causes of the Wealth of Nations* (Oxford: Oxford University Press, 1976), 456.

603 Smith, *An Inquiry into the Nature and Causes of the Wealth of Nations*, 26.

604 Smith, *An Inquiry into the Nature and Causes of the Wealth of Nations*, 26.

It's true that "man has almost constant occasion for the help of his brethren,"[605] Smith wrote. But the tie that binds society is self-interest, not benevolence.

However, Smith also felt that man's desire to improve could serve society in more ways than just the financial. In his 1993 book *Adam Smith in His Time and Ours: Designing the Decent Society*, Jerry Muller argues that

> far from being an individualist, Smith believed that it is the influence of society that transforms people into moral beings. He thought that people often misjudge their own self-interest. He never used the term "laissez-faire," and he believed that governmental expenses were bound to increase as civilization advanced. He regarded the attempt to explain all human behavior on the basis of self-interest as analytically misguided and morally pernicious. In the society he intended to promote, men and women were freer from the traditional, direct controls of political lords and state churches. But that had been made possible, he showed, only by the growth of central government, and it would only be desirable when coupled with a panoply of social institutions which fostered self-control. The "liberty" Smith advocated was not "freedom" from all control, but freedom to control one's own passions. That freedom would be learned from and encouraged by such social institutions as the market, the family, religious communities, and the law. Adam Smith is best known as an advocate of "natural liberty." But the understanding of what liberty means and of why it is worth having has changed radically from his day to ours. If Smith's association of liberty with institutionally fostered self-control sounds strange to us, it is because we have adopted the assumption that the most "authentic" self is the self that is least inhibited by external standards, and so many have come to identify liberty with the absence of legal constraint, social constraint, and even self-restraint—with unbounded will and unconstrained desire; and imagine that Adam Smith offered the ultimate rationale for "doing as one likes."[606]

But that may have been an easy—perhaps even deliberate—mistake for some to make. Consider some other, undeniably selfish views which Hume's skepticism also inspired.

605 Smith, *An Inquiry into the Nature and Causes of the Wealth of Nations*, 26.

606 Jerry Z. Muller, *Adam Smith in His Time and Ours: Designing the Decent Society* (New York: The Free Press,1993), 2–3.

The British philosopher Jeremy Bentham was an aspiring lawyer when he read Hume's *A Treatise of Human Nature*. He "felt as if scales had fallen from my eyes."[607]

Bentham was struck by Hume's refinement of Aristotle's three types of value judgments. We do things because they're pleasant, because they're useful, or because they're virtuous. Because Hume had eliminated virtue as something that we couldn't really know, that left just two possibilities: "to pursue what gave ease or pleasure."[608]

The philosophy Bentham proposed was called *utilitarianism*. He laid out the principle in a document published in 1776, the year Hume died. "It is the greatest happiness of the greatest number that is the measure of right and wrong."[609]

Bentham later defined *utility* as "that property in any object" which "tends to produce benefit, advantage, good or happiness."[610] Pleasure is good. Pain is bad. What gives pleasure to the most people has the most utility.

Even in death, Bentham tried to live up to this maxim. He asked that his corpse be displayed publicly, to encourage people to donate their bodies for medical research. His skeleton, crowned with a wax replica of his head, can still be seen at University College London.

Bentham's protégé, John Stuart Mill, meanwhile, is part of nearly every debate over free speech. We've all heard someone quote the saying, "Your right to swing your fist ends where my nose begins." That's a paraphrase of the "harm principle," from Mill's 1859 book *On Liberty*.

Mill wrote that "the only purpose for which power can be rightfully exercised over any member of a civilised community, against his will, is to prevent harm to others."[611]

That means an individual *can't* be stopped from doing something "because it will be better for him to do so, because it will make him happier, because, in the opinion of others, to do so would be wise, or even right.... Over himself, over his own body and mind, the individual is sovereign."[612]

[607] James Crimmins, "Jeremy Bentham," *Stanford Encyclopedia of Philosophy*, March 17, 2015, https://plato.stanford.edu/entries/bentham/.

[608] Hume, *An Enquiry Concerning Human Understanding*, 105.

[609] Crimmins, "Jeremy Bentham."

[610] Crimmins, "Jeremy Bentham."

[611] John Stuart Mill, *On Liberty*, ed. Michael B. Mathias (New York: Routledge, 2007), 31.

[612] Mill, *On Liberty*, 70–71.

The key question, of course, is what counts as "harm" to others. Physical harm is easy to quantify; other types of harm are trickier to gauge.

There is evidence that Mill, like Smith, was far less permissive than many believe. While he was a defender of liberty, he also advocated limits to control people's behavior. Yet again, people only heard the line they wanted to hear: that they could do as they pleased.

Utilitarianism turned out to be an extraordinarily far-reaching philosophy. "The greatest good for the greater number" is a principle that we see in both free societies and totalitarian ones.

Yet the overriding idea — the thing that unites all the thinkers in this chapter — is a belief in the individual. There's a direct connection between Locke and Berkeley's belief that the material world is essentially a mystery, Hume's denial of any real knowledge, the economic theories of Adam Smith, and the utilitarianism of Bentham and Mill.

God may be the thing that holds reality together, or He may not exist at all. Either way, freedom reigns. For good or ill, we're sovereign — and on our own.

CHAPTER FOURTEEN

CHILDREN'S CRUSADE

1.

The innocence of children represents to me the source of infinite creativity, and I feel this is where all my creative source comes from. This is not an intellectual kind of intelligence but an intelligence that is full of wonder, magic, mystery and adventure. In this intelligence there is love, there is trust, there is joy and there is beauty. It's the kind of intelligence that will heal the world.

But by the time you are an adult, you're conditioned; you're so conditioned by the things about you and it goes.... Children are loving, they don't gossip, they don't complain, they're just open-hearted. They're ready for you. They don't judge. They don't see things by way of color.... That's the problem with adults; they lose that child-like quality.[613]

—Michael Jackson, 1992

613 The first quotation comes from remarks made by Jackson during a visit to the American Consulate in Tokyo, December 10, 1992. The occasion was the Heal the World Foundation Donation Ceremony (YouTube: https://www.youtube.com/watch?v=BIEvInkbIzI). The second quotation is from an interview with *Ebony Magazine*, May 1992, http://www.jackson.ch/ebony1.htm.

Given the controversies that began dogging Michael Jackson the very next year, and which overshadowed the final decade and a half of his career, these quotes seem truly unfortunate now.

But what's even more disturbing is how perfectly they reflect the philosophy of Jean-Jacques Rousseau.

Whether the King of Pop was ever aware of this eighteenth-century Swiss philosopher is unknown. He certainly understood Rousseau's worldview, though. He definitely picked up on the sentimentality. The alleged link between innocence and creativity. The love of animals, which he sometimes treated better than people. And, of course, the romanticization of children, and the ways in which the world "conditions" us into all sorts of evils.

It's the sort of philosophy, in short, that could only appeal to a child—or someone who wanted badly to remain a child forever. That, of course, was the perfect description of Michael Jackson. And it was the perfect description of Rousseau as well. The similarities between their careers are striking—including the apologists who defended them both in the face of substantial damning evidence.

"My idea of happiness," Rousseau once wrote, "is never to have to do anything I don't wish to do."[614] Like a true star, he did his best to live up—or down—to that ideal.

2.

The historian Paul Johnson called Rousseau the first of the modern intellectuals. Johnson identified five qualities that characterized these people. In the history of philosophy, the third category may be most important: utter self-absorption.

"He took the discovery of the individual, the prime achievement of the Renaissance, a giant step further," Johnson wrote.[615] Even that is an understatement.

We're speaking of a man who wrote a dozen volumes of his own autobiography, *Confessions*—and then followed it up with two more books on his favorite subject: himself. We're speaking of a man who gave seventeen-hour

614 Paul Johnson, *Intellectuals* (New York: Harper Perennial, 1990), 13. Another similarity between Rousseau and the King of Pop: Rousseau also had great success as a composer. He had a huge hit opera in the early 1750s, *Le Devin du Village* ("The Village Soothsayer"), and it led King Louis XV to offer Rousseau a lifetime pension. Incredibly (especially for Rousseau), he turned it down.

615 Johnson, *Intellectuals*, 3.

readings from his memoirs. We're speaking of a man who freely shared his private thoughts and sexual escapades, believing the public's curiosity about him was insatiable.

Rousseau wanted, he said earnestly, to know himself. If, in the end, he didn't — and his capacity for delusion was immense — no one can claim he didn't try his hardest. And yet, if you'd asked him, he would have sworn that he did all that self-analysis for the rest of us.

"He believed he had a unique love for humanity and had been endowed with unprecedented gifts and insights to increase its felicity," said Johnson. "An astonishing number of people, in his own day and since, have taken him at his own valuation."[616]

However, the people who knew Rousseau best despised him the most. He fell out with nearly every male friend he ever had, and with several female admirers as well. His mentor, the French philosopher and writer Denis Diderot, called him "deceitful, vain as Satan, ungrateful, cruel, hypocritical and full of malice." His peer Voltaire described him as "a monster of vanity and vileness."[617]

Even David Hume, who helped bring him to England and got him a government pension, later told Rousseau that he had "wantonly and voluntarily, thrown away all these advantages.... I can not be surprized after this; that you are my enemy. Adieu and for ever."[618]

But that was nothing compared to how Rousseau treated those even closer to him. He "showed no affection, or indeed interest in, other members of his family." His father, Isaac, a watchmaker in Geneva, "meant nothing to him, and his death was merely an opportunity to inherit."[619]

In 1745, Rousseau took a mistress: Thérèse Levasseur, an illiterate laundress. They stayed together until his death, even though he admitted he "never felt the least glimmering of love for her."[620] She fulfilled all his needs, both sexual and practical — including changing the painful catheter he had to wear.

616 Johnson, *Intellectuals*, 26.

617 Johnson, *Intellectuals*, 26.

618 Daniel Klein, Jason Briggeman, and Jacob Hall. "Foreword to 'Hume's Manuscript Account of the Extraordinary Affair between Him and Rousseau,'" *Econ Journal Watch* 18, no. 2 (October 2021): 278–326, https://econjwatch.org/File+download/1205/HumeSept2021.pdf?mimetype=pdf. The complete account of Hume and Rousseau's friendship and falling out, available online, is utterly remarkable.

619 Johnson, *Intellectuals*, 18.

620 Johnson, *Intellectuals*, 19.

Thérèse also bore him five children — all of which he forced her to give up for adoption. The last four were dropped off anonymously at the Hôpital des Enfants-trouvés, where two-thirds of the babies died in their first year, and only five percent lived to adulthood. The man who loved children didn't even bother to name his own.

Dr. I. W. Allen, who wrote a biography of Thérèse Levasseur, described Rousseau as a "masochist, exhibitionist, neurasthenic, hypochondriac, onanist, latent homosexual afflicted by the typical urge for repeated displacements, incapable of normal or parental affection, incipient paranoiac, narcissistic introvert rendered unsocial by his illness, filled with guilt feelings, pathologically timid, a kleptomaniac, infantilist, irritable and miserly."[621] But otherwise, a wonderful human being.

And then there was his legendary self-pity. It started from the beginning: "my birth cost my mother her life, and was the first of my misfortunes."[622] In one of the most honest sentences he ever wrote, in his *Confessions*, he admitted, "Frequently, when in possession of everything that could make life pleasing, I have been the most miserable of mortals."[623]

Yet Rousseau lacked neither admirers nor talent. He wasn't just a skillful writer, but a successful one, who understood how readers can be swept up by powerful emotions. His 1761 novel *Julie, or the New Heloise*, became a runaway bestseller: it was so hard to keep in stock that bookshops rented it out by the hour.

In a series of letters, *Julie* told the story of a doomed affair between a young woman and her tutor. The allusion to the affair between the student Heloise and her tutor, the medieval philosopher Peter Abelard (described in chapter 8), gave the book some extra spice. This led to the Catholic Church condemning it, which undoubtedly helped boost sales.

The fan mail — especially from society ladies, Rousseau's target audience — was ecstatic. Those admirers also loved the follow-up, 1762's *Émile, or On Education.* Part novel, part manual for Rousseau's theory of education, it follows the fictional Émile through his young life. The section about giving a child a "natural religion,"[624] rather than a Christian one, also got this book

[621] Johnson, *Intellectuals*, 26.

[622] Jean-Jacques Rousseau, *The Confessions of Jean Jacques Rousseau — Complete*, Project Gutenberg, August 15, 2004; last updated February 26, 2021, https://gutenberg.org/cache/epub/3913/pg3913-images.html.

[623] Rousseau, *The Confessions*.

[624] Jean-Jacques Rousseau, *Émile, or on Education*, trans. Allan David Bloom (New York: Basic Books, 1979), 295.

banned. Part of Rousseau's genius was knowing how to push the buttons of his adversaries to promote his work.

His educational views were hardly surprising for a man who willingly abandoned his own babies. Rousseau believed the government's job is to socially engineer its citizens. And he approvingly cited Plato's ideas about the state, rather than parents, raising children.

Not everyone agreed with Rousseau on the subject of education. The early feminist Mary Wollstonecraft took particular issue with his idea that boys and girls should be taught differently. Her 1792 book *A Vindication of the Rights of Women* was a tart response to *Émile*. "Let woman share the rights," Wollstonecraft argued, "and she will emulate the virtues of man."[625]

Wollstonecraft's view would win out in the end, but at the time, Rousseau was ascendant. In *Émile*—and in a work of nonfiction, *The Social Contract*, published the same year—his full philosophy emerged. Like Rousseau himself, it was incredibly contradictory, incredibly cruel—and nevertheless, incredibly influential.

3.

Rousseau coined his catchphrase in the opening sentence of *The Social Contract*: "Man is born free, and everywhere he is in chains."[626] Like Thomas Hobbes and John Locke, Rousseau agreed that man makes a social contract to form society. Unlike them, he thought it was an inherently bad deal.

Simply put, man is born perfect, and society corrupts. In his essay *On Cannibals*, the sixteenth-century French philosopher Michel de Montaigne had called this idealized character "Nature's Gentleman." The more common term today is "noble savage," and it was Rousseau who popularized the idea.

Rousseau's 1755 essay *Discourse on the Origin and Foundations of Inequality Among Men* had already identified the root of man's problem: private property. Property ownership, he insisted, had corrupted man's perfect nature by introducing envy and competition. This, in turn, led to inequality and vice.

> The first man who, having enclosed a piece of land, thought of saying "This is mine" and found people simple enough to believe him, was the true founder of civil society. How many crimes, wars, murders; how

[625] Buckingham, *The Philosophy Book*, 175.

[626] Jean-Jacques Rousseau, *Of the Social Contract* (Brunswick, OH: King's Court Communications, 1978), 2.

> much misery and horror the human race would have been spared if someone had pulled up the stakes and filled in the ditch and cried out to his fellow men: "Beware of listening to this impostor. You are lost if you forget the fruits of the earth belong to everyone and that the earth itself belongs to no one."[627]

It was, Rousseau sadly admitted, too late to go back to this utopia. But like Hobbes and Locke, he also had a solution for how we could still be free and live in harmony.

The answer was something called the "General Will." John Locke had insisted rulers must have the consent of the governed, but Rousseau's idea went much, much further. People voluntarily give their freedom to a collective body, which, in theory, will work on their behalf. On paper, it sounds like true democracy: one citizen, one vote.

Rousseau described the General Will in mystical terms — almost as if people's collective will would be transformed into a new person. But that person was just a more oppressive version of Thomas Hobbes's Leviathan.

Once the General Will was decided, there could be no dissent. People must be "forced to be free,"[628] because the General Will "is always righteous."[629] Man must give up his selfish desires and surrender his heart to the state. Only then will he be happy again.

This authoritarian concept has been copied by dictators ever since. As just one example, the revolutionary Pol Pot closely studied Rousseau. The ideas of the "noble savage" and the General Will directly inspired the Khmer Rouge genocide in Cambodia during the late 1970s.

Rousseau inspired other madmen much closer to his own time. His writings were often cited as the spark that ignited the French Revolution. He was a hero to Maximilian Robespierre, the bloodthirsty lawyer who presided over the Terror that sent thousands of French citizens — including priests, nuns, children, and the elderly — to their deaths.

[627] Jean-Jacques Rousseau, *A Discourse upon the Origin and the Foundation of the Inequality among Mankind*, Project Gutenberg, February 1, 2004. https://www.gutenberg.org/cache/epub/11136/pg11136-images.html.

[628] Rousseau, *Of the Social Contract*, 12.

[629] Johnson, *Intellectuals*, 24.

"Rousseau is the one man who, through the loftiness of his soul and the grandeur of his character, showed himself worthy of the role of teacher of mankind," Robespierre said gratefully.[630]

Considering the judgement Robespierre handed down on the *un*worthy — the guillotine — this was quite a compliment.[631] But Rousseau was safely dead by the time the revolution began in 1789. In fact, the Assembly — a legislative version of what he had in mind with his General Will — voted to transfer his ashes to the Panthéon.[632]

Most had forgotten that Rousseau had, at times, warned against such an uprising. "People who make revolutions nearly always end by handing themselves over to tempters who make their chains heavier than before," he'd observed.[633] That's a pretty good description of how Napoleon Bonaparte came to power when the French Revolution finally ended.

But the French revolutionaries weren't wrong to acknowledge Rousseau. For years, he had stoked class resentments and threatened violence. At one of his last epic readings, he said that anyone who disagreed with his version of events "is himself a man who deserves to be strangled."[634]

Paul Johnson thought Rousseau's "true revolution" could be summarized in a single quotation: "Everything is at root dependent on politics."[635] Rousseau "moved the political process to the very centre of human existence by making the legislator . . . into the new Messiah, capable of solving all human problems by creating New Men."[636]

This is undoubtedly true — especially in nations that have suffered under the dictatorship of the General Will. But in the West, Rousseau's other noteworthy accomplishment is less often acknowledged.

[630] Johnson, *Intellectuals*, 2.

[631] Of course, the guillotine eventually came for Robespierre, too, in 1794, as the Terror finally concluded. He first tried to kill himself with a pistol, but failed, only shattering his jaw. The next morning, when he took his place on the platform, the executioner removed the bandage holding Robespierre's jaw in place, causing him to scream in pain until the blade came down. Knowing a happy ending when they saw one, the onlookers reportedly cheered for fifteen minutes afterward.

[632] The Panthéon was originally designed as a church. King Louis XV planned for it to be dedicated to Paris's patron saint, St. Genevieve. It was her relics — and not Rousseau's ashes — which were intended to be housed there.

[633] Johnson, *Intellectuals*, 23.

[634] Johnson, *Intellectuals*, 16.

[635] Johnson, *Intellectuals*, 26.

[636] Johnson, *Intellectuals*, 26.

By pursuing the ultimate individualism — making his life inseparable from his thought — Rousseau is the true creator of the culture of feeling. He reduced everything to the level of emotion. This tendency, along with his idealized view of nature, inspired the Romantic movement in the late eighteenth century, and the hippies in the twentieth.

But even though his tears flowed freely — no one cried more in print than Rousseau — there was steel underneath them. Find someone who is offended or "harmed" — who has suffered "violence" from someone's words or beliefs and now demands satisfaction — and you can imagine Jean-Jacques Rousseau's sulky spirit sniffling angrily behind them.

4.

During the Enlightenment, there was one philosopher in particular who didn't drink the Kool-Aid of individualism. In fact, he wrote that "religion is the basis of civil society, and the source of all good and all comfort." Unlike many of his contemporaries, he seems to have actually believed this.

And unlike many of his contemporaries, he refused to embrace the French Revolution. Instead, as it was beginning, he wrote a book that correctly predicted how things were likely to end. (Badly, in other words.) And he placed the blame where it belonged: on Jean-Jacques Rousseau, the "insane Socrates"[637] who had inspired it all.

Naturally, Edmund Burke therefore gets written out of many histories of philosophy. Or he receives a few lines that acknowledge he was out of step with the times. But the evidence shows that he was wiser by far than many of his peers.

Burke was an Irishman from Dublin, who served nearly thirty years in the British Parliament. He was a member of the House of Commons from the Whig Party, and many of his views, like his party's, were liberal.[638]

He supported the American colonists' complaints about unfair taxation. He led impeachment proceedings against the Indian colonial governor Warren

637 Herman, *The Cave and the Light*, 404.

638 Edmund Burke's mother, Mary Nagle, was a lifelong Catholic from County Cork. His wife, Jane Nugent, was also a Catholic, although they had to marry in the Anglican Church, since Roman Catholic weddings were then illegal.

Hastings, and supported the rights of the Indian people. "Every rupee of profit made by an Englishman," he declared, "is lost for ever to India."[639]

But he was also a defender of tradition. At the peak of the Enlightenment, when science and politics seemed ready to liberate people from every restriction, Burke saw this lie for what it was, and named it.

The social contract was not, as Locke and Rousseau had argued, something that could be broken on a whim.

> Society is, indeed, a contract. Subordinate contracts for objects of mere occasional interest may be dissolved at pleasure; but the state ought not to be considered as nothing better than a partnership agreement in a trade of pepper and coffee, calico or tobacco, or some other such low concern, to be taken up for a little temporary interest, and to be dissolved by the fancy of the parties. It is to be looked on with other reverence; because it is not a partnership in things subservient only to the gross animal existence of a temporary and perishable nature. It is a partnership in all science, a partnership in all art, a partnership in every virtue and in all perfection.
>
> As the ends of such a partnership cannot be obtained in many generations, it becomes a partnership not only between those who are living, but between those who are living, those who are dead, and those who are to be born.[640]

Burke insisted we don't just have a connection to the past, but that we also owe a *debt* to it. Here is where he was clearly against the spirit of his age. The excitement of the Enlightenment was all about progress and liberation, not tradition and gratitude.

This is why so few people recognized the French Revolution for what it was as quickly as Burke. He wasn't looking towards a glorious future. He had his eyes on the past, instead — and he didn't like how he saw it repeating in the present.

[639] Edmund Burke, "Mr. Burke's Speech, on the 1st December 1783," Eighteenth Century Collections Online, https://quod.lib.umich.edu/cgi/t/text/text-idx?cc=ecco.

[640] Edmund Burke, *Reflections on the Revolution in France* (Amherst, NY: Prometheus Books, 1987), 100.

5.

When it came to religious freedom, Burke —unlike many of his contemporaries — practiced what he preached. He was a lifelong Anglican who spoke out in defense of Catholics — especially when things turned ugly.

Anti-Catholic laws had been on the books in England and Ireland since the days of King Henry VIII. But in 1778, the Papist Act proposed relaxing some of the harshest restrictions on education and inheritance.

Two years later, Lord George Gordon and his Protestant followers marched on Parliament to protest the legislation. These demonstrations quickly became violent, and London burned that summer. The Gordon Riots, as they were called, revealed the depths of Britain's prejudice. They were also, Burke realized, a warning about what lay just beneath the veneer of "enlightenment."

"Wild and savage insurrection quitted the woods, and prowled about our streets in the name of reform," he wrote in "A Letter to a Noble Lord."[641]

This ugly incident reminded Burke that history was something to be studied — not transcended. Pretending that human nature was something science and politics could change, he thought, was the height of folly.

"The legislators who framed the ancient republics knew that their business was too arduous to be accomplished with no better apparatus than the metaphysics of an undergraduate and the mathematics and arithmetic of an exciseman," he said. "They had to do with men, and they were obliged to study human nature."[642]

That was exactly what Rousseau and the revolutionaries inspired by him *hadn't* done. The secret of Rousseau's success, Burke realized, was that "to strike and interest the public, the marvellous must be produced."[643] By "marvellous," Burke meant "novel" and "untried."

[641] Edmund Burke, "A Letter from the Right Honourable Edmund Burke to a Noble Lord" (1796), Eighteenth Century Collections Online, https://quod.lib.umich.edu/cgi/t/text/text-idx?c=ecco. Burke wrote this letter to the Duke of Bedford. He had retired from Parliament in 1794 and received a pension; the Duke and the Earl of Lauderdale criticized it as too generous. The letter highlighted the hypocrisy of these peers, who had received huge royal grants while providing far less service to the Crown.

[642] Burke, *Reflections on the Revolution in France*, 188.

[643] Burke, *Reflections on the Revolution in France*, 175. Burke noted in this passage that David Hume had shared with him this advice about the public's interest in the "marvellous." Hume had heard this wisdom from Jean-Jacques Rousseau himself.

Rousseau's General Will, and the way it was being manifested in France's National Assembly, was just such a "marvellous" experiment. This was what linked Rousseau to the more scientific philosophers of the seventeenth and eighteenth centuries: the burning desire to test a hypothesis that might lead to progress — or disaster. This time, French citizens would be the guinea pigs.

In 1789, Burke had received a letter from a young Frenchman named Charles-Jean-François Depont. The revolution had just begun, and an enthusiastic Depont wanted to know what Burke thought of it.

Burke responded with caution rather than congratulations. He later expanded on these troubled thoughts in *Reflections on the Revolution in France*, published the next year. The book, which also took the form of a letter, gave many warnings — especially of the way the French were trading tradition for novelty.

"Some very unusual appearances of wisdom ought to display themselves on the face of the designs of those who appeal to no practice and who copy after no model," Burke wrote. "Has any such been manifested?"[644]

The answer, as he suggested, was no. France would neither be the first, nor the worst, example of this mistake.

6.

Another key to Burke's prediction was that he understood the interplay between three major groups in society: the individual, the state, and the "little platoons" in between them.

Rousseau's political theory was all about liberating the individual. But to do this required the intervention of the state. And in Rousseau's concept, that intervention would be absolute. To become "free," the individual had to pledge his soul to the government — which would, in theory, reward him with the society he wanted and deserved.

The fly in the ointment was the "little platoons." When he used this term, Burke appears to have been talking about nobility. But others have pointed out that "little platoons" can also apply to churches, communities, and especially

[644] Burke, *Reflections on the Revolution in France*, 188.

families. What all these groups have in common is that they make claims on individuals and restrict their freedom.[645]

The love of one's country "is not extinguished by this subordinate partiality"[646] to these smaller groups, Burke argued. But the reformers and revolutionaries did not agree. In their view, the little platoons had to be circumvented or eliminated.

Locke, and especially Rousseau, had initiated this process. The French revolutionaries sped it up in many ways, from making marriage an easily dissolved civil contract to plundering churches and brutalizing the clergy. And the marginalization of the little platoons continues to this day, in societies both free and unfree.

Whether Burke was talking about aristocrats, grandparents, or the owners of a local store, his point was about *obligation* — what we owe others. But in the revolutionary view, the state is our only creditor.

7.

In the end, Burke correctly predicted just about everything. He foresaw that the French Revolution would end "in open violence and rapine," with "every description of tyranny and cruelty."[647] Like Rousseau, he foresaw that only a violent man would put an end to it: a "popular general" who would become "the master of your Assembly, the master of your whole republic."[648] Enter Napoleon.

And Burke believed that, especially after the Gordon Riots, the British were too smart to copy the French. "At home we behold similar beginnings," he wrote. "We are on our guard against similar conclusions."[649]

[645] The great conservative writer Russell Kirk is probably the person who popularized the idea that "little platoons" equaled families. In a 1977 speech at Hillsdale College, Kirk made this case: "In the phrase of Edmund Burke, the family is the origin of 'the little platoon we belong to in society,' and it is 'the germ of public affections' " (Kirk, "The Little Platoon We Belong to in Society," 1977). However, in a 2018 piece for *The American Conservative,* "Knock It Off With the 'Little Platoons' Already," James McElroy argues that Burke was talking about aristocrats and not families. He cites Yuval Levin's 2013 book *The Great Debate: Edmund Burke, Thomas Paine, and the Birth of Right and Left,* which states that "in its context in the *Reflections* the passage is very clearly a reference to social class."

[646] Burke, *Reflections on the Revolution in France,* 201.

[647] Burke, *Reflections on the Revolution in France,* 109, 127.

[648] Burke, *Reflections on the Revolution in France,* 224.

[649] Burke, *Reflections on the Revolution in France,* 109.

Criticizing the French Revolution, however, made Burke unpopular in many quarters. Some felt that by defending the monarchy he'd turned conservative and was abandoning his liberal principles and friends.

One was the reformer Thomas Paine, the author of *Common Sense* — the pamphlet that had helped launch the American Revolution. He felt betrayed by Burke, who had supported the colonists.[650]

After reading *Reflections*, Paine quickly assembled his own response. *Rights of Man*, published in 1791, was a passionate defense of the French Revolution. It was also a personal attack on Burke.

As author Yuval Levin notes, Burke and Paine had a surprising amount in common. "Each was an outsider who transformed himself, by force of intellect and personality, into the great champion of a society in which he was not born."[651] But *Reflections* and *Rights* made crystal clear the difference between the two men, and between the movements they would represent.

Paine believed that "nothing of reform on the political world ought to be held improbable." If that meant burning the entire system down and starting over, then so be it.[652]

But where the progressive Paine imagined possibility, the conservative Burke saw the guillotine. Respecting, learning from, and preserving the past were the only ways to avoid it.

One of Paine's criticisms of Burke continues to the present day: that he didn't know enough about France to assess the situation. Paine had seen the revolution firsthand; Burke had not.

Burke had already anticipated that complaint. It was better to lack firsthand experience, he felt, than to be ignorant of how men really are.

"I do not pretend to know France as correctly as some others," he wrote, "but I have endeavored through my whole life to make myself acquainted with human nature — otherwise I should be unfit to take even my humble part in the service of mankind."[653]

650 In a 2022 piece in *The Imaginative Conservative*, historian Bradley Birzer makes the case that Edmund Burke was actually a much stronger supporter of the American Revolution than most scholars realize: https://theimaginativeconservative.org/2022/07/edmund-burke-support-american-revolution-bradley-birzer.html.

651 Yuval Levin, *The Great Debate: Edmund Burke, Thomas Paine, and the Birth of Right and Left* (New York: Basic Books, 2014), 23.

652 Levin, *The Great Debate*, 70.

653 Burke, *Reflections on the Revolution in France*, 140.

That humble part is often overlooked in the history of philosophy. Yet Burke's unglamorous conclusions may still be the best way to keep the blood and fire of revolution at bay.

SECTION FOUR

THE DARKENING WOOD

Not everyone realized it at the time. But as England fought against rebels on foreign soil, and France drew closer to its own revolution, the philosophical torch was being passed.

Throughout the nineteenth century, it burned brightest in Germany. Or more accurately, in the German-speaking territories — primarily Prussia — that were considering their own revolutionary act: reunification.

The German world was not without its optimism, nor did it lack brilliant men. But for the most part, the Enlightenment had convinced them to banish God from the conversation. If He existed, He was outside the picture frame and unknowable — or He was really just us, a trick we played on ourselves.

And the rise of Germanic thought also gave us the philosopher-as-professional-academic, who wrote in intentionally baffling language. So the philosophical torch now cast shadows, rather than creating illumination.

As the century changed, the philosophies of German thinkers grew to resemble a solitary man, carrying a light through a dense and forbidding forest. This was the allegedly liberated individual of the Enlightenment, but he seemed to be following the breadcrumbs straight to the witch's house.

While he stumbled along, weird shapes that his torch created would stretch far beyond this darkening wood. Those images would haunt the rest of the world for decades afterward, well into the twentieth century. In fact, they haunt it still.

CHAPTER FIFTEEN

GERMAN ENGINEERING

1.

The professor is out for his afternoon walk.

His lectures at the university are over. He's had his usual lunch at his usual pub. Now it's time to muse while he travels the avenues of Königsberg.

It's a cloudy day, so he's wearing his gray overcoat. The professor is a tiny man — just over five feet — but he strides briskly along the avenue, in the shade of the linden trees. He taps his walking stick gently on the ground as he strolls.

Behind the professor, his faithful servant lurks, carrying in the crook of his arm an umbrella, in case it rains. The professor barely seems to notice. Sometimes he has additional company on these walks, but today he's by himself, deep in thought.

The professor has actually been deep in thought for most of the past decade. He's nearly sixty years old, and he's been wrestling with several dilemmas. Some of them are old problems for philosophers. What can we know, and how can we know it? And where does our sense of morality come from?

No one will know it today, on this afternoon near the end of the 1770s, but the professor has come up with some answers for these vexing questions.

Over the next few years, he'll publish them in a series of books. These books will be notoriously difficult to read: the professor is a better teacher and conversationalist than he is a writer. But enough people will fight through these dense texts that the professor's ideas will alter philosophy.

Later, people will caricature the professor and his predictable habits: his early morning coffee and his pub lunches; his walks and his gray overcoat. They'll compare his lifestyle to the clock of the nearby cathedral — except they'll joke that the clock is more passionate and less regular. They'll say the professor is just a mechanical man, an automaton.

This will all, of course, be an exaggeration. It ignores the fact that the professor is no hermit: he's a popular dinner guest and spirited conversationalist. In his youth, he was a dandy, but even as he's aged, his cheeks have stayed ruddy and his piercing blue eyes remain lively and curious.

In fact, the professor will argue that what makes men "more than machines" is free thought — the very sort he's about to share in his books.

"Have courage to use your own understanding!" he will urge. "That is the motto of enlightenment."[654] *Some will claim that Enlightenment with a capital "E" is what the professor and his ideas have saved.*

2.

Depending on whom you ask, Immanuel Kant is one of two things.

He's the man who rescued philosophy from David Hume's skepticism and reconciled the long war between reason and the senses. Or he's the philosopher who came up with an impractical system that few could grasp, in language almost no one could understand.

It's possible he was both.

[654] Immanuel Kant, "What Is Enlightenment?" (1784), trans. Ted Humphrey, New York Public Library, https://www.nypl.org/sites/default/files/kant_whatisenlightenment.pdf. Material from Manfred Kuehn's 2002 biography of Immanuel Kant also figures into this opening sequence.

For most of his life, Kant worked quietly in his hometown of Königsberg, a port along the Baltic Sea in what was then Prussia. Today it's the Russian city of Kaliningrad.

Kant attended the local university, taught there, and became the chair of logic and metaphysics in 1770. Two philosophers proved especially important in his daily readings, and filled his mind as he walked the streets of the city.

One was Jean-Jacques Rousseau. This still seems an odd choice to many people. What could the sober university professor have seen in the over-the-top fiction of Rousseau? And why was Rousseau's portrait one of the only decorations in Kant's spartan bachelor apartment?[655]

They both shared an interest in education, for starters. There's a story—probably another exaggeration, but a telling one—that Kant interrupted his daily walks only once: to keep reading Rousseau's book *Émile,* which outlined plans for an ideal system of learning. And both men were also interested in morality. Where, specifically, does it come from?

Kant would, in the end, disagree with most of Rousseau's conclusions. But he acknowledged that it was Rousseau who "set me right."[656]

Kant found the skepticism of David Hume even more challenging. Later he admitted, in a famous quote, that Hume "first interrupted my dogmatic slumber and gave my investigations in the field of speculative philosophy a quite new direction."[657]

The goal Kant set for himself was to solve "the execution of Hume's problem in its widest extent."[658] But this was no overnight job. Hume had seemingly demolished the foundations of philosophy. How could we know *anything* for certain?

Kant spent ten years ruminating on this dilemma. He considered it in his rented rooms in the Löbenicht Town Hall, and later in a drafty apartment on the Ochsenmarkte. He brought it up in his university lectures. And of course, he weighed the possibilities on his strolls around Königsberg.

When the *Critique of Pure Reason* finally appeared in 1781, then, it was the result of thousands of hours of thought. Kant's thesis was that "traditional metaphysics rests on a fundamental mistake."[659]

655 A useful survey of Kant's classrooms and private quarters (which were sometimes in the same places) can be found at https://users.manchester.edu/facstaff/ssnaragon/kant/lectures/lecturesClassrooms.htm.

656 Manfred Kuehn, *Kant: A Biography* (Cambridge: Cambridge University Press, 2002), 131.

657 Kuehn, *Kant: A Biography*, 230.

658 Kuehn, *Kant: A Biography*, 231.

659 Kuehn, *Kant: A Biography*, 242.

The mistake, Kant thought, was thinking that reason could help us know anything concrete about the world around us. He would spend the last twenty-plus years of his life trying to correct this error.

3.

René Descartes had created his philosophy by splitting the mind and the body. Immanuel Kant would rejoin them. To do this, however, Kant insisted on a different sort of separation: a separation of the world.

For Kant, there were really two worlds: the *phenomenal* and the *noumenal.*

The phenomenal world is the world of phenomena: the world of things as they *appear* to be. This is the world of sensory perception. In this realm, we use our senses to get impressions of the things we encounter: the color and taste of an apple; the scent and feel of a rose; the length and weight of a bottle.

The noumenal world, meanwhile, is the world of things as they truly are — as *things-in-themselves.* This is a world *beyond* our perception. Kant insisted that we're "incompetent" if we try to go "beyond the conditions of our sensibility, and to assume the existence of objects of pure thought."[660]

These objects of pure thought include things-in-themselves, as well as God and the immortal soul. Kant doesn't *deny* their existence. He just walls them off from inquiry. His explanation, in the preface to the second edition of *Critique of Pure Reason,* was, "I had to deny knowledge in order to make room for faith."[661] Medieval philosophers like John Duns Scotus and William of Ockham had insisted on a similar denial.

The three big questions for Kant were *What can I know? What must I do?* and *What may I hope?* His answer to the first question was fairly simple: we can only know things in the phenomenal realm.

But we can't know them as they *really* are, as things-in-themselves. And we should stop trying. We don't have the sensory apparatus to penetrate this noumenal world beyond our experience. "It is precisely in knowing its limits," Kant advised, "that philosophy exists."[662]

[660] Immanuel Kant, *The Critique of Pure Reason* (Chicago: Encyclopedia Britannica, 1952), 106.

[661] Kuehn, *Kant: A Biography,* 262.

[662] Buckingham, *The Philosophy Book,* 167.

So far, Kant's idea of a limited phenomenal world sounds a lot like the ideas of the British empiricists. It's similar to John Locke's admission that the substance underneath an object's qualities is just a "something, I know not what." And it has something in common with the skeptical empiricism of George Berkeley and David Hume.

Here is where Kant brought rationalism into the picture. Locke, Berkeley, and Hume had all denied the possibility of *a priori* knowledge—knowledge we're born with. This was a tradition in empirical thought that went all the way back to Aristotle. The idea was that man is born with a mind like a *tabula rasa*—a blank slate. As we experience things, this slate gets filled up with sensory data.

Kant, however, argued that our minds actually play a critical role in processing the sensory data we receive. And he thought they do so because humans *do* have *a priori* knowledge. We're preprogrammed, Kant said, with a sort of template that helps us understand the world around us.

This template includes a dozen different categories related to quantity, quality, relation, and modality (meaning whether a thing is *possible, actual,* or *necessary*). Kant called these categories "principles of pure understanding."[663]

The categories in this template, Kant believed, are how we interpret the world. Every time we encounter an object, we automatically fit it into this preprogrammed structure.

This rational structure is just a template: it's useless without the empirical, sensory data we feed into it. But the template, for Kant, solved the problem of Hume's skepticism. Having this preprogrammed understanding "grants also the existence of things in themselves."[664] We can at least be sure that the world around us exists—even if we can't know anything deeper about it.

This is Kant's truly radical break—what he immodestly claimed as his Copernican revolution. Almost every previous empiricist had claimed that the objects in the world define reality for us. Those objects generate sensory representations, which we interpret.

But Kant claimed that *we* create reality, every time we apply the template in our mind to the objects we encounter. This template is what creates our representations of those objects. And it's those representations, Kant thought, that actually make the objects exist.

663 Kant, *The Critique of Pure Reason*, 10.
664 Cahn, *Classics of Western Philosophy*, 1016.

It's a startling idea. But by insisting on this structure, Kant also felt he'd solved another problem that had plagued both rationalists *and* empiricists. They had struggled to explain how we can really talk about the world around us, if we can't be sure that the objects we encounter exist outside our own minds.

Kant's even more surprising answer was that "we would not have knowledge of the states of our own minds ... if we were not simultaneously aware of permanent substances in space, outside of the mind."[665] In other words, it's the existence of the world around us that proves our minds are working—and not the other way around.

This combination of rationalism (the preprogrammed template in our minds) and empiricism (using this template to translate sensory data) generated controversy—and plenty of confusion. So did Kant's term for it: *transcendental idealism.*

He seemed to mean that our knowledge of the world goes beyond sensory evidence (that's the transcendental part) and requires us to also understand how our minds process that evidence (that's the idealism part).

It was a hard sell for critics. Some felt Kant's concept of a world we can't truly know wasn't much different than Hume's skepticism. This resulted in several negative reviews for *Critique of Pure Reason*.

Kant was stung especially by the criticisms that his work was written in "hierogylphics."[666] He not only revised the book substantially but returned two years later with a much shorter version, the *Prolegomena*. It somehow managed to be every bit as dense and obscure.

Nevertheless, Kant had at least tried to answer one of his three major questions: What can I know? That left two others: What must I do? and What may I hope? He took up those inquiries next.

4.

There's a knock at your door.

When you answer it, you find your best friend, disheveled and clearly panicked. He tumbles into the room and begs you to hide him. When you ask why, he stutters out an explanation: he's being

[665] Tim Jankowiak, "Kant, Immanuel," *Internet Encyclopedia of Philosophy*," 2023, https://iep.utm.edu/kantview/.

[666] Frederick C. Beiser, *The Fate of Reason: German Philosophy from Kant to Fichte* (Cambridge, MA: Harvard University Press, 1987), 172–173.

chased by an axe murderer named Bob, who is right on his heels. Shaken, you agree to let your friend hide in your basement.

Barely two minutes later, your door shudders as someone pounds against it. You swallow, take a deep breath, and open the door. You find an angry-looking man holding a bloody axe. He introduces himself as Bob and asks if your friend is there.

When you ask why, Bob says that he's looking for your friend. He fixes you with a scarifying stare. Then he asks you again, and more insistently, if your friend is there.

How should you answer him?[667]

5.

Like many Enlightenment philosophers, it's difficult to pin down Kant's spiritual views. The vagueness was undoubtedly intentional. Unorthodox religious beliefs were still, in most cases, bad for one's career.

Kant's belief in some sort of deity is easily established. What sort of deity he believed in is not. His biographer Manfred Kuehn points out that Kant was often heard to "scoff at prayer and other religious practices. Organized religion filled him with ire.

[667] This section is a reimagining of a dilemma posed by Kant as an extreme test of his Categorical Imperative. In his 1797 essay "On the Supposed Right to Lie from Benevolent Motives," he responded to criticism from the French philosopher Benjamin Constant, who insisted, "To tell the truth is a duty, but only towards him who has a right to the truth." Kant disagreed. He pointed out that by telling a lie, you might unknowingly cause a murderer and his potential victim to meet.

For, if you had spoken the truth as well as you knew it, perhaps the murderer while seeking for his enemy in the house might have been caught by neighbours coming up and the deed been prevented. Whoever then tells a lie, however good his intentions may be, must answer for the consequences of it, even before the civil tribunal, and must pay the penalty for them, however unforeseen they may have been; because truthfulness is a duty that must be regarded as the basis of all duties founded on contract, the laws of which would be rendered uncertain and useless if even the least exception to them were admitted (Immanuel Kant, "On the Supposed Right to Lie from Benevolent Motives," 1797. http://www.sophia-project.org/uploads/1/3/9/5/13955288/kant_lying.pdf).

Kant's point was that lying for a good cause can have unforeseen consequences. This probably won't convince most people to turn a friend over to an axe murderer, but Kant was at least consistent in his principles.

"It was clear to anyone who knew Kant personally that he had no faith in a personal God," Kuehn writes. "Having postulated God and immortality, he himself did not believe in either."[668]

In *Critique of Pure Reason,* Kant had tried to show the "impossibility" of three common proofs for God's existence: the ontological proof, the cosmological proof, and the physico-theological proof—otherwise known as the teleological argument, which argues that nature shows evidence of design.

Kant was most sympathetic to the last argument. But he claimed it ended up borrowing from the other two arguments—which invalidated it, too.

As Kant was at pains to point out, that didn't mean God does not exist. The "boundary principle"—that some things are simply beyond our experience—helped keep discussions about God out of his philosophy. Kant's influence ensured that many future philosophers would follow his example.

The exception came when Kant began seriously wrestling with the problem of morality. He had to concede "that morality inevitably leads us to the acceptance of certain tenets of traditional theism."[669] So, to mean anything, morality couldn't simply be relative or manmade: it had to be universal instead. And if morality was universal, Kant realized, then it had to come from somewhere beyond the phenomenal world.

Our moral "intuitions"—our inner sense of right and wrong—give us our major clue about the existence of the noumenal world. Even "in the absence of knowledge of absolute reality," Kant concluded, "morality has a claim on us that is itself absolute and incontrovertible."[670]

This moral claim is what "elevates us above the beasts. It shows us to be rational in the way that Plato had insisted that we are rational."[671] And it also suggests that humans must have free will, which also comes from the noumenal world.

We can't experience free will with our senses. But morality makes no sense without it. So if we believe in the concepts of right and wrong—and Kant acknowledged that even people who seem to act *immorally* think they should be treated morally, too—then we must also believe in free will.

These conclusions would be the basis of *Groundwork of the Metaphysics of Morals,* published in 1785. In this book, Kant tried to nail down a supreme moral principle. His conclusion was that it meant having a "good will"—acting

[668] Kuehn, *Kant: A Biography*, 3.
[669] Kuehn, *Kant: A Biography*, 250.
[670] Kuehn, *Kant: A Biography*, 265.
[671] Kuehn, *Kant: A Biography*, 265.

as we know we should, with no ulterior motives. We can't treat people as means to our own selfish ends, but instead as ends in themselves.

From this "good will," Kant proposed a concept he later called the Categorical Imperative. This is a principle to evaluate our actions. It goes like this: "I ought never to act except in such a way that I could also will that my maxim should become a universal law."[672]

So before we act, we should ask ourselves a question. *What would happen if the law forced everyone in similar circumstances to do what I'm about to do?* If we admit this would create problems, then we shouldn't do what we're about to do.

Obviously, there are problems with using the Categorical Imperative as a moral yardstick. In some cases, it seems to be a helpful guide. *What would happen if every time someone gets angry at a child, they were required to beat them bloody?* The answer there seems clear.

In other cases — as in the case of Bob the axe murderer — it's much trickier.

Kant took the position that we're obligated to tell the truth, no matter what. So even if we think we're doing the right thing by lying to Bob and saving our friend, we are also treating Bob as a means to an end and depriving him of the chance to act morally.

Naturally, most people won't agree with this idea — especially not if they find themselves confronted by Bob. And as Edward Feser points out, applying the Categorical Imperative under more normal circumstances still involves so many conditions and qualifications that it quickly becomes useless.

But Kant's theory of morality, like his attempt to solve Hume's problem of skepticism, seemed to offer an attractive compromise for Enlightenment thinkers. Both ideas appealed to reason, without committing to God. They confirmed that the material world does exist, while insisting humans can operate freely within it. And they preserved a secular world for Kant's descendants. There, science could work unimpeded because faith was a purely private affair.

At least, Kant's philosophy offered a compromise for those who could *understand* it. He wrote in the sort of dry, technical style we've come to associate with academics — and philosophers. Some argue this has been Kant's greatest influence. The authors of *A Short History of Philosophy* note dryly, "With Kant, philosophy had become resolutely an academic discipline. (It has never recovered.)"[673]

[672] Kuehn, *Kant: A Biography*, 265.

[673] Robert C. Solomon and Kathleen Marie Higgins, *A Short History of Philosophy* (New York: Oxford University Press, 1996), 216.

But there was also something hollow at the core of Kant's teaching. The limits he placed on what we could know meant that his far-reaching system occupied a much smaller space than it seemed.

Kant understood this himself. In the *Prolegomena,* he admitted, "On a cursory view of the present work it may seem that its results are merely negative, warning us that we must never venture beyond the limits of experience. Such is in fact its primary use."[674] Those limits meant that his system was quickly replaced.

Kant was only the first of a series of German philosophers who dominated the nineteenth century. Their ideas would range far, far beyond the guidelines he'd tried to impose. They found his unverifiable God easy not just to ignore, but also to refute.

And while Kant's transcendental idealism had a great effect on philosophy, some of the thinkers who followed him would have a much more practical influence on the world. The body counts alone would prove it.

6.

The problem with Kant's philosophy, for many critics, was that it was actually two different philosophies.

Kant had tried to reconcile rationalism and empiricism. He'd also tried to avoid the mind-body dualism of Descartes. But in doing all this, he'd created a dualism of his own.

His natural philosophy insisted that the material world actually exists — but that we can know nothing certain about it. It's the noumenal world, of things as they truly are. But Kant's moral philosophy claimed that we *can* know something about this noumenal world — that it's the source of our moral intuitions.

This idea, in the view of some of his German academic rivals, was incoherent. So they set out to fix it.

Two of the first contestants were Johann Fichte and Friedrich Schelling. Both were university professors, like Kant. Each man essentially focused on the half of Kant's philosophy he preferred.

For Fichte, that was Kant's ideas about morality. Fichte wrote, "What sort of philosophy one chooses depends on what sort of person one is."[675]

[674] Cahn, *Classics of Western Philosophy,* 1239.

[675] Magee, *The Story of Philosophy,* 155.

Kant had said that we create reality through the "template" in our minds that we apply to our experiences. Fichte adapted this view. He agreed that we create reality. But we create it not for the sake of knowledge, but because we are "moral beings."[676]

If we actually have free will, then we need a material world where we can use it. This material world has to be separate from each of us, or else we wouldn't truly be free. So we create a material world through our *morality,* Fichte said — to give ourselves a place to prove our virtue.

This concept wasn't for everyone. But Fichte was a great orator. And his ethical worldview had more influence when he applied it to another cause: the growing desire in the nineteenth century to unify the German states, like Prussia and Austria, into a single nation. Fichte became known as one of the founding fathers of German nationalism.[677]

Friedrich Schelling, meanwhile, focused on Kant's natural philosophy — specifically, nature. Nature, Schelling thought, is a continually evolving and unified entity. Man is part of that unity, and that evolution.

Man's self-awareness puts him at the top of nature's food chain. And because he is self-aware, he can also create. In the art he makes, man tries to understand nature. This, Schelling believed, meant that the artist actually helps capital-*N* Nature — the single entity that we're all a part of — become self-aware.

Schelling's *Philosophy of Nature* sounds a lot like the pantheism of Baruch Spinoza and the ancient Stoics. But because it was so artist-centric, artists — naturally — loved it.

Germans like Johann Wolfgang von Goethe — the author of the play *Faust* — and the composer Carl Maria von Weber became fans. And Schelling, writes Bryan Magee, became "the house philosopher of the Romantic Movement"[678] in England. Poet Samuel Taylor Coleridge, who wrote "Kubla Khan" and "The Rime of the Ancient Mariner," spread the gospel according to Schelling.

Yet it would be a college friend of Schelling's who became Kant's true rival and unlikely successor. That was Georg W. F. Hegel.

[676] Magee, *The Story of Philosophy,* 155.

[677] The movement in favor of a unified German nation-state began early in the nineteenth century, after Napoleon's invasion of Prussia. The European revolutions of 1848 saw nationalists come to power in several German states. By 1871, when the German Empire was formed, nationalists' views were dominated by Prussian and Protestant influence.

[678] Magee, *The Story of Philosophy,* 157.

It took Hegel quite some time to get his ideas off the ground. Born in Stuttgart in 1770, he attended a Protestant seminary with Schelling and the poet Friedrich Hölderlin. He would borrow heavily from both men, but his own work was first confined to a series of essays written while he worked as a private tutor.

In 1801, Hegel finally landed a teaching position at the university in Jena, a city located southwest of Leipzig. But Schelling was the school's philosophical star. Hegel's lectures, by contrast, drew fewer than a dozen students.

A description of a typical class helps explain why:

> His students saw a plain, old-fashioned face, without life or lustre — a figure that had never looked young and was now prematurely aged. Sitting with his snuffbox before him and his head bent down, he looked ill at ease and kept turning the folios of his notes. His utterance was interrupted by frequent coughing; every sentence came out with a struggle.[679]

Yet Hegel kept working steadily to develop both a style and a philosophy. His early essays had been surprisingly clear and jargon-free. Now he realized that the way to go was to copy Kant's "ponderous, sometimes tortured" writing.[680]

Hegel completed his first book in 1806. *The Phenomenology of Spirit* was reportedly finished to the sound of gunfire that October. On a plateau outside the city, Napoleon was winning the Battle of Jena.

You might think Hegel was dismayed to see Prussia defeated by the French emperor. Hegel and his friends had been enthusiastic supporters of the French Revolution — so you might also think he'd be disappointed that the result of it all was a military dictator.

Both guesses would be incorrect. When Hegel saw Napoleon enter the city just before the battle, he gushed to a friend, "I saw the Emperor — this world-spirit — riding out of the city on reconnaissance. It is indeed a wonderful sensation to see such an individual, who, concentrated here at a single point, astride a horse, reaches out over the world and masters it."[681]

Napoleon's victory meant hardship for Hegel. Enrollment at the university dropped after the battle, and Hegel had to take a job in Bamberg as a newspaper

679 T. Malcolm Knox, "Georg Wilhelm Friedrich Hegel," *Britannica*, last updated November 10, 2023, https://www.britannica.com/biography/Georg-Wilhelm-Friedrich-Hegel/At-Berlin.

680 Solomon and Higgins, *A Short History of Philosophy*, 216.

681 Terry P. Pinkard, *Hegel: A Biography* (Cambridge: Cambridge University Press, 2001), 228.

editor. But that didn't matter. The rise of Napoleon fit perfectly into Hegel's emerging philosophy.

It was ambitious: Hegel was developing a system to replace Kant's. This system included elements of art, religion — and history, in particular. Today we take for granted that philosophy will also focus on history. But at the time, this idea made Hegel unique.

When Hegel looked around him, he saw Germanic genius in full flower. For example, the composer Ludwig van Beethoven, who was born the same year as Hegel, was just about to debut his famous Fifth Symphony. But Beethoven, like all artists, was a product of history. He could not have existed in any other time. He and his work were infused with the spirit of the age — the *Zeitgeist.*

History, for Hegel, was a continuous, evolving process. This process is called the *dialectic,* which we first saw all the way back in chapter 2. There are three parts: the *thesis,* the *antithesis,* and the *synthesis.*

In history, everything begins with an idea: a thesis. But every thesis contains an opposing idea, a contradiction. This is the antithesis. And the thesis and antithesis are destined to clash. When they do, the result isn't just one side winning. There is always some sort of synthesis — a combination of the thesis and antithesis.

Of course, every synthesis also contains contradictions. That leads to further conflict, and the cycle begins again.

"When Hegel's theses and antitheses collide," Arthur Herman observes, "they tend to collide on the battlefield, in bitter, violent street clashes, in torture chambers and prison cells, and in revolutions."[682] But all these events, even the bloody ones, are necessary, Hegel insisted.

In fact, "periods of happiness" are "empty pages" in history. Nothing is *happening* during these times of peace. "Let insecurity finally come in the form of Hussars with glistening sabers," Hegel enthused, "and show its earnest activity!"[683]

History, in short, was not just a *process* for Hegel. It was also the story of *progress*. And progress can't happen without the conflict of the dialectic.

But what is all this progress leading us *to*? How will we know when we've reached our goal? Here, we reach the heart of Hegel's philosophy. Or rather, its *Geist.*

682 Herman, *The Cave and the Light*, 437.

683 Herman, *The Cave and the Light*, 437.

7.

Hegel had been struck by an idea of his friend Friedrich Schelling: the concept of a pantheistic Nature trying to become self-aware.

Hegel, however, was no Romantic. So he substituted something else for Nature. That was a thing called *Geist*, a German word somewhere between "spirit" and "mind."

Hegel's *Geist* is at war with itself as it tries to achieve self-awareness — the knowledge that everything is really a single thing. This is similar in many ways to ideas we have seen from older philosophers.

Plotinus and the Neoplatonists had argued that everything is just part of the One. Muslim philosophers like Averroës and Hindu thinkers had made the same claim.

But Hegel traced out a long chain of steps to explain how this happens. We start with "sense certainty"[684] — the simple idea that the things we experience are real objects. Next, we recognize universals, like the color red, or triangles, or dogs.

Soon we reach self-consciousness, which brings knowledge, but also conflict — the *Geist* at war with itself. And eventually, we reach a stage of "unhappy consciousness,"[685] where we project the ideas of our ideal selves onto a godlike figure.

This creates *alienation*, an important concept in Hegel's philosophy. We're alienated because we haven't yet realized that we are all one — and therefore, all *Geist*. And *Geist* can be called many things besides "Spirit" or "World Spirit": Mind, the Absolute, or God.

Hegel described Christianity as the "absolute religion."[686] But that was less because he was an orthodox Christian and more because he saw Christianity as a critical later stage in his own philosophy. He viewed Christ as a singular man who had achieved the enlightenment Hegel described: recognizing that he was one with God. This, according to Hegel, is the job for the rest of us, following Christ's example.

Once we accept this challenge, and once the *Geist* finally recognizes itself, we will reach the end of history. There will be no more conflict and no more dialectic, because there will be no need. Unity will have been achieved.

How will we know when this happens? Conveniently enough, by listening to Hegel. This is another way his philosophy was unique: Hegel not only gave

[684] Kreeft, *Socrates' Children*, vol. 3, ch. 67.

[685] Kreeft, *Socrates' Children*, vol. 3, ch. 67.

[686] Kreeft, *Socrates' Children*, vol. 3, ch. 67.

us "the key to understanding reality" but made himself "the culmination of the world-historical process, the embodiment of reality's purposes as regards understanding, the very incarnation of our enlightenment."[687]

As Peter Kreeft jokes, "Not a bad job for a dull professor: to be the intellectual obstetrician for God's birth."[688]

But this self-promotion worked — at least in raising Hegel's profile. By the time he moved on to teach at Heidelberg and Berlin, his lectures were attended by hundreds of students. In the German-speaking world, he'd become a bigger star than Fichte or Schelling could have dreamed.

Hegel died in 1831 during a cholera epidemic in Berlin, at age sixty-one. Evidently, the fame he achieved was no reassurance that his complex philosophy had landed with his audience. "There was only one man who ever understood me," Hegel reportedly observed on his deathbed, "and even he didn't understand me."[689]

The story of those last words was probably apocryphal.[690] But they were prophetic nonetheless. After his death, Hegel's supporters split into two camps — with two very different understandings of his ideas.

Both groups were inspired by Hegel's belief that "man owes his entire existence to the State."[691] For Hegel, the group was always more important than the individual. He believed that the social contract thinkers like Hobbes and Locke had it backwards. They'd taught that man acts as an individual to create a society. But for Hegel, it's *society* that creates the individual.

"Individuality begins to appear only *within* an interpersonal context," write Robert Solomon and Kathleen Higgins in their *Short History of Philosophy*. "What people basically want and need is not only security and material comfort but *recognition*."[692]

This desire reflects the essential unity of human beings. But it also means that the State is the highest authority. It trumps "the laws and interests of the

687 Magee, *The Story of Philosophy*, 161.

688 Kreeft, *Socrates' Children*, vol. 3, ch. 67.

689 Heinrich Heine, *The Works of Heinrich Heine* (London: William Heinemann, 1892), 157.

690 Hegel's biographer Terry Pinkard dismisses Hegel's deathbed quote as a fabrication that enemies of Hegel used to dismiss him. He claims that Hegel "became the voice that many proponents of modern life wished to ignore, or, if they could not ignore him, to dismiss him with a sneer" (*Hegel: A Biography*, 662).

691 Magee, *The Story of Philosophy*, 161.

692 Solomon and Higgins, *A Short History of Philosophy*, 218.

family and community," which "are subject and dependent" to the State.[693] The State, in fact, is "the Spirit of the People itself."[694]

Here, Hegel reached a similar, paradoxical conclusion to Rousseau: the only thing that can give us individual freedom is the State. The Renaissance had liberated man from medieval society; the Reformation had liberated him from Catholicism. Capitalism had liberated him from home and hearth, but it also isolated and alienated.

The State was the ultimate answer. "Its development as an autonomous actor in history is in fact the next and final stage of freedom beyond commercial society."[695]

But what *kind* of state? That was where Hegel's followers were split.

The Right Hegelians shared Hegel's enthusiasm for Prussia's constitutional monarchy. He had suggested that it was the ideal form of the State. Of course, that meant Hegel himself might be around to witness the end of history—a tempting and convenient conclusion.

That didn't happen, of course, but Right Hegelians stayed committed to the concept. All the way back to his praise of Napoleon, Hegel had subscribed to what is called the "Great Man" theory of history. Certain outstanding individuals come along every now and then, and they have a major effect on world affairs. This is good, Hegel thought, because they speed up the process of the *Geist* realizing itself.

Combine the love of a dominant state with the belief in powerful leaders—"Great Men," free to act outside traditional ethical guidelines. Then add the growing desire for German nationalism to this Right Hegelian mix. The result is an intellectual justification for the rise of Hitler and the Third Reich.

The Left Hegelians certainly didn't view the Prussian monarchy as the best form of government. They saw inequality and alienation, all right—but they could find no great men, and no ideal state, that could deal with these problems. So they believed the State would have to go much, much further.

The best known of the Left Hegelians was Karl Marx. But one of the first, and most influential, was one of Hegel's former students: a Bavarian named Ludwig Feuerbach.

Feuerbach borrowed Hegel's idea of alienation. The big difference was that Feuerbach was an atheist. So he disagreed with Hegel's idea that man is alienated because he doesn't recognize he's really at one with God.

[693] Georg Hegel, *The Philosophy of Right* (Kitchener, ON: Batoche Books, 2001), 249.

[694] Herman, *The Cave and the Light*, 437.

[695] Herman, *The Cave and the Light*, 436.

In his 1841 book *The Essence of Christianity*, Feuerbach argued that man is alienated instead because he's projected all his best qualities onto a being that doesn't exist. We try vainly to live up to a moral perfection we can never hope to attain, becoming more and more unhappy.

This idea of perfection not only "proclaims to me what I ought to be, it also tells me to my face, without any flattery, what I am not," Feuerbach wrote. "And religion renders this disunion all the more painful, all the more terrible, that it sets man's own nature before him as a separate nature, and moreover as a personal being, who hates and curses sinners, and excludes them from his grace, the source of all salvation and happiness."[696]

Love is the only answer, Feuerbach insisted — along with liberation from the destructive idea of a separate, judgmental God. "Love is God himself, and apart from it there is no God," he declared. "Love makes man God and God man.

"Hence, if man is to find contentment in God," concluded Feuerbach, "he must find himself in God."[697]

Hegel had seen a version of this philosophy while Feuerbach was his student, and reportedly hadn't been impressed. But Feuerbach's idea is closer to Hegel's than the master would likely have admitted. Both men were essentially saying that man creates God throughout history. Feuerbach just thought there was no actual God behind this process.

The battles between the Right and Left Hegelians raged well into the twentieth century. Long after he died, Hegel — like Rousseau — would win the dubious distinction of being an "intellectual grandfather of both Nazism and communism."[698]

But we should also point out a third strain of Hegel's thought. That's the kind we find in most Western democracies. We could call it Center Hegelianism — but the more common term is the "nanny state."

"Unemployment insurance, health and safety regulations, minimum wage laws and aid to dependent children, the income tax and federal deposit insurance,"

[696] Ludwig Feuerbach, *The Essence of Christianity*, trans. Marian Evans (London: Kegan Paul, Trench, Trübner, & Co., 1890), Project Gutenberg, https://www.gutenberg.org/cache/epub/47025/pg47025-images.html.

[697] Feuerbach, *The Essence of Christianity*.

[698] Magee, *The Story of Philosophy*, 162.

Arthur Herman notes. "All these become justified as the State acting to protect us from ourselves, because the State is our Better and Higher Self."[699]

So, what, in the end, is the real Hegelianism? Is his focus on history, as Peter Kreeft writes, "Hegel's lasting legacy" — specifically, his belief that "history is the story of progress"?[700] Is it the devastation unleashed in Germany, Russia, and China by his twentieth-century followers, as they proved his theory spectacularly wrong? Or is it the safety net that an activist state stretches out to save its citizens — whether they want to be saved or not?

The final irony of Hegel's philosophy of unity is that it continues to divide us — more than two hundred years after the fact.

8.

It was the summer of 1820, and Georg Hegel was near the peak of his fame.

His speaking delivery hadn't improved much since his early days as a professor: he still "stuttered, moved rigidly, gasped for breath, and tirelessly repeated 'Also.'"[701] But he was the chair of philosophy at the University of Berlin, and his lectures were standing-room-only affairs.

So the university registrar could hardly believe his ears when a new lecturer made a special request. The lecturer was just thirty-two years old, and a complete unknown.

His course was called "Universal Philosophy," and the lecturer insisted he wanted it scheduled at the exact same time as Hegel's class. This was no accident. He thought Hegel was "a flat-headed, insipid, nauseating, illiterate charlatan" and was confident students would reach the same conclusion. So the incredulous registrar shrugged and granted the young professor's strange demand.

If it seems like this is going to be one of those incredible stories of overcoming adversity, think again. Only five students signed up for the course. The next semester, exactly *zero* students registered. And that was the end of the young lecturer's university career.

It was not, however, the end of Arthur Schopenhauer's *philosophical* career. He came from a family of wealthy merchants in Danzig, and he didn't need a university position. But this story perfectly reflects Schopenhauer the individual, as well as his philosophy: difficult, stubborn, proud, and uncompromising.

[699] Herman, *The Cave and the Light*, 436–437.

[700] Kreeft, *Socrates' Children*, vol. 3, ch. 67.

[701] Frederick Beiser, *Hegel* (New York: Routledge, 2007), 17.

Look at a photo of Schopenhauer as an old man, and you'll get the picture. The wild tufts of white hair; the set of his jaw. He's almost a caricature of the mad philosopher.

He once assaulted his neighbor during an argument, when she refused to stop talking outside his apartment. What really happened in Schopenhauer's altercation with forty-seven-year-old seamstress Caroline Louise Marquet remains unknown. But Schopenhauer was forced to pay her compensation for the rest of her life. And when she died twenty years later, he reportedly wrote "Obit anus, abit onus" — *The old lady died, the burden is gone* — on a copy of her death certificate.[702]

Had the students at the University of Berlin known anything about Schopenhauer's philosophy, he might not have gotten even five of them to sign up for his course. In his 1818 book *The World as Will and Representation,* he laid out his views in all their discouraging glory.

The driving force of the cosmos, Schopenhauer claimed, was *will.* This, he believed, was what existed in Kant's noumenal realm. The will is an energy without "mind or consciousness. It is a wholly mindless phenomenon, blind, without personality or intelligence, and therefore without purposes or aims or goals, an utterly impersonal force."[703]

In Schopenhauer's view, "We are perpetually in an unsatisfied state, and our very existence itself is a source of suffering to us. . . . He took the blackest view of our existence it seems possible for anyone to take and still remain sane. Indeed, as one might expect, he derived a certain grim pleasure from it."[704]

So why would anyone sign up for such a ruthless philosophy? There were three mitigating factors in Schopenhauer's thought, and each of them set him apart.

He was the first Western philosopher to seriously study Eastern thought. Schopenhauer read Hindu and Buddhist texts in translation — some of them were just becoming available in the West — and he was struck by the similarities between his beliefs and Eastern philosophy.

Schopenhauer was especially drawn to the Upanishads, the Hindu holy texts. In 1814, at his local library, he found a Latin translation from the original Sanskrit. Nearly forty years later, he confessed that this book had been "the most

702 David E. Cartwright, *Schopenhauer: A Biography* (Cambridge: Cambridge University Press, 2010), 411.

703 Magee, *The Story of Philosophy*, 141.

704 Magee, *The Story of Philosophy*, 144.

profitable and sublime reading that is possible in the world; it has been the consolation of my life and will be of my death."[705]

The Buddha had taught that overcoming desire was a key to enlightenment. This teaching struck a nerve with Schopenhauer. He struggled to overcome his own desires, especially the sexual ones. He wrote to a friend late in life, "As far as women are concerned, I was fond of them — had they only wanted to have me."[706]

The second thing that humanized Schopenhauer was his belief in compassion. Kant had said that our moral impulses give us clues about the noumenal world. Schopenhauer had a different idea. In his noumenal world, everything is just a single thing: will.

But since this reality is monistic, we recognize, at some level, that we're all actually connected. If we hurt others, we're actually hurting ourselves. So compassion, Schopenhauer believed, is the true source of morality. We have to act toward others as if they are an "I, once more,"[707] and treat their suffering like it's our own.

Schopenhauer advanced this idea in his 1839 essay *On the Basis of Morality*. Like Hindus and Buddhists, he also included animals in his moral universe, since "the same will is manifest in all living things, and to exclude animals from the moral community signifies ignorance and a cold, indifferent hardness of heart."[708]

The third, and most significant, quality that blunted Schopenhauer's pessimism was his love of the arts. In fact, in his view, blunting pessimism is exactly what art is supposed to do. When we're absorbed in a great piece of art, he thought, "we can find momentary release from our imprisonment in the dark dungeon of this world."[709]

Art, he felt, can make us feel like we're outside our bodies — even outside space and time. Only Schelling had made the arts so important in his philosophy.

Music even convinced this otherwise devout atheist to attend Mass at a "magnificent Catholic church" in Dresden, just so he could hear the "glorious church music."[710] (Schopenhauer, in fact, played the flute for many years, and even dabbled with the guitar.)

And music, Schopenhauer thought, was the greatest of all the arts. It "conveyed truth to a higher degree than any other art," because it "completely ignores the world

705 Cartwright, *Schopenhauer: A Biography*, 269.
706 Cartwright, *Schopenhauer: A Biography*, 22.
707 Cartwright, *Schopenhauer: A Biography*, 510.
708 Cartwright, *Schopenhauer: A Biography*, 329.
709 Magee, *The Story of Philosophy*, 144.
710 Cartwright, *Schopenhauer: A Biography*, 277.

of appearances."[711] Unlike painting, poetry, and dance, music has no visual element. This, he thought, make it the closest that art could get to the universal Will.

Music, however, couldn't relieve all Schopenhauer's frustrations. He felt he was ignored by the public, which rewarded men clearly his inferior. So he bashed nearly every German philosopher of his day, including Fichte, Schelling, and especially Hegel. They had all, he thought, gone backwards trying — and failing — to come up with an answer to Immanuel Kant's transcendental idealism.

Schopenhauer believed he had done it — and that therefore, he was Kant's true successor. "There is no philosophy between Kant and myself," he said, "only University charlatanism."[712]

Toward the end of his life, interest in Schopenhauer began to awaken. An enthusiastic cult of followers began hunting for first editions of *The World as Will and Representation.* They traded paintings, photos, and sketches of the philosopher, "as if his image became a fetish."[713]

The German composer Richard Wagner, who created the epic opera cycle *The Ring,* became a diehard admirer. His "activity on Schopenhauer's behalf may have done more to enhance Schopenhauer's popularity than the activities of the philosopher's evangelists."[714]

Schopenhauer was flattered and bemused by most of the attention. But it was after his death, in 1860 at age seventy-two, that his fortunes really began to turn. The fortunes of his nemesis, Georg Hegel, turned at the same time — in the opposite direction.

Hegel had once been the imperious German rock-star philosopher, while Schopenhauer couldn't even get a half-dozen students to sign up for his class. Yet as the nineteenth century progressed, it was Schopenhauer's books that began to sell, while Hegel's collected cobwebs on the shelves.

"For many, Schopenhauer's pessimism set the philosophical agenda in the second half of the nineteenth-century and beyond, while Hegel's Enlightenment optimism became the object of ridicule," writes Joshua Dienstag. "What had happened?"[715]

[711] Cartwright, *Schopenhauer: A Biography*, 317.

[712] Kreeft, *Socrates' Children*, vol. 3, ch. 68.

[713] Cartwright, *Schopenhauer: A Biography*, 532.

[714] Cartwright, *Schopenhauer: A Biography*, 540.

[715] Joshua Dienstag, "Schopenhauer vs Hegel: Progress or Pessimism," IAI News, March 15, 2023, https://iai.tv/articles/schopenhauer-vs-hegel-progress-or-pessimism-joshua-dienstag-auid-2416.

For one thing, Dienstag points out, it became obvious that Hegel's story of progress was too Eurocentric. It neglected areas like the Americas and Africa, which he knew little about. For another, even the Eurocentric parts of Hegel's story had become suspect by the turn of the century.

The year 1848 had seen a series of revolutions across the globe, including a third revolution in France. Unrest simmered during the rest of the century, and by 1900, a much bigger war loomed over the continent. It would be the sort of war that had never been seen before.

Hegel had claimed that conflict was just part of the dialectic, part of the progress. But that optimism became harder and harder to maintain.

Schopenhauer, meanwhile, made more and more sense to more and more influential, disaffected people. The philosopher Friedrich Nietzsche, the psychoanalyst Sigmund Freud, the author Albert Camus — all owed something to his work.

All three men were notorious for their pessimism, even though it took different forms. Maybe that's the greatest truth of Arthur Schopenhauer's strangely alluring philosophy: misery really does love company.

9.

A hundred feet overhead, light streams through the twenty windows of the great dome. They circle the ceiling like a halo, and the blue, cream, and gold paint adds to the heavenly effect.

The man sitting at a desk below, in the Reading Room of the British Museum, is certainly not thinking about Heaven. He's as unimpressive as the room is magnificent. The man is short, squat, and dirty. He has a mane of coal-black hair, and an unkempt beard covers the top of his misbuttoned frock coat.

What he's actually thinking about right now are boils. He has one at the end of his nose, and another on his ass — which means sitting here all day is particularly painful. The man gets these boils because he rarely bathes. But he believes that they — like most other things in life — are someone else's fault.

He'll endure the pain, however, because he has research to conduct. He spends most days here in the Reading Room, as he'll do for nearly thirty-five years. You might think he loves books, but that's not quite the truth. "I am a machine condemned to devour them," he will tell his daughter, years later, "and then, throw them, in a changed form, on the dunghill of history."[716] *So he fills out another ticket and begins trying again to find facts that will suit his arguments.*

They are arguments born in anger, because the man is often angry: "I will annihilate you" is one of his favorite phrases.[717] *He's trying to write a history of capital, and how it causes workers to be exploited. But it's hard for him to separate his views from his own financial despair.*

He rarely has any money, and he always spends more than he has — so he's always on the verge of financial ruin. His wife's jewelry is often in the pawnshop. And it's no wonder he prefers to spend his days in this vast, quiet room. It's the exact opposite of his cramped two-room apartment, where everything is dusty and broken and his children's toys lie on top of his manuscripts. When he's there, he prefers to fall asleep, fully clothed, on the threadbare couch. He sometimes dozes well into the afternoon, oblivious to the chaos of his unhappy household.

The one thing the man will almost never do, as he works slowly on his book about working people, is actually talk *to any — or even observe them. He'll never visit a factory, a mill, or a mine. Instead, he'll keep filling out tickets in the Reading Room and keep looking for the facts he needs. He knows he'll find them — even if they need a little editing. Or a lot.*

His powerful, unshakable belief is what will carry him through every hardship. As he wrote a few years earlier, in the manifesto that defined his movement, "The workers have nothing to lose but their chains. They have a world to gain." And this scruffy, boil-pocked messiah, writhing on his chair in the heart of capitalist London, is going to lead them to it.

[716] Karl Marx, *The Letters of Karl Marx* (Englewood Cliffs, NJ: Prentice-Hall, 1979), 250.
[717] Johnson, *Intellectuals*, 71.

10.

The best description of Karl Marx's philosophy is found in Arthur Herman's book *The Cave and the Light.* Marx stripped "Hegel's Platonizing vision of history to its bare steel skeleton and recast it as the specter of global apocalypse."[718]

The best introduction to Marx's thought is found in Paul Johnson's book *Intellectuals.* There, in a single chapter, Johnson lays bare the deceptions, evasions, half-truths, and outright lies that allowed the creation of Marx's masterpiece, *Das Kapital.*

And the best thing about most philosophers is that their wildest ideas stayed on the page. Had Plato's vision of the perfect society come to pass, we might well remember him as a monster.

Unfortunately, the same can't be said for Marx. "The only person in history whose ideas ever conquered more of the world than Marx's," Peter Kreeft writes, "was Jesus Christ."[719] Marx is, therefore, the most influential philosopher in history.

Marx insisted that his philosophy was a science. It was no such thing, but his experiment has been carried out on millions of people across the world regardless. "No other philosophy has ever been proved more conclusively, decisively, and disastrously wrong about nearly everything it claimed to be true," asserts Kreeft, "both by philosophical reasoning and by the events of history."[720]

Despite the more than 100 million people who have lost their lives under some version of Marx's philosophy, it will always retain its appeal because of what it promises. That promise is as irresistible as the happy ending of a romance novel or a Hallmark movie.

"From each according to his ability," Marx wrote, "to each according to his needs."[721] It sounds undeniably fair, utterly humane — and it's completely impractical, since it completely ignores human nature.

Human nature was something Marx seldom experienced in the Reading Room. But alone beneath that celestial dome, he conjured into being what every utopian philosopher has dreamed of from the very beginning: Heaven right here on earth.

[718] Herman, *The Cave and the Light*, 438.

[719] Kreeft, *Socrates' Children*, vol. 3, ch. 72.

[720] Kreeft, *Socrates' Children*, vol. 3, ch. 72.

[721] Karl Marx, "Critique of the Gotha Programme," in *Marx: Later Political Writings*, 208–226, Cambridge University Press, June 5, 2022, https://doi.org/10.1017/cbo9780511810695.011.

11.

From the beginning, Karl Marx was full of contradictions.

He was born in 1818 into a middle-class, Jewish family in Prussia. There were rabbis and Talmudic scholars in Marx's family tree, but his parents became Lutherans because Jews were forbidden to become doctors or lawyers. Marx became anti-Semitic, only the most unusual of his prejudices.

Not surprisingly, given his family's lukewarm religious convictions, he also turned into an atheist. He got a secular education in Bonn and Berlin, and received his doctorate at Jena University, the former home of Hegel and many other great German philosophers.

In fact, Marx was well-educated in the classics, and for a while, he was a serious poet. His verses helped win the heart of the girl next door: Jenny von Westphalen, descended from Scottish nobility. Her reward was a life of poverty and heartbreak.

Marx's anger burns through many of his poems, especially those that tackle his other great theme: apocalypse. His imagery of burning cities, captives chained to marble blocks, and a vengeful God shouting, "I shall howl gigantic curses at mankind,"[722] set the stage for his political writing. And there are multiple deals with the devil:

> Thus Heaven I've forfeited,
> I know it full well.
> My soul, once true to God,
> Is chosen for Hell.[723]

As Paul Johnson points out, "The poet in Marx was much more important than generally supposed."[724] When you combine his romantic poetry and his poems of violent revenge, you get a perfect preview of the system he would create.

Marx never had the discipline to carry off the "scientific" research he promised. But he did possess a true gift for memorable images and slogans. He used this talent well in his early years as a political journalist, and it became the

[722] Johnson, *Intellectuals*, 55.

[723] Paul Kengor, *The Devil and Karl Marx: Communism's Long March of Death, Deception, and Infiltration* (Gastonia, NC: TAN Books, 2020), 51. Kengor devotes a chapter to Marx's poetry and its significance to his political thought.

[724] Johnson, *Intellectuals*, 54.

strongest part of his later writing. "The workers have nothing to lose but their chains" is one of a handful of philosophy's most memorable catchphrases.[725]

Newspaper career aside, one of the countless ironies of Marx's life was that the champion of the working man barely ever held a job. He was supported for most of his life by his writing partner, Friedrich Engels.

Engels grew up in a wealthy Prussian family that owned several cotton textile mills. But like many a rich young radical, he rebelled against his upbringing. He spent time at his family's mill in Manchester, England, and was horrified by the conditions there. (His girlfriend, the Irish rabble-rouser Mary Burns, helpfully pointed him toward the worst spots.) Engels wrote about his experiences in radical newspapers, and later in a book.

A correspondence with Marx — and soon, a partnership — followed. By 1844, Marx had already sketched out the outline of what would become his philosophy. He'd borrowed a key idea from Georg Hegel and Ludwig Feuerbach: the concept of alienation.

For Marx, alienation perfectly described the condition of workers under capitalism. In a perfect world, Marx wrote, "Our products would be so many mirrors in which we saw reflected our essential nature."[726] But that was increasingly untrue in an industrial society, he pointed out. Adam Smith's division of labor meant that a worker was just a cog, who might not even see the final result of his work. How could he help but be alienated?

Marx and Engels were commissioned to write a pamphlet explaining the principles of the Communist League, an underground movement of workers and radicals they had joined. This became *The Communist Manifesto,* whose final draft was written by Marx, and published in 1848.

It opens with one of Marx's greatest, most evocative lines: "A spectre is haunting Europe — the spectre of communism."[727]

[725] Karl Marx and Friedrich Engels, *The Communist Manifesto with Related Documents,* ed. John E. Toews (Boston: Bedford St. Martin's, 1999), 96. The actual word used is "proletarians" instead of "workers," to correspond, as a footnote states, "to the recently approved motto of the Communist League."

[726] Karl Marx, "Abstract from the Contribution to the Critique of Hegel's Philosophy of Law" (1844), Marx/Engels Internet Archive, https://www.marxists.org/archive/marx/works/1844/df-jahrbucher/law-abs.htm.

[727] Marx and Engels, *The Communist Manifesto,* 63.

In this pamphlet, Hegel's idea of the dialectic was hijacked. Hegel's philosophy had been called *dialectical idealism,* because it suggested the dialectic was working to bring about spiritual progress: the self-realization of *Geist.*

For Marx, the method was appealing, but Hegel's idea of *Geist* was twaddle. Marx was, like Thomas Hobbes, a materialist who had no use for invisible spirits. So he proposed instead a *dialectical materialism.*

History was still Hegel's story of progress, advancing through the conflict of the dialectic. But in Marx's view, "the entire so-called history of the world is nothing but the creation of man through human labour."[728] So now we were progressing toward something material and tangible: what would later be called a "workers' paradise."[729]

How would we get there? Marx identified five economic stages, from hunter-gatherers who practiced a form of primitive communism, to ancient slave societies, to medieval feudalism, and then to capitalism.

Capitalism was in some ways the worst system yet. In it, the workers — the *proletariat* — were ruthlessly exploited by the owners and bosses — the *bourgeoisie.* These were the people with money. Not coincidentally, they were also the money *lenders* — the people Marx hated most of all, since he was constantly in debt to them.

Yet capitalism was also a necessary evil. Each succeeding system had to destroy the system before it. And capitalism was a required fourth step before man could reach the pinnacle: communism.

Communism for Marx was like the self-realization of *Geist* for Hegel. It would be the end of history. The workers would overthrow their bosses and seize the means of production, which they would share freely. No further progress would be possible, and conflict would cease forever.

Of course, there was one small catch. Just before communism ushered in the "workers' paradise," history would have to go through an initial phase of

728 Karl Marx, "Private Property and Communism" (1844), Marx/Engels Internet Archive, https://www.marxists.org/archive/marx/works/1844/manuscripts/comm.htm.

729 In fairness to Marx and Engels, the phrase "workers' paradise" does not appear in any of the common translations of their writings. Marx's famous quote about what life would be like for workers under communism — that they would be able to spend their mornings hunting, their afternoons fishing, and their evenings raising cattle, then offering critiques after dinner — may be equally fanciful, but it's clear, at least, that he said it.

"crude communism."[730] In this stage, we would see what was later called the "dictatorship of the proletariat."[731]

That meant that every vestige of the old capitalist society—from law and art to religion and the family—would be suppressed by force, if necessary. Greed would take center stage, and the rich would be humbled. The "entire world of wealth" would pass "from the relationship of exclusive marriage with the owner of private property to a state of universal prostitution with the community."[732] As in Marx's old poetry, the world would be cleansed by fire.

"Crude communism," Marx explained, "is only the culmination of this envy and of this levelling-down."[733] So perhaps it's unfair to say that all Marx's predictions were untrue. Nearly everywhere communism has been tried, crude communism has inevitably been the result.

12.

The Communist Manifesto had claimed that "All the Powers of old Europe have entered into a holy alliance to exorcise" the specter of communism.[734] That was a prescient warning.

The year of its publication, 1848, was the year of the third French Revolution, which spread throughout Europe. The "Springtime of Nations" was not a communist movement, and it didn't last long. But it made rulers and their governments nervous, and known radicals like Marx became suspect.

He was expelled from Belgium, and bounced from Paris to Prussia to Paris again, before settling in London in 1849. Marx would spend the rest of his life there, abandoning the dingy squalor of his rooms—and escaping his family in the bargain—for his research under the dome of the British Museum.

Marx's plan for a six-part epic that would explain in detail the ideas of *The Communist Manifesto* dwindled down to a single volume on capital—plus a disorganized series of notes that Engels cobbled into two further books.

[730] "Crude communism" is sometimes translated as "raw communism."

[731] The term "dictatorship of the proletariat" was apparently coined by the communist revolutionary and journalist Joseph Weydemeyer in 1852. His idea, however, followed Marx and Engels: that the goals of communists "can be attained only by the forcible overthrow of all existing social conditions" (Marx and Engels, *The Communist Manifesto*, 96).

[732] Marx, "Private Property and Communism."

[733] Marx, "Private Property and Communism."

[734] Marx and Engels, *The Communist Manifesto*, 63.

The truth was that, with the *Communist Manifesto,* Marx had already done most of his important work. Finally published in 1867, *Das Kapital* is based on a series of errors both large — for starters, that the expansion of capitalism inevitably means worse conditions for workers — and small.

The small mistakes were mostly deliberate. As early as the 1880s, two Cambridge scholars began investigating the veracity of *Das Kapital.* They uncovered numerous invented and doctored quotes, and a "criminal recklessness"[735] in using sources. One of those sources was Engels's own book, *The Condition of the Working Class in England* — which was itself filled with inaccurate and faked information.

To be fair to Marx and Engels, the conditions they described had been all too real. They didn't have to fabricate the abuses of the Industrial Revolution. But by using long out-of-date statistics, they ignored a simple fact: conditions for workers *had* improved, and it was capital that had helped them improve — because it was in the best interests of the *bourgeoisie* for this to happen. Bigger manufacturers *wanted* better working conditions to be enforced by the authorities, since it put their smaller competitors at a disadvantage.

Marx and Engels also weren't wrong about unchecked capitalism being a destructive force. It encouraged greed and rootlessness. And what it hurt most were the "little platoons" of society: the church, the family, and the community. But these were things Marx, especially, cared little about. He was a wandering atheist whose family paid the cost for his single-minded vision. That vision was the same as Rousseau's and Hegel's: the individual "liberated" by the all-powerful state.

"From start to finish, not just *Capital* but all his work reflects a disregard for truth which at times amounts to contempt," writes Paul Johnson. "That is the primary reason why Marxism, as a system, cannot produce the results claimed for it; and to call it 'scientific' is preposterous."[736]

But here we reach the other legacy of Marx's philosophy, the one that has found its way into even the strongholds of capitalism. It may be his greatest idea, and his ultimate victory, even though he might not have claimed it. That is the concept of *ideology.*

Ideology is a term that dates from the end of the first French revolution. In its original meaning, ideology described a political or social worldview that might require struggle to accomplish. It also needed a commitment from its followers.

735 Johnson, *Intellectuals,* 67.

736 Johnson, *Intellectuals,* 69.

In the definition of Marx and Engels, ideology was another word for the "false consciousness" of the bourgeoisie. This was the way the rich and the bosses stayed in power: by manipulating reality to distract us from class differences.

When we buy something, we only see the price tag: not the (exploited) labor that went into making the product. And we don't notice what *we* might have in common with those workers. Simply put, for Marx and Engels, ideology meant that truth was subservient to a political goal.

If you combine the original definition with Marx's, then nothing could better describe his *own* system of thought, with its deliberate obfuscations and outright falsehoods—all for the good of the inevitable revolution. His view of morality was purely practical: he redefined Kant's categorical imperative as the need "to overthrow all relations in which man is a debased, enslaved, forsaken, despicable being."[737]

And who decides this? Man himself. "The criticism of religion ends with the teaching that *man is the highest being for man*," declared Marx.[738] We're back to Protagoras: Man is the measure of all things, and truth is relative.

Marx's Russian disciples, Lenin, Trotsky, and Stalin, would rephrase this idea to defend the communist revolution and its aftermath. "Who, whom?" is a phrase reminding party members that truth is subordinate to results. It all depends on *who* is doing what to *whom*.

Today we take for granted that ideology, or to be "ideological," means ignoring inconvenient facts, if necessary, to achieve a larger goal. "Who, whom?" seems to be the operating principle in politics. It was Marx (and Engels) who truly showed us the way.

And it was Marx himself, with his knack for a memorable phrase, who summed it up best. He did it so well that it became his epitaph. If you visit Highgate Cemetery in London, the city where he spent most of his life in political exile, you can read these words on his tomb. Beneath his somber, bearded bust is the perfect reflection of his action-over-reflection worldview.

"The philosophers have only interpreted the world, in various ways," reads the inscription. "The point, however, is to change it."[739]

737 Karl Marx, "Economic Manuscripts: Comments on James Mill by Karl Marx" (1844), Marx/Engels Internet Archive, https://www.marxists.org/archive/marx/works/1844/james-mill/.

738 Marx, "Economic Manuscripts: Comments on James Mill by Karl Marx."

739 The quote on Marx's tombstone comes from the end of his 1845 essay "Theses on Feuerbach." (The other inscription is from the close of the *Communist Manifesto*: "Workers of all lands unite.")

13.

Speaking of philosophical quotations, one of the most famous ones in history may also be the most misattributed.

It wasn't Friedrich Nietzsche who said, "If God is dead, then everything is permitted." The phrase actually comes — in heavily paraphrased form — from Fyodor Dostoyevsky's 1880 novel *The Brothers Karamazov*.[740]

Nietzsche *did* say — multiple times — that God is dead. He put these words into the mouth of a "madman" in a parable from his 1882 book *The Gay Science*:

> God is dead. God remains dead. And we have killed him. How shall we comfort ourselves, the murderers of all murderers? What was holiest and mightiest of all that the world has yet owned has bled to death under our knives: who will wipe this blood off us? What water is there for us to clean ourselves? What festivals of atonement, what sacred games shall we have to invent? Is not the greatness of this deed too great for us? Must we ourselves not become gods simply to appear worthy of it?[741]

What Nietzsche saw clearly — long before most others — was that centuries of weakened belief in Christianity had led to *dis*belief. The insistence, dating all the way back to John Duns Scotus and William of Ockham, that God could only be known by faith, had eroded the foundations of religion.

The philosophers who followed them had mostly agreed. A few, like David Hume and Arthur Schopenhauer, saw no need for God at all. Many others, like John Locke and Immanuel Kant, had downgraded God's involvement in the world. It was usually secondary to man's own goals, or something it would be better not to talk about at all.

So the pillars that held up Christianity rotted steadily over the centuries. To the naked eye, the Church seemed as solid as ever. That was true even after the shocks of the nineteenth century, like the publication of Charles Darwin's *The*

[740] In *The Brothers Karamazov*, Dmitri Karamazov poses the question of what would happen to mankind "without God and the future life," asking whether this means "everything is permitted now, one can do anything." The cynical seminarian Ratkin responds, "Didn't you know? Everything is permitted to the intelligent man." Fyodor Dostoyevsky, Richard Pevear, and Larissa Volokhonsky, *The Brothers Karamazov: A Novel in Four Parts with Epilogue* (New York: Farrar, Straus and Giroux, 2002), 589.

[741] Friedrich Nietzsche, *The Gay Science: With a Prelude in Rhymes and an Appendix of Songs*, trans. Walter Kaufmann (New York: Random House, 1974), 181.

Origin of Species—which proposed a theory of evolution that challenged Scripture. The West was still a Christian culture, and old habits died hard—and slowly.

But Nietzsche recognized the decay below the surface. He was very much the "madman" of his little fable. He warned the crowds what had happened to God, but also realized they probably wouldn't listen. "This tremendous event is still on its way, still wandering," the madman admitted. It "has not yet reached the ears of men."[742]

The phrase "Don't shoot the messenger" could apply to Nietzsche's entire career. Most of his philosophy is based on telling the truth about the state of the world near the end of the nineteenth century. It wasn't a popular truth, nor—in his lifetime, at least—was it a popular philosophy. He was a little like a secular John the Baptist: preparing the way for someone, or some*thing*, else.

To be clear, Nietzsche thought the death of God was a necessary step. The key line in the madman's speech is his question to the crowd: "Must we ourselves not become gods simply to appear worthy" of God's demise?[743]

Even the perpetually miserable Schopenhauer, who was an early influence on Nietzsche, had suggested there was *something* beyond this world. Nietzsche disagreed. This idea, he felt, only held man back. There was just one world—this one—and "we should live our lives to the full in it, and get everything we can out of it. The central question posed by Nietzsche's philosophy is how best to do this in a godless, meaningless world."[744]

With Nietzsche's philosophy, we reach the end of many things—including the end of man's centuries-long quest for freedom. We are free—radically free. But that also means it's our job to finally remake the world in our image. It's an awesome responsibility.

What makes a hero? According to Nietzsche, it is "going out to meet at the same time one's highest suffering and one's highest hope."[745] That sums up his career, and really, his life—with the emphasis on *suffering*.

14.

If you're ever feeling discouraged, you should consider reading a biography of Friedrich Nietzsche. You'll feel much better by comparison.

[742] Nietzsche, *The Gay Science*, 182.
[743] Nietzsche, *The Gay Science*, 181.
[744] Magee, *The Story of Philosophy*, 172.
[745] Nietzsche, *The Gay Science*, 219.

The novelist Stefan Zweig, who wrote one of those books, summed up Nietzsche's lonely existence this way:

> The tragedy of Friedrich Nietzsche is a monodrama: no other figure is present on the brief lived stage of his existence. Across the acts of this tragedy, which crash down and surge on like an avalanche, the isolated combatant stands alone beneath the stormy sky of his own destiny; nobody is alongside him, nobody is opposing him and no woman is there to momentarily relax the overstrung atmosphere with her presence.... Not a single being dare properly enter the inner sanctum of that destiny; always Nietzsche speaks, struggles, suffers for himself alone. He addresses no one and no one responds. Worst of all: no one is even listening.[746]

Born in the Prussian province of Saxony in 1844, Nietzsche was plagued by illness almost from the start. He suffered from crippling migraines throughout his life, and his vision began failing when he was a young man.

He lost his faith even earlier. He was the son of a Lutheran pastor who died suddenly when Friedrich was just four years old. Afterward, he lived in fear that the illness that took his father at age thirty-five would lead to his early death as well.

Nietzsche grew into an outstanding student, but the influence of works like Ludwig Feuerbach *The Essence of Christianity* and David Strauss's *The Life of Jesus*—a "historical biography" of Christ that denied his divinity—led Nietzsche to atheism.

The young man had clear talents. When he was just twenty-four, he became a professor of classical philology at Switzerland's University of Basel. And when he spent a year as a volunteer in the Prussian army, he quickly became a captain, and got the reputation as an outstanding horseman.

However, Nietzsche had a difficult personality that alienated his fellow academics, and his promising career quickly stalled out. Meanwhile, a riding accident in the army further compromised his already delicate health. To make matters worse, at some point during his youth, he may have contracted syphilis from a prostitute. Some contend this disease—if he had it—contributed to his ultimate collapse.[747]

746 Stefan Zweig and William Stone, *Nietzsche* (London: Hesperus Press, 2013), 3.

747 Nietzsche himself denied to his doctor that he had ever had syphilis. He admitted he had gotten gonorrhea as a student—probably from visiting brothels, which seems to have been his only source of female contact. Julian Young, *Friedrich Nietzsche: A Philosophical Biography* (Cambridge: Cambridge University Press, 2010), 240.

Nietzsche became part of the composer Richard Wagner's inner circle, but the two later fell out: Nietzsche admired the composer's abilities, less so the vain and egotistical man and the cult around him. Wagner's wife, Cosima, was in many ways Nietzsche's ideal woman — despite the anti-Semitism she shared with her husband. Many believe Nietzsche was in love with her.

Yet the great unrequited affair of his life was with Lou Salomé, a Russian-born writer nearly twenty years his junior. They met in Rome in 1882. And for several years, Nietzsche, the author Paul Rée, and Salomé tried to form a kind of threesome — they called it an "intellectual commune."[748]

Nietzsche unsuccessfully proposed to Salomé three times. But he kept hanging around until jealousy undid the trio. He blamed Rée, and also his own sister Elisabeth — who hated Salomé — for causing the relationship to end.

It was Elisabeth, however, who eventually took Nietzsche in after he had a breakdown in 1889. The popular story is that Nietzsche witnessed a horse being flogged in the streets of Turin, Italy. He intervened, hugging the neck of the horse and refusing to let go, and was arrested.

This tale was first told years afterward, and the facts behind it are sketchy.[749] But Nietzsche's mental deterioration was all too real. For the last decade of his life, he descended even more deeply into madness, eventually refusing to communicate. Then a series of strokes left him paralyzed, and he spent his final two years unable to walk or speak.

Yet success, finally, had arrived. A new book appeared for his growing audience: *Twilight of the Idols*, an introduction to Nietzsche's thought. While staying at his mother's house,

> pilgrims from all over Germany and beyond began to come to Naumburg to stand before the house on Weingarten, hoping to catch a glimpse of the deranged philosopher at his upstairs window. In the age of mad-women-in-the-attic Victorian novels, Nietzsche's madness can only have increased the fascination with his philosophy.[750]

[748] Young, *Friedrich Nietzsche*, 341. Lou Salomé later dumped Paul Rée, before taking up with the much younger poet Rainer Maria Rilke. Rée died while hiking in the Swiss Alps in October 1901. It's not clear whether his death was accidental or suicide.

[749] You can read a closer examination of the fabled incident of Friedrich Nietzsche and the horse at the Faena Aleph website: https://www.faena.com/aleph/the-true-story-of-the-turin-horse-or-nietzsches-horse.

[750] Young, *Friedrich Nietzsche*, 553.

Even before their mother died, Elisabeth correctly saw that the Nietzsche business was turning into big business. So she "devoted her enormous reserves of energy [and] ruthless lack of scruple ... to obtaining sole control over both his works and what remained of his life."[751]

She began to market his work to the wider audience she knew it deserved. Unfortunately, that included Adolf Hitler — who supported the Nietzsche Archive that Elisabeth created and attended her funeral in 1935 — and other members of the Nazi Party.

Nietzsche was neither a strong German nationalist nor an anti-Semite. So the adoption of his ideas by the Nazis seems like the final cruel joke played on a man whose life was full of them. Yet what was true of many modern philosophers is also true of the last great one: the hubris they showed in playing with fire ensured that many, many people would get burned.

15.

Arthur Schopenhauer had imagined the engine that drives the world, from the invisible noumenal world, is simply a will to *live*. He included animals in his philosophy because he thought human striving was similar. We're led by our desires; if we're lucky enough to have them satisfied temporarily, we'll then be bored — and still unhappy.

This wasn't good enough for Nietzsche, a physically weak man who dreamed of heroism. This was one reason he criticized Richard Wagner's operas. He saw them as decadent, glamorizing a "will to death."[752] Nietzsche, instead, saw man's will to *power* as his potential liberating force. This idea was the "chief thing"[753] in his existence.

Man was naturally violent: there was no doubt. Nietzsche had seen this himself, even during the brief month he served during the Franco-Prussian War. But Nietzsche saw Judeo-Christian ethics as no answer. They were a "slave morality"[754] — a worldview that defended the weak against the strong.

This not only went against man's true nature, it stopped the progress of civilization. Man's "terrible potentialities which are regarded as inhuman,"

751 Young, *Friedrich Nietzsche*, 554.
752 Young, *Friedrich Nietzsche*, 494.
753 Young, *Friedrich Nietzsche*, 460.
754 Young, *Friedrich Nietzsche*, 464.

Nietzsche wrote, are "in fact the fruitful soil from which alone everything humane, in feelings, deeds, and works can grow forth."[755]

The Greeks and Romans, he felt, had a better handle on how to channel man's violent impulses. But leaders like Jesus, who said that the meek shall inherit the earth, were just preserving the mediocre and inferior — while the world's natural leaders and innovators (like Nietzsche) were "un-selfed."[756]

It's not certain whether Nietzsche ever read Charles Darwin, but the similarities between his will-to-power world and Darwin's theory of natural selection are obvious. The weak are weeded out in favor of the strong, and civilization progresses. In the twentieth century, this "social Darwinism" would take many ugly forms, from eugenics to Nazism — under the guise of "progress."

Ultimately, Nietzsche's own goal was to make way for the *Übermensch* — usually translated as "overman" or "superman." The Übermensch was the next frontier of human development. These men and women would be totally free of Judeo-Christian morality. They would create their *own* morality — since Nietzsche believed, like Protagoras, that only man can be the measure of how to act.

What Nietzsche also saw was a hypocrisy the rest of the world preferred to ignore. The West, it seemed, had moved beyond Christianity. The decline had been ongoing for centuries, and the reasons were numerous — from the Industrial Revolution to the Enlightenment to Darwinism to philosophers whose number one project was increasing man's freedom, as we've seen throughout this book.

So why were people still held back by a "slave morality" they no longer believed? They needed to shape a new morality based on the views they *actually* held — not the ones they paid lip service to every Sunday. Abolishing Judeo-Christianity also meant no more self-hatred — which is what focusing on the next world, and not this one, inspired. There *is* no next world, Nietzsche insisted.

However, he *did* believe in a form of redemption. That was a concept he called the *eternal return*. Time moves in cycles, Nietzsche thought. So everything we do now will inevitably be repeated in the future. Therefore, we should live as fully as possible while we can, because those are actions worth repeating.

It's part Epicurus's old idea that "Death is nothing to us," and part reincarnation. But for Nietzsche, it was the closest thing "to eternal life as it is possible to get in a world that is finite and bounded."[757]

[755] Young, *Friedrich Nietzsche*, 141.

[756] Magee, *The Story of Philosophy*, 177.

[757] Magee, *The Story of Philosophy*, 175.

16.

The playwright George Bernard Shaw, one of many artists inspired by Nietzsche, once said you could sum up his philosophy in three lines from Shakespeare's *Richard III*:

> Conscience is but a word that cowards use
> Devised at first to keep the strong in awe.
> Our strong arms be our conscience, swords our law![758]

Nietzsche recognized the dangers that "the raging of the blond, Germanic beast"[759] could create. This creature was represented in the past by the Vikings and Germanic tribes. And of course, it would be reborn after his death in the myth of the Aryan Superman, the symbol of the Nazis and their master race.

But Nietzsche, like every modern philosopher before him, believed advancing the cause of man was worth the risks he suggested. And like every modern philosopher, he died before he could see those gambles come to terrible fruition in the twentieth century.

Perhaps it's unfair to link him to the Nazis. But Nietzsche's reputation has survived. He stands alone, as the last great German thinker of the 1800s, and as the first modern philosopher who truly saw the way the world was headed, and wasn't afraid to say it.

In that sense, he is both the Omega and the Alpha of Western thought. He is the real end of the centuries-long project described in this book, the project to liberate the individual. With his characteristic realism, Nietzsche realized that no person could ever live up to the impossible standards he'd set—which is why he longed for an imaginary superman who could.

His philosophy promises the Romantic grandeur of German painter Caspar David Friedrich's 1818 *Wanderer Above the Sea of Fog*.[760] A lone man stands

758 Magee, *The Story of Philosophy*, 178.

759 Young, *Friedrich Nietzsche*, 464.

760 Painter Caspar Friedrich's work was also appropriated by the Nazis. And like Nietzsche, he was always haunted by a childhood death. His brother drowned saving him from an ice-skating accident on the Baltic Sea. As an adult, Friedrich tried to slit his own throat, but the suicide attempt failed. As *The Encyclopedia Britannica* notes, "The relationship between trauma and inspiration is evident in Friedrich's statement that 'The painter should paint not only what he has in front of him, but also what he sees inside himself. If he sees nothing within, then he should stop painting what is in front of him.'" Ana

triumphant at the summit, taking in a landscape both thrilling and terrifying. Yet the reality of Nietzsche was, is, and always will be lonely men in lonely rooms, determined to speak fantasy into reality.

Brave, miserable, and yet strangely optimistic, he appeals to every unhappy individual who believes the world is holding him back. And he promises a way to leap those hurdles by embracing life and looking out for the self, in a way he never could.

"Only the day after tomorrow belongs to me," Nietzsche wrote, with his usual uncanny prescience. "Some are born posthumously."[761]

Finel Honigman, "Wanderer above the Sea of Fog (painting by Friedrich)," Britannica, n.d., accessed September 3, 2023, www.britannica.comhttps://www.britannica.com/topic/Wanderer-Above-the-Sea-of-Fog#ref1304950.

761 Friedrich Nietzsche, *The Portable Nietzsche*, ed. Walter Kaufman (New York: Penguin Books, 1976) 568.

CHAPTER SIXTEEN

LOST ON THE TIGHTROPE

1.

"Nietzsche's fundamental metaphysical position," Martin Heidegger once wrote, "is the end of Western philosophy."[762]

Heidegger wasn't literally arguing that Western philosophy was over. After all, he was a philosopher himself. Heidegger was really claiming that the old question of *metaphysics* — what is the nature of reality? — had been exhausted by the start of the twentieth century. It was time to investigate other questions.

Metaphysics was "at an end. That seems a bootless, comfortless insight, a conclusion which like a dying tone signals ultimate cessation," Heidegger said. "Yet such is not the case."[763]

But sometimes statements reveal an unintended truth. The "dying tone" was a telling metaphor. After Nietzsche, *all* kinds of philosophy floundered — not just metaphysical thought.

Echoes of the German philosophers of the eighteenth and nineteenth centuries — Kant, Hegel, Marx, Nietzsche — would ring out for decades. The fatal consequences of their big-picture metaphysical systems were still to come. Yet there was widespread confusion about where philosophy could go next.

[762] Martin Heidegger, *Nietzsche*, trans. David Farrell Krell and Joan Stambaugh (San Francisco: Harper San Francisco, 1991), 204.

[763] Heidegger, *Nietzsche*, 205.

This is easy to understand when you consider that for more than five hundred years, the primary contribution of Western philosophy had been doubt. From Duns Scotus and Ockham to Descartes and Locke to Hume and Kant, the overriding insistence had been on what we *couldn't* know, rather than what we could. And the reason for this insistence had been to free the individual.

Now, after Nietzsche, the individual was alone at last. William of Ockham had gleefully walked a tightrope back in the 1300s, razor in hand, doing his daring philosophical act. The rest of us were now on that tightrope, too, following his footsteps, unarmed and unassisted in a heavy fog. God couldn't help us, and neither could science. How could we take one more step forward?

Out of the mist, and over the dying tones of the nineteenth century, emerged a multitude of new voices. None rose above the crowd, and none were particularly compelling. But they all clamored for attention.

These were the contemporary philosophers of the twentieth century, directing Western civilization on the long tightrope where each person teetered. If the directions seemed contradictory or even, at times, insane — how could anyone truly judge? And if people fell into the abyss, well, what had truly been lost? We either were returning to the void, or perhaps we never existed in the first place.

The old Sophist, Protagoras, must have been smiling somewhere as he watched this tightrope procession. Man was finally, utterly, the measure of all things. It looked like he'd won at last.

2.

Metaphysics might have been dead by 1900. Man's search for certainty was not.

For centuries, the futility of this task had dominated philosophy. We couldn't know God. We couldn't know the material world. We couldn't even, according to the skeptics, know ourselves.

It's not surprising, then, that language became the thing philosophers grabbed onto like a life preserver. Ever since the days of Aristotle, there had been logic, of course, and logic was a language-based activity. But now it was language, not nature, that would be "put on the rack." Every statement would be parsed relentlessly for hidden meanings and — even more important — contradictions.

Out of this analysis, the ultimate, unshakable truth would emerge — or so the story went.

This ignored a fundamental insight made by Bryan Magee, who worked with some of the great linguistic philosophers of this era. "Almost none of the things that matter to us most," he wrote, "can be adequately expressed in language."[764] This was a minority view among philosophers in the first half of the twentieth century.

The roots of linguistic philosophy lie with a German thinker — and, paradoxically, with math.

Gottlob Frege was an academic at the University of Jena in the late nineteenth century. His work was overshadowed by the idealism of Kant, Hegel, and Schopenhauer. But he was a brilliant mathematician who believed that "there is nothing more objective than the laws of mathematics."[765]

This was a belief, of course, that went all the way back to Pythagoras and Plato. But Frege pointed out that logical relationships are — like mathematical equations — also independent of human thought.

This led Frege to conclude that logic and math were inevitably intertwined. In fact, he thought "all the unproven assumptions and rules" that make math possible "could be derived from the most elementary principles of logic."[766]

Those "assumptions and rules" that we take for granted when we do math are "unproven" because they're not based on our direct experience. They're "free-floating," in a sense. When we say, for example, that one million divided by twenty-five equals 400,000, we believe the answer is correct because we trust the *rule*, not because we've experienced this math problem directly.

But what if we could validate those mathematical rules by using logic, instead? This was Frege's project.

Because of it, "the study of logic underwent a transformation into a vast and highly technical field overlapping with mathematics, and is now taught and researched as such in every major university in the world."[767] But the main reason for that was actually the British philosopher Bertrand Russell.

Russell was the grandson of Lord John Russell, and was a precocious mathematician from childhood. In his autobiography, he told the story of how his older brother, Frank, tried to teach him geometry. Russell insisted on knowing *why* the rules existed, which frustrated Frank.

[764] Bryan Magee, *Confessions of a Philosopher: A Personal Journey through Western Philosophy from Plato to Popper* (New York: Modern Library, 1997), 79.

[765] Magee, *The Story of Philosophy*, 195.

[766] Magee, *The Story of Philosophy*, 195.

[767] Magee, *The Story of Philosophy*, 195.

Russell eventually went along with the lesson and discovered a passion for math that was "as dazzling as first love."[768] But he never gave up wanting to justify mathematical rules. So he worked on this project for years — not realizing Frege was doing the same thing in Germany.

When Russell finally discovered Frege, he helped bring the older man to the public's attention. And he published the results of his project in *The Principles of Mathematics* in 1903, and the three-volume *Principia Mathematica,* with his Cambridge math professor, Alfred North Whitehead, between 1910 and 1913.

The *Principia Mathematica* was "regarded by many as the greatest single contribution to logic since Aristotle." And it was undoubtedly a "gargangtuan achievement."[769]

But a larger question often went unasked: What did it all *mean*? What difference did it make to the average person, for example, whether a dot was used for "punctuation" or "conjunction"? And if math could be validated by logic, so what? Would that really change how people have done math for centuries?

As *The Encyclopedia Britannica* admits, "The philosophical significance of the work as a whole is still a matter of debate. Does it demonstrate that mathematics is logic? Only if one regards the theory of types as a logical truth, and about that there is much more room for doubt than there was about the trivial truisms upon which Russell had originally intended to build mathematics."[770]

Russell would eventually abandon his effort to combine math and logic, and he turned to more general philosophy and social activism. His *History of Western Philosophy,* published in 1946, became a deserved international best-seller. It's still one of the best surveys of Western thought around.

He's also remembered today for *Why I Am Not a Christian,* a 1927 lecture he gave that was later published as a pamphlet. In this talk, Russell gave the usual refutations of God's existence. For example, he cited the "Who caused God?" argument that Aquinas had dealt with almost a millennium earlier.

Russell also claimed, "There is one very serious defect to my mind in Christ's moral character, and that is that He believed in hell. I do not myself feel that any person who is really profoundly humane can believe in everlasting punishment."[771] Christianity, he felt, was based on fear, and that fear caused it to oppose science.

[768] Magee, *Confessions of a Philosopher,* 168.

[769] Magee, *Confessions of a Philosopher,* 197.

[770] Ray Monk, "Bertrand Russell," *Britannica,* last updated October 1, 2023, https://www.britannica.com/biography/Bertrand-Russell.

[771] Bertrand Russell, *Why I Am Not a Christian, and Other Essays on Religion and Related Subjects,* ed. Paul Edwards (New York: Simon and Schuster, 1957), 17.

"I say quite deliberately that the Christian religion, as organised in its Churches," Russell said, "has been and still is the principal enemy of moral progress in the world."[772]

Russell's own moral progress took a number of unusual twists and turns over the years. That included his belief that the United States should have used the H-bomb to wipe out Soviet Russia after World War II — something he later denied saying. (Russell was a foe of communism, but he was no conservative: what he hoped to see instead was a world government.)

Many found Russell's work outside of mathematics lacking. The Austrian philosopher Ludwig Wittgenstein spoke for them when he said, "Russell's books should be bound in two colours . . . those dealing with mathematical logic in red — and all students of philosophy should read them; those dealing with ethics and politics in blue — and no one should be allowed to read them."[773]

Wittgenstein was the most prominent thinker to pick up where Russell had left off in linguistic philosophy. In his lifetime, he only published a single book: the brief but dense *Tractatus Logico-Philosophicus*, written while he was a soldier in the Austrian army during World War I. It was less than a hundred pages long and consisted of terse, numbered statements. Nevertheless, it made Wittgenstein one of the twentieth century's best-known philosophers.

Wittgenstein was the son of an Austrian steel magnate. He'd planned to become an engineer. But when he read Russell's *Principles of Mathematics*, he decided to study philosophy with Russell at Cambridge instead.

Wittgenstein was influenced by the view of reality that philosophers like Immanuel Kant and Arthur Schopenhauer had described. There are two worlds: a phenomenal world we can know something about, and a noumenal world that we can't.

But Wittgenstein thought we *could* use language to talk more precisely about the phenomenal world. His lifelong task was exploring the link between language and what it describes.

There were two distinct phases to this project. The first, in the *Tractatus*, centered around what came to be known as the "picture theory" of meaning. A statement was only meaningful, Wittgenstein felt, if it could be pictured.

[772] Russell, *Why I Am Not a Christian*, 21.
[773] Ray Monk, *Ludwig Wittgenstein: The Duty of Genius* (New York: Vintage, 1990), 471.

This idea had come to him while he was in the army on the Eastern Front. He read a magazine story about a French court case concerning a car accident. The lawyers had prepared toy models to represent the cars, houses, and people at the accident scene.

Wittgenstein realized that language works in a similar way. The models related to the accident in the same way language relates to reality. We understand a sentence not just because a word stands for something, but also because of the structure of these words — the way they're arranged. This arrangement, he thought, mirrors the arrangement of objects in real life.

Yet Wittgenstein's picture theory — like much previous philosophy — ruled out big chunks of thought. In section 6.421 of the *Tractatus,* he declared, "It is clear that ethics cannot be expressed. Ethics is transcendental. (Ethics and æsthetics are one.)"[774]

Any metaphysical speculating was therefore out of bounds. It's to Wittgenstein's credit that he realized this disqualified his own statements in the *Tractatus.*

"My propositions are elucidatory in this way: he who understands me finally recognizes them as senseless, when he has climbed out through them, on them, over them," he admitted. "(He must, so to speak, throw away the ladder, after he has climbed up on it.)"[775]

A better metaphor might have been someone sawing off the tree branch where they were sitting. After years of thought, Wittgenstein seemed to agree.

Toward the end of his life, he rejected picture theory in favor of a more realistic approach. In *Philosophical Investigations,* a book published after his death from prostate cancer in 1951, Wittgenstein admitted that language was far more fluid than he'd made out before. His new theory reflected this more open-minded approach. He called it the "language-game."

The idea of picture theory — where one word stood for one image — was too limiting. Wittgenstein now compared language to a tool, which might have many different uses, depending on the context. The one absolute he insisted upon was that language is a public act: a "private language" doesn't really make sense.

Not everyone was happy with this new, playful Wittgenstein. Bertrand Russell was puzzled by his former student's final book. He claimed Wittgenstein had

[774] Ludwig Wittgenstein, *Tractatus Logico-Philosophicus* (New York: Harcourt, Brace, 1922), 88.
[775] Wittgenstein, *Tractatus Logico-Philosophicus,* 90.

"grown tired of serious thinking," and felt the language game turned philosophy into an "idle tea-table amusement."[776]

It was the old Wittgenstein, meanwhile, who inspired a whole new school of thought. A. J. Ayer, a British professor, studied at the University of Vienna in the 1920s with a number of thinkers who developed a style known as *logical positivism*. This was yet another attempt to find truth by eliminating uncertainty.

The logical positivists wanted to strip language down to its chassis to avoid misunderstanding. They were inspired by Wittgenstein's *Tractatus*. Only verifiable statements had any meaning: talking about things like aesthetics, and ethics, and religion was worthless. That was convenient, since many logical positivists, like Ayer, were devout atheists.

A person interested in metaphysics "produces sentences which fail to conform to the conditions under which alone a sentence can be literally significant. Nor are we ourselves obliged to talk nonsense in order to show that all sentences of a certain type are necessarily devoid of literal significance," sniffed Ayer in 1936's *Language, Truth, and Logic*.[777]

This was a practical approach — and also incredibly dull. Only an academic could love the torturous way the logical positivists parsed sentences. That's probably why this thinking found a home at universities.

The logical positivists' successors were the linguistic philosophers, led by Ayer's rival at Oxford, J. L. Austin. Austin became known for his description of the "speech-act." This is a statement like "I now pronounce you man and wife," which not only describes what someone is doing but actually *does* it at the same time.

Compared to logical positivism, linguistic philosophy was a barrel of laughs. But Austin's 1955 book *How to Do Things with Words* was also full of high-level terminology suitable only for a college course: *phemes* (sentences in English) and *rhemes* (English sentences with a definite meaning) and *illocutionary acts* (asking questions or giving commands) and *perlocutionary acts* (getting someone to answer a question).

All these thinkers can broadly be called *analytic*, in the sense that they believed their job was to analyze language. But for the average person, the difference between logical positivism and linguistic philosophy was negligible.

[776] Bertrand Russell, *My Philosophical Development* (New York: Simon and Schuster, 1959), 217.

[777] Alfred Ayer, *Language, Truth, and Logic* (London: Pelican Books, 1971), 15.

Even Sir Geoffrey Warnock, a philosopher who later became vice-chancellor at Oxford, admitted that while he enjoyed Austin's work, "I did not believe that it was likely to contribute to the solution of the problems of the post-war world; I did not believe that it would contribute, certainly or necessarily, to the solution of any problems of philosophy."

But Warnock added that "it was enormously enjoyable; it was not easy; it exercised the wits; and those who think they know that it cannot ever be valuably instructive have simply never tried, or perhaps are no good at it."[778]

All this linguistic activity, centered at Oxford University, was probably inevitable. Modern philosophers had been shrinking their field of inquiry for centuries. What was left to talk about except talking itself?

However, as Warnock's quote suggests, many of these young, language-based philosophers and their students were also full of themselves. They believed philosophy was a dying art that only they were smart enough to redeem. Using the rigorous standards of mathematics, logic, and linguistics would solve the remaining problems, and then everyone could stop thinking and go home. As Bryan Magee recalled it, "The way these philosophers conducted themselves sowed a lasting hostility towards philosophy among gifted people in other disciplines."[779]

The analytic style is still the most common form of philosophy. It's almost exclusively confined to universities, the zoos in which what's left of philosophy still lives. Curious people can visit — at great expense. But most people aren't curious anymore. That may be the true legacy of analytic thought.

3.

It's when philosophy goes wandering off its academic game preserve that most of us encounter it.

America began developing its own philosophical schools in the nineteenth century. The New England Transcendentalists, who included authors Ralph Waldo Emerson and Henry David Thoreau, were deeply influenced by Hegel as well as the Romantic movement in England.

The Transcendentalists were optimistic and nature-centered, and skeptical of organized religion. They looked instead for Heaven on earth — which helped explain their social activism, including support of abolition and women's suffrage.

[778] Magee, *Confessions of a Philosopher*, 66.

[779] Magee, *Confessions of a Philosopher*, 66.

Their followers took a somewhat different path, one that had more tangible effects on society. The American Pragmatists also had little use for traditional ideas about God. As their name suggests, they valued *usefulness*. This meant that, as was the case with the analytic philosophers, talking about metaphysics was out.

William James, the brother of the prominent novelist Henry James, famously defended people's right to religious belief. But that wasn't because James was actually a believer himself. If religion brought people comfort and cheer, he thought, then it was *useful*.

It's John Dewey, though, who best represented the Pragmatists. He called his theory of knowledge "instrumentalism," which reflected his practical nature. Learning is not something we do for its own sake. The goal is to *accomplish* things.

A Vermont native who taught at the University of Chicago, Dewey was a picture-perfect progressive of the early twentieth century. He was a defender of democracy and labor unions; an apologist for the Soviet Union; a fervent believer in Darwin's evolutionary theories; and the leading supporter of hands-on learning.

This was, and is, a student-centered approach, based not just on what children *need* to know, but what they *want* to know. So learning was based on a student's "ordinary life-experience."[780]

It's not hard to trace the effect this idea has had on schools over the past century. So it's no stretch to say Dewey has probably had more influence on American education than any other individual. That influence reflects a now-familiar set of ideas: Metaphysics are a waste of time. Individual freedom, as enforced by the state, is the ultimate goal. And if we follow these plans, progress is inevitable.

While Dewey was implementing his educational reforms, another influential school was setting up shop at an American university. The members of the Institute for Social Research began their studies in the 1920s at Goethe University in Frankfurt. The goal was to study Marxism, but when the Nazis came to power, they chased the professors out. So in 1935, the group relocated to Columbia, in New York City.

They soon became better known as the Frankfurt School. This group of intellectuals laid out their manifesto in the 1937 book *Traditional and Critical Theory*, by Max Horkheimer. One of Critical Theory's main objectives was to cast doubt on objective knowledge. That was, Horkheimer said, because all of us are biased observers who can't separate our perceptions from our experience.

[780] John Dewey, *Experience and Education* (New York: Free Press, 1938), 74.

As he wrote, "The facts which our senses present to us are socially preformed in two ways: through the historical character of the object perceived and through the historical character of the perceiving organ."[781]

It's new phrasing, but an old, old idea. Man, once again, is the measure of things, and objective truth is impossible. So what are we supposed to do?

For one thing, we shouldn't "fetishize" knowledge. We should *use* it, instead, for "social emancipation. In the light of such finalities, knowledge becomes social criticism and the latter translates itself into social action, that is, into the transformation of reality."[782] And the Frankfurt philosophers add that "action-transformation" should also include "revolutionary action."[783]

Here we see the payoff of several strands of philosophy. The German philosophers all contributed to this thinking. Kant's skepticism about knowledge and God, Hegel and Marx's belief in historical progress, and Nietzsche's need to *act* in this world to "transform social reality," even if violence is involved: all combine to inspire the Frankfurt School.

But there are echoes of other thinkers here. From Protagoras to the Skeptics, from the doubtful René Descartes to tolerant John Locke to the cheerful negativity of David Hume, all the way up to the American Pragmatists — the Frankfurt School had many parents.

First-generation Frankfurt scholars like Horkheimer, Theodor Adorno, and Herbert Marcuse still loom large. Their views — especially the concept of Critical Theory — have spread well beyond college campuses. These ideas have mutated into a variety of "liberation" movements. Many of these movements share analytic philosophy's obsession with language — especially how the way we speak (and how we *don't* speak) can "transform social reality."

The fallout of all this theorizing has been huge. You can see it in the battles over using Critical Theory to introduce skepticism in the classroom. You can see it in the language-policing now common in journalism and social media, as well as academia. And you can see it everywhere objective reality is denied in favor of "liberation."

Yet the real goals of the Frankfurt School — the goals that philosophers have been pining after for centuries — remain elusive. The "realistic utopias" that the third generation of Frankfurt scholars have investigated are as oxymoronic as ever.

[781] Claudio Corradetti, "Frankfurt School and Critical Theory," *Internet Encyclopedia of Philosophy*, n.d., https://iep.utm.edu/critical-theory-frankfurt-school/.

[782] Corradetti, "Frankfurt School and Critical Theory."

[783] Corradetti, "Frankfurt School and Critical Theory."

"What has been noticed," the *Internet Encyclopedia of Philosophy* concedes, "is that whereas Critical Theory has aimed at fostering human emancipation, it has remained incapable of specifying a political action-strategy for social change."

As the history of philosophy shows, those repeated failures will likely never stop anyone from trying.

4.

The analytic philosophers and the Critical Theorists weren't the only people who looked for ways that language might alter reality.

The structuralists took their cues from Ferdinand de Saussure. He was a Swiss philosopher who was one of the founding fathers of linguistics, the scientific study of language.

Most people didn't learn about Saussure's ideas until decades after his death in 1913. His posthumously published book *Course in General Linguistics* gave us the idea that language is a system of signs. Saussure developed this concept into a branch of linguistics called semiotics.

All signs have a dyadic, or two-part, model, according to Saussure. The *signifier* is the form that a sign takes, and the *signified* is what the sign represents.

For example, when we see the word "stop" on a stop sign, the signifier is the word "STOP." The signified is the meaning: that cars should stop before they reach the sign.

That might sound straightforward, but Saussure pointed out that values in language are always shifting. He compared language to a game of chess. Our words are like chess pieces: their values "depend above all else on an unchangeable convention, the set of rules that exists before a game begins and persists after each move. Rules that are agreed upon once and for all exist in language too; they are the constant principles of semiology."[784]

But within the rules of a chess game, there can be big changes. "A certain move can revolutionize the whole game and even affect pieces that are not immediately involved," he wrote. "Exactly the same holds for language."[785]

Here, Saussure seems to be anticipating Ludwig Wittgenstein's "language-game." Language is too complex and ever-changing to reduce to simple

784 Ferdinand de Saussure, *Course in General Linguistics* (New York: McGraw-Hill, 1966), 88.

785 De Saussure, *Course in General Linguistics*, 89.

one-to-one relationships. Saussure thought it was, instead, the *systems* — the rules of the game — that gave words their meaning.

As we've seen, philosophers have always been suckers for a good system. Other philosophers tried to use Saussure's structuralist theories about the system of language to interpret larger systems — eventually, whole societies.

The Belgian anthropologist Clause Levi-Strauss was one of the best known examples. His 1962 book *The Savage Mind* suggested that even in indigenous societies, people create complex systems of meaning — linguistic and otherwise. And they do this, Levi-Strauss thought, through a process of *bricolage* — taking bits and pieces of whatever's available to construct new systems.

Levi-Strauss compared these *bricoleurs* to engineers in Western societies. Both make new things, but they do so in different ways. Bricoleurs are like mythologists, who reuse existing material to make new stories. Engineers, on the other hand, create their own specific models and specifications to complete buildings.

That was enough bait for a French-Algerian provocateur named Jacques Derrida. One of the other recurring themes throughout Western thought that we've seen is this: when someone proposes a structure that claims to have all the answers, it prompts someone else who wants to knock down the whole thing.

In 1966, Derrida responded to Levi-Strauss's bricolage idea in an essay called "Structure, Sign, and Play in the Discourse of the Human Sciences." Derrida presented the essay at an American conference on structuralism, but his talk contained the seeds of structuralism's demise.

Derrida criticized Levi-Strauss's contrast between engineers and bricoleurs. We're *all* bricoleurs, Derrida argued. And bricoleurs are pragmatic: they don't care about what materials they're using to make a system. They just want the system to work.

The engineer, by contrast, wants a "centered" system. He will "privilege" or "center" certain ideas to create this system. That means it's probably going to be stable. But for Derrida, it's also going to be boring.

The "play" in the title of Derrida's essay is a reminder that language can be fun when words have multiple meanings. It's how we create puns, for example. (It's also a reminder that "fun" is a term that few would apply to Derrida's own densely academic writing.)

But Derrida's real game here was to argue for a much more complete "decentering"[786] of language. For bricoleurs, he said, meanings — and therefore,

[786] Jacques Derrida, *Writing and Difference* (Chicago: University of Chicago Press, 1978), 260.

truth — are in a constant state of flux. All systems — even the stable, centered ones — are ultimately unstable, Derrida thought. And we could prove this through a theory he proposed that came to be known as "deconstruction."

Derrida's deconstruction of texts includes the concept of *binary opposition*. This is a term that originated with Saussure, but Derrida used it for different purposes. If we replace "man" with "woman" in a text, for example, we allegedly uncover the fact that men have been privileged, and women have been excluded, in Western societies.

The same trick can be performed with "white" and "black," "straight" and "gay," and numerous other "opposites." Derrida believed that these contrasts show us more than just the marginalization of certain groups: they remind us that the "privileged"[787] group can't truly exist without the oppressed group. Women, to use one example, help to define men.

The kernel of truth contained in this observation grew into a cornfield that blocked out the sun and threatened to make all distinctions meaningless — which was, ultimately, the point. Turning every statement into its opposite didn't necessarily *reveal* the instability of systems — but it did *create* instability, in language and in life. It continues to do so today.

Derrida insisted that "the undoing, decomposing, and desedimenting of structures ... was not a negative operation. Rather than destroying, it was also necessary to understand how an 'ensemble' was constituted and to reconstruct it to this end."[788]

But most people recognized this as a feeble defense. Mid-twentieth-century postmodernism was, after all, a rejection of the certainties of modernism. Those included both reason and science.

Yet the postmodernists' goal was exactly the same as the modernists': the liberation of the individual. The postmodernists simply recognized that *every* type of certainty had to go if people were ever truly going to be "free."

Language was no exception. Analytic philosophy had promised to turn language into math. But that project, too — even though it largely failed — was a threat to freedom. So deconstructionism ultimately meant that everyone's words (including, of course, Derrida's) were just so much nonsense.

787 Derrida, *Writing and Difference*, 257.

788 David Wood and Robert Bernasconi, *Derrida and Différance* (Evanston, IL: Northwestern University Press, 1988), 3.

In that respect, Derrida — who died in 2004 — was something like a modern David Hume: a fun-loving skeptic who could only shrug at the devastation he left in his wake.

5.

Amidst this obsession with language, Western thought did produce one truly intriguing philosophical movement in the twentieth century. However, existentialism actually started a hundred years earlier — with a Danish theologian named Søren Kierkegaard.

The word often used to describe Kierkegaard is "unusual." He had long, stork-like legs, but walked with a slump so pronounced that some called him a hunchback. He studied for a decade to get his theology degree, but never became a pastor. He broke off a yearlong engagement to a girl, explaining that melancholy made him unfit for marriage — and then seemed to write callously about the affair in his book *Either/Or*.

And while he loved walking the streets of Copenhagen and greeting the poor, he spent much of his time alone with his journals. He poured out his thoughts onto more than seven thousand pages. Yet even in these entries, his true personality is elusive: he had a habit of writing in pseudonyms, and some speculate he exaggerated details of his unhappy family life.

But unhappiness, Kierkegaard believed, was fundamental to the human condition. "There is not a single human being who does not despair at least a little, in whose innermost being there does not dwell an uneasiness, an unquiet, a discordance, an anxiety in the face of an unknown something," he wrote in *The Sickness Unto Death*, published in 1849.[789] Denying this truth only makes things worse.

The source of our anxiety, he thought, was the knowledge of our absolute free will. Kierkegaard used the example of standing on a cliff: we feel anxiety because we realize that we could jump off the edge. He called this the "dizziness of freedom"[790] — but it wasn't necessarily bad. This intense sensation also reminds us that we shouldn't just go through the motions of life.

That, Kierkegaard felt, was what many of his fellow Christians were doing. He had harsh criticism for the state-controlled Lutheran Church of Denmark. He

[789] Adam Kirsch, "Søren Kierkegaard's Struggle with Himself," *New Yorker*, April 29, 2020. https://www.newyorker.com/magazine/2020/05/11/soren-kierkegaards-struggle-with-himself.

[790] Buckingham, *The Philosophy Book*, 195.

believed it was more concerned with worldly affairs, and that it was encouraging people to believe it was enough to be a nominal Christian in a Christian society.

Kierkegaard particularly disliked Georg Hegel's insistence that the state is more important than the individual. So it's not surprising that he took this position about the Danish Church. He insisted instead that "subjectivity" — the experience of the individual — "is truth."[791] And he said the doubt that inevitably comes with subjectivity — are our perceptions really accurate? — is actually a crucial part of faith. Doubt proves that we're really *thinking* about our beliefs.

But Kierkegaard felt we had to do more than just ruminate. He believed that unless we obeyed God's will in "every secret desire and thought," our unhappiness and anxiety would never end.

How could we know God's will? By developing a completely personal connection to God. This was an idea among Protestants that went all the way back to Martin Luther. But Kierkegaard took it further.

The "dizziness of freedom" tells us it's our job to pursue a unique, individual relationship with God. Revelation comes to individuals, Kierkegaard thought — not to groups. And we can't just lean on Scripture for guidance. We have to accept responsibility for every thought and action, and for trying to discern whether they align with God's will.

It's an awesome task, and a daunting one. "A Christian, for Kierkegaard, isn't something you are born; it is something you have to become through terrific inner effort."[792]

Kierkegaard died in 1855, just forty-two years old and not knowing whether his work had convinced anyone that this terrific inner effort was worthwhile. He'd lived off his inheritance and self-published his books, which sold poorly.

At the start of the twentieth century, a new wave of philosophers would take up Kierkegaard's cross, so to speak. They would also take God out of the picture.

6.

First, however, came the phenomenologists.

If by "phenomenology" we mean "a study of phenomena," then it had been going on for centuries. But as a separate branch of philosophy, it really came into

[791] Søren Kierkegaard, *Concluding Unscientific Postscript to Philosophical Fragments* (Princeton, NJ: Princeton University Press, 1992), 50.

[792] Kirsch, "Søren Kierkegaard's Struggle with Himself."

its own in the early 1900s. And the primary figure was a Moravian mathematician and philosopher named Edmund Husserl.

Husserl had a lot in common with René Descartes. He wanted to eliminate uncertainty, and hoped to turn philosophy into the "first science."[793] His first step was to agree with Descartes: we can be sure of our own consciousness.

The next step was trickier: trying to prove the existence of an external world beyond our minds. Many philosophers had gotten bogged down here, as we've seen. The best they could suggest was that we know we're *perceiving* objects — not that the objects actually exist.

Husserl's big idea was that we were overlooking a major source of information. We should stop focusing on the objects themselves. Instead, we should pay attention to our *perception* of objects, and what we could learn from it. This became a study of consciousness known as *phenomenology.*

This way of thinking meant, for Husserl, that we should try to eliminate any preconceptions we might have about an object or experience. He thought we should "bracket" those preconceptions — including all prior knowledge — and set them to one side. This process of bracketing, Husserl called *Epoché.*

What we hope to describe, and study, is our pure experience of perception. Husserl named this process *phenomenological reduction.*

An important aspect of Husserl's thought is something called *intentionality*. This was an old idea, dating back to the Scholastic philosophers of the medieval era. Simply put, it stated that our thoughts are intentional, in the sense that they're directed *toward* something. Even dreams, thoughts about imaginary beings, or hallucinations are all intentional in this sense.

The problem with Husserl's work was the same issue that had been plaguing philosophers since Descartes reopened the divide between mind and body. That is, if the only thing that's certain is the contents of our minds, how can we know that anything else in the world exists? How do we know it's not all just a dream? This is the problem of *solipsism*.

In his *Cartesian Meditations,* Husserl tried to answer this criticism with an idea he called *transcendental intersubjectivity*. It's a weighty term, but the underlying concept is simpler: empathy.

[793] Jitendranath N. Mohanty, *Phenomenology: Between Essentialism and Transcendental Philosophy* (Evanston, IL: Northwestern University Press, 1998), 2.

We believe that other beings who seem to look and act like us will have similar perceptions to our own. And we all perform these actions, and have these perceptions, against a similar backdrop that Husserl called the "lifeworld."[794]

So we empathize with others. We believe that their acts are intentional in the same way ours are. We put ourselves in their shoes, believing that we're similar beings operating in a similar environment — and that allows us to overcome the aloneness of solipsism.

Not everyone was convinced by what was essentially a leap of faith. Especially not those who had no faith at all. Enter Martin Heidegger.

Heidegger was a German academic who studied with Husserl. In fact, he dedicated his greatest work, 1927's *Being and Time,* to his teacher. But as the Nazis rose to power in Germany, Heidegger joined the party. This severed for good his connection with Husserl, whose parents were Jews before converting to Christianity.

The controversy over Heidegger's Nazi involvement rages to this day. He claimed that he soon became an adversary of the party. But he never left it, nor did he apologize for talking about "the glory and the greatness of the Hitler revolution."[795] And he continued making ambiguous statements about the Nazis, even after World War II concluded.

Heidegger's philosophical disagreement with Husserl — and with other, older philosophers — was their focus on knowledge rather than existence. Most thinkers since Descartes had focused on epistemology: how we learn about the world around us. This assumed that man was separate from the world he was trying to learn about.

But Heidegger disagreed with this separation of subjects and objects. People are an inextricable part of the world, he said. It's the setting for all our experience. Heidegger even came up with the term *Dasein* to represent the unity of man "being there," or "being in the world."[796]

So our focus should be, he felt, on *ontology* — on *being*: the mystery of our own existence, and why it is we're here. Ignoring these questions — falling "out of being"[797] — Heidegger speculated, was responsible for humanity's decline.

[794] Mohanty, *Phenomenology*, 1–3.

[795] Peter Kreeft, *Socrates' Children,* vol. 4, *Contemporary Philosophers* (Elk Grove Village, IL: Word on Fire, 2022, e-book), ch. 75.

[796] A fuller explanation of Heidegger's *Dasein* is given by the translators of his *Introduction to Metaphysics*. Martin Heidegger, *Introduction to Metaphysics,* trans. Gregory Fried and Richard Polt (New Haven, CT: Yale University Press, 2000), xi–xii.

[797] Heidegger, *Introduction to Metaphysics*, 39.

Time, he concluded, is *the* integral part of being. Time is what shapes our existence, and the big, unavoidable marker — the thing that makes existence finite — is death. So the main job for us, in the time we have as we live lives of "being-towards-death,"[798] is to figure out what it means to be an authentic human being. Here, Heidegger borrowed from Nietzsche, who also felt man wasn't making the best use of the time he had on earth.

On the other hand, as Peter Kreeft points out, if you substitute "God" for "Being," there's a profoundly religious aspect to Heidegger's philosophy.[799] Especially since Heidegger had a mystical term for "Being itself" — he called it *Sein*.

Despite their break, Heidegger kept something in common with his mentor, Husserl. Both men felt that their attempts at solving the questions they set out to answer were unsuccessful.

Phenomenology became a popular field of study, especially when applied to other disciplines. But it never made philosophy the "first science" that Husserl hoped. Meanwhile, Heidegger's version of phenomenology, which focused on existence rather than knowledge, remained unfinished.

The person who some believe finished it would become the best known and most commercially successful philosopher of the twentieth century. He went back to the old question of essence and existence and gave it a surprisingly popular new twist.

7.

Jean-Paul Sartre's focus on the question of existence may have started early. He was born in Paris in 1905, an only child. Throughout his childhood, he dominated attention in his family.

His father died when Sartre was just a year old, something Sartre later claimed he was glad about: "Had he lived, my father would have laid down on me at full length, and would have crushed me."[800] He was brought up by his doting mother, and his grandfather allowed the boy free rein in his library.

[798] Martin Heidegger, *Being and Time*, trans. Dennis J. Schmidt and Joan Stambaugh (Albany: State University of New York Press, 1996), 216–221.

[799] Perhaps worth noting: Heidegger attended Jesuit seminary in 1909, but left for health reasons. Peter Kreeft explains the religious aspects of Heidegger's philosophy in *Socrates' Children*, vol. 4, ch. 75.

[800] Jean-Paul Sartre, *The Words* (New York: George Braziller, 1964), 19.

When he was four, Sartre developed a sty in his right eye. The sty left him permanently walleyed, and when he got to school, he discovered that his mother had lied. He wasn't a beautiful prince: he looked more like a frog instead.

But he received an excellent education, and seemed never to lack for confidence, despite his appearance. He was a womanizer his entire life, and he started early. One of his first conquests was Simone de Beauvoir, a fellow high school student and academic competitor. Beauvoir would become one of the most prominent feminist writers of the century, but she remained loyal throughout her life to Sartre — no matter how many times his affairs humiliated her.

The other women were often students. Sartre was an academic — a poor one, whose classes were chaotic. But it would be as a writer that he found his true calling.

World War II took a considerable toll on France. After the Nazi invasion of 1940, it fell under the control of the puppet Vichy government. But Sartre, as author Paul Johnson pointed out, "had a good war."[801] He spent most of it writing in cafes, rather than helping the French Resistance oppose the Nazis. And in 1944, his play *No Exit* made him famous.

No Exit is the story of three characters who have died and are together in a waiting room of Hell. Relations between the trio grow increasingly tense as they reveal the reasons they've been condemned. The final revelation is summed up in Sartre's famous phrase: "Hell is other people."[802] The three realize that *this* is their torture: to be stuck with one another for eternity.

The next year, Sartre followed up the play with the book most consider his greatest: *Being and Nothingness*. In it, he contributed substantially to the foundations of a philosophy that came to be known as *existentialism*.[803]

His Big Idea was that man has no essence prior to his existence. Instead, it's man's job — his lifetime project — to determine his *own* essence. Until then, he's just an empty shell.

Kierkegaard had at least suggested that there's another entity — God — who created us for some purpose. But Sartre called faith in God "bad faith." Like Nietzsche, he believed there is no God to help us figure out why we're here. We're entirely on our own.

801 Johnson, *Intellectuals*, 228.

802 Jean-Paul Sartre, *No Exit, and Three Other Plays* (New York: Vintage Books, 1955), 47.

803 Kierkegaard is often considered the first true existentialist, although Nietzsche, Heidegger, and the Catholic philosopher Gabriel Marcel all made significant contributions as well.

Not only are we alone, but we're destined to make mistakes as we wander through a barren landscape free of morals or guidance. Those mistakes will lead to guilt. For Sartre, the "dizziness of freedom" led inevitably to nausea — the title of Satre's early philosophical novel.

The philosophy was bleak, but it was timed perfectly to resonate with a France — and a Europe — devastated by war and the Holocaust. Sartre became a continental, and later a worldwide, celebrity. He was joined by other existentialists — including the Algerian writer Albert Camus, who wrestled with the "absurdity" of man's existence in a meaningless universe and who wrote, "There is only one serious philosophical problem, and that is suicide."[804]

Camus had a lot in common with the ancient Stoics. He believed that even if the universe was pointless, man should rebel nobly against that fate and seek out a meaningful life anyway. For that reason, Camus was sometimes described as "a saint without a God."[805]

Sartre, by contrast, descended into incoherence, even as his fame spread through the decades. He flirted with Marxism and communism, even though they directly contradicted his own individualistic philosophy. But he accepted Marx's idea that violence is necessary.

He became the sponsor of Frantz Fanon, a psychiatrist from the French colony of Martinique. Fanon, who died of leukemia at age thirty-six, dictated his book *The Wretched of the Earth* from his sickbed. In that influential work, Fanon preached violent revolution against colonizers in his native Africa.

Sartre agreed to write a preface. In it, he declared, "For in the first days of the revolt you must kill: to shoot down a European is to kill two birds with one stone, to destroy an oppressor and the man he oppresses at the same time." Of course, Sartre clearly wasn't talking about himself.[806]

He continued, until the end, to pursue multiple women, even while mostly blind and increasingly drunk. When Sartre died in April 1980, a crowd of fifty thousand mourners processed through the streets of Paris, on the way to Montparnasse Cemetery. People climbed trees to get a better view of the coffin, which was covered with roses, lilies, and gladioli. One eager spectator reportedly fell onto the casket itself.

It was a sendoff fit for the greatest of philosophers. What they were celebrating, exactly, was far less clear. Paul Johnson put it best: "What faith, what

[804] Magee, *The Story of Philosophy*, 217.

[805] Magee, *The Story of Philosophy*, 217.

[806] Frantz Fanon, *The Wretched of the Earth* (New York: Grove Press, 1966), 18.

luminous truth about humanity, were they asserting by their mass presence? We may well ask."[807]

8.

Many philosophers of this era seemed to be calling a halt to philosophy. How could it go any further?

One of the more sensible was Karl Popper, an Austrian-born academic. Popper was something like the modern version of John Locke. Locke had developed a way that philosophy could respond to the scientific genius of Sir Isaac Newton, who had revolutionized science through his laws of motion.

Popper, like many intellectuals of his day, realized that philosophy would now have to deal with the work of Albert Einstein. Einstein's theories of relativity had upended the Newtonian universe. What everyone had assumed was "settled science" was now unsettled. So what could we do?

According to Popper, we should abandon, once and for all, the search for philosophical certainty. Like Locke — and Hume, and Kant, and other philosophers — Popper insisted that the material world could never truly be known.

The best we could do, Popper thought, was to develop theories about this world. A theory is good for as long as it works . . . and then another theory takes its place. We can't prove ultimate truths — but we can prove ultimate *untruths*.

That is, statements that can be contradicted are ruled out. In explaining his Falsification Principle, Popper used the example of swans. If we say, "All swans are white," and then we see a black swan, then we know the statement is false.

This means that knowledge is developed critically, by finding inconsistencies and getting rid of them. This, Popper said, is how science, and progress, works.

Therefore, societies that allow people to critically examine things — not just science, but also politics — are the best ones. "The secret of intellectual excellence is the spirit of criticism; it is intellectual independence," Popper wrote.[808]

This belief led him to dismantle Marxism in his 1945 book *The Open Society and Its Enemies*. By the end of World War II, Popper had come to realize that communism was a gigantic threat to human progress. Its unrealizable idea of the

[807] Johnson, *Intellectuals*, 251.

[808] Karl Raimund Popper, *The Open Society and Its Enemies*, vol. 1 (New York: Routledge, 1966), 134.

perfect society made everyone who opposed it a traitor. "The enemies of freedom," he warned, "have always charged its defenders with subversion."[809]

So Popper's "open society" sounded a lot like John Locke's: open to inquiry and criticism, willing to examine alternative viewpoints, and tolerant of dissenters. To believe in God is one viewpoint among many, but God's existence can never be proven.

Yet just as Locke had drawn the line at tolerating atheists, Popper foresaw the problem of unlimited tolerance in an open society. One of his quotes is especially prophetic.

"If we extend unlimited tolerance even to those who are intolerant, if we are not prepared to defend a tolerant society against the onslaught of the intolerant," he wrote, "then the tolerant will be destroyed, and tolerance with them."[810]

Left unanswered then, as now, is: Who is intolerant? The philosophers of the twenty-first century will have to reclaim that question from society's gatekeepers.

9.

Taken in total, this chapter seems to represent a bleak philosophical landscape. It's appropriate for a bleak century, in which nearly 200 million people died in wars. Millions upon millions more died of starvation, execution, and forced labor in communist regimes. The numbers mocked Hegel and Marx, and their story of history's inevitable progress.

And yet, there was a major development that you almost never read about in the histories of philosophy. That was the unexpected resurgence of the Catholic philosophical tradition.

During the twentieth century, an astonishing variety of Catholic thinkers appeared. They represented a wide range of philosophical traditions, from Neo-Thomism to analytical philosophy to existentialism. There are far too many noteworthy ones to fit into this book, but the list includes such well-known names as scholastic philosophers Josef Pieper, Etienne Gilson and Jacques Maritain, along with Edmund Husserl's academic assistant Edith Stein and his student Dietrich von Hildebrand.

The best of them offered a return to the sanity and stability that modernism had abandoned during the medieval era. And some of them were popes, who rarely get credit for the philosophical content of their writings.

[809] Popper, *The Open Society and Its Enemies,* vol. 1, 88.

[810] Popper, *The Open Society and Its Enemies,* vol. 1, 265.

This rebirth really started at the end of the 1800s, with Pope Leo XIII's encyclical *Aeterni Patris*. An encyclical is a letter from the pope, addressed to Catholic religious leaders. This tradition began in 1740, and Leo was the most prolific issuer of encyclicals: he released eighty-five during his pontificate.

In the 1878 encyclical *Aeterni Patris*, Leo — a native of Rome who had just become pope eighteen months earlier — called for a "Restoration of Christian Philosophy in Catholic Schools in the Spirit of the Angelic Doctor, St. Thomas Aquinas." The document was an early call to arms: philosophy needs theology, and theology needs philosophy. And Thomistic philosophy was the best antidote to corrosive modernity.

Leo practiced what he preached with 1891's *Rerum Novarum*. Encyclicals often deal with a current problem and offer remedies that are faithful to Catholic teaching. The problem in this case was the same one that Karl Marx had made a career of addressing: conditions for workers worldwide in the aftermath of the Industrial Revolution.

Rerum Novarum defended free enterprise, and it recognized that socialism was "directly contrary to the natural rights of mankind."[811] But it also defended the rights of workers — especially the working poor. "Wage-earners, since they mostly belong in the mass of the needy, should be specially cared for and protected by the government."[812]

It's widely believed that much of *Rerum Novarum* was written by a professor named Tommaso Maria Zigliara. He was a well-known Thomistic philosopher who cited Aquinas at the beginning of the document, defending private property. And the entire encyclical has Aquinas's calm, reasoned philosophical tone.

Rerum Novarum didn't shy, however, from the challenge of Marxism. "The great mistake made in regard to the matter now under consideration," it read, "is to take up with the notion that class is naturally hostile to class, and that the wealthy and the working men are intended by nature to live in mutual conflict."[813]

But the encyclical defended the right of workers to organize in labor unions — and it insisted on fair wages. Employers and workers should be free to make their own arrangements, but "there underlies a dictate of natural justice more

811 Pope Leo XIII, "Aeterni Patris," August 4, 1879, www.vatican.va,. https://www.vatican.va/content/leo-xiii/en/encyclicals/documents/hf_l-xiii_enc_04081879_aeterni-patris.html.

812 Pope Leo XIII, "Aeterni Patris."

813 Pope Leo XIII, "Aeterni Patris."

imperious and ancient than any bargain between man and man, namely, that wages ought not to be insufficient to support a frugal and well-behaved wage-earner."[814]

At all times, employers and workers need to remember the Church's teachings — and their obligations to one another. "If Christian precepts prevail, the respective classes will not only be united in the bonds of friendship, but also in those of brotherly love."[815]

The devil is always in those details, of course. Yet *Rerum Novarum* managed, in a tiny fraction of the space taken up by Marx's bloated *Das Kapital,* to offer a humane, sensible capitalism that didn't need to be overthrown. It's hard not to wonder how history might have changed if more people had listened.

You could say the same thing about Pope Paul VI's 1968 encyclical *Humanae Vitae,* which warned about the dangers of artificial contraception. As author Mary Eberstadt notes, it's been mocked widely — even by Catholics — since its release.

"The encyclical warned of four resulting trends: a general lowering of moral standards throughout society; a rise in infidelity; a lessening of respect for women by men; and the coercive use of reproductive technologies by governments," Eberstadt writes.

"All of these predictions have come to pass, as well as a link between contraception and abortion that even secular thinkers have admitted. The joke is on society, and it's been an increasingly expensive, needless, and tragic one."[816]

Before he became pope, and while participating in Vatican II as a cardinal, Karol Wojtyla wrote the book *Osoba i czyn*. Published in 1969, *Person and Act* was the work of a serious philosopher. The book tackled one of the fundamental questions of history — what makes a person a person?

Wojtyla used the work of Thomas Aquinas as his base. He went back to Aquinas's definition of the "human act" as a voluntary, goal-oriented expression of free will. But *Person and Act* also showed the influence of modern phenomenologists like Edmund Husserl. In particular, Husserl's idea of intersubjectivity as a force that unites people played a key role in the book.

In the end, Wojtyla argued, like Aquinas, for an approach that combined reason and the evidence of the senses. There's more to a person than just what our senses tell us. But we're not just trapped in our own minds, either. It's a

[814] Pope Leo XIII, "Aeterni Patris."

[815] Pope Leo XIII, "Aeterni Patris."

[816] Mary Eberstadt, "The Vindication of Humanae Vitae," *First Things*, August 2008. https://www.firstthings.com/article/2008/08/002-the-vindication-of-ihumanae-vitaei.

person's actions — and what those actions reveal about them — that show us their humanity, and connect us to them.

"Action," Wojtyla wrote, "constitutes the specific moment where the person is revealed."[817]

After becoming Pope John Paul II, Wojtyla gave a series of addresses on the sacrament of marriage, sexuality, and the human body. These talks drew again on Aquinas and Husserl, as well as *Humanae Vitae* and Wojtyla's own *Person and Act*. They were eventually collected as the *Theology of the Body*.

Although they were delivered over a period of six years — from 1979 to 1984 — the addresses offered a coherent and complete argument for the way that a person's body reveals God.

"The body in fact, and it alone," Pope John Paul II wrote, "is capable of making visible what is invisible: the spiritual and divine."[818]

For John Paul, the evidence that modern philosophers had been seeking vainly for centuries — the missing link that would finally solve Descartes's mind and body problem, the bridge between Kant's phenomenal and noumenal worlds, and the explanation of the existentialists' "authentic" experience — had been as close as the mirror the whole time.

10.

Two of the most important Catholic philosophers of the twentieth century have a great deal in common.

Both are, or were, Catholic converts. Both had roots in secular philosophical movements, like Marxism and analytic philosophy. And both ultimately reached back to the work of St. Thomas Aquinas for inspiration.

The first also happens to be, in the view of many, the greatest female philosopher in history. That was Gertrude Elizabeth Margaret Anscombe — usually called "Elizabeth," "G. E. M.", or just "Miss Anscombe." (One of the people who used the last term was her husband, Peter Geach, a formidable Catholic philosopher in his own right.[819])

817 Cardinal Karol Wojtyla, *Person and Act* (Boston: D. Reidel, 1979), 11.

818 Pope John Paul II, *The Redemption of the Body and Sacramentality of Marriage (Theology of the Body)*, The Catholic Primer, 2006, https://stmarys-waco.org/documents/2016/9/theology_of_the_body.pdf.

819 Geach and Anscombe co-wrote the 1961 book *Three Philosophers: Aristotle, Aquinas, Frege*.

Anscombe was born in 1919. She was a native of Ireland who converted to Catholicism in her teens. Anscombe was a brilliant student at Oxford, and, while she was at Cambridge, became a protégé of Ludwig Wittgenstein. The Austrian analytic philosopher was well known for "his general dislike of academic women and especially of female philosophers."[820] But Anscombe was the exception.

Perhaps it was because she seemed absolutely fearless. One of the most famous examples came when she debated author C. S. Lewis at Oxford's Socratic Club.

Lewis was the president of this club, which met every Monday evening during the school year. He had set the group up as a way of defending Christianity against its critics, and debated many well-known atheists over the years. But on this night in February 1948, his opponent was no unbeliever, but Anscombe, a devout Catholic. She took issue with the way he attacked naturalism in his most recent book, *Miracles*.

It wasn't that Anscombe was defending naturalism — which is, simply put, the idea that there is nothing beyond nature. But Anscombe felt Lewis had been imprecise in his language, which undercut his argument.

History records Anscombe as the knockout winner of the debate: Lewis has been described as despondent afterward. Some contend this exchange humiliated Lewis so much that he gave up philosophical arguments and turned to children's literature instead.

Even Anscombe recognized that this was all an exaggeration. As she reflected, "The meeting of the Socratic Club at which I read my paper has been described by several of his friends as a horrible and shocking experience which upset him very much.... My own recollection is that it was an occasion of sober discussion of certain quite definite criticisms."[821]

However, as she noted, Lewis did eventually revise the chapter of *Miracles* that she criticized. And perhaps the debate is less significant for the technical points she raised, and serves more as an illustration of her take-no-prisoners personality.

What may be Anscombe's most widely known work is another case in point. In 1956, Oxford decided to honor former U.S. President Harry S. Truman with an honorary degree. Anscombe, who was on the faculty at the time, was appalled.

[820] Julia Driver, "Gertrude Elizabeth Margaret Anscombe," *Stanford Encyclopedia of Philosophy*, July 21, 2009; revised May 30, 2022, https://plato.stanford.edu/entries/anscombe/.

[821] Christopher Mitchell, "University Battles — C. S. Lewis and the Oxford University Socratic Club," C. S. Lewis Institute, January 7, 2010, https://www.cslewisinstitute.org/resources/university-battles-c-s-lewis-and-the-oxford-university-socratic-club/.

She felt Truman's decision to drop atomic bombs on Hiroshima and Nagasaki during World War II was indefensible, and she wrote a pamphlet in protest of Oxford's decision.

"Mr. Truman's Degree" applied Anscombe's ethical views to one of the most controversial decisions in history. The pamphlet anticipated her 1957 book, *Intention.* The key question, she insisted, was understanding the intention behind our actions — because only then can we assign responsibility.

While the language in Anscombe's work was sometimes spiky and difficult, this pamphlet showed she could be short, clear, and devastating. Truman, she felt, had committed mass murder, and her words conveyed her outrage.

"In the bombing of these cities it was certainly decided to kill the innocent as a means to an end," she wrote. "And a very large number of them, all at once, without warning."[822] These civilians could not escape or take shelter, she added. The decision was not rash or accidental, but premeditated.

Many argued that Truman had averted greater loss of life by avoiding an invasion of Japan. Anscombe acknowledged this — but questioned whether Japan's total defeat was truly necessary. The "fixation on unconditional surrender"[823] was also what made the bombing evil, she contended.

How had we gotten to the point where Oxford had decided to honor a man Anscombe believed was responsible for the deliberate murder of thousands? "I get some small light on the subject when I consider the productions of Oxford moral philosophy since the First World War, which I have lately had occasion to read," she wrote.

"Its character can easily be briefly demonstrated. Up to the Second World War the prevailing moral philosophy in Oxford taught that an action can be 'morally good' no matter how objectionable the thing done may be."[824]

It might be surprising to learn, then, that in "Modern Moral Philosophy," a paper released around the same time, Anscombe argued that "it is not profitable for us at present to do moral philosophy." At least, she continued, not until "we have an adequate philosophy of psychology, in which we are conspicuously lacking."[825]

Why would Anscombe make such a case? Philosophers have debated this for decades, but the answer seems to be a fairly simple one: because Anscombe

822 Elizabeth Anscombe, "Mr. Truman's Degree" (1956), The Integrity Project, https://projectintegrity.files.wordpress.com/2015/07/mr_trumans_degree.pdf.

823 Anscombe, "Mr. Truman's Degree."

824 Anscombe, "Mr. Truman's Degree."

825 Driver, "Gertrude Elizabeth Margaret Anscombe."

was a practicing Catholic who believed that divine law was superior to any secular philosophy.

The Stanford Encyclopedia of Philosophy points out that Anscombe wasn't calling for an end to *morals*—only moral *philosophy*. This, the editors add, would make perfect sense to Christians.

"If you and your audience trust that God has promised each of you that it is in your interest to avoid injustice," they write, "you don't need to deeply understand the concept of flourishing or of virtue in order to talk to one another about how to live."[826]

And they note that no less an authority than Thomas Aquinas believed "it's possible to think that morality is based upon God and also believe that we need to understand the nature of our psychology in order to adequately understand morality."[827]

It's yet another reminder of just how open the medieval church really was to science—something we continue to need reminding of, eight hundred years after the fact.

11.

> What matters at this stage is the construction of local forms of community within which civility and the intellectual and moral life can be sustained through the new dark ages which are already upon us. And if the tradition of the virtues was able to survive the horrors of the last dark ages, we are not entirely without grounds for hope. This time however the barbarians are not waiting beyond the frontiers; they have already been governing us for quite some time. And it is our lack of consciousness of this that constitutes part of our predicament. We are waiting not for a Godot, but for another—doubtless very different—St. Benedict.[828]

The last paragraph of Alasdair MacIntyre's 1981 work *After Virtue* sounds like the warning of a disenchanted Catholic believer. It isn't—or at least, it wasn't at the time.

It was only after the publication of *After Virtue*, when he was trying to talk his university students out of the virtues of Thomism, that MacIntyre became a convert—first to Aquinas's philosophy, and then to the Catholic faith.

[826] Driver, "Gertrude Elizabeth Margaret Anscombe."

[827] Driver, "Gertrude Elizabeth Margaret Anscombe."

[828] Alasdair MacIntyre, *After Virtue*, 3rd ed. (Notre Dame, IN: University of Notre Dame Press, 2007), 278.

At ninety-four, MacIntyre is, at the time of this writing, the only living philosopher mentioned in this book. Born in Glasgow in 1929 to a pair of doctors, he's become the world's leading ethical thinker.

His life also contains one of the most intriguing journeys and juxtapositions of any modern philosopher. As his "intellectual biographer," the late Émile Perreau-Saussine, put it, "He is one of the rare thinkers today to have remained faithful to the antiliberalism of his youth, one of the rare critics of liberalism not to have stopped thinking after the fall of communism, and one of the rare thinkers to have been able to reorient his outlook in a new direction."[829]

As a young man at Oxford, MacIntyre drew inspiration from three major sources: the Swiss Protestant theologian Karl Barth, who argued that the Bible only becomes the Word of God when it's received by faith; the economic theories of Karl Marx; and the precision of analytic philosophy.

Raised Presbyterian, MacIntyre lost his faith in the 1950s and cast about for "something that he wanted to say."[830] He considered and rejected Hume, Kant, and the utilitarians — as well as Soviet communism, after the 1956 invasion of Hungary.

MacIntyre grew increasingly conscious that the Enlightenment had failed in a fundamental way, and that abandoning Aristotle might have been a critical mistake. In *After Virtue*, the chapter "Nietzsche or Aristotle?" weighs each philosopher's set of ethics. MacIntyre points out that Nietzsche's view — that man's raw will reigns supreme — is the result of modern philosophers who failed to establish a rational basis for morality.

"The defensibility of the Nietzschean position turns in the end on the answer to the question: was it right in the first place to reject Aristotle?" he writes. "For if Aristotle's position in ethics and politics — or something very like it — could be sustained, the whole Nietzschean enterprise would be pointless."[831]

"And thus the key question does indeed become: can Aristotle's ethics, or something very like it, after all be vindicated?" In the end, MacIntyre argues that it can — and that led him to Aquinas.[832]

[829] Émile Perreau-Saussine, *Alasdair MacIntyre: An Intellectual Biography* (South Bend, IN: University of Notre Dame Press, 2022), 12.

[830] John Cornwell, "MacIntyre on Money," Prospect, October 20, 2010. http://www.prospectmagazine.co.uk/essays/54612/macintyre-on-money.

[831] MacIntyre, *After Virtue*, 133.

[832] MacIntyre, *After Virtue*, 133–134.

"I became a Thomist after writing *After Virtue* in part because I became convinced that Aquinas was in some respects a better Aristotelian than Aristotle," he wrote in an introduction to a revised version of the book. "Not only was he an excellent interpreter of Aristotle's texts, but ... he had been able to extend and deepen both Aristotle's metaphysical and his moral enquiries."[833]

This has led MacIntyre to defend "a Thomistic position that looks to escape both the universalism of the Enlightenment and 'postmodern' relativism, a position that looks to render faith neither superfluous nor unintelligible."[834]

In short, MacIntyre argues for a return to the moral philosophy of the ancients and the medieval Christians. It's a three-part theory. There are people as they are in nature, and people as they could be. Virtue is the link: how we get from the way we are to the way we know we ought to be.

The modern philosophers spent hundreds and hundreds of years searching for alternatives, shortcuts, or escape clauses. They all failed. The only answer, MacIntyre tells us, is to go back to the future.

"The hard work of morality," he says, "consists in the transformation of desires, so that we aim at the good and respect the precepts of the natural law."[835]

And as he famously reminds us in *After Virtue*, the skies grow increasingly dark. The barbarians have been inside the walls for quite some time, and the hour for such changes has grown late indeed.

[833] MacIntyre, *After Virtue*, 7.

[834] Perreau-Saussine, *Alasdair MacIntyre*, 144.

[835] Cornwell, "MacIntyre on Money."

EPILOGUE

Sometimes, it's not a joke that best conveys a difficult truth. A meme is often better.

There's a popular one featuring actor Zac Efron, of *High School Musical* fame and infamy. In response to the question, "So how did you become interested in philosophy?" a smiling Efron holds up a sign that reads, "Needing a coping mechanism for existing that makes more sense than God."[836]

That nicely sums up the past eight centuries in philosophy. "Making more sense than God" was the project of many of the men in this book.

Many were well intentioned. Some were Christians. None succeeded.

Yes, they helped make a modern world for which we can, in many ways, be profoundly grateful. They've also dragged untold millions of people along on their wild goose chase into the cave, to find morality and meaning without God. This book has been, in large part, the story of their Pyrrhic victory. The result has been more freedom — along with more alienation, isolation, recrimination, and desolation.

And ultimately, considering all those burdens, less freedom after all.

Some days, it's hard not to think the late Malcolm Muggeridge was spot-on when he said, back in 1985,

[836] You can find this Zac Efron philosophy meme wherever classic memes are displayed.

> So the final conclusion would surely be that whereas other civilizations have been brought down by attacks of barbarians from without, ours had the unique distinction of training its own destroyers at its own educational institutions, and then providing them with facilities for propagating their destructive ideology far and wide, all at the public expense.
>
> Thus did Western Man decide to abolish himself...[837]

And yet, the hopeful signs are there for those who can spot them. In the final chapter of his refutation of atheism, *The Last Superstition*, Edward Feser relates examples of how science has turned — albeit often silently and reluctantly — back in the direction of Aristotle and Aquinas. This is, as he explains, "rationally unavoidable"[838] for those who want to perform science.

If the weight of millennia can't extinguish the common sense of Socrates, Plato, and Aristotle, then it's unlikely to be crushed. Conversely, if Christ's own disciples couldn't follow his teachings, it should hardly be a surprise that much of the world now ignores Augustine and Aquinas.

But if you believe in truth — and almost everyone does, no matter what they say or do — then you must also believe it's stubborn. Indestructible. And eternal. That means it will return, even when people try to bury it.

Nearly a hundred years ago, in the wake of a brutal and senseless world war, and on the eve of even more unimaginable cataclysms, G. K. Chesterton wrote:

> The earth is an earthquake, a ceaseless and apparently endless earthquake, for the moderns for whom Newton has been scrapped along with Ptolemy. And for them there is something more steep and even incredible than a mountain: a piece of really solid ground; the level of the level-headed man.[839]

He was talking about St. Thomas Aquinas, the Dumb Ox who took the best parts of Plato, Aristotle, and Augustine, and used them to lay a foundation of thought as balanced and unshakable as he was — because it rests on everlasting bedrock.

A lot of needless clutter has been laid on top of that foundation, but it's still there, clean and plain and humble. This book has been an attempt to move just

[837] Malcolm Muggeridge, *Vintage Muggeridge: Religion and Society*, ed. Geoffrey Barlow (Grand Rapids, MI: William B. Eerdmans, 1985).

[838] Feser, *The Last Superstition*, 266.

[839] Chesterton, *St. Thomas Aquinas*, 18.

a little of the clutter aside so that the floor — the eternal truth — can become visible again.

And once you've seen it, you're free to reject it. But once you've seen it, you can never *truly* be free again — because you never truly were free in the first place. As Jesus says in John's Gospel, only the truth can set us free. It's the same truth history's greatest philosophers — from Socrates, Plato, and Aristotle to Alisdair McIntyre — have been seeking for centuries.

In their quest, however, many philosophers — some great, and some minor — have been leading us all in the opposite way for quite some time. May this book be able to point even a single reader back in the right direction.

SELECTED BIBLIOGRAPHY

Abelard, Peter. *Historia Calamitatum: The Story of My Misfortunes*. Translated by Henry Adams Bellows. New York: Macmillan, 1922. Medieval Sourcebook, Fordham University. https://sourcebooks.fordham.edu/basis/abelard-histcal.asp.

Ambury, James M. "Socrates." Internet Encyclopedia of Philosophy. https://iep.utm.edu/socrates/.

Anscombe, Elizabeth. "Mr. Truman's Degree." The Integrity Project, https://projectintegrity.files.wordpress.com/2015/07/mr_trumans_degree.pdf. Printed, 1956.

Aristotle. *Metaphysics*. Edited by W. D. Ross. Oxford: Clarendon Press, 1908.

———. *The Nicomachean Ethics of Aristotle*. Edited by W. D. Ross. Oxford: Clarendon Press, 1908.

Augustine, Saint. *Eighty-three Different Questions*, trans. David L. Mosher. Washington, D.C.: Catholic University of America Press, 1982.

Augustine, Saint. *The City of God*. Edited by Marcus Dods. Edinburgh: T. & T. Clark, 1871.

Augustine, Saint. *The Confessions: With an Introduction and Contemporary Criticism*. Translated by Maria Boulding. Edited by David Vincent Meconi, S.J. San Francisco: Ignatius Press, 2012.

Aune, Bruce. *Metaphysics*. Minneapolis: University of Minnesota Press, 1985.

Aurelius, Marcus. *The Meditations*. Edited by George Long. Mineola, NY: Dover Publications, 1997.

Ayer, Alfred. *Language, Truth, and Logic*. London: Pelican Books, 1971.

Bacon, Francis. *The Works of Francis Bacon*. Edited by James Spedding, Robert Leslie Ellis, and Douglas Denon Heath. Cambridge: Cambridge University Press, 2011.

Baker, Alan. "Simplicity." *Stanford Encyclopedia of Philosophy*. October 29, 2004; revised May 16, 2022. https://plato.stanford.edu/entries/simplicity/.

Barr, Stephen M. "St. Augustine's Relativistic Theory of Time." *Church Life Journal.* February 7, 2020. https://churchlifejournal.nd.edu/articles/augustines-push-against-the-limits-of-time/.

Beckwith, Christopher I. *Warriors of the Cloisters: The Central Asian Origins of Science in the Medieval World.* Princeton, NJ: Princeton University Press, 2012.

Beiser, Frederick C. *The Fate of Reason: German Philosophy from Kant to Fichte.* Cambridge, MA: Harvard University Press, 1987.

———. *Hegel.* New York: Routledge, 2007.

Bellarmine, Robert. "Letter from Bellarmine to Father Foscarini," April 4, 1615. Famous Trials. https://www.famous-trials.com/galileotrial/1024-bellarmineletter.

Berkeley, George. *A Treatise Concerning the Principles of Human Knowledge.* New York: Barnes & Noble, 2006.

Berryman, Sylvia. "Ancient Atomism." *Stanford Encyclopedia of Philosophy* Archive. August 23, 2005; revised December 15, 2016. https://plato.stanford.edu/Archives/win2021/entries/atomism-ancient/.

Blumenau, Ralph. "Free Will and Predestination." *Philosophy Now* (1998). https://philosophynow.org/issues/20/Free_will_and_Predestination.

Bobro, Marc E. "The Optimistic Science of Leibniz." *New Atlantis* (2014). https://www.thenewatlantis.com/publications/the-optimistic-science-of-leibniz.

Boethius. *Consolation of Philosophy.* Indianapolis: Hackett Publishing, 2001.

Bonazzi, Mauro. "Protagoras." *Stanford Encyclopedia of Philosophy* (Fall 2020; revised Fall 2023). https://plato.stanford.edu/entries/protagoras/.

Boswell, James. "Death and David Hume," Scotland's Pages –Timeline – 1776. National Library of Scotland. https://digital.nls.uk/scotlandspages/timeline/17762.html.

Buckingham, Will. *The Philosophy Book.* 1st ed. London: Penguin, 2011.

Burke, Edmund. *Reflections on the Revolution in France.* Amherst, NY: Prometheus Books, 1987.

———. "Mr. Burke's Speech, on the 1st December 1783." Eighteenth Century Collections Online. https://quod.lib.umich.edu/cgi/t/text/text-idx?cc=ecco.

———. "A Letter from the Right Honourable Edmund Burke to a Noble Lord." 1796. Eighteenth Century Collections Online. https://quod.lib.umich.edu/cgi/t/text/text-idx?c=ecco.

Burnet, John. *Early Greek Philosophy.* First Rate Publishers, 2014.

Cahn, Steven M., ed. *Classics of Western Philosophy.* 4th ed. Indianapolis: Hackett, 1995.

Cartwright, David E. *Schopenhauer: A Biography*. Cambridge: Cambridge University Press, 2010.

Chesterton, G. K. *St. Thomas Aquinas: The Dumb Ox*. Mansfield Centre, CT: Martino Publishing, 2011.

Cohen, S. Marc, Patricia Curd, and C. D. C. Reeve, eds. *Readings in Ancient Greek Philosophy: From Thales to Aristotle*. Indianapolis: Hackett, 2011.

Connor, James A. *Pascal's Wager*. New York: Harper Collins, 2009.

"Constitutio Dogmatica Dei Filius." April 24, 1870. Vatican website. https://www.vatican.va/content/pius-ix/la/documents/constitutio-dogmatica-dei-filius-24-aprilis-1870.html.

Cornwell, John. "MacIntyre on Money." Prospect, October 20, 2010. http://www.prospectmagazine.co.uk/essays/54612/macintyre-on-money.

Corradetti, Claudio. "Frankfurt School and Critical Theory." *Internet Encyclopedia of Philosophy*. n.d. https://iep.utm.edu/critical-theory-frankfurt-school/.

Cranston, Maurice. *Locke*. New York: Macmillan Company, 1957.

Crimmins, James. "Jeremy Bentham." *Stanford Encyclopedia of Philosophy*. March 17, 2015. https://plato.stanford.edu/entries/bentham/.

Critchley, Simon. "Athens in Pieces: In Aristotle's Garden." *New York Times*, February 18, 2019. https://www.nytimes.com/2019/02/18/opinion/aristotle-lyceum.html.

Cuvier, Georges. *Cuvier's History of the Natural Sciences*. Paris: Publications scientifiques du Muséum, 2019.

De Saussure, Ferdinand. *Course in General Linguistics*. New York: McGraw-Hill, 1966.

Deneen, Patrick J. *Why Liberalism Failed*. New Haven, CT: Yale University Press, 2018.

Derrida, Jacques. *Writing and Difference*. Chicago: University of Chicago Press, 1978.

Descartes, René. *The Philosophical Writings of Descartes*. Vol. 1, translated by John Cottingham, Robert Stoothoff, and Dugald Murdoch. Cambridge: Cambridge University Press, 1985.

Dewey, John. *Experience and Education*. New York: Free Press, 1938.

DeWitt, Norman Wentworth. *Epicurus and His Philosophy*. Minneapolis: University of Minnesota Press, 1954.

Dienstag, Joshua. "Schopenhauer vs Hegel: Progress or Pessimism." IAI News. March 15, 2023. https://iai.tv/articles/schopenhauer-vs-hegel-progress-or-pessimism-joshua-dienstag-auid-2416.

Diogenes Laërtius. *Lives of the Eminent Philosophers*. Edited by Robert Drew Hicks. Cambridge, MA: Harvard University Press, 1979.

———. *The Lives and Opinions of Eminent Philosophers*. Translated by C. D. Yonge. London: G. Bell and Sons, 1915. Project Gutenberg. https://www.gutenberg.org/files/57342/57342-h/57342-h.htm.

Dostoyevsky, Fyodor. *The Brothers Karamazov: A Novel in Four Parts with Epilogue*. Translated by Richard Pevear and Larissa Volokhonsky. New York: Farrar, Straus and Giroux, 2002.

Driver, Julia. "Gertrude Elizabeth Margaret Anscombe." *Stanford Encyclopedia of Philosophy*. July 21, 2009; revised May 30, 2022. https://plato.stanford.edu/entries/anscombe/.

Eberstadt, Mary. "The Vindication of Humanae Vitae." *First Things*. August 2008. https://www.firstthings.com/article/2008/08/002-the-vindication-of-ihumanae-vitaei.

Eckhart, Meister. *The Complete Mystical Works of Meister Eckhart*. Translated and edited by Maurice O'C. Walshe. New York: Crossroad Publishing, 2009.

Einstein, Albert. *The Ultimate Quotable Einstein*. Edited by Alice Calaprice. Princeton, NJ: Princeton University Press, 2013.

Epictetus. *Epictetus: A Stoic and Socratic Guide to Life*. Edited by Arthur Anthony Long. Oxford: Clarendon Press, 1904.

———. *Discourses*. Edited by George Long. New York: Appleton, 1904.

Erasmus, Desiderius. *In Praise of Folly*. Edited by John Wilson. Mineola, NY: Dover Publications, 2012.

Falcon, Andrea. "Commentators on Aristotle: Andronicus of Rhodes." *Stanford Encyclopedia of Philosophy*. 2021. https://plato.stanford.edu/entries/aristotle-commentators/supplement.html.

Fanon, Frantz. *The Wretched of the Earth*. New York: Grove Press, 1966.

Feser, Edward. *The Last Superstition*. South Bend, IN: St. Augustine's Press, 2008.

_____. *Locke*. New York: Oneworld Publications, 2013.

Feuerbach, Ludwig. *The Essence of Christianity*. Translated by Marian Evans. London: Kegan Paul, Trench, Trübner, & Co, 1890. Project Gutenberg. https://www.gutenberg.org/cache/epub/47025/pg47025-images.html.

Ford, Laura. "An Encounter to Remember." Kosmos Society. February 2, 2016. https://kosmossociety.chs.harvard.edu/an-encounter-to-remember/.

Gerson, Lloyd. "Plotinus." *Stanford Encyclopedia of Philosophy*. June 30, 2003; revised June 28, 2018. https://plato.stanford.edu/entries/plotinus/#:~:text=The%20human%20person%20is%20essentiall.

Guerber, H. A. *The Story of the Greeks*. New York: American Book Company, 1896. Project Gutenberg. https://www.gutenberg.org/files/23495/23495-h/23495-h.htm.

Hampden, Renn Dickson. *The Life of Thomas Aquinas*. London: John J. Griffin, 1848.

Harris, Sam. *The End of Faith: Religion, Terror, and the Future of Reason*. New York: W. W. Norton, 2005.

Hegel, Georg. *The Philosophy of Right*. Kitchener, ON: Batoche Books, 2001.

Heidegger, Martin. *Nietzsche*. Translated by David Farrell Krell and Joan Stambaugh. San Francisco: Harper San Francisco, 1991.

Heidegger, Martin. *Introduction to Metaphysics*. Translated by Gregory Fried and Richard Polt. New Haven, CT: Yale University Press, 2000.

Heidegger, Martin. *Being and Time*. Translated by Dennis J. Schmidt and Joan Stambaugh. Albany: State University of New York Press, 1996.

Heine, Heinrich. *The Works of Heinrich Heine*. London: William Heinemann, 1892.

Herman, Arthur. *The Cave and the Light: Plato versus Aristotle, and the Struggle for the Soul of Western Civilization*. New York: Random House, 2013.

Himma, Kenneth. "Anselm: Ontological Argument for God's Existence." *Internet Encyclopedia of Philosophy*. https://iep.utm.edu/anselm-ontological-argument/.

Hitchens, Christopher. *God Is Not Great*. New York: Twelve, 2007.

Hobbes, Thomas. *Leviathan*. 1651. Early English Books Online. https://quod.lib.umich.edu/cgi/t/text/text-idx?c=eebo.

———. *The Life of Mr. Thomas Hobbes of Malmesbury Written by Himself in a Latine Poem, and Now Translated into English*. 1680. Ann Arbor: Text Creation Partnership. https://quod.lib.umich.edu/e/eebo/A44004.0001.001/1:2?rgn=div1.

Honigman, Ana Finel. "Wanderer above the Sea of Fog (painting by Friedrich)," Britannica. n.d. Accessed September 3, 2023. https://www.britannica.com/topic/Wanderer-Above-the-Sea-of-Fog#ref1304950.

Hume, David. *An Enquiry Concerning Human Understanding*. Hume Texts Online. http://www.davidhume.org.

———. *A Treatise of Human Nature: Being an Attempt to Introduce the Experimental Method of Reasoning into Moral Subjects*. Hume Texts Online. http://www.davidhume.org.

Husserl, Edmund. *Cartesian Meditations: An Introduction to Phenomenology*. Translation by Dorion Cairns. Dordrecht: Springer-Science+Business Media, B.V., 1960.

Iamblichus. *Life of Pythagoras, or, Pythagoric Life. Accompanied by Fragments of the Ethical Writings of Certain Pythagoreans in the Doric Dialect …* Translated by Thomas Taylor. London: A. J. Valpy, 1818.

Jackson, Michael. Interview in *Ebony Magazine*. May 1992. http://www.jackson.ch/ebony1.htm.

Jankowiak, Tim. "Kant, Immanuel." *Internet Encyclopedia of Philosophy*." 2023. https://iep.utm.edu/kantview/.

John Paul II. *The Redemption of the Body and Sacramentality of Marriage (Theology of the Body)*. The Catholic Primer, 2006. https://stmarys-waco.org/documents/2016/9/theology_of_the_body.pdf.

Johnson, Paul. *Intellectuals*. New York: Harper Perennial, 1990.

———. *Socrates: A Man for Our Times*. New York: Classic Penguin, 2011.

Jones, Howard. *The Epicurean Tradition*. New York: Routledge, 1989.

Jones, Tom. *George Berkeley: A Philosophical Life*. Princeton, NJ: Princeton University Press, 2021.

Kang, Minsoo. "The Mechanical Daughter of René Descartes." *Modern Intellectual History* 14, no. 3 (2016): 633–660. https://doi.org/10.1017/s147924431600024x.

Kant, Immanuel. "On the Supposed Right to Lie from Benevolent Motives." Excerpt from *Critique of Practical Reason*, 4th ed., 1889. Sophia Project Philosophy Archives. http://www.sophia-project.org/uploads/1/3/9/5/13955288/kant_lying.pdf.

———. *The Critique of Pure Reason*. Chicago: Encyclopedia Britannica, 1952.

———. "What Is Enlightenment?" 1784. Translated by Ted Humphrey. New York Public Library. https://www.nypl.org/sites/default/files/kant_whatisenlightenment.pdf

Kengor, Paul. *The Devil and Karl Marx: Communism's Long March of Death, Deception, and Infiltration*. Gastonia, NC: Tan Books, 2020.

Kenny, Sir Anthony. *Aquinas on Mind*. New York: Routledge, 1994.

Kierkegaard, Søren. *Concluding Unscientific Postscript to Philosophical Fragments*. Princeton, NJ: Princeton University Press. 1992.

Kirk, Russell. "The Little Platoon We Belong to in Society." *Imprimis*. November 1, 1977. https://imprimis.hillsdale.edu/the-little-platoon-we-belong-to-in-society-november-1977/.

Kirsch, Adam. "Søren Kierkegaard's Struggle with Himself." *New Yorker*. April 29, 2020. https://www.newyorker.com/magazine/2020/05/11/soren-kierkegaards-struggle-with-himself.

Klein, Daniel B., Jason Briggeman, and Jacob R. Hall. "Foreword to 'Hume's Manuscript Account of the Extraordinary Affair between Him and Rousseau.'" *Econ Journal W*atch 18, no. 2 (October 2021): 278–326. https://econjwatch.org/File+download/1205/HumeSept2021.pdf?mimetype=pdf.

Knox, T. Malcolm. "Georg Wilhelm Friedrich Hegel." *Britannica*. Last updated November 10, 2023. https://www.britannica.com/biography/Georg-Wilhelm-Friedrich-Hegel/.

Kreeft, Peter. *Socrates' Children*. Vol. 2, *Medieval Philosophers*. South Bend, IN: St. Augustine Press, 2019.

———. *Socrates' Children*. Vol. 1, *Ancient Philosophers*. Elk Grove Village, IL: Word on Fire, 2022, e-book.

———. *Socrates' Children*. Vol. 3, *Modern Philosophers*. Elk Grove Village, IL: Word on Fire, 2022, e-book.

———. *Socrates' Children*. Vol. 4, *Contemporary Philosophers*. Elk Grove Village, IL: Word on Fire, 2022, e-book .

———. *Philosophy*. San Francisco: Ignatius Press, 2023.

Kuehn, Manfred. *Kant: A Biography*. Cambridge: Cambridge University Press, 2002.

Leaman, Oliver. *Moses Maimonides*. New York: Routledge, 2013.

Leibniz, Gottfried. "Monadology." 1714. Oliver Knill, Harvard University, January 7, 2017. https://people.math.harvard.edu/~knill/various/monadology/index.html#:~:text=known%20in%20another.

Leo XIII. Encyclical Letter *Aeterni Patris* (August 4, 1879). https://www.vatican.va/content/leo-xiii/en/encyclicals/documents/hf_l-xiii_enc_04081879_aeterni-patris.html.

———. Encyclical Letter *Rerum Novarum* (May 15, 1891). https://www.vatican.va/content/leo-xiii/en/encyclicals/documents/hf_l-xiii_enc_15051891_rerum-novarum.html.

Levin, Yuval. *The Great Debate: Edmund Burke, Thomas Paine, and the Birth of Right and Left*. New York: Basic Books, 2014.

Locke, John. *The Works, Vol. 5 Four Letters Concerning Toleration*. 1685. Online Library of Liberty. https://oll.libertyfund.org/title/locke-the-works-vol-5-four-letters-concerning-toleration.

———. *The Two Treatises of Civil Government (Hollis Ed.)*. Online Library of Liberty. 1689. https://oll.libertyfund.org/title/hollis-the-two-treatises-of-civil-government-hollis-ed.

———. *The Works, Vol. 1 An Essay Concerning Human Understanding Part 1*. 1689. Online Library of Liberty. https://oll.libertyfund.org/title/locke-the-works-vol-1-an-essay-concerning-human-understanding-part-1.

"Logicism." *Britannica*. n.d. https://www.britannica.com/topic/logicism.

Luther, Martin. "Martin Luther's 1517 Disputation against Scholastic Theology." William Roach. August 21, 2017. https://williamroach.org/2017/08/20/martin-luthers-1517-disputation-against-scholastic-theology/.

Lynch, John Patrick. *Aristotle's School; a Study of a Greek Educational Institution*. Berkeley: University of California Press, 1972.

Machiavelli, Niccolò. *The Prince*. Translated by Daniel John Donno. New York: Bantam Classics, 1985.

Magee, Bryan. *Confessions of a Philosopher: A Personal Journey through Western Philosophy from Plato to Popper*. New York: Modern Library, 1997.

———. *The Story of Philosophy*. New York: Dorling Kindersley Publishing, 1998.

Maimonides, Moses. *The Guide of the Perplexed,* Vol. 1. Chicago: University of Chicago Press, 1963.

Manent, Pierre. *An Intellectual History of Liberalism*. Princeton, NJ: Princeton University Press, 1995.

Marder, Michael. "The Philosopher's Plant 6.0: Avicenna's Celery." *Project Syndicate*. April 4, 2013. https://www.project-syndicate.org/blog/the-philosopher-s-plant-6-0--avicenna-s-celery.

Marenbon, John. "Why We Should Read Boethius's *Consolation of Philosophy* Today." *Aeon*. October 9, 2020. https://aeon.co/essays/why-we-should-read-boethiuss-consolation-of-philosophy-today.

Maritain, Jacques. *St. Thomas Aquinas*. 1958. https://www3.nd.edu/~maritain/jmc/etext/thomas1.htm

Martinich, A. P. *Thomas Hobbes*. New York: St. Martin's Press. 1997.

Marx, Karl. "Abstract from the Contribution to the Critique of Hegel's Philosophy of Law." 1844. Marx/Engels Internet Archive. https://www.marxists.org/archive/marx/works/1844/df-jahrbucher/law-abs.htm.

———. "Comments on James Mill, *Éléments D'économie Politique*." 1844. Marx/Engels Internet Archive. https://www.marxists.org/archive/marx/works/1844/james-mill/.

———. "Private Property and Communism." 1844. Marx/Engels Internet Archive. https://www.marxists.org/archive/marx/works/1844/manuscripts/comm.htm.

———. "Critique of the Gotha Programme." In *Marx: Later Political Writings*, 208–226. Cambridge University Press, June 5, 2022. https://doi.org/10.1017/cbo9780511810695.011.

———. *The Letters of Karl Marx*. Englewood Cliffs, NJ: Prentice-Hall, 1979.

Marx, Karl, and Friedrich Engels *The Communist Manifesto with Related Documents*. Edited by John E. Toews. Boston: Bedford St. Martin's, 1999.

McElroy, James. "Knock It off with the 'Little Platoons' Already." *The American Conservative*. June 28, 2018. https://www.theamericanconservative.com/knock-it-off-with-the-little-platoons-already/.

McInerny, Ralph. "The End of Philosophy." *Anuario Filosófico* (January 2002).

MacIntyre, Alasdair. *After Virtue*. 3rd ed. Notre Dame, IN: University of Notre Dame Press, 2007.

McKenna, Michael, and Coates, D. Justin. "Compatibilism." *Stanford Encyclopedia of Philosophy*. April 26, 2004; revised November 26, 2019. https://plato.stanford.edu/entries/compatibilism/.

McLuhan, Marshall, Eric McLuhan, and Jacek Szlarek. *The Medium and the Light: Reflections on Religion*. Eugene, OR: Wipf & Stock, 2010.

Meenan, John Paul. "The Seraphic Doctor: Saint Bonaventure." Catholic Insight. July 15, 2023. https://catholicinsight.com/the-seraphic-bonaventure/.

"Introduction to Meister Eckhart." *Esoterica*. n.d. Accessed September 3, 2023. http://esoteric.msu.edu/REL275/EckhartIntroduction.html.

Mill, John Stuart. *On Liberty*. Edited by Michael B. Mathias. New York: Routledge, 2007.

Miller, Clyde Lee. "Cusanus, Nicolaus [Nicolas of Cusa]." *Stanford Encyclopedia of Philosophy*. July 10, 2009; revised November 9, 2021. https://plato.stanford.edu/entries/cusanus/.

Mitchell, Christopher. "University Battles — C.S. Lewis and the Oxford University Socratic Club." C. S. Lewis Institute. January 7, 2010. https://www.cslewisinstitute.org/resources/university-battles-c-s-lewis-and-the-oxford-university-socratic-club/.

Mohanty, Jitendranath N. *Phenomenology: Between Essentialism and Transcendental Philosophy*. Evanston, IL: Northwestern University Press, 1998.

Monk, Ray. *Ludwig Wittgenstein: The Duty of Genius*. New York: Vintage, 1990.

———. "Bertrand Russell." *Britannica*. Last updated October 1, 2023. https://www.britannica.com/biography/Bertrand-Russell.

Morris, Errol. "The Ashtray: Hippasus of Metapontum (Part 3)." Opinionator, *New York Times*. March 9, 2011. https://archive.nytimes.com/opinionator.blogs.nytimes.com/2011/03/08/the-ashtray-hippasus-of-metapontum-part-3/.

Muggeridge, Malcolm. *Vintage Muggeridge: Religion and Society*. Edited by Geoffrey Barlow. Grand Rapids, MI: William B. Eerdmans, 1985.

Muller, Jerry Z. *Adam Smith in His Time and Ours: Designing the Decent Society*. New York: The Free Press. 1993.

Nadler, Steven M. *Spinoza and Medieval Jewish Philosophy*. Cambridge: Cambridge University Press, 2014.

Natali, Carlo. *Aristotle: His Life and School.* Princeton, NJ: Princeton University Press, 2013.

Nietzsche, Friedrich Wilhelm. *Beyond Good and Evil: The Philosophy Classic.* Translated by Helen Zimmern. Hoboken, NJ: Wiley, 2020.

Nietzsche, Friedrich. "Twilight of the Idols." 1895. Handprint.com. http://www.handprint.com/SC/NIE/GotDamer.html.

———. *The Gay Science: With a Prelude in Rhymes and an Appendix of Songs*: Translated, with commentary by Walter Kaufmann. New York: Random House, 1974

———. *The Portable Nietzsche*. Edited by Walter Kaufman. New York: Penguin Books, 1976.

Oberman, Heiko Augustinus. *The Harvest of Medieval Theology: Gabriel Biel and Late Medieval Nominalism*. Cambridge, MA: Harvard University Press, 1963.

Olson, Carl. "The Error of Nominalism." *Catholic Answers*. October 1, 2005. https://www.catholic.com/magazine/print-edition/whats-in-a-name-2.

Ozment, Steven. *The Age of Reform, 1250–1550*. New Haven, CT: Yale University Press, 1980.

Pascal, Blaise. *Pascal's Pensées*. New York: E. P. Dutton, 1958. Project Gutenberg. https://www.gutenberg.org/files/18269/18269-h/18269-h.htm.

Perreau-Saussine, Émile. *Alasdair MacIntyre: An Intellectual Biography*. South Bend, IN: University of Notre Dame Press, 2022.

Pierpont, Claudia Roth. "The Florentine." *New Yorker*. September 8, 2008. https://www.newyorker.com/magazine/2008/09/15/the-florentine.

Pinkard, Terry P. *Hegel: A Biography*. Cambridge: Cambridge University Press, 2001.

Planned Parenthood of Southeastern Pennsylvania v. Casey (1992). Legal Information Institute. https://www.law.cornell.edu/supremecourt/text/505/833.

Plato. *Apology* (Section 31d). *Plato in Twelve Volumes*. Vol. 1. Edited by Harold North Fowler. Cambridge, MA: Harvard University Press, 1966. Perseus Digital Library. https://www.perseus.tufts.edu/hopper/text?doc=Perseus:text:1999.01.0170:text=Apol.:section=31d&highlight=voice.

———. *Phaedrus*. Translated by Benjamin Jowett. Project Gutenberg. Last updated January 15, 2013. https://www.gutenberg.org/files/1636/1636-h/1636-h.htm.

———. *The Republic*. Translated by Benjamin Jowett. Project Gutenberg. July 26, 2017. https://www.gutenberg.org/files/55201/55201-h/55201-h.htm.

———. *Phaedo*. Translated by Benjamin Jowett. Center for Hellenic Studies. December 12, 2018. https://chs.harvard.edu/primary-source/plato-phaedo-sb/.

———. *Euthydemus*. Translated by Benjamin Jowett. Internet Classics Archive. http://classics.mit.edu/Plato/euthydemus.html.

Plotinos and Porphyry. *Plotinos: Complete Works, v. 1*. Translated by Kenneth Sylvan Guthrie. Project Gutenberg. June 13, 2013. https://www.gutenberg.org/files/42930/42930-h/42930-h.htm.

Popper, Karl Raimund. *The Open Society and Its Enemies*. Vol. 1. New York: Routledge, 1966.

———. *The Open Society and Its Enemies*. Vol. 2. New York: Routledge, 1966b.

———. "Back to the Pre-Socratics: The Presidential Address." Proceedings of the Aristotelian Society 59, no. 1 (June 1959): 1–24. https://doi.org/10.1093/aristotelian/59.1.1.

Rasmussen, Dennis C. *The Infidel and the Professor: David Hume, Adam Smith, and the Friendship That Shaped Modern Thought*. Princeton, NJ: Princeton University Press, 2017.

Relihan, Joel C. *The Prisoner's Philosophy: Life and Death in Boethius's* Consolation. With a contribution on the medieval Boethius by William Earnshaw Heise. South Bend, IN: University of Notre Dame Press, 2007.

Ridolfi, Roberto. *The Life of Niccoló Machiavelli*. Chicago: University of Chicago Press, 1963.

Robinson, Andrew. "Did Einstein Really Say That?" *Nature* 557 (April 2018): 30. https://doi.org/10.1038/d41586-018-05004-4.

Robinson, Dave, and Judy Groves. *Introducing Plato*. Duxford, U.K.: Icon Books, 2000.

Rousseau, Jean-Jacques. *Émile or on Education*. Translated by Allan David Bloom. New York: Basic Books, 1979.

Rousseau, Jean-Jacques. *Of the Social Contract*. Brunswick, OH: King's Court Communications, 1978.

———. *A Discourse Upon the Origin and the Foundation of the Inequality Among Mankind*. Project Gutenberg. February 1, 2004. https://www.gutenberg.org/cache/epub/11136/pg11136-images.html.

———. *The Confessions of Jean Jacques Rousseau — Complete*. Project Gutenberg. August 15, 2004; last updated February 26, 2021. https://gutenberg.org/cache/epub/3913/pg3913-images.html.

Rubenstein, Richard E. *Aristotle's Children*. New York: Harvest Book/Harcourt, 2003.

Russell, Bertrand. *A History of Western Philosophy, and Its Connection with Political and Social Circumstances from the Earliest Times to the Present Day*. New York: Simon and Schuster, 1945.

———. *Why I Am Not a Christian, and Other Essays on Religion and Related Subjects*. Edited, with an Appendix on the Bertrand Russell Case, by Paul Edwards. New York: Simon and Schuster, 1957.

———. *My Philosophical Development*. New York: Simon and Schuster, 1959.

Ryle, Gilbert. *The Concept of Mind*. New York: Barnes & Noble, 1949.

Sanders, Fred. "Thomas Aquinas' Big Pile of Straw." *The Scriptorium Daily*. December 6, 2010. https://scriptoriumdaily.com/thomas-aquinas-big-pile-of-straw/.

Sartre, Jean-Paul. *No Exit, and Three Other Plays*. New York: Vintage Books, 1955.

———. *The Words*. New York: George Braziller, 1964.

Schindler, D. C. *Freedom from Reality: The Diabolical Character of Modern Liberty*. South Bend, IN: University of Notre Dame Press, 2019.

Scruton, Roger. *A Short History of Modern Philosophy: From Descartes to Wittgenstein*. London: Routledge, 1995.

Shea, William R., and Mariano Artigas. *Galileo in Rome: The Rise and Fall of a Troublesome Genius*. Oxford: Oxford University Press, 2004.

Shields, Christopher. "Aristotle." *Stanford Encyclopedia of Philosophy*. September 25, 2008. https://plato.stanford.edu/entries/aristotle/.

Shorto, Russell. *Descartes' Bones: A Skeletal History of the Conflict between Faith and Reason*. New York: Vintage Books, 2008.

Smith, Adam. *An Inquiry into the Nature and Causes of the Wealth of Nations*. Oxford: Oxford University Press, 1976.

Smith, George H. "Freethought and Freedom: Francis Bacon and the Rise of Secularism." Libertarianism.org. May 15, 2015. https://www.libertarianism.org/columns/freethought-freedom-francis-bacon-rise-secularism.

Solomon, Robert C., and Kathleen Marie Higgins. *A Short History of Philosophy*. New York: Oxford University Press, 1996.

Spade, Paul Vincent, ed. *The Cambridge Companion to Ockham*. Cambridge: Cambridge University Press, 1999.

Spinoza, Benedict de. *The Ethics*. Project Gutenberg. Last updated December 11, 2017. https://www.gutenberg.org/files/3800/3800-h/3800-h.htm.

Springborg, Patricia. *The Cambridge Companion to Hobbes's* Leviathan. Edited by Tom Sorrell. Cambridge: Cambridge University Press, 2007.

Stone, I. F. *The Trial of Socrates*. Boston: Little, Brown, 1989.

Strathern, Paul. *Plato in 90 Minutes*. Chicago: Ivan R. Dee, 1996.

———. *Aristotle in 90 Minutes*. Chicago: Ivan R. Dee, 1996.

———. *Socrates in 90 Minutes*. Chicago: Ivan R. Dee, 1997.

The Bible. "Official King James Bible Online." Kingjamesbibleonline.org. 2018. https://www.kingjamesbibleonline.org/.

Thorburn, William. "The Myth of Ockham's Razor." *Mind* 27, no. 3 (January 1918): 345–353. https://doi.org/10.1093/mind/xxvii.3.345.

Tierney, Brian. *Origins of Papal Infallibility, 1150–1350: A Study on the Concepts of Infallibility, Sovereignty and Tradition in the Middle Ages*. Leiden, Netherlands: E. J. Brill. 1972.

Turner, Denys. *Thomas Aquinas: A Portrait*. New Haven, CT: Yale University Press, 2013.

Van Steenberghen, Fernand. *The Philosophical Movement in the Thirteenth Century*. Edinburgh: Nelson, 1955.

Vincelette, Alan. *A Reader in Recent Catholic Philosophy*. St. Louis: En Route Books, 2020.

Voltaire. *Candide, Or, Optimism*. Translated by Burton Raffel. New Haven, CT: Yale University Press, 2005.

Walton, Geri. "David Hume: Anecdotes Related to Him." GeriWalton.com. April 27, 2015. https://www.geriwalton.com/anecdotes-of-david-hume/.

Weaver, Richard M. *Ideas Have Consequences*. Chicago: University of Chicago Press, 2013

West, Rebecca. *The Essential Rebecca West*. New York: Penguin Books, 1983.

Whitehead, Alfred North. *Process and Reality*. New York: Free Press, 1978.

William of Ockham. *Philosophical Writings: A Selection*. Translated by Philotheus Boehner. Indianapolis: Bobbs-Merrill, 1964.

William of Ockham. *Quodlibetal Questions*. Translated by Alfred J. Freddoso and Francis E. Kelley. New Haven, CT: Yale University Press, 1998.

Wittgenstein, Ludwig. *Philisophische Untersuchungen. Philosophical Investigations*. Translated by Elizabeth Anscombe. Oxford: Basil Blackwell, 1986.

———. *Tractatus Logico-Philosophicus*. New York: Harcourt, Brace, 1922.

Wojtyla, Cardinal Karol. *Person and Act*. Boston: D. Reidel Publishing Company. 1979.

Wood, David, and Robert Bernasconi. *Derrida and Différance*. Evanston, IL: Northwestern University Press, 1988.

Young, Julian. *Friedrich Nietzsche: A Philosophical Biography*. Cambridge: Cambridge University Press, 2010.

Zweig, Stefan, and William Stone. *Nietzsche*. London: Hesperus Press, 2013.

About the Author

Dan LeRoy is an author, journalist, and teacher who is the director of the Writing and Publishing Department at Lincoln Park Performing Arts Charter School in Midland, Pennsylvania. His writing about music and politics has appeared in the *New York Times, Rolling Stone, Newsweek,* the *Village Voice, Alternative Press, Esquire,* and *National Review Online*. He is certainly the only person in history to have contributed to publications founded by William F. Buckley, Jr. and by Gene Simmons of KISS. Meanwhile, his speculative fiction has appeared in several anthologies, and on the *No Sleep* podcast.

His books include a volume for Bloomsbury's 33 1/3 series about the Beastie Boys classic *Paul's Boutique; Dancing to the Drum Machine: How Electronic Percussion Conquered the World;* and a previous volume for Sophia Institute Press, *Liberty's Lions: The Catholic Revolutionaries Who Established America*. For more information, visit his website, danleroy.com, or subscribe to his Substack newsletter, danleroysbonusbeats/substack.com

Sophia Institute

Sophia Institute is a nonprofit institution that seeks to nurture the spiritual, moral, and cultural life of souls and to spread the gospel of Christ in conformity with the authentic teachings of the Roman Catholic Church.

Sophia Institute Press fulfills this mission by offering translations, reprints, and new publications that afford readers a rich source of the enduring wisdom of mankind.

Sophia Institute also operates the popular online resource CatholicExchange.com. *Catholic Exchange* provides world news from a Catholic perspective as well as daily devotionals and articles that will help readers to grow in holiness and live a life consistent with the teachings of the Church.

In 2013, Sophia Institute launched Sophia Institute for Teachers to renew and rebuild Catholic culture through service to Catholic education. With the goal of nurturing the spiritual, moral, and cultural life of souls, and an abiding respect for the role and work of teachers, we strive to provide materials and programs that are at once enlightening to the mind and ennobling to the heart; faithful and complete, as well as useful and practical.

Sophia Institute gratefully recognizes the Solidarity Association for preserving and encouraging the growth of our apostolate over the course of many years. Without their generous and timely support, this book would not be in your hands.

www.SophiaInstitute.com
www.CatholicExchange.com
www.SophiaInstituteforTeachers.org

Sophia Institute Press is a registered trademark of Sophia Institute.
Sophia Institute is a tax-exempt institution as defined by the Internal Revenue Code, Section 501(c)(3). Tax ID 22-2548708.